UNDERSTANDING
the WAR in
KOSOVO

D1103144

UNDERSTANDING
the WAR in
KOSOVO

Editors

FLORIAN BIEBER
European Center for Minority Issues, Belgrade

ŽIDAS DASKALOVSKI
Central European University, Budapest

FRANK CASS
LONDON • PORTLAND, OR

First published in 2003 in Great Britain by
FRANK CASS PUBLISHERS
Crown House, 47 Chase Side, Southgate
London N14 5BP

and in the United States of America by
FRANK CASS PUBLISHERS
c/o ISBS, 920 NE 58th Avenue, Suite 300
Portland, Oregon, 97213-3786

Website: www.frankcass.com

British Library Cataloguing in Publication Data

Understanding the war in Kosovo
1. Kosovo (Serbia) – History – Civil War, 1998– 2. Kosovo
(Serbia) – History – Civil War, 1998 – Causes 3. Kosovo
(Serbia) – Foreign relations
I. Bieber, Florian II. Daskalovski, Zhidas
949.7'103

ISBN 0-7146-5391-8 (cloth)
ISBN 0-7146-8327-2 (paper)

Library of Congress Cataloging-in-Publication Data

Understanding the war in Kosovo/edited by Florian Bieber, Zhidas Daskalovski.
   p. cm.
   Includes bibliographical references and index.
   ISBN 0-7146-5391-8 (cloth) – ISBN 0-7146-8327-2 (pbk.)
   1. Kosovo (Serbia)–History–Civil War, 1998– 2. Kosovo (Serbia)–Ethnic relations.
   3. Balkan Peninsula–Politics and government–1989– 4. North Atlantic Treaty
Organization–Yugoslavia. I. Bieber, Florian. II. Daskalovski, Zhidas.

DR2087.U53 2003
949.7103–dc21
                                                                    2002041473

Typeset in 10.25/12pt Sabon by Vitaset, Paddock Wood, Kent
Printed in Great Britain by
MPG Books Ltd, Victoria Square, Bodmin, Cornwall

Contents

Contributors' Biographies

Florian Bieber is a senior non-resident research associate of the European Centre for Minority Issues, based in Belgrade, and recipient of the International Policy Fellowship of the Open Society Institute. He also teaches at the Central European University, Budapest and University of Sarajevo. He completed his Ph.D. in political science at the University of Vienna on contemporary nationalism in Serbia. He holds an MA in Southeast European Studies from the Central European University and an MA in History and Political Science from the University of Vienna. He has published articles on nationalism and politics in south-eastern Europe in *Nationalities Papers*, *Third World Quarterly*, *Current History*, *Rethinking History* and other journals. He is co-editor of the journal *Southeast European Politics* and founder and editor of *Balkan Academic News*.

Marina Blagojević has a Ph.D. in sociology. She is currently a Senior Researcher at the Institute for Criminological and Sociological Research in Belgrade. She was Associate Professor at Belgrade University (until 1998) and has been visiting professor in the United States, Hungary (Central European University 1998–2001, and ELTE) and Germany (2000–01). She was the President of the Sociological Association of Serbia and the Director of the Institute for Sociological Research, Belgrade. Currently she is an appointed member of the Editorial Board of the magazine *East Central Europe*. Her recent research projects focus on Kosovo, Hungarian and Serbian relations in Hungary and institution building in eastern and central Europe. Her major fields of interest are the sociology of gender and the sociology of inter-ethnic relations and she has published numerous articles in these fields in Serbian, English, German and Hungarian. She is the co-author (with R. Petrović) of the book *Migrations of Serbs and Montenegrins from Kosovo and Metohija*, and author and editor of five other books, including the most recent one: *Mapping Misogyny in Serbia: Discourses and Practices* (Belgrade, AŽIN, 2000). She has been included in several international projects related to Kosovo.

Isa Blumi is currently a Fulbright-Hayes fellow and is based in Istanbul, Turkey, where he is conducting archival research into late Ottoman Albania and Yemen. His work focuses on the impact of institutional transformations of the modern period and its impact on collective and individual identities in both the Balkans and the Arabic-speaking world. Formally a SSRC-IDRF (Social Science Research Council – International Dissertation Field Research Fellowship) fellow, Isa Blumi has an MA in Political Theory from the New School for Social Research and is a Ph.D. candidate for the joint History/Middle Eastern Studies programme at New York University. He has published a number of articles on aspects of Ottoman rule in Albania and Yemen, as well as post-First World War social history in Albania and Kosova.

Aldo Bumci has been deputy Executive Director of the Albanian Institute for International Studies since October 1999 and is a part-time professor at Tirana University, teaching International Relations Theory. He received his BA in International Relations at the Eastern Mediterranean University in northern Cyprus and his MA in International Relations at Bilkent University in Ankara, Turkey, in 1999.

Židas Daskalovski is a doctoral candidate in political science at Central European University, Budapest, Hungary. His dissertation topic is 'Liberalism and Interethnic Justice'. He has been the Macedonian Studies Teacher/ Fellow at the School of Slavonic and East European Studies, University College London. In addition, he has received a number of scholarships and awards including the CEU/Dahrendorf Fellowship at St Antony's, Oxford University. He has published a number of articles on topics related to the politics and history of south-east Europe, Macedonia in particular.

Elizabeth Allen Dauphinee is a doctoral candidate in the Department of Political Science at York University in Toronto, Canada, and a researcher with the York Centre for International and Security Studies. She holds a Social Sciences and Humanities Research Council of Canada doctoral fellowship and is currently pursuing projects dealing with security in south-eastern Europe, ethics and military intervention/peacekeeping, and political processes of identity formation.

Dejan Guzina is an Assistant Professor in comparative politics at Wilfrid Laurier University, Waterloo, Canada. He has published in several international journals. His most recent article 'The Self-Destruction of Yugoslavia' was published in *Canadian Review of Studies in Nationalism* (2000). His current research is on the relationship between state sovereignty, national self-determination and minority rights in the post-communist Balkans (south-eastern Europe).

Goran Janev is a doctoral candidate in social anthropology at Oxford University. He obtained his BA in Ethnology and MA in Sociology from Sts Cyril and Methodius University in Skopje. He is also an assistant at the Centre for Ethnic Relations at the Institute for Sociological and Political and Juridical Research, Sts Cyril and Methodius University. His research interests include political anthropology and, particularly, ethnicity and plural societies, the relations between Albanians and Macedonians in Macedonia.

Laurie Johnston is a Ph.D. candidate in Theological Ethics at Boston College. Originally from Washington, DC, she earned an Interdisciplinary BA from the University of Virginia in 1997, where she was a Jefferson Scholar. She also holds a Masters of Divinity degree from Harvard Divinity School, where she founded the Committee on Religion and International Relations. She has been actively involved in the Restorative Justice movement in Boston. She organized a conference in Switzerland on 'Religious Leadership After Conflict', for theology students from throughout the former Yugoslavia, under the auspices of the Boston Theological Institute. She is a member of the Community of Sant'Egidio.

Leon Malazogu teaches at the Political Science Department of the University of Pristina and is affiliated with the Princeton-based Project on Ethnic Relations. He has an MA degree in International Peace Studies from the University of Notre Dame and a BA degree in International Relations and Mass Communications from the American University in Bulgaria. He established the College for Alternative Humanistic Studies in Pristina and worked for the European Centre for Minority Issues as a regional representative in Pristina. He co-authored the curriculum for the newly opened department of Political Science/Public Administration at the University of Pristina and is a board member of the Albanian Political Science Association. He was scholar in residence at the Arizona State University for a semester, researching public administration curriculum and developing a course on local government.

Cristina Churruca Muguruza is a Research Fellow at the Institut for International Law of Peace and Armed Conflict Institute (IFHV), Ruhr University of Bochum, Germany. In 1998–2000 she was a Marie Curie Fellow at the IFHV. She holds a Ph.D. in International Relations from the University of the Basque Country. She has done research into the role of the European Union (EU) in humanitarian crises, the Western European Union (WEU) as a defence component of the EU and on the EU as an international actor. She has published articles on the common foreign policy of the European Union. Her book contributions include: 'The European Union's foreign policy and the promotion of respect of international humanitarian law: the problem of internally displaced persons', Institut für Friedenversicherung und Völkerrecht (ed.), *50 Jahre Genfer Konventionen: Aktuelle Rechtsfragen* (Berlin: Berlin-Verlag, forthcoming) and 'The development of political/ humanitarian strategies in Europe. The EU's political and humanitarian objectives: a contradiction in or a logical interdependence?' in H. Fischer (ed.), *Europa und die Zukunft der Humanitären Hilfe. Aus Krisen Lernen* (Bochum: IFHV, 2001). She is writing a book on the formulation and implementation of the European Union's common foreign policy.

Lazar Nikolić is tutor of Social Pathology at the Faculty of Philosophy, University of Belgrade. He is the coordinator of and a participant in the Sociological Dictionary project (Institute for Sociology, Faculty of Philosophy, 2000–01). He is a contributor to Blagojević, M. (ed.), *Mapping Misogyny in Serbia*. His articles and reviews have been published in the journals *Sociology, Sociological Review, Psychiatry Today, Gledista, New Serbian Political Thought, Intergraph* and *Socjologia i Wyzwania Spoleczne* (Krakow Academy of Economics). He was a researcher on the Humanitarian Law Research Team analyzing Belgrade printed media for hate speech and subliminal war propaganda (Humanitarian Law Center, 1996–98).

Besnik Pula is a Ph.D. candidate at the University of Michigan. He has an MA in Russian and East European Studies from Georgetown University. His thesis research was on the rise of the Albanian movement in Kosova from 1989–92. He has worked for the UN Mission in Kosovo (UNMIK). Previously, he acted as the regional representative for the European Centre for Minority Issues in Pristina.

Jens Stilhoff Sörensen is a Ph.D. candidate at the European University Institute, Florence. He was previously a doctoral Fellow at the Department for Ethnic Studies, University of Linköping Campus in Norrkoping, Sweden. His research focuses on aid policy and social reconstruction in the context of inter-ethnic relations in the Balkans, with particular emphasis on Serbian–Albanian relations. His publications include *The Threatening Precedent – Kosovo and the Remaking of Crisis* (1999) and 'Balkanism and the New Radical Interventionism – A Structural Critique', *Journal of International Peacekeeping* (Spring 2002).

Gábor Sulyok is an Assistant Lecturer of Public International Law at the Széchenyi István University, in Györ, Hungary, as well as a junior research fellow of the Hungarian Academy of Sciences, Institute for Legal Studies. He also pursues his Ph.D. studies in the Department of International Law at the University of Miskolc, concentrating on the issues of human rights and humanitarian intervention. His publications include 'Humanitarian Intervention: A Historical and Theoretical Overview', *Acta Juridica*

Hungarica (2000), and 'Operation Allied Force: A Legal Evaluation', *Sfera* (October 2000).

Stefan Wolff is Lecturer in the Department of European Studies, University of Bath, England. He graduated from Leipzig University and received his M.Phil. from the University of Cambridge and his Ph.D. from the London School of Economics. Apart from numerous articles and book chapters, Wolff is the author of, *Disputed Territories: The Transnational Dynamics of Ethnic Conflict Settlement*; editor of, *German Minorities in Europe: Ethnic Identity and Cultural Belonging* and co-editor of, *Coming Home to Germany: The Integration of Ethnic Germans from Central and Eastern Europe in the Federal Republic* and of *Peace at Last? The Impact of the Good Friday Agreement on Northern Ireland*. Wolff is also editor of *The Global Review of Ethnopolitics* and general editor of the series *Studies in Ethnopolitics* published by Berghahn Books in New York and Oxford. Since 1999, Wolff has been the co-chairman of the Specialist Group on Ethnic Politics, an international network of academics and practitioners associated with the Political Studies Association of the UK.

Foreword

In late January 1996, I rode a bus from Skopje to Pristina. At the Yugoslav border station 'Djeneral Janković', all passengers were ordered to unload their luggage into the mud of a parking lot for a rude inspection. At two checkpoints on the road to Priština, special forces members with automatic weapons entered the bus to double-check passports and visas. Not a word was spoken. Upon arrival at Priština's central bus station, armoured troop carriers pointed their machine guns at the main entrance. 'This, surely, is the grimmest spot in Europe', wrote the *Economist* at the time, 'the crucible, some fear, of its next war.'[1]

Indeed, a few weeks later, in April 1996, a militant Kosovar Albanian group carried out the first assassination attempts on Serb army and police officers in Kosovo. Disappointment and frustration with the Dayton Peace Agreement and its neglect of the Kosovo issue could no longer be controlled by the moderate leadership of Fehmi Agani's and Ibrahim Rugova's pacifist Democratic League of Kosovo (LDK). Already in January, this turning of the tide had been quite obvious. By that time, three currents could be identified in the Kosovar Albanian political spectrum. First, the LDK demanded independence for Kosovo by opting for peaceful means, hoping for the support of the international community as a reward. Secondly, a heterogeneous group of elder statesmen as well as younger realists still had not given up completely on the idea of negotiating a new *modus vivendi* with Belgrade, be it '1974 Plus', 'Federalization' or even a new 'Balkania'. Thirdly, young hotspurs and 'old' radicals, for the first time since the dramatic years of 1989 to 1992, openly discussed the organization of a Kosovar Albanian *intifada* movement against Serbian occupation-type rule.

The threat of escalation of the conflict during the first months of 1996, brought about by militant Kosovar Albanians, had a visible impact on the Milošević regime and thus opened a window of opportunity for international mediation. While the EU failed to act upon an urgent appeal by the European Parliament of 18 April 1996 to open a permanent office in Pristina, the US did act. On 5 June 1996, a United States Information Service office was opened in the presence of both LDK Chairman Rugova and

Serbian Deputy Governor for Kosovo Miloš Nešović. With Belgrade admitting at least a small degree of internationalization of the conflict, the LDK message to the Kosovar Albanians of not turning to violence but waiting for international intervention was considerably enforced. Finally, on 1 September 1996, the Catholic laymen organization, Comunità di Sant'Egidio of Rome, succeeded in brokering the first agreement between Pristina and Belgrade since 1992. A Memorandum of Understanding signed by Milošević and Rugova provided for the return of Kosovar Albanian students and teachers back to schools from which they had been banned for years.

The momentum brought about by the beginning of an international-ization of the conflict was not followed up by the international community for a whole year. Instead, the diplomatic formula of 'deep concern' was coined and stereotypically repeated. Yet, as the Serbian, Kosovar and Montenegrin branches of the International Helsinki Federation for Human Rights aptly remarked, 'concern is not a policy'.[2] When the situation escalated again in the fall of 1997, it turned out to be too late for therapeutic conflict intervention, or any kind of conflict prevention at all.

By early 1998 both sides to this asymetric and increasingly hot conflict were determined to try to solve it by violent means. Accordingly, the low intensity war of 1998 turned out to be just round one and thus the prelude to a much fiercer round two in 1999. From September 1998 both sides applied an all-or-nothing strategy: Milošević went for the total ethnic cleansing of Albanians from Kosovo, and the recently emerged Kosovo Liberation Army (KLA) applied the high risk tactic of provoking a superior adversary to overreact, which on their behalf would trigger international military intervention. The latter concept proved to be successful – albeit at the cost of some 10,000 civilians and combatants killed and up to 900,000 Kosovar Albanians temporarily displaced. Since 1999, the international community is – in the literal sense of the word – paying dearly for its hesitation and reluctance towards pro-active conflict prevention and minimal invasive intervention in 1996 and 1997.

In 1994, at a remarkable first conference on the conflict in Kosovo held in Nijmegen in the Netherlands, Milenko Karan, Serbian *homme de lettres* and psychologist from Pristina, made a gloomy prediction: 'Whatever happens, we will have to negotiate, but I'm afraid – knowing our mentality – that this will occur only after major bloodshed, which would make all talks useless: in the cemetery, to the best of my knowledge, there is no dialogue'.[3] Eight years later, after massive bloodshed indeed had happened, the future is still clouded although there is at least a silver lining: the parallel processes of democratization in post-war Kosovo as well as in post-Milošević Serbia do give some hope for the renewal of Serbian-Albanian dialogue over Kosovo and ultimately for an internationally mediated consensual solution.

A completely different question is, however, whether the international community's first and foremost aim in Kosovo, the 'reconstruction of the multi-ethnic society', is realistic. In my view, it is not – and this not due to a general impossibility of bringing the toothpaste back into the tube but because of the specific nature of Kosovo as a colony governed by Belgrade since 1912. Only during the fifteen years of territorial autonomy, from 1974 to 1989, was this colonial status suspended. Whereas in the Yugoslav republic of Bosnia and Herzegovina, up until 1992, the major ethnic groups were basically on an equal footing – the pre-condition for multi-ethnic society – the Serbs and Albanians in Kosovo were not. Here apartheid prevailed, and this is also the explanation for the racist undertones on the Serbian side as well as partly on the Albanian one before and after 1999. So in understanding the state of the Kosovo problem today – and even more so in coming up with solutions for the future – taking the post-Ottoman period into account is crucial. Hence the shorter terms of Serbian, Bulgarian, Italian, and German occupation during the Balkan Wars and the two World Wars, the three longer periods of Yugoslav colonial rule over Kosovo of 1918 to 1941, 1944 to 1974, and 1989 to 1999, are of particular importance.

The editors of this collection of essays, aimed at understanding the war in Kosovo, are therefore to be congratulated for carefully balancing perspectives of the past, present *and* future. In order to create a common future for the Balkans, the regional political actors have to put aside their respective ethno-centric master narratives and face the difficult task of getting acquainted with their past. This book, I am sure, will help them to do so.

Stefan Troebst
Professor of East European Cultural Studies
University of Leipzig

NOTES

1. 'Europe's Roughest Neighbourhood', in: A Ghost of Chance: A Survey of the Balkans, p. 4, supplement to *The Economist*, 22 January 1998.
2. IHF, 'Kosovo: Urgent Appeal for Courage, Leadership, and Cooperation', Belgrade, Pristine, Podgorica, 21 January 1998.
3. Milenko Karan, 'Kosovo: From Tomorrow to Yesterday', in (eds), Ger Duijzings, Dušan Janjć and Shkëlzen Maliqi, *Kosovo – Kosova: Confrontation or Coexistence* (Nijmegen: Peace Research Instituts, University of Nijmegen, 1997), p. 176.

Acknowledgements

More than three years after the end of the war over Kosovo in June 1999, Kosovo remains a controversial issue for regional and international politics. Although the fall of the Milošević regime also put an end to large-scale regional conflict, as was the case in Croatia, Bosnia and Kosovo, the low-intensity fighting in southern Serbia and Macedonia highlighted the continued danger emanating from ethnic mobilization and nationalism. Reconciliation and dialogue between most Serbs and Albanians remains difficult and only few steps have been taken in the last years.

The conference 'Kosovo: Understanding the Past – Looking Ahead', held in April 2000 in Budapest, where most papers included here were first presented, did not aim to bring about reconciliation, but merely help re-establish discussion and communication between young Serb and Albanian scholars. The papers presented at the conference by young researchers, mostly from Serbia, Kosovo and south-eastern Europe, as well as western Europe and North America, addressed the most sensitive issues pertaining to Kosovo – its history, the nature of the conflict and state of Kosovo after the end of the war. The participants did not represent their community but just themselves, in an attempt to understand Kosovo.

While most chapters included in this volume were presented at the conference, some additional contributions were included to present a coherent volume on Kosovo, its historical background, the conflict and the international administration. The nature of the contributions is not purely descriptive, but rather seeks to stimulate discussion, be controversial and at times contradictory. This volume cannot and does not seek to present a single interpretation of the Kosovo conflict, but rather wants to question any simplistic approach to understanding the complexities underlying the conflict and its origins.

The conference and the book were made possible only by the great personal involvement of a number of people who we would like to thank here: Frank Burgdörfer, Altin Ilirjani, Marijana Trivunović and Minna Nikolova. Furthermore, a number of institutions and organizations deserve mention for their logistical and financial support for the success of this project: the Central European University, especially the International Relations and European Studies Department for providing the facilities of the conference and the European Youth Foundation of the Council of Europe, for their generous financial support for the conference and the publication and the organizational and logistical support of the International Politics Working Group of the European student organization AEGEE.

Florian Bieber and Židas Daskalovski
October 2002

Introduction

Florian Bieber

Few places in Europe of the size and population of Kosovo have received any comparable amount of attention both among policy makers and academics. Why is Kosovo important? The significance of Kosovo for European and even transatlantic politics thrust itself upon decision makers in the West in 1998, when the escalating conflict between the Yugoslav security forces and the Kosovo Liberation Army threatened to escalate into a full-fledged war. The conflict in Kosovo, emerging in 1981, and again in 1989, remained a concern throughout the wars of Yugoslavia's disintegration and as the war in Kosovo escalated it seemed the last piece in a series of war – both the most dangerous but also the last.

Although the confrontation between the Albanian leadership in the province and the Serbian regime had been simmering throughout the 1990s and had been visible even to the non-expert observer, the conflict seemingly caught most Western policy makers unprepared. The intensive attempts by different international actors, including the contact group – including the United States, Russia, France, Germany, Italy and Great Britain – raised the stakes for Western governments. A lesson from the Bosnian war had seemingly been that limited use of aerial bombardment against Serb position could end the conflict. When the threat of such strikes in October 1998 brought about the entry of the OSCE Kosovo Verification Mission (KVM), the calculation seemed to have paid off. Only a few months later, however, after the failed Rambouillet peace talks, the threat was deemed no longer sufficient to restrain the Serbian and Yugoslav security forces and led to the three-month war of the North Atlantic Treaty Organization (NATO) against Yugoslavia, while the Serbian and Yugoslav authorities engaged in a ferocious campaign of ethnic cleansing against the Albanian population.

The end of the conflict saw the entry of a strong international peace mission, led by the Kosovo Force (KFOR) from the military angle and the United Nations Interim Administration in Kosovo (UNMIK) for most civilian aspects. The beginning of the international presence in Kosovo did not, however, put an end to the conflict, which ensued with expulsion of non-Albanian inhabitants from Kosovo and the emergence of Serb enclaves.

1

Unlike Bosnia, where most power structures from the war remained in place during peacetime, Kosovo's institutions emerged and continue to emerge in the post-conflict period.

Returning to the original question of the importance of Kosovo. It could be argued that the significance of Kosovo by far exceeds its size. We can map out five factors which have contributed to the importance of Kosovo:

1. The conflict over Kosovo emerged in 1981 between Serb claims for re-centralization and reducing disadvantages felt by the Serb population of Kosovo, and Albanian demands for a further enhancement of the province's status to the level of republic. This was the key impetus to the re-emergence of Serbian nationalism throughout the 1980s. It can be assumed that the rise to power of Slobodan Milošević would not have happened, or if so under quite different circumstances, were it not for rising concern in Serbia for Kosovo. In the ensuing Slovene–Serb dispute over the future of Yugoslavia Kosovo was again of great symbolic importance for both sides.[1]

2. Absence of war but the existence of conflict in and over Kosovo during the 1990s raised the key question of how to engage in conflict prevention. Whereas the first conflict prevention mission in the United Nations history was launched in Macedonia,[2] Kosovo was largely excluded from international attempts at preventing an escalation of the conflict.[3] Arguably the sidelining of Kosovo from international mediation in former Yugoslavia, especially in the Dayton Peace Accords for Bosnia, helped accelerate the conflict in Kosovo.[4]

3. The war itself has raised a number of key questions – whose significance transcends Kosovo – regarding the appropriateness of international response to ethnic cleansing. While preventive action was largely made impossible by the primacy of state sovereignty, the bombing by NATO sought to limit the sovereignty of a state when it comes to the massive violation of the human rights of its citizens. Not only the legal aspects of this campaign, but also the nature in which NATO chose to respond to the conflict, have raised debates which have yet to be decided.[5]

4. Together with Bosnia, Kosovo is an example of a new type of international intervention, which in part can also be found outside of Europe, i.e., in East Timor and Afghanistan. The presence of both a massive military force and a strong civilian presence intrinsically involved in the governance of the territory are expressions of international commitment to Kosovo, but the jury is still out on assessing the outcome of this type of intervention.[6] Critiques have charged that this type of intervention has brought at worst many of the vestiges of colonialism, and at best the difficulties of local ownership in governance.[7]

5. Finally, Kosovo is a challenge to advocates of inter-ethnic co-existence

2

and tolerance. While Bosnia had a rich history of co-existence and cooperation before the war, Kosovo's history in the twentieth century has been shaped significantly by the confrontation between the Serb and Albanian population. The post-war experience has provided little additional evidence in terms of possibilities for co-existence.

It is to these larger questions that the contributions in this volume are seeking to give answers.

Kosovo has two histories, often mutually exclusive and frequently antagonistic. As most nationalist movements project their interpretation of the nation into the past and thus become the prime primordialists of the nation so do those of Kosovo. Recollecting past events in a mythological light has been a key component of nationalist mobilization of the past two decades, with the memory of perceived past injustices (even if they weren't) and victories, politics of exclusion could be justified. Such rhetorics have often been promoted by political leaders in Kosovo[8] and throughout former Yugoslavia, and permeate the educational system of the region.[9] Židas Daskalovski, in his contribution, outlines nationalist 'fairy tales' and demonstrates the way in which Albanian and Serbian national history of Kosovo has been mythologized. He suggests that the constructed nature of these narratives deprives them of their validity as claims to territory, suggesting that other criteria need to be taken into account when determining the claims to Kosovo. The contribution by Dejan Guzina continues into the post-World War II period the exploration of the two interlocking nationalisms in Kosovo. Focusing particularly on the 1990s, Guzina explores the absence of communication between the communities and the difficulties, even among the political and intellectual opposition to Milošević in Serbia, of striking up a meaningful dialogue with the Albanian elite in Kosovo. The few informal instances of inter-community contact throughout that period have been a dialogue of the 'deaf' or a conversation between intellectuals and politicians who lacked sufficient support within their own community.[10] These difficulties were, however, not only rooted within the elite, but found their reflection in general misperceptions between the communities. As Lazar Nikolić elucidates on the basis of sociological studies on ethnic distance and stereotypes, a pattern of mutual suspicion emerges over a considerable period, pre-dating the political conflict of the late 1980s and 1990s. He suggests that the antagonistic relationship between Serbs and Albanians is reflected in a pendulum of domination over Kosovo, which has seen alternating periods of dominance, by one community then the other, but no examples of joint governance and coexistence in the course of the twentieth century. In conclusion, he notes that with the forceful entry of the international community onto the stage of Kosovo, the stereotyping of the international community of the Balkans, and both Albanians and Serbs, needs to be taken into account. This

3

assessment is drawn upon in later chapters in the evaluation of the performance of the international mission in Kosovo.

Against this backdrop of ethnic relations and the escalation of conflict in the late 1980s with the coming to power of Slobodan Milošević, international governmental and non-governmental organizations started becoming active in the late 1980s. The first initiatives originated with human rights organizations that noted the increasing repression of the Albanian population in Kosovo. They also noted the profound failure of the Kosovo political leadership prior to the take-over by Milošević:

> Kosovo's previous political authorities thus failed in their human rights obligations in two ways. First, they failed to protect Kosovo's minorities from abuse. Second, rather than creating a criminal justice system that would offer protection to everyone in Kosovo, they exhausted themselves and their moral authority in striving to outlaw and punish separatist, nationalist speech in Kosovo.[11]

The efforts of international organizations often failed due to the invocation of the primacy of territorial integrity and realpolitik, which sought to solve the more pressing conflict of Bosnia at the expense of addressing the unresolved dispute over Kosovo.[12] Stefan Wolff revisits the attempts of the international community to find a solution to the conflict against this backdrop in the two years preceding the conflict. He suggests that the international community itself lacked the internal coherence and coercive pressure on both sides to engage in successful conflict prevention. In addition, the internal dynamics of the conflict at the time of its escalation in 1998 narrowed the space for finding a common ground.

The failure of resolving the conflict before NATO bombing has been closely tied with the negotiations at Rambouillet, the only comprehensive attempt at finding a temporary solution for the status of Kosovo. The Rambouillet proposal stands in a line of attempts by the international community to end conflict in former Yugoslavia through a combination of ceasefire and institutional reform. Ranging from the first plans in 1991, for all of Yugoslavia, to the numerous peace initiatives for Croatia and Bosnia, the international community, represented first by the United Nations and the European Community (later Union), and subsequently by the Contact Group, these plans were an innovation from previous attempts at conflict resolution and mostly failures, due to the hesitancy of the international actors to use some degree of coercion to ensure their implementation. Rambouillet has been particularly controversial among these plans, as negotiations were carried out against the backdrop of the threat of NATO air strikes. Marc Weller, a participant during the negotiations points out that '[i]n terms of substance, the Rambouillet settlement represents a further step in the development of innovative mechanisms to address, if not resolve, self-determination conflicts'. At the same time, he notes that '[i]n terms of process, the Rambouillet conference on Kosovo represented a significant departure in international mediation. The presence of the parties at the talks had been ensured through the threat of force by NATO.'[13]

It is this inherent conflict in the Rambouillet talks which Elizabeth Allen Dauphinee traces in her reassessment of the talks in the light of the subsequent NATO air strikes against Yugoslavia. She suggests that the proposed substance of the talks contained a degree of ambiguity that rendered support by the different parties difficult to secure. Dauphinee furthermore points to the alterations, or rather suspension, of the Rambouillet proposal with the beginning of the international administration of Kosovo. These ambiguities were in part caused by misperceptions of Western policy makers concerning the conflict and how to resolve it, as outlined by the author. While it remains unclear whether Rambouillet was a window of opportunity or its failure a foregone conclusion, it was the last effort before the war which effectively precluded any substantial compromise on the status of Kosovo. With the beginning of the ethnic cleansing in Kosovo by the Serbian and Yugoslav forces, the possibility and desirability of a negotiated settlement further faded.

Leon Malazogu and Gábor Sulyok examine the nature of NATO intervention from the moral, political and legal point of view. While both authors support the bombardment of Yugoslavia by NATO, they raise a number of concerns, including the absence of a UN Security Council mandate, and conclude, from different points of view, that it is the United Nations which should be enabled to engage in such actions in the future, rather than a regional alliance.

The implications of the conflict were broad and did not exhaust themselves in its military aspects. A key player in the conflict was the media, both the tightly controlled media in Yugoslavia, which came under increasing pressure in the months before the Kosovo war, and the Western media, largely unaware of the background to the conflict. Marina Blagojević argues that the media in Yugoslavia, both among Serbs and Albanians, played a crucial role in mobilizing nationalist sentiment and constructing conflict. In fact, the media was less an actor of its own but more frequently the instrument of the authoritarian regime in the pursuit of its policies.[14] Unlike the late 1980s the production of hate speech and nationalist mobilization by regime-controlled media was, at the time of the Kosovo war, part and parcel of the suppression of critical and independent media outlets. Blagojević argues that although Western media operated in a different environment and possessed independence Serbian and Albanian media lacked, the reporting similarly 'constructed' the conflict.

Next to the media, religious communities have been a key actor in Kosovo. Whereas religion as such played no significant role in the conflict, religious communities have been particularly important in the nationalist movements of Yugoslavia during its disintegration. As religious communities largely coincide with nations in former Yugoslavia, with the exception of Albanians, religion has been a symbol of nationhood. At the same time, as Laurie Johnston points out, religious leaders have sought to play a positive role during the conflict. In the case of Kosovo, some Serbian-Orthodox religious leaders, especially Bishop Artemije, shifted from a hardline position in the early 1990s to moderation, seeking dialogue with Albanians. Johnston argues that religious leaders can thus play a crucial role in seeking reconciliation and accommodation. In the case of Serbia, however, the church has been largely compromised due to its rather strong support for the nationalist policies of the regime and parts of the opposition during the 1990s.[15]

The following chapters turn to the post-war order in Kosovo. The end of the Kosovo war in June 1999 dramatically shifted the agenda for Kosovo. The challenge to be met by the international community was no longer ending the campaign by the Serbian security forces against Kosovo Albanians, but establishing security and building institutions in Kosovo where institutions has existed either underground or as part of a repressive system for more than a decade. Unlike Bosnia, security concerns continued to shape international priorities. Pressure against minorities, and the confrontation in Mitrovica between the Serb-controlled north of the city and the Albanian controlled south preventing normalization in Kosovo for more than three years are of special concern.[16] Whereas in Bosnia, where international involvement in post-war reconstruction has been comparable, institutions were part of the peace accord, the international organizations entered Kosovo without set institutions. This has been both an opportunity to build institutions that are more viable for Kosovo and a hurdle in stabilizing the post-war political situation. Besnik Pula and Isa Blumi assess the performance of the United Mission to Kosovo in its effort to build a democratic polity in Kosovo. Pula traces the difficulties in the first phase to establish new institutions and tackle key problems, such as the economic reconstruction of the province. Blumi turns to the perception of the UN in Kosovo and how it conceived the polity. He argues that the approach chosen by the international administration has been largely a failure, overemphasizing ethnicity over other forms of identity and downplaying pre-existing institutions at the local level.

In addition to the United Nations in Kosovo, a host of other international organizations have shaped and continue to shape the post-war development of Kosovo. The European Union has been an especially crucial actor for two reasons: firstly, it has been a key source of financial support, both in terms of humanitarian aid and post-war reconstruction. Secondly, the long-term prospect of EU integration is an incentive for all countries of south-eastern Europe to seek cooperation with the EU. While the membership of Kosovo in the European Union is by all assessments at best a long-term prospect, the launch of the Stability Pact during the Kosovo war and subsequently the beginning of the Stabilization and Association Process signifies EU commitment to the region.

Cristina Churruca Muguruza explores the involvement of the European Union in Kosovo and frames it in the larger context of the Union's policies during the disintegration of Yugoslavia throughout the 1990s. While the author assesses that the EU, for the first time, faced its responsibilities during the Kosovo war towards the western Balkans, it still lacks adequate instruments in addressing some of the key problems in the region, most prominently the uncertain status of Kosovo. The EU involvement through Javier Solana, as coordinator of the Common Foreign and Security Policy in Macedonia in 2001 and 2002 in the relations between Serbia and Montenegro demonstrates the willingness of the EU to reach beyond its earlier emphasis on economic and humanitarian support to active conflict prevention. Assessments of the extension of EU activities into conflict prevention have been, however, mixed.[17]

Following on the previous discussion of EU support for Kosovo, Jens Stilhoff Sörensen explores in great detail the underlying assumptions in the reconstruction aid provided to Kosovo.

In the three closing chapters, the impact of the war in Kosovo, its current position under international administration and options for future status are examined from the perspective of the surrounding countries. Aldo Bumci discusses the possible impact of an independent Kosovo for Albania and Macedonia. He argues that independence for Kosovo might have a stabilizing effect on both countries, especially Macedonia. Bumci questions both the prevalence of domino theories regarding regional conflict and refutes the suggestion that the idea of a 'Greater Albania' would elicit much support in Albania.

The interconnectedness between Kosovo and Macedonia was demonstrated during the conflict in Macedonia in Spring 2001, which had causes in neighbouring Kosovo (if not its roots). Goran Janev traces the impact of the status of Kosovo on inter-ethnic relations in Macedonia. He sees the danger for inter-ethnic relations in Macedonia less in an eventual independence of Kosovo, but rather in a rise of nationalism in Macedonia, as was exemplified during the conflict in 2001. While the stability of Macedonia is closely tied to Kosovo, the relevance of Kosovo for Serbia has gradually diminished since the end of the war. The impact of the conflict over Kosovo on the democratic changes in October 2000 remains hard to assess. On one side, did NATO bombing of Yugoslavia help marginalize the opposition and create some deep suspicions towards Western policy, possibly delaying transition to democracy? On the other side, the loss of Kosovo and further decline in living standards as a result of the war, might have helped undermine the Milošević regime. After the (semi-negotiated) revolution of 5 October 2000 the main energy of the new authorities has been directed towards economic reconstruction and internal infighting. Kosovo disappeared from the main political agenda. Nevertheless, responsibility for crimes in Kosovo remain largely taboo and Serbian politicians have been reluctant to discuss the long-term relations between Serbia and Kosovo.

More than three years after the end of the war over Kosovo, Kosovo has not yet become a stable area. The conflicts in its vicinity, even after the democratic changes in Serbia, such as in the areas of Preševo, Bujanovac and Medvedja, and in Macedonia, evidence the instability of the region. With the future status of Kosovo not only open, but also largely undiscussed,[18] it is hard to assess the success or failure of the post-war efforts of the international community in Kosovo and the part Kosovo will have in the larger region of south-eastern Europe.

NOTES

1. Wolfgang Petritsch, Karl Kaser and Robert Pichler, *Kosovo. Kosova. Mythen, Daten, Fakten* (Klagenfurt: Wieser, 1999), pp. 154–207.
2. Abioudun Williams, *Preventing War. The United Nations and Macedonia* (Lanham: Rowman & Littlefield, 2000).
3. Only the Carrington Plan in 1991 for Yugoslavia addressed Kosovo and the brief CSCE missions of Long Duration to Kosovo, Sanjak and Vojvodina 1992–93.
4. Stefan Troebst, *Conflict in Kosovo: Failure of Prevention? An Analytical Documentation, 1992–98*. European Centre for Minority Issues Working Paper 1 (Flensburg: ECMI, 1998).
5. Kurt R. Spillmann and Joachim Krause (eds), *Kosovo: Lessons Learnt for International Cooperative Security* (Bern: Peter Lang, 2000).
6. Alexandros Yannis, *Kosovo under International Administration. An Unfinished Conflict* (Athens: ELIAMEP & PSIS, 2001).
7. David Chandler, *Bosnia: Faking Democracy After Dayton* (London: Pluto, 2000).
8. Florian Bieber, 'Nationalist Mobilization and Stories of Serb Suffering. The Kosovo Myth from 600th Anniversary to the Present', *Rethinking History*, vol. 6, no. 1 (Spring 2002), pp. 95–110.
9. Christina Koulouri (ed.), *The Teaching of History of Southeastern Europe* (Thessaloniki: Centre for Democracy and Reconciliation in South-eastern Europe & South-east European Joint History Project, 2001).
10. See Bahri Cani and Cvijetin Milivojević (eds), *Kosmet ili Kosovo* (Belgrade: NEA, 1996); *Srpsko-Albanski Dijalog, Beograd 21–22 Novembar 1998* (Belgrade: Helsinški odbor za ljudska prava u Srbiji, 1999).
11. Helsinki Watch & International Helsinki Federation, *Yugoslavia. Crisis in Kosovo*, March 1990, p. 25.
12. See Troebst, *Conflict in Kosovo: Failure of Prevention?*
13. Marc Weller, 'The Rambouillet conference on Kosovo,' *International Affairs 75*, no. 2 (1999), pp. 249–50.
14. Dragoš Ivanović, *Plot Against the Public* (Belgrade: Republika, 1999).
15. Milorad Tomanić, *Srpska crkva u ratu i ratovi u njoj* (Belgrade: Medijska knjižara Krug, 2001).
16. International Crisis Group, *UNMIK's Kosovo Albatross. Tackling Division in*

Mitrovica, 3 June 2002; UNHCR and OSCE, *Ninth Assessment of the Situation of Ethnic Minorities in Kosovo (September 2001–April 2002)*, (May 2002).

17. Ulrich Schneckener, 'Developing and Applying EU Crisis Management. The Test Case of Macedonia', *ECMI Working Paper*, no. 14 (January 2002); International Crisis Group, *Still Buying Time. Montenegro, Serbia and the European Union*, 7 Mary 2002.

18. Discussions on the final status have to date been held mostly with policy advisors and academic circles, see Dana H. Allin et al., 'What Status for Kosovo?', *Chaillot Paper*, no. 50 (October 2001); International Crisis Group, *A Kosovo Roadmap (I). Addressing Final Status*, 1 March 2002; The Independent International Commission on Kosovo, *The Kosovo Report* (Oxford: Oxford University Press, 2000).

PART I
BACKGROUND TO THE CONFLICT

Claims to Kosovo: Nationalism and Self-Determination

Židas Daskalovski

The aim of this chapter is to answer the question of whether claims by different national movements are to be seen in the light of the 'particularity' of their cases. As Yael Tamir has put it, '[M]ost nationalists, however, tend to repress the knowledge that their nation is but a reiteration of a world-wide phenomenon ... they tend to emphasize the particular'.[1] Using the case of Kosovo, I will illustrate how nationalist claims are certainly not so dramatically different that they each can be judged as specific and therefore meriting special attention. More specifically, I will show the congruence of the claims of Albanian and Serbian nationalists for the right to rule over Kosovo. As it will become evident, both sides, Serbian and Albanian, try to present to the international community their case as being particular and therefore deserving particular attention and consideration. However, if both cases are presented as being particular, but both claims rest on more or less equivalent arguments, then we face a dilemma – how to evaluate Serbian or Kosovo Albanian assertions for political right to rule this province.

If both of the claims are based on a supposed distinctness of 'their case' but this uniqueness is a mere illusion, then a neutral observer deciding upon particular present day disputes between the 'Kosovo Albanians' and the 'Serbs' must evaluate the claims, decide which one of them has the veracity and, therefore, merits attention. In other words, if the Kosovo Albanians' claim to independence is not based on an unique argumentation, as Albanian nationalists would like us to believe it is, but is indeed similarly constructed to the Serbian argument, then the Albanian assertion over the 'rule of Kosovo' would fail the test of originality and we would have to look at which one of the cases is accurate. Given that the 'ordinariness' of the Albanian claims for the 'right to rule Kosovo' is established, then 'particularity' of the case cannot be taken as a measure for passing rightful decisions on the Kosovo question. Instead, careful analysis of the reliability of the claims themselves may be the alternative solution. To reiterate, as the

Kosovo case study will evince, nationalist claims are typically not unique, and cannot be judged on the basis of their proclaimed particularity. Before looking for substitute solutions we should consider whether a careful analysis of the reliability of the claims of the two sides can conceivably be an alternative answer. However, is not that clear whether we can duly assess the opposing claims through comparative analysis of the arguments presented by the two sides. For Serbian and Kosovo Albanian arguments for 'rights', like many other nationalistic mythologies, are based on a complex interpretation of a combination of historical, legal and demographic details rendering the evaluation of the rightness of the intricate claims.

If the claims by national groups cannot be justifiably considered on the basis of the particularity of their situation question then there would be a need for an alternative mechanism for adjudicating nationalistic demands. This chapter, however, stops at this point. Its aim, based on evidence from the Kosovo case study, is to show that there is a need on the part of social scientists to construct a universal mechanism for evaluating nationalistic claims, a 'just theory of nationalism'. This chapter, in other words, attempts to illustrate that confronting nationalistic claims cannot be assessed by relying on their supposed particularity. Hence, this analysis will promote different approaches to the study of nationalism, be they liberal, communitarian or other.

THE SERBIAN PERSPECTIVE

The Beginnings

The Serbian 'fairy tale'[2] starts with one of the least disputable events in early European history, the arrival of the Slavs in Europe in the fourth century AD, the time of the great migrations. These were the times when the ethnic map of Europe that largely exists today was formed, and every claim of territorial rights that relies on the ethnic map of premigration Europe is simply impossible today, for in this period there were no states or nations of today.[3] The Slavs were separated into three groups, one of them made up by south Slavs who settled the Balkans. Among those south Slavs three distinct groups could be observed – the ancestors of the present-day Serbs, Croats and Slovenes.[4] Kosovo was the area where the Serbs settled between the seventh and tenth centuries.[5] They were mainly crop farmers and thus inhabited only the plains and river valleys of present-day Albania, leaving the mountains to the early Balkan shepherds – Vlachs and ancestors of modern Albanians.[6] Prior to the sixteenth century, the time of the conversion of great numbers of Albanians to Islam, 'Serbo-Albanian relations … can be regarded rather as a symbiosis.'[7]

In the late twelfth century, Kosovo and Metohija were incorporated into the Serbian medieval empire. By this time, Kosovo was, 'the heart of Serbia',[8] or in other words, 'the state, political, economic and cultural centre of the Serbian nation'.[9] Studded with more churches and monasteries than any other Serbian land, 'Kosovo and Metohija became the spiritual nucleus of Serbs'.[10]

Stefan Dušan's (1331–55) time was the peak of the Serbian medieval state for it then incorporated territories from Belgrade, across Albania, Epirus, Thessaly and Macedonia to the Aegean. Dušan was influenced by medieval ideas of the state, which were never national in the modern sense of the word' and, accordingly, called himself 'Emperor of the Serbs, Greeks, Bulgars and Arbanasi [Albanians]'.[11] However, by 1385 the Serbian medieval empire was mostly broken into pieces, falling under Turkish domination. Serbia itself (much divided among feudal lords) clashed with the Ottoman armies at the battle of Kosovo Polje, on 28 June (Vidovdan or St Vitus Day) 1389.

Whether this battle '[was] one of the greatest armed confrontations in Europe, [that] can even be compared ... to the Battle of Thermopile (480 BC)'[12] or just an insignificant event for world history, didn't matter to generations of Serbs. What matters is that 'of all Kosovo battles only one counts in the formation of the psyche of a Serb'.[13] Thus, for some Serbian historians 'Kosovo [is not] a myth, but a historical idea, which helps a nation to forge a link with its real historical past'.[14] The myth and legend of Kosovo and Vidovdan were 'transmitted to posterity by the popular epic poetry, by the Serbian Orthodox Church, by intellectuals and historians, as well as by national and political leaders in modern times'.[15] For Serbs, the legend of 'lost' Kosovo, regardless of how everything really happened, was another indispensable factor that kept the Serbian national consciousness alive and contributed to the successful end of the struggle for independence.

The Ottoman Rule and the Liberation Movements

The Turkish invasion caused Serbs to migrate to the north. Since the Ottoman Empire saw itself as a religious organization,[16] anyone who embraced the 'true faith' of Islam had the same rights as the Ottomans themselves. This resulted in mass conversions, forced or voluntary. The rule of the law of discrimination and the absolute authority of Islam were the factors that contributed largely to the demographic changes that took place in the eighteenth and nineteenth centuries.[17] In the great Austro-Turkish wars Serbs fought, together with other Christian inhabitants of the Balkans, on the Austrian side to overturn the 'Turkish yoke'. After the Austrians were defeated, reprisals followed and Serbs migrated north in large numbers, partly because of actual reprisals by the Turks and partly out of fear of reprisals.

The great migrations of the Serbs (the first estimated at some 185,000) greatly weakened the Serbian ethnic element in Kosovo and in other regions as well, but it wasn't before the eighteenth century that Kosovo started to lose its distinctly Serbian ethnic homogeneity. That was the time of the greatest and most numerous Albanian penetrations.[18] The new Albanian settlers, mostly Muslims by faith, were additionally protected by Ottoman authorities or previously settled ethnic Albanians.[19] According to Dimitrije Bogdanović, a Serbian historian, this mass colonization meant genocide for the Slav population.[20] The nineteenth century was marked by the national revolutions of the Balkan nations, and by the 1860s Serbs had won autonomy. In 1875 there was unrest in Bosnia. Serbia and Montenegro declared war on the Turks in 1876. The international crisis that followed was resolved first with the Treaty of San Stefano in 1878 and then with its revision, the Congress of Berlin in the same year. Both were a shock to Serbs since they had hoped to win back the 'Old Serbia' (Kosovo) and the Sanjak of Novi Pazar.

From the Congress of Berlin to the First World War

The Albanians who moved from the newly liberated Serbian territories contributed to the changes of the demographic picture of Kosovo.[21] Serbian ethnographer Niko Zupancić, for example, declared that 150,000 Serbs left Kosovo between 1876 and 1912.[22] Serbian official Branislav Nusić, compiled statistics for the villages in the Peć region, from which he concluded that 15,756 Serbs had left in the period 1870–95.[23] The creation of the independent Albania and Serbia's territorial gains in the Balkan wars – including Kosovo – did not solve the Serbian–Albanian problems. Serbia maintained – after the Balkan wars and later – that Kosovo *had* to be a part of the Serbian state, whether the Albanians made up the majority of the population or not.[24] Upon these premises the policy of the Serbian State towards the Albanian minority has been conducted ever since.

The Albanian Minority and the Yugoslav State from 1914 to 1989

During the Kingdom of the Serbs, Croats and Slovenes, the policy of moving the Albanian population out (for it was seen as the remnant of Ottoman dominance) was never approached systematically, although it was suggested by Turkey in 1914 and completed in respect to the other Muslims, from Romania, Bulgaria and Serbia 'proper'.[25] However, by this time, it had become absurd to consider the Albanians as strangers on Serbian land – people who should, in due time, be expelled from it. The developments during and after the Second World War firmly established them as a native population of Kosovo and they came to think of Kosovo as their land, that was unjustly not a part of a 'greater' Albanian state.

During the Second World War Kosovo became a part of Greater Albania, created by Italy, and huge numbers of Albanians flooded into the region.[26] This period of Serbian history is marked by a reign of terror – there were mass and single killings of Serbs in Kosovo and a 'campaign of expulsion and extermination [was conducted] against the Serbian population in the ... area'.[27] According to the Serbian historian, author Predrag Živančević, 60,000 Serbs and Montenegrins were killed during the war.[28] However, the outcome of all this was the incorporation of Kosovo not into Albania, but into a new, socialist Yugoslavia. Kosovo (or Kosovo-Metohija, more precisely, also called Kosmet) was until 1966 an autonomous 'region'. In 1974 Kosovo was bestowed a constitution separate from that of Serbia, the status of the Socialist Autonomous Province with rights equal to those of the nations of Yugoslavia.

After Tito's death in 1980, the manifestations of Albanian nationalism became more frequent. Many private assaults against Serbian persons and property were reported, as well as various other cases of rapes, beatings, destruction of graves and murders. Some monasteries and churches had also been defaced – all for reasons of ethnic hatred.[29] The pattern was emerging, that of systematic pressure on the Serbs and Montenegrins to leave Kosovo, sell everything they had and go to Serbia. (The percentage of the Serbian population in Kosovo fell from 23.6 per cent in 1961 to 13.2 per cent in 1981. It is now less than 10 per cent.[30]) In 1981[31] the secessionist tendencies of the Albanian population culminated in the so-called March riots. The central message of these mass protests was the demand for Kosovo to become a republic of Yugoslavia and the final aim of the protesters was union with their mother-state – Albania. A state of emergency was declared and the Yugoslav People's Army had to crush the revolt and restore order in Kosmet.

Even after these events the Albanian pressure and abuse of the Serbs and the Montenegrins continued. In 1990 Serbian historians alleged that in the previous two decades some 400,000 Serbs were forced to leave Kosovo.[32] They were ignored both by the Kosovo and the federal government. Resentment for the state that could not and did not want to protect its own citizens was rising. That, together with the coming six-hundredth anniversary of the famous battle of Kosovo created an atmosphere conducive to the rise of Serbian nationalism. Slobodan Milošević, an emerging figure on the political scene, used the emotions of the people and their dissatisfaction to gain power. Milošević only did what most of the Serbian people wished for: the centralization of the Serbian Republic. The first step was the abolishment of the autonomous provinces of Kosovo and Vojvodina.

Yugoslav Disintegration and Kosovo

Martial law was imposed on Kosovo in February 1989 and when a new wave of revolts erupted at the beginning of 1990, the army was sent to 'prevent civil war between ethnic Albanians and potential armed Serb militias'.[33] The Albanians and their leaders were explicit in their demands and thought that international recognition would come, together with the support from the mother-state. An illegal referendum was held in September 1991 and the outlawed Kosova Republican Assembly met on 19 October to declare that 'the Republic of Kosova is a sovereign and independent state' with Ibrahim Rugova as its 'president'. A few days later it was recognized by Albania.[34] Nevertheless, 'The Republic of Kosovo' was never a political reality in spite of the creation of a parallel system that covered all aspects of public life (for example, the Serbian state schools and the University of Pristina were boycotted by the Albanian students and an alternative educational system was introduced).

THE KOSOVA ALBANIAN PERSPECTIVE

The Beginnings [35]

For the Albanians the ethnic and cultural continuity between the early Illirians and the medieval Albanians is legitimate and well established fact.[36] The Albanian side points out that only in the twelfth century did the Serbs begin to populate the land of the Albanians in an organized way. According to Albanian sources, the aim of the Serbs and Montenegrins ever since they colonized a part of the Balkan Peninsula, has been to occupy the land of the Illirians–Albanians.[37] Pulaha, for example, states that 'the expansion of the Serb State in Kosova, during the twelfth century onward was by no means a "liberation" of the Serb lands but an annexation and occupation of Albanian territories'.[38] Even after the Ottomans occupied the Balkans, the Serbs, despite being under the Ottoman Empire, received the blessings of the Orthodox Church and Russia and organized two uprisings, at the beginning of the nineteenth century, and won their local autonomy. Since that time, the Serbian Orthodox Church, intellectuals and leaders have intended to invade the land of the Albanians.

From the Berlin Congress to the Balkan Wars

The Albanian side claims that all-Albanian populated lands, including Kosova, in the second half of the nineteenth century were objects of Serbian and Greek state aspirations. These aspirations became stronger 'particularly during and after the Eastern Crisis (1875–78) through propagandistic campaigns, and later through occupations and ethnic cleansing of these territories'.[39] According to Albanian sources, Albanians populated a wide area between 'Niš, Leskovac and Vranje in the north; Kumanova[o], Prilep and Manastir [present day Bitola] in the east and to Konitza, Janina and Preveza in the south'.[40] The Albanian side provides numerous cartographic

18

evidences about the 'real picture of the regions of ethnic Albanians in the twentieth century'.[41] According to Albanian historians, Serbian plans for an expansionist policy toward Albanian lands were outlined in the programme of Ilija Garašanin, the Minister of Internal Affairs of Serbia and one of the most outstanding Serbian officials in the nineteenth century, known by the name 'Načertanija'.[42] 'According to the Albanian side "Načertanija" of Garašanin transmitted ideas for multiple falsifications of Serbian historiography between 1870 and the 1880s on the land of the Albanians, such as Kosova, baptized by the name "Old Serbia".' (Stara Srbija).

The national ideology and Serbian state policy coming out of 'Načertanija' of Garašanin had 'the intention to occupy other's territories, to denationalize, assimilate and expatriate the other peoples, and the Serbian expansion, colonization and creation of a greater Serbia were foreseen instead'.[43] The Serbian–Ottoman wars 1877/1878, followed mass and forceful movements of Albanians from their native territories. By the end of 1878 there were 60,000 Albanian refugees in Macedonia and 60,000–70,000 in the *villayet* of Kosova.[44] At the 1878 Congress of Berlin, the Albanian territories of Niš, Prokuple, Kuršumlia, Vranje and Leskovac were given to Serbia; Montenegro was given the areas of Tivar, Podgorica, Plava, Gucia, Rugova and Kolašin.

From the Balkan Wars to Tito's Yugoslavia

The Balkan Wars brought about great changes on the geographic map of the Balkans. Although an Albanian state was established, much of the Albanian ethnic space, Kosovo included, was occupied by Serbian and Greek armies. Even the census organized by the Serbian military regime evidenced that the majority of the population of Kosova was Albanian. In order to change the ethnic balance of Kosova, the Serbian government undertook extreme measures, including regular killings of Albanians, forced expulsion and colonization by Serbians from Serbia. According to Albanian sources

> in the period between 1913 and 1939, 'flying detachments' of military and policemen acted to punish and massacre the population. From 1918 to 1938, the military burned and destroyed 320 villages with Albanian populations; only between 1918 and 1921, it killed 12,346 persons, put 22,160 people into prison, plundered 50,515 houses and burned down 6,125 houses.[45]

In the period between 1912 and 1941 at least 300,000 Albanians were expelled from Kosova, while 14,000 Serbian families settled in the region.[46] In short, 'the "Serbianization" of Kosova continued from 1912 until 1941 and the territory for the Serbian national element was created'.[47] As a consequence of ethnic cleansing and colonization of the Albanian land, a significant change of the ethnic structure of the population resulted. While the Albanians comprised 90 per cent of the population in these regions in 1912, it was down to 70 per cent in 1941.

Kosova in Tito's Yugoslavia

After the end of the Second World War, the Albanians of Kosova and other parts of Yugoslavia, were prevented from uniting with Albania. The Serbian regime continuously implemented the pre-war policies, the Kosova Albanians 'felt the annexation of Kosova to Serbia as the negation of their war and betrayal of the partisan leadership to them'.[48] Due to the persecutions, terror, violence and genocide inflicted on them, many Albanians – between 3,000 and 4,000 people – were forced to flee abroad, particularly the members of political and democratic organizations and groups with Western orientation that did not accept the new slavery in Kosova.[49] At the end of January 1953, the President of Yugoslavia, Josip Broz Tito, and the Turkish Foreign Minister, Fuad Kuprili, bowed for a gentlemen's agreement between Yugoslavia and Turkey. The agreement provided for expatriation of Kosova Albanians to Turkey; indeed more than 400,000 Albanians were forced to leave their homes and emigrate to Turkey in the period between 1950 and 1966.[50] The treatment of ethnic Albanians within Kosovo took 'an especially brutal turn with the reign of Alexander Ranković as the head of the secret police (1953–63)'.[51] Ranković's regime carried out acts of violence, terror and harassment against Kosovo Albanians.

Serbian domination of the province continued after 1966, despite Yugoslav constitutional changes in 1974 that upgraded the status of Kosova into autonomy. Meanwhile the economy stagnated and as a result, in the period between 1971 and 1981, 45,000 Albanians left the province.[52] Albanian historians estimate that out of a population of 1.5 million, only 178, 000 had jobs in all forms of state run enterprises (civil service, schools, hospitals, factories and so on). A significant ethnic imbalance was still in place, with the Serbs and Montenegrins, who formed 15 per cent of the population, holding 30 per cent of these jobs.[53] Dissatisfied with their position of being subjugated to Serbian power, Albanian students and youth organized demonstrations in 1981 with the main mobilizing slogan – Kosova Republic. Although the whole Albanian population supported them the Yugoslav leadership decided that the demonstrations threatened the territorial integrity and sovereignty of Yugoslavia. According to Fekrat, as a result of the crack down, 'hundreds were believed to have been killed, thousands arrested, and many provincial leaders were purged for their inability to control the unrest'.[54] A state of emergency was declared in the province, and large numbers of security forces occupied the region.

Kosova 1989–1999

Under Milošević Serbia wished to change its constitution and abolish Kosovo autonomy. Not only did the Albanians of Kosova not accept the proposals for abolishment of their autonomy, they advocated its upgrading. At the time of voting for changes to the Serbian Constitution, 'the building of the Assembly of Kosova was surrounded by tanks, military and police, and members of the secret police were present in the hall too'.[55] In conditions of a 'state of emergency', without the required quorum, without numbering the votes and by voting of persons that were found in the hall but were not delegates, the President of the Assembly of Kosova, who was a Serb, proclaimed on 23 March 1989 the approval of the constitutional amendments, and in addition to them some amendments that had not been in public discussion.[56] Therefore, the decision of the assembly of Serbia passed on 28 March 1989, to approve amendments 9–49 of the Constitution of Serbia was illegal. Meanwhile, the Albanian delegates of the Assembly of Kosova approved a Declaration of the Independence of Kosova on 2 July 1990, that preceded the Constitution of the Republic of Kosova, approved on 7 September 1990.

Despite the repressive regime in the 1990s the peaceful struggle against the Serbian occupation continued. After the Dayton Agreement in 1995 radical Kosova Albanians started advocating a military solution to their demands. Disappointed with the slow pace of their community's struggle for independence in early 1997 they started an armed rebellion against the institutions of the Serbian state. The conflict took some 2,000 lives, created thousands of refugees and caused enormous material damage. In addition, during the war in 1999, Kosovo saw an unprecedented level of material destruction, while thousands of refugees poured into Albania and Macedonia.

THE PROBLEM SEEN FROM THE SERBIAN SIDE[57]

The underlying principle of the Albanian struggle, the principle of self-determination, was originally intended for the colonial peoples.[58] It is 'the aspiration of the people to rule themselves and not be controlled by others', and as it can be both a force for convergence and for divergence, it can be destructive.[59] The denial of the right to self-determination is justified either by the need to preserve the territorial integrity of a state or the affirmation that civil freedoms and rights make the exercise of the right of self-determination redundant. On the other hand, 'this right is seen as absolute in claims that an ethnic community can pursue its freedom and preserve its identity only if it is constituted as a separate state'.[60] Therefore, justice and law can be, and are, in agreement with this principle if it is achieved within the boundaries of the state. However, separatists around the world, including the Kosovo Albanians, reject autonomy, 'as weak half-way measures'.[61] That is when the self-determination principle becomes destructive and violates international order and justice.

Because separatist movements want to change internationally recognized borders, they are a threat to international order. The Albanians in Kosovo (and potentially in north-western Macedonia) thought that they could repeat the strategy of Serbs in Bosnia and Croatia to change internationally recognized borders. But the international community has maintained its firm stance that self-determination of Serbs in ex-Yugoslav republics and, therefore, the self-determination of Albanians in Kosovo, has to be realized within the existing borders of the states, no matter how justly or unjustly they were once drawn. For Serbian authorities and nationalists alike, it is the right of the Serbian state to keep its territory; the succession of a part of the state – however centralized or decentralized that state might be – would mean violation of the interstate justice as envisioned by various international legal norms and resolutions.[62]

THE PROBLEM SEEN FROM ALBANIAN PERSPECTIVE[63]

Ignoring the Serb political system, Albanians proclaimed the independence of Kosova in 1990 and elected Ibrahim Rugova as their president. Albanians and their elite were convinced that the international community would respect the principles of self-determination and the right of the people to choose their own regime. However, from 1989 to 1999, Kosova has continued to be a colony of Serbia and the international community failed to recognize Kosova's independence. The international community insisted that Kosova was an integral part of Serbia and there was no willingness on its part to deal with it on a par with the other successor states.[64] Deciding that the peaceful and non-violent movement of Rugova had brought no results for the 'Albanian cause' radicalized Kosova Albanians organized a clandestine military organization, the Kosovo Liberation Army (KLA), and took up an armed struggle as a solution to their demands. The Kosova Albanians base their call for self-determination on the particular circumstances of their case. Oppressed and subject to discrimination, the Albanians' demand for independence 'is justified on both moral and legal grounds, as they do not ask for the change of frontiers by force'.[65] Given the fact that Kosovo autonomy was unlawfully abolished, that today Kosova comprises a clearly defined territory inhabited by a population of over two million, 90 per cent of whom are Albanians, and who has through referendum asked for independence and, finally, given the present day Serbian regime's brutal oppression, the right to have an independent Kosova Albanian state is justified.[66]

22

THE CLASH OF TWIN CLAIMS

Although the Albanian as well as the Serbian side claim their right to Kosovo/a as being specific, both give a very similar argumentation in favour of this right. On one hand, the Serbs state that their 'right to Kosovo' is based on the fact that Serbs migrated to this region in the tenth century, founded a great medieval empire, the Serbian Orthodox Church and a number of churches and monasteries, etc. The Serbian side refutes the Albanian claim that Albanians are descendants of Illirians. In addition, the Serbs maintain that even if the link between Illirians and Albanians is true, it does not count since every claim of territorial rights that relies on the ethnic map of premigration Europe is 'simply impossible today', for in that period there were no states or nations as we know them today. In short, the Serbian argument of historical right over Kosovo is one of first occupancy: 'we were there first and although in Kosovo there might have been other ethnic groups in the time of our migration they had not had any meaningful forms of organization, neither did they have national consciousness.' Although the argument is supposed to be specific, it is in fact quite similar to the Albanian 'historical claim'. The Albanian side notes that Illirians, the predecessors of present day Albanians, were the majority on the territory of Kosovo and that Serbs began migrating there from the tenth century. Despite Serbian colonization, mass deportations, killings and other methods of oppression, Albanians remained the bulk of the population of Kosova until the present day. Unlike the Serbs, Albanians explain that the fact that they, as the biggest ethnic group in Kosova, did not have a state or national consciousness adds to their right to claim Kosova. Although they do not agree on the question of what counts as meaningful presence in the region, both Serbs and Albanians state that they were the 'first inhabitants' of Kosovo/a. In order to support their claim Serbs explain that it was exactly in Kosovo where they formed their medieval state, the Patriarchy, many monasteries, churches and so on. Albanians, on the other hand, note that although they did not, or rather could not, create national institutions like the Serbs did, they were nevertheless the bulk of the population of Kosova in the same period. Even though Albanians rely on 'numbers' while Serbs use 'numbers plus institutions' as proofs of their right to Kosovo/a, obviously both sides want to present it as being historically 'theirs' in a similar fashion.

Besides historical arguments both parties in the conflict also call upon legal evidence to prove the right to Kosovo/a. Again, both sides employ a more or less similar argument in support of their legal right to Kosovo. The Serbian argument notes that Kosovo is an internal affair of Serbia and that Kosovo Albanians can be granted some sort of autonomy but certainly not independence. Actions by the Kosovo Liberation Army are categorized as 'terrorist deeds' while the operations of the Serbian police and the paramilitary units are seen as legitimate. Kosovo Albanians do not want even to consider being granted autonomous rights by what they see as being a 'Nazi-like' regime. For them Serbia unlawfully abolished the autonomy of Kosova in 1989. Following the disintegration of former Yugoslavia in which the other federal constituent units (Slovenia, Macedonia, et al.) disassociated from Belgrade, the legally established Assembly of Kosova declared independence and proclaimed the Constitution of the Republic of Kosova based on the principles of self-determination, equality and sovereignty. The claim to independence was supported by the general will of the population of Kosova which was and is overwhelmingly ethnic Albanian. For Serbs, the abolishment of Kosovo's autonomy by the Serbian parliament in 1989 was a legal step, this act is perceived as illegal by the Kosova Albanians. Notwithstanding the dispute over the legitimacy of the abolishment of Kosovo's autonomy within the Yugoslav federation, it is apparent that the claims of Serbs and Albanians to have a legal right to rule this province are ubiquitously similar. On the one hand, the Serbs interpret that after the fall of communism Kosovo became Serbia's internal matter and that based on this fact they can decide whether to 'give' Kosovo Albanians rights to self-rule or not. Kosova Albanians, on the other hand, construe that due to the disintegration of former Yugoslavia, Kosova's autonomy was upgraded to an independent status, and that therefore Serbia has nothing to do with the province and should withdraw its 'occupational forces'. Paradoxically then, Serb and Albanian interpretations of the legal developments and status of the region are identical – both claim that the other party has 'nothing to do with us – we have the legal basis to rule over Kosovo/a'. Although both sides' legal arguments are dubious, nevertheless they exist as 'real' in nationalist rhetoric. In other words, the interpretation of the legal developments exists as part of the justification of both Serbian and Albanian nationalists of the right to rule over Kosovo/a no matter which side *actually* is right as far as law is concerned.

Evidently, both Serbian and Albanian argumentation over the right to Kosovo/a is similar and cannot be evaluated by the principle of 'particularity' as nationalists from both camps would like us to do. What would happen if we insist on accepting the arguments of either side? Imagine that we are the omnipotent ruler of life on the earth. Let's say one day we are confronted by a Kosovo Albanian who says that based on historical rights, legal status and demographics Kosova should become a free Albanian state. After listening to this point of view we decide to fulfil his demand and declare Kosova independent. The next day, however, a Serbian comes to visit our office. He states that Kosovo should be returned to Serbia because Serbs have first occupancy rights in the region and, legally speaking, Kosovo was/is a part of the Serbian state. He also insists that Kosovo Albanians are but a minority in Serbia and therefore cannot succeed. Upon hearing his arguments we decide to return Kosovo to Serbian rule.

Of course, the following day the Kosova Albanian knocks on our door with a different story. The point I am trying to make is that we cannot rely on the particularized nationalistic claims, for as the Kosovo case study evinces, they are conflicting and therefore impossible to adjudicate.

Moreover, both sides' arguments are similar to those of many other nationalist groups, be they the Basques or the Chechens. The problem we have to overcome is how to reconcile two diametrically opposing interpretations of historical and legal developments. Although there are cases in which we can stand back and evaluate different nationalist historical and legal interpretations of the opposing claims these instances are rare. Nevertheless, even if we can imagine that we can find the truth about the history, legal status or demography of the region we still do not have the ultimate answer to which of these concepts to base decisions about the right to rule over a territory. Thus if, for example, historical facts show that Serbs were the first inhabitants of Kosovo, the Serbian side will call this the right principle for adjudicating between their claims and the Albanian counter claims. In this scenario the Albanian side will evince the principle of self-determination based on the demographics of the region. On the other side the Serbs might counter this proposal by one which calls for self-determination of the whole population of Serbia. Again we are faced with a problem of what maxims to use in determining the rightness of nationalist claims. Obviously then what we need is a framework, or some general principles which can tell us how to adjudicate between nationalist claims.

If the claims of national groups cannot be justifiably considered on the basis of the uniqueness of the situation of the groups in question then what should be done? As the Kosovo case study shows, there is a need on the part of social scientists to construct a 'just theory of nationalism'. Such an analysis would not only distinguish between just and unjust nation-building processes, but would also outline a framework of minority rights and make a generalized statement as to when and under what conditions nations do have a right to territorial self-determination. Therefore, such a theory would look at questions regarding which nationalist claims are justifiable and through what kind of mechanisms they can be realized.

NOTES

1. Yael Tamir, 'The Enigma of Nationalism', *World Politics*, April 1995, p. 419.
2. This is the Serbian interpretation of the history of Kosovo, and therefore does not necessarily correspond to an objective view of the history of the region. Indeed, here it is not my aim to present a 'correct' history of this region, but only to give an account of the Serbian reading of the history no matter how biased it might be.
3. Dimitrije Bogdanović, *Knjiga o Kosovu* (Belgrade: SANU, 1986), p. 284.
4. Jovan Ilić, 'The Balkan Geopolitical Knot and the Serbian Question: Characteristics and Importance of the Geographical Position of the Balkan

Peninsula', in Ilić, *Serbian Question in the Balkans* (Belgrade: University of Belgrade, 1995), at members.tripod.com/Balkania/resources/history/ilic_balkan_knot.html.

5. Dusan Bataković, 'Kosovo and Metohija: a Historical Survey', in Bataković, *Kosovo Chronicles* (Belgrade: Plato, 1992), at www.kosovo.com/history/kosovo_chronicles/kc_part1b.html.
6. See Bogdanović, *Knjiga*, p. 284.
7. Ibid., p. 285.
8. Slobodan Milošević, quoted in 'Will Blood Again Drench Kosovo?' *Observer*, 5 May 1994, p. 32.
9. See Bogdanović, *Knjiga*, p. 285
10. See Bataković, 'Historical Survey'.
11. See Bogdanović, *Knjiga*, p. 285.
12. Ibid., p. 286.
13. Alex Dragnich and Slavko Todorović, 'Kosovo Battle', in Alex Dragnich and Slavko Todorović, *The Saga of Kosovo* (New York: Columbia University Press, 1984), at www.kosovo.com/history/kosovo_saga/saga03.html.
14. See Bogdanović, *Knjiga*, p. 286.
15. Dimitrije Djordjević, 'The Role of St. Vitus Day in Modern Serbia', in William Dorich, *Kosovo* (Alhambra: Kosovo Charity Fund, 1992), at www.kosovo.com/history/dorich_kosovo/kosovo18.html.
16. See Bogdanović, *Knjiga*, pp. 286–7.
17. Barbara Jelavich, *History of the Balkans* vol. 2 (Cambridge: Cambridge University Press, 1991), p. 1.
18. Ibid., p. 84.
19. Alex Dragnich and Slavka Todorović, 'Migrations, Ethnic Vacuum, Shifts in Center of Serbdom', in Alex Dragnich and Slavko Todorović, *The Saga of Kosovo.*
20. For more information see: Radovan Samardzić et al., *Kosovo i Metohija u srpskoj istoriji* [Kosovo and Metohija in the Serbian History] (Belgrade: Srpska knjizevna zadruga, 1989); see also D. T. Bataković (ed.), *Savremenici o Kosovu i Metohiji 1852–1912* [Contemporaries on Kosovo and Metohija 1852–1912] (Belgrade: Srpska knjizevna zadruga, 1988).
21. See Bogdanović, *Knjiga*, p. 288.
22. Alex Dragnich and Slavka Todorović, 'The Albanians of the Nineteenth Century', in Dragnich and Todorović, *The Saga of Kosovo.*
23. See Niko Zupančić, *Altserbien und due Albanesische Frage* (Vienna, 1912), as cited in Noel Malcolm, *Kosovo* (London: Macmillan, 1998, 1995).
24. See Jelavich, *History of the Balkans*, p. 84.
25. Memorandum of the Serbian Delegation to the Peace Conference of 1913, quoted in Bogdanović, *Knjiga*, p. 173.
26. See Jelavich, *History of the Balkans*, p. 273, and Bogdanović, *Knjiga*, p. 292.
27. M. Vucković and G. Nikolić, in *Stanovnistvo Kosova u Razdoblju od 1918 do 1991* (Munich, 1996), cite a figure of 100,000.
28. Steven L. Burg, *Conflict and Cohesion in Socialist Yugoslavia* (Princeton, NJ: Princeton University Press, 1983), p. 48.
29. Helsinki Watch Report, pp. 21–2.
30. See statistics in Marina Blagojević and Ruza Petrović, *The Migrations of Serbs and Montenegrins from Kosovo and Metohija* (Belgrade: SANU, 1992), at members.tripod.com/Balkania/resources/history/migrations/mk_3.html.
31. Tito died on 4 May 1980, in Ljubljana.
32. See Malcolm, *Kosovo*, p. 329.
33. Helsinki Watch Report, p. 30.

34. David Rinder, 'Yugoslavia's Albanians Seek Foreign Affirmation', *New York Times*, 3 November 1991.
35. What follows is the Kosova Albanian account of the historical developments in the regions. Again the reader must be warned that this version of history might not correspond to an objective historic account of the region.
36. See, for example, Selami Pulaha, 'On the Autochthony of Albanians in Kosovo and the Postulated Massive Serb Migration at the End of the Seventeenth Century', in *International Journal of Albanian Studies* vol. 2, no. 1 (1997), at www.albanian.com/IJAS/vol2/is1/art2.html#top. For a good discussion of the topic see Alain Ducellier, 'Did the Albanians Occupy Kosova?' at www.albanian.com/main/countries/kosova/index.html.
37. Dr Aleksander Stipčević, *The Question of Illirian–Albanian Continuity and its Political Topicality Today*, at www.kosovainfo.com.
38. See Pulaha, 'On the Autochthony of Albanians in Kosovo'.
39. The Institute of History, Pristina, *Expulsions of Albanians and Colonization of Kosova* (Pristina: QIK [KIC – Kosova Information Centre], 1997), at www.kosova.com.
40. Ibid. The Albanian side of the argument is well synthesized in *Expulsions* from where most of the subsequent quotes are taken. Sami Frashëri, *Dheshkronjë* [Geography] (Bucharest, 1886), quoted after Rexhep Qosja, *Çështja shqiptare – Historia dhe Politika* [Albanian Question – History and Politics] (Pristina: IA, 1994), p. 29.
41. Quoted after Hamit Kokalari, *Kosova Djep i Shqiptarizmit* [Kosova the Cradle of the Albanians] (1962), p. 87.
42. Dr Hakif Bajrami, *Ilija Garashanini dhe Politika e tij Shtetnrore 1844–1874* [Ilija Garašanin and His State Policy Between 1844–1874], *Vjetar* (Annual), XIV, AK (Pristina: 1988), pp. 103–38.
43. See *Expulsions of Albanians*.
44. See E. Pllana, 'Les Raisons et la maniere de L'Exode Des Refugies Albanais du Territoire du Sandjak de Nish a Kosove (1877–1878)', in G. Reichenkron and A. Schmaus (eds), *Die Kultur Sudosteuropas: Ihre Geschichte und Ihre Ausdrucksformen* (Wiesbaden: Harrassowitz, 1964); and S. Rizaj 'Nente Dokumente Angleze Mbi Lidhjen Shqiptare te Ptizrenit (1878–1880)' in, *Gjurmine Albanologjike, Seria e Shkencave Historike* vol. 10 (1981), both cited in Malcolm, *Kosovo*.
45. See *Expulsions of Albanians*.
46. Zamir Shtylla, 'The Forced Deportation of Albanians in the Years 1912–1941', in Kristaq Prifti et al. (eds), *The Truth on Kosova* (Tirana: Encyclopedia Publishing House, 1993), p. 147.
47. See *Expulsions of Albanians*.
48. Ibid.
49. Sinan Hasani, *Kosovo, Istine i Zablude* [Kosova, Truths and Misconceptions] (Zagreb: Centar za informacije i publicitet, 1986), p. 130.
50. See Zamir Shtylla, 'The Deportation of Albanians in Yugoslavia After the Second World War', in Prifti et al., *The Truth on Kosova*, p. 239, and *Expulsions of Albanians*. Another Albanian historian, H. Islaimi, states that roughly 246,000 people emigrated to Turkey from the *whole of Yugoslavia* (emphasis added). See his 'Demokratski Problemi Kosova i Njihovo Tumacenje', in S. Gaber and T. Kuzmanic (eds), *Zbornik–Kosovo–Srbija–Jugoslavija* (Ljubljana: Universitetna Konferenca ZSMS and Knijžnica Revolutionarne Teorije, 1989), p. 52. Malcolm estimates that 100,000 were emigrants from Kosova.
51. Bruce Fekrat, 'Albanians in the Kosovo Region of Yugoslavia', report for

Minorities at Risk Project, at www.bsos.umd.edu/cidcm/mar/yugalban.html.

52. P. Prifti, 'Kosova's Economy: Problems and Perspectives', in A. Pipa and S. Repishti (eds), *Studies on Kosova* (New York: East European Monographs, 1984), p. 129.
53. See Malcolm, *Kosovo*, p. 337.
54. See Fekrat, 'Albanians'.
55. See *Expulsions of Albanians*.
56. Ibid. and see A. Gashi, *The Denial of Human and National Rights of Albanians in Kosova* (New York: Illyria, 1992), pp. 102–3.
57. This section presents the Serbian perception of the problem – it does not necessarily correspond with 'actual' facts or arguments.
58. Ljubivoje Ačimović, 'The Principle of Self-determination of Peoples', speech from the conference 'Self-determination in International Law: Applications to the Kosovo Case' (Belgrade, 21–22 November 1998), organized by the Yugoslav Helsinki Committee.
59. Louis L. Snyder, *Encyclopedia of Nationalism* (New York: Paragon House, 1990), p. 212.
60. Milenko Marković, 'Self-determination of Peoples', speech from the conference 'Self-determination in International Law'.
61. Ibid., p. 234.
62. See Zlatko Isaković, 'Kosovo under International Receivership: The Territorial Integrity versus Self-determination', *EuroBalkans* no. 37–8 (Spring–Summer, 2000).
63. The arguments are presented from the Albanian side in this section.
64. Shinasi Rama, 'The Serb–Albanian War and the International Community's Miscalculations', *International Journal for Albanian Studies*, Spring 1998.
65. Sami Repishti, abstract from 'The Question of Kosova and the Albanians in the Former Yugoslavia', symposium held jointly by the Academy of Sciences of Albania and the Academy of Sciences and Arts of Kosova (Tirana, 15 and 16 April 1993), at www.kosovainfo.com/english/politics/politics3.html.
66. See, for example, the wording used in 'The Declaration of Kosova's Independence' and in the 'Decision on the Proclamation of the Constitution of the Republic of Kosova', in Prifti et al., *The Truth on Kosova* (Tirana: Encyclopedia Publishing House), pp. 329 and 330. Also see 'A Political Declaration', p. 338, and 'Letter to the Extraordinary EPC meeting of Brussels' (16 December 1991), p. 341.

REFERENCES

Bajrami, H., *Ilija Garashanini dhe Ppolitika e tij Shtetnrore 1844–1874, Vjetar* (Annual), XIV, AK (Pristina, 1988).

Bataković, D., *Kosovo Chronicles* (Belgrade: Plato, 1992), at www.kosovo.com/history/kosovo_chronicles/kc_part1b.html.

Blagojević, M. and Petrović, R., *The Migrations of Serbs and Montenegrins from Kosovo and Metohija* (Belgrade: SANU, 1992), at www.members.tripod.com/Balkania/resources/history/migrations/mk_3.html.

Bogdanović, D., *Knjiga o Kosovu* (Belgrade: SANU, 1986).

Burg, S. L., *Conflict and Cohesion in Socialist Yugoslavia* (Princeton, NJ: Princeton University Press, 1983).

Dragnich, A. and Todorović, S., *The Saga of Kosovo* (New York: Columbia University Press, 1984), at www.kosovo.com/history/kosovo_saga.

Djordjević, D., 'The Role of St. Vitus Day in Modern Serbia', in William Dorich, *Kosovo* (Alhambra: Kosovo Charity Fund, 1992), at www.kosovo.com/history/dorich_kosovo/kosovo18.html.

Engelberg, S., 'Carving Out A Greater Serbia', *New York Times*, 1 September 1991.

Fekrat, B., 'Albanians in the Kosovo Region of Yugoslavia', report for Minorities at Risk Project, at www.bsos.umd.edu/cidcm/mar/yugalban.html.

Gashi, A. A., *The Denial of Human and National Rights of Albanians in Kosova* (New York: Illyria, 1992).

Hadri, A., *Istorija Albanskog Naroda za Osnovnu Školu* (Pristina: Zavod za Udzbenike i Nastavna Sredstva, 1974).

Hasani, S., *Kosovo, Istine i Zablude* (Zagreb: Centar za informatcije i publicitet, 1986).

Ilić, J., 'The Balkan Geopolitical Knot and the Serbian Question' (Characteristics and Importance of the Geographical Position of the Balkan Peninsula), in Ilić, *Serbian Question in the Balkans* (Belgrade: University of Belgrade, 1995), at www.members.tripod.com/Balkania/resources/history/ilic_balkan_knot.html.

The Institute of History, Pristina, *Expulsions of Albanians and Colonization of Kosova* (Pristina: QIK (or KIC – Kosova Information Centre), 1997), at www.kosova.com.

Isaković, Z., 'Kosovo under International Receivership: The Territorial Integrity versus Self-determination', in *EuroBalkans* no. 37–8 (Spring–Summer 2000).

Islami, H., 'Demokratski Problemi Kosova i Njihovo Tumacenje', in S. Gaber and T. Kuzmanić (eds), *Zbornik–Kosovo–Srbija–Jugoslavija* (Ljubljana: Univerzitetna Konferenca ZSMS and Knjižnica Revolutionarne Teorije, 1989).

Jelavich, B., *History of the Balkans* vol. 2. (Cambridge: Cambridge University Press, 1991).

Kaplan, R. D., *Balkan Ghosts: A Journey Through History* (New York: Vintage Departures, 1994).

Kokalari, H., *Kosova Djep i Shqiptarizmit* (1962).

Malcolm, N., *Kosovo* (London: Macmillan, 1998).

Marković, M., 'Self-determination of Peoples', speech from the conference 'Self-Determination in International Law: Applications to the Kosovo Case' (Belgrade, 21–22 November 1998), organized by the Yugoslav Helsinki Committee.

Prifti, K. et al. (eds), *The Truth on Kosova* (Tirana: Encyclopedia Publishing House, 1993).

Prifti, P., 'Kosova's Economy: Problems and Perspectives', in A. Pipa, and S. Repishti (eds), *Studies on Kosova* (New York: East European Monographs, 1984).

Rama, S., 'The Serb–Albanian War and the International Community's Miscalculations', in *International Journal for Albanian Studies*, Spring 1998.

Repishti, S., abstract from 'The Question of Kosova and the Albanians in the Former Yugoslavia', symposium held jointly by the Academy of Sciences of Albania and the Academy of Sciences and Arts of Kosova (Tirana, 15 and 16 April 1993), at www.kosovainfo.com/english/politics/politics3.html.

Rinder, D., 'Yugoslavia's Albanians Seek Foreign Affirmation', *New York Times*, 3 November 1991.

Sabit, U., *Dëbimi me dhunë i shqiptarëve nga Sanxhaku i Nishit (1877–1878), Gjenocidi dhe aktet gjenocidale të pushtetit serb ndaj shqiptarëve nga Kriza Lindore e këndej* (Pristina: ASHAK, 1995).

Selami, P., 'On the Autochthony of Albanians in Kosovo and the Postulated Massive Serb Migration at the end of the Seventeenth Century', *International Journal of Albanian Studies* vol. 2, no. 1 (1997), at www.albanian.com/IJAS/vol2/is1/art2.html#top.

Serbian Delegation, 'Memorandum to the Peace Conference' 1913.

Shtylla, Z., 'The Forced Deportation of Albanians in the Years 1912–1941', in Kristaq

Prifti et al. (eds), *The Truth on Kosova* (Tirana: Encyclopedia Publishing House, 1993).

Snyder, L. L., *Encyclopedia of Nationalism* (New York: Paragon House, 1990).

Stipcević, A., *The Question of Illirian–Albanian Continuity and its Political Topicality Today*, at www.kosovainfo.com.

Tamir, Y., 'The Enigma of Nationalism', *World Politics*, April 1995.

'Will Blood Again Drench Kosovo', *Observer*, 5 May 1994.

Xhemajl, A., *Ndjekja dhe politika ndëshkrimore për delikte politike në Kosovë në periudhën 1981–1990* (Pristina: Bota e Re, 1995).

2

Kosovo or Kosova – Could It Be Both? The Case of Interlocking Serbian and Albanian Nationalisms

Dejan Guzina

To the frustration of outside observers, virtually everything seems to represent a bone of contention between the Serbian and Kosovar Albanian communities. Caught between two 'truths on Kosovo' – the Serbian one and the Albanian one – analysts often seek refuge, as Julie Mertus observes, in three lines of rhetoric: complexity, denial or Balkan primordialism. In combination, these offer a powerful 'vision' that nothing ever changes in the Balkans: people simply keep killing each other for unknown and unintelligible reasons buried deep in the past.[1]

The situation becomes even more complex if one takes account of the contributions of local national historiographies towards understanding the Kosovo issue. These aim to enlighten foreign observers as to the truth of Kosovo, building sympathy for their own territorial claims. But their constant references to historical events in Kosovo – such as the battle between the Serbs and the Ottoman Turks in 1389, the Serbian exodus from Kosovo in the 1690s, the Albanian League of Prizren in 1878, the Serbian *reconquista* (or, from the Albanian perspective, invasion) of Kosovo in 1912 – only reinforce the Western myth of Balkan complexities.[2]

The Kosovo crisis can and needs to be addressed from a different perspective, unburdened by mythical recountings of Serbian and Albanian pasts. Such a viewpoint would not deny the significance of the key events in Serbian and Kosovo Albanian histories, but it must avoid instrumentalizing these events as evidence for one side over the other, and instead recognize the extent to which both sides invoke historical events to try to legitimize present territorial claims. This would shift the focus from sterile debate about the relative historical significance of this or that group's presence in the region to serious analysis of the contemporary reasons for the conflict over Kosovo.[3]

31

Before looking in detail at the origins of the present crisis, it is instructive to clarify some terminological points. As from 1990, the official Serbian name of the province is Kosovo and Metohija (or Kosmet in abbreviated form).[4] However, the former name of the province – Kosovo – is still widespread in the Serbian media and has usually been the most popular term abroad. During the recent Serb–Albanian conflict, however, the Albanianized version of the term – Kosova (which can also be written as Kosovë) – gained popularity in foreign accounts of the situation, perhaps reflecting heightened sympathy at the time with the plight and political objectives of Kosovo/a Albanians.[5]

There is similar terminological confusion over the name for the inhabitants of the region. After 1945, in pursuit of a policy of national equality, the Communist Party designated the Albanian community as 'Šiptari' (Shqiptare, in Albanian), the term used by Albanians themselves to mark the ethnic identity of any member of the Albanian nation, whether living in Albania or elsewhere. This was a step forward, as it replaced older, pejorative Serbian terms such as 'Arbanasi', and 'Arnauti' (a word of Turkish origin). However, with the increased territorial autonomy of Kosovo in the late 1960s, the Albanian leadership requested that the term 'Albanians' be used instead – thus stressing national, rather than ethnic, self-identification of the Kosovar population. The term 'Albanians' was accepted and included in the 1974 Yugoslav Constitution.

In the process, however, the Serbian version of the Albanian term for ethnic Albanians – 'Šiptari' – had acquired an openly pejorative flavour, implying cultural and racial inferiority. Nowadays, even though in the documents of post-socialist Serbia the term 'Albanians' is accepted as official, many state and opposition party leaders use the term 'Šiptari' indiscriminately in an effort to relegate the Kosovo Albanians to the status of one among many minority groups in Serbia. Thus the quarrel over the terms used to identify the region and its inhabitants has acquired a powerful emotional and political significance for both communities.

At the heart of these disputes is the question of identity, the extent to which Kosovar Albanians have not been recognized as a fully sovereign national group in Serbia and Yugoslavia. From this primordial disagreement over the question of identity, other political disagreements follow. If Albanians are a minority, should not the Serbian regime have the right to protect territorial integrity of the Serbian state? On the other side, if Albanians are a (sovereign) people, should they not be granted full rights to national self-determination, including the right to a state of their own? Who has the legitimate right to diagnose (that is, to decide on) the status of a particular national group as a minority or a majority? Does Serbian repression constitute a violation of group rights or a 'gross violation of human rights', etc.?

These dilemmas are the focus of the following pages. The first part presents an overview of the autonomous status of Kosovo province in socialist Yugoslavia. The second part discusses the regime's politics of systemic discrimination against Kosovar Albanians. It also explores various forms of political resistance against the Serbian regime. The chapter does not deal with the issues opened by NATO (North Atlantic Treaty Organization) intervention in Kosovo and Serbia in March–June 1999, nor with international aspects of the question of the final political and territorial status of Kosovo.

KOSOVO'S AUTONOMY, 1945–1989

In hindsight, and especially in the light of the armed Serbian–Albanian conflict in Kosovo in 1998 and the NATO military intervention against Serbia in March 1999, it is hard to argue with the often repeated view that Kosovo has always been subject to two irreconcilable claims to sovereignty. This argument emphasizes Albanian perceptions of Kosova as the birthplace of modern Albanian nationalism, only left out of Albania because of Serbian occupation in 1912. It similarly stresses Serb views of Kosovo as the crucible of Serbian nationhood, justly liberated and reintegrated with Serbia in 1912 after five centuries under the Ottoman Turkish 'yoke'. Neither narrative leaves space for the existence of the other in the region. Kosovo, or Kosova, could be either Serbian or Albanian, but not both.[6] Yet the communist elite tried to reconcile these two claims within the framework of the socialist, federal Yugoslavia: Kosovo remained a part of Serbia, while being a part of the federation as well.[7] This was done by gradually enhancing Kosovo's territorial autonomy and the status of Kosovo Albanians. In the end, under the 1974 Yugoslav constitutional system, Kosovo emerged as the de facto seventh federal unit, while formally still being a part of Serbia.

Serbia gradually lost its powers in relation to the status of the autonomous provinces. Following constitutional amendments in 1971, it was obliged to coordinate the provincial status of Vojvodina and Kosovo with the provincial authorities and a Federal Assembly. Finally, in 1974, the provinces were granted their own constitutions, which regulated their economic, social, cultural and political affairs independently of the Serbian Constitution. This effectively deprived Serbia of control over the provinces, even though technically they remained a part of its territory. In the 1980s, neither Vojvodina nor Kosovo were integrated into the legal system of the Serbian federal unit to which they (officially) belonged. This fuelled Serbian nationalism.[8]

Among the early signs of crisis in the 'Yugoslav socialist paradise' were Kosova Albanian demonstrations in 1981 and the (interpretation of) census results of the same year. The mass student protests in Kosovo in 1981 might seem puzzling, given the political emancipation of Kosovo between 1968 and 1981. Over this period, Kosova Albanians gained full control of the province's political, social and cultural affairs. The University of Pristina (capital of Kosovo) opened in 1969 and the Kosovo Academy of Sciences and Arts in 1978.

The period also saw the development of strong cultural ties between Kosovo and Albania, which had been frozen for most of the time since 1945.[9] Moreover, as a result of the so-called 'national key' policy (a Yugoslav socialist version of affirmative action), Albanians took over many top managerial positions in the region formerly reserved for Serbs, while leading federal posts were regularly filled with Kosovo Albanian politicians. In 1978–79, a leading Kosovo Albanian politician, Fadil Hoxha, became a vice-president of the Yugoslav Presidency. Thus it seemed that Kosovo Albanians had finally been recognized fully, on equal terms with the members of Slavic nations in the country, and that they might eventually be granted the long-coveted status of one of Yugoslavia's nations.[10]

Yet the economic development of the province did not keep pace with its political and cultural progress, and by 1981 its economy was in dire straits. Despite huge federal financial injections during the 1970s and 1980s, all initiatives to develop the region failed dismally. Paradoxically, the very nature of the Yugoslav socialist, planned economy effectively undermined all federal economic incentives. The gap between the high prices of industrial goods and low prices of raw materials and agricultural produce trapped the least developed regions in Yugoslavia – Kosovo was the out-standing example – in poverty.[11] Of course, a strategy of investing in labour-intensive industries might have reduced unemployment and helped spark the economy, but this did not enter the administrative logic of the socialist model of self management and directed development.

During the late 1970s, provincial economic and social conditions deteriorated almost by the month, resulting in high unemployment (27.5 per cent in 1981), hyperinflation and increasing poverty. Moreover Kosovo's health and social services were far below the Yugoslav average, and its educational system failed to address the challenges posed by shortcomings of the communist model of modernization. Thus, during the 1970s, Pristina University specialized almost exclusively in Albanian history, literature and arts, while training in modern technical disciplines was neglected. A large number of young people enrolled, mainly in order to postpone unemployment. By 1981 Pristina had the highest proportion of students of any Yugoslav city.[12]

This mass of young Albanian liberal arts graduates became the backbone of the Albanian nationalist movement in the 1980s.[13] Their nationalist 'baptism' occurred on 11 March 1981, when they organized demonstrations on the streets of Pristina. The first demonstrations represented, in the words of Helen Lindholm, 'mainly a peaceful outburst of despair and frustration', provoked by the rapid economic and social deterioration of the province.[14] However, the intervention of special federal police sharpened the students' demands for republican status and the possibility of uniting with Albania. Finally, in the first week of April, police repression provoked a mass revolt throughout the province, which was eventually quelled by Yugoslav army troops.[15]

Hence, what started as peaceful student rallies against Kosovo's social and economic problems turned into a mass uprising of the Kosovo Albanian population to demand rights they thought to have already gained in 1974. Caught by surprise by discontented Albanian students, the federal communist leadership resorted to labelling the 1981 demonstrations as counter-revolutionary; a slogan already at that time devoid of any meaning, but which allowed police and the state-controlled judiciary to 'discover' more than 200 'hostile and counter-revolutionary groups'.[16] At a series of mass show-trials without independent monitoring, 226 students and younger workers were sentenced to up to 15 years each in prison for counter-revolutionary and irredentist activities.[17] The socialist Yugoslav regime hoped that such draconian measures would preclude further demands for self-determination. In the event, they only rallied more Kosovo Albanians around the struggle for republican status and recognition as a constitutive nation in Yugoslavia.

The 1981 Albanian demonstrations and the harsh governmental response not only radicalized the Albanian population, they also fostered the rise of the Serbian nationalist movement. From the Kosovo Serbs' perspective, the extension of Kosovo's autonomy in 1974 was at the expense of their political, cultural and economic status in the province. The Kosovar Serbs feared that, even though Kosovo remained officially part of Serbia, they had been effectively relegated to the status of a minority in their 'own' state. The events of 1981 – the uprising and subsequent 'discovery' of irredentist activities – seemed to confirm this.

The 1981 census results fuelled further controversy. They showed that 77.5 per cent of the Kosovo population was Albanian (1,226,736) and only 13.2 per cent Serb (210,000). The remaining 9.3 per cent consisted of Muslims, Romanies (gypsies), Turks and Croats. This confirmed a declining trend in the number of Serbs already noted at the 1971 census. From 1948 to 1961 the share of Albanians had remained around 67 per cent, with 23.5 per cent Serbs. Thus the 1981 results showed a marked change.[18]

At first hesitantly, then later in the 1980s in a flood of articles and interviews, leading Serbian national figures tried to portray the Kosovo Albanians' birth rate – the highest in Europe – as an anti-Serbian plot, designed to turn the province into an ethnic Albanian enclave. They also used the census results to show that increasing numbers of Kosovo Serbs were leaving for central Serbia. Without a shred of evidence, the Serbian migrations from Kosovo were branded with the terms 'pogrom' and 'genocide'.[19]

In 1990 a group of independent Yugoslav intellectuals finally reacted to Serbian policies based on attributing 'genocidal' motives to Albanians in

Kosovo. Although their analysis was long overdue, it passed unnoticed as the Yugoslav socialist system neared collapse and Serbian populism raged under the guidance of Slobodan Milošević. Yet it is worth careful consideration, because it still represents the most complete report on the Kosovo crisis or, as they put it, the Kosovo knot.[20]

So who, or what, was most responsible for the ethnic shift and the emigration of Serbs and Montenegrins from Kosovo? The report commenced its answer to this question by stating that of the three possible models of organizing relations among different groups – co-existence, assimilation and domination – domination had always characterized the situation in Kosovo. This cultural–historic pattern had been repeated by both Serbs and Albanians, and had its roots in the history of the region. Whichever political group gained ascendancy during a particular period would monopolize positions of power. The ethnic differences in the region then meant that the authoritarian character of government was confused with the ethnicity of the oppressor. Immediately after 1945, the Serbs, being far more numerous in Communist Party ranks than Albanians, dominated the administration. Although this was essentially just the expression of an antidemocratic order, the Albanian population perceived it as primarily the product of a Serbian regime.[21]

In the mid-1960s, the fall of Serbian strongman Aleksandar Ranković, led to genuine reforms in Kosovo, and an extension of its autonomy vis-à-vis Serbia. These sweeping changes not only enhanced the status of the Albanian population in the province; they also allowed the full Albanization of Kosovo's Communist Party. While Serbs had previously controlled the party, in the 1970s it was the Kosovar Albanians' turn. This nurtured Kosovo's 'internal sovereignty' in full accordance with the 1974 constitution. By then, the ethnic principle seemed more legitimate than in the late 1950s and early 1960s, when the ideology of socialism still dominated that of nationhood. In any case, the underlying model of domination remained, but this time it was the Serbs who were pushed out of their previous favoured position into increasing subordination.[22]

Moreover, as a result of the ethnification of the Yugoslav political system, in the 1970s people started migrating to their kin-republic. Serbs from Croatia migrated to Serbia, Croats from Vojvodina to Croatia, Serbs and Croats from Bosnia to Serbia and Croatia, and Muslims from Croatia and Serbia to Bosnia. So Serb and Montenegrin migrations from Kosovo to Serbia and Montenegro were part of a general Yugoslav trend, sharpened by the poor economic and social conditions in the province.[23] While there were various forms of ethnic pressure against Serbs and Montenegrins, their departures mainly reflected complex economic, political, social and cultural factors rather than any 'devious' Albanian plan.[24]

The rise of Milošević in the late 1980s brought a new twist to the model of domination in Kosovo. Inflammatory anti-Albanian rhetoric in the

Serbian media and by prominent Serbian nationally oriented intellectuals served to justify a new round of Serbian domination in Kosovo. The air was thick with claims of intimidation of the Serbian and Montenegrin population by the local police, forced sales of property by Serbs, and even systematic rape of Serbian women as an instrument of ethnic repression. None of these accusations were ever fully substantiated. In fact the evidence suggests that throughout the period of the so-called Albanian terror in the province, Albanians remained the prime target of repression by the Yugoslav political system. For example, Albanians continued to provide the greatest number of political prisoners in the country. Similarly, available data on the frequency of inter-ethnic rapes suggest that the rate of such crimes was actually declining.

If there was any 'crime' committed by the Albanians in the 1970s, it was the same as that committed by the Serbs before 1966 and after 1989. But by the late 1970s and early 1980s the break between the two ethnic communities in Kosovo was virtually complete. It simply became difficult for them to come into contact with one another, and intermarriages virtually ceased.[25] The accelerating separation of the Serb and Albanian communities was met with total inaction on the part of the Kosovo ethnic elites. Then, as later, the only solution to the Kosovo knot would have been rejection of the domination model in favour of one based on the coexistence of different ethnic groups sharing the same territory.[26]

By 1990, such political suggestions could only fall on deaf ears, for by then socialist Yugoslavia was in disarray, while the Serbian regime was celebrating the adoption of the new constitution of the (finally) united Serbia. Not surprisingly, it tried to halt the process of political self-identification by the Kosovar Albanians by reducing the province's substantive autonomous status to that of an administrative region within Serbia. But it was already too late. The period 1974–89 had heightened Kosovar Albanians' national consciousness and accustomed them to substantial autonomy with the region's own territorial boundaries, history and symbols. 'This genie [of self-determination]', as Andrew March and Rudra Sil nicely explain, 'once let out of the bottle, prohibits the Kosovo question from ever being viewed as a matter of greater or lesser minority rights granted or revoked by Serbia'.[27] The Serbian regime learnt this lesson repeatedly in the 1990s.

THE REPUBLIC OF KOSOVA – A STATE WITHIN A STATE, 1990–1998

In 1990, the struggle for the unification of Serbia seemed to be over. The old Yugoslav plan of a three-part Serbia was in ruins (as was Yugoslavia itself), and the Serbian regime felt it was high time to legally and insti-tutionally incorporate the Serbian provinces into a new centralized system of government. But this required, in the words of Muhamedin Kulaši (Muhamedin Kullashi), 'surgical cuts into Kosovo's institutional and legal system to root out any traces of provincial autonomy'.[28]

The first step towards legal unification of Serbia was the adoption of the Programme for the Attainment of Peace, Freedom, Equality and Prosperity in Kosovo by the still socialist Serbian Assembly (March 1990). The Programme provided the ideological and legal framework of a new political orthodoxy in the country. Under the pretext of protecting all national communities in Kosovo (Serbs, Montenegrins, Muslims, Turks, Romanies and Croats), and while pointing out that Albanians enjoyed rights 'unparalleled by any other national minority in the world', it claimed that Serbia, as a legal state, had a legitimate right to stop Albanian separatism. 'All means of the legal state' should be used to protect 'endangered nations and nationalities' in Kosovo from further menace. The Programme foreshadowed 'specific measures for preservation of order, peace, freedom, equality, and the constitution and integrity of Serbia', and empowered the Serbian Assembly to annul any laws and decrees of the then still functioning Assembly of Kosovo judged contrary to the Programme.[29]

New republican laws and regulations soon mushroomed. Within a year more than 20 new laws were adopted. They abolished nationality rights in Kosovo in the spheres of education, health care, self-government, information, economy, culture, sport, etc. A key early step was the Law on Actions of the Republican Administration in Exceptional Circumstances, which allowed 'temporary' (that is, emergency) measures to be introduced in the province. Using this law as a legal shield, the Serbian government replaced the entire ruling Albanian political and managerial elite with Kosovar Serbs. This law and the Law on Labour Relations in Exceptional Conditions (adopted with the proviso that it should be used only in Kosovo), allowed more than 100,000 Albanians to be dismissed from their jobs.[30] These draconian acts were justified by reference to alleged serious violations of public interest, failure to fulfil legal obligations, and severely disrupted self-management relations.[31]

The Law on the Termination of the Work of the Assembly and the Executive Council of Kosovo was adopted in July 1990. It prepared the ground for the imposition of colonial administrative rule of the province. At the same time, a new Law on Information effectively usurped the rights of the Albanian population in this sphere: the regime quickly banned the most influential Kosovar Albanian daily, *Rilindja*, and took over Kosovo radio and television. The most important Kosovar Albanian cultural institutions were also closed down – the Kosovo Academy of Science and Arts, the Kosovo Institute for History, the Institute for Albanian Studies, the Kosovo Bureau for Textbooks, etc.[32] Belgrade viewed these institutions as hotbeds of Albanian nationalism.

On 7 August 1990, the Serbian Parliament abrogated all province-specific aspects of the educational system, including special programmes in history, the Albanian language, geography, arts and music. Instead, it mandated uniform elementary and secondary school programmes for all schools in Serbia, including those in Kosovo, Vojvodina and Sandžak (Sanjak), irrespective of the cultural needs of the various national communities. Albanian teachers refused to implement the new social sciences and humanities curricula, and the Serbian authorities then cut off funding to Albanian schools in Kosovo.[33]

The enrolment of Albanians in secondary schools was also restricted. Whereas practically all Serbian children went to secondary school, the ratio for Albanian youngsters fell to about one in three. The situation deteriorated further at the beginning of the 1991/92 school year, when the Serbian authorities banned Albanian teachers and students from using school buildings unless they agreed to follow the Serbian curricula. Similar restrictions had already been imposed in 1990 at Pristina University, including the Kosovo Textbook Publishing Company and the University Student Centre. The Law on Labour Relations in Exceptional Conditions legalized these actions, and allowed the authorities to dismiss 18,000 teaching and non-teaching staff, many for reasons such as arriving late for work, leaving work without the permission of the dean and the like.[34]

A legal keystone of the new, united Serbia was laid on 27 November 1992, when the Serbian Parliament adopted the Declaration on Human Rights and Rights of Members of National Minorities. Its first section states that the Republic of Serbia is a 'state of equal citizens living in it', and nominally prohibits discrimination against citizens on the basis of their national affiliation. It specifically mentions the Kosovar Albanian national minority, whose rights are described as 'far above international standards'. Section two enumerates their rights: use of the Albanian mother tongue, health protection, free profession of religion, free access to information in Albanian, organization of constitutionally established territorial autonomy, etc.[35] However, from section three to the end of the document, the language changes from that of human and minority rights protection towards a version of the arguments in the infamous 1986 Memorandum of the Serbian Academy of Science and Art. For example, the declaration explicitly states that the Albanization of Kosovo and Metohija represents the greatest ethnic cleansing in Europe and that the demographic change against the Serbian population was done in an openly uncivilized and forced manner. Thus an ostensible declaration of human rights actually anathematizes Kosovar Albanians as an uncivilized people. In effect they were accused of a 150-year long campaign of ethnic cleansing against the Serbs, designed to alter the ethnic composition of Kosovo by force and eventually create a Greater Albania.[36]

In sum, from the beginning of the unified Serbia, a formal depreciation of the status of Kosovar Albanians permeated all Serbian laws and regulations governing economic, social, cultural and political life in Kosovo. The politics of oppression was, moreover, fully institutionalized and it amounted, in the words of Djerdj Rrapi, 'to formal, ideological and informal discrimination against the Albanian population'.[37] Formal and informal discrimination was practised on a day-to-day basis by the Serbian police in Kosovo, who used physical violence, open threats, insults and other forms of intimidation against Albanians. Ideological discrimination, on the other side, was in the attitude of those Kosovar Serbs who supported the Serbianization of Kosovo based on ideas of Serbian 'sacred land' and ethnic superiority.[38]

What was the Kosovar Albanian response to the Serbian state's policies of ethnic discrimination? Just as in Serbia, the Kosovo political scene became increasingly pluralized in the late 1980s to the early 1990s. But there were some important differences. In Serbia, former communists emerged as authoritarian socialist nationalists. In Kosovo, the Kosovar Communist Party had been politically liquidated by the Serbian regime, and the first seedlings of pluralism emerged in 1988 among members of the Association of Writers of Kosova and the Kosova Association of Philosophers and Sociologists. They, like the Serbian intellectuals in the mid-1980s, tried to raise the Kosovar Albanian question from a non-socialist (either communitarian–nationalist or a more civic–democratic) perspective.[39]

As in Belgrade, the Kosovar process of pluralization was eventually taken over by nationalist political parties, while democratic ones remained on the fringe. The marginalization of democratic alternatives in Kosova was perhaps inevitable after the Serbian regime suspended the autonomy of the province. The so-called civic option could not survive in a situation viewed by the Kosovar Albanians as one of police and military occupation of Kosovo. Political groups giving absolute priority to the status of Kosova quickly drowned the civic parties' arguments in support of democratic processes both at the level of Kosova and Yugoslavia.[40]

In other words, Serbian repression in the late 1980s stimulated Kosovar Albanians to press their claims for full territorial sovereignty. In 1990, the Kosovar Albanian delegates to the banned provincial assembly were just as enthusiastic for their own state as any other group in the former Yugoslavia. In July, they adopted the Declaration of Independence of the Republic of Kosova. Then in September they met in secret in Kačanik to endorse the so-called Kačanik Constitution, the Electoral Law and the Law on Political Association. Finally, in September 1991, a referendum was held at which, according to Albanian sources, 87 per cent of eligible voters supported the declaration and sovereignty for the Republic of Kosova.[41]

In the process of political pluralization, the Democratic League of Kosova (LDK) headed by Ibrahim Rugova emerged as the strongest national Kosovar Albanian party. Within months the LDK claimed to have 700,000 registered members. Although this figure must be exaggerated, since it would include almost every adult in Kosova, the party had clearly established its claim to embody the Kosovar Albanian national will.[42]

The LDK nurtured strong ties with the Albanian national parties in Macedonia and Montenegro. In October 1991, the Coordinating Committee of Albanian Political Parties in Yugoslavia, headed by Rugova, put forward a political platform that to a great extent still represents the Kosovar Albanian solution of the Albanian question. The platform set out the Albanian Kosovar position in three possible cases.

1. If the external and internal borders of socialist Yugoslavia remained unchanged, ethnic Albanians within Serbia, Macedonia and Montenegro should enjoy the status of a nation, not a national minority. This implied elevating Kosovo to the status of a republic.
2. If Yugoslavia's internal borders change, Yugoslav Albanians have the right to unite into an Albanian Republic within Yugoslavia. Then Kosova would incorporate territory in central Serbia, Montenegro and Macedonia populated by Albanians.
3. If Yugoslavia's external borders were changed, that is, if the country was dissolved, all Albanian lands in the Balkans should be united on the basis of 'ethnic boundaries' as envisioned by the First Prizren League of 1878.[43]

Thus by 1991 the Albanian nationalist movement became a mirror image of the nationalist projects raging throughout the former Yugoslavia. Responding to projects for Greater Serbia and Greater Croatia, Albanian national leaders proposed a Greater Albania. In all three cases the legitimizing principle would be ethnic monism. But the unfolding Yugoslav drama soon forced Albanian parties in Macedonia and Montenegro to accept these former republics as their own home. Kosovar Albanians then concentrated on trying to establish a sovereign Kosova. They agreed to postpone questions of democratic reform until they achieved full territorial sovereignty. To quote Lutovac, their strategic commitment was to pan-Albanian unification, while differences 'arose only in tactical approaches to this strategic goal'.[44]

But in spite of their maximalist claims, the LDK opted for minimalist methods, employing Gandhi-like tactics of non-violent opposition to Serbian administration in Kosova. All Kosovar Albanian parties undertook an active, peaceful boycott of the Serbian provincial administration. As a result, a complete set of parallel institutions was created between 1992 and 1996, leading to total separation of the Serb-controlled Kosovo administration from the Albanian-controlled Kosovar society.[45]

Responding to the regime's attempt at full colonialization of the province, Kosovar Albanians organized their own parliamentary and presidential elections in May 1992. These were deemed illegal by the Serbian

41

administration. Yet they were the act, as Vickers puts it, of a 'mini-state in the making'.[46] Given that by then, the process of national homogenization of Kosovar Albanians was complete, it is not surprising that Rugova's party won a reported 99.5 per cent of the vote, while Rugova himself was elected president of the Republic of Kosova with 95 per cent of the vote.[47]

The Kosovar Albanians boycotted the December 1992 Yugoslav elections on the pretext that the 'Republic of Kosova' was no longer part of Yugoslavia, defying substantial international pressure to support reform-minded federal Prime Minister Milan Panić in his struggle against Milošević's warmongering in Croatia and Bosnia and Herzegovina. Many Serbian intellectuals regarded the boycott as proof of extreme Albanian nationalism. Vladimir Cvetković, a Serbian philosopher, criticizes the Kosovar Albanian minority's 'continuous and almost fanatical boycotting' of all of Serbian and Yugoslav elections.[48] Dušan Janjić, a sociologist and *spiritus movens* of many informal contacts between Albanian and Serbian intellectuals in the 1990s, is more restrained. He believes that the Kosovar Albanian leaders confused questions of the Serbian state's legitimacy with the legality of various forms of political struggle against the oppressive Serbian regime. In his view, participating in elections would not have implied accepting the legitimacy of the Serbian regime or the state, or precluded future negotiations between the two sides, but simply represented Kosovar Albanian recognition of basic democratic principles. By renouncing democratic means of political struggle, they were left with options reflecting a strong communitarian bias, promoting collective Albanian rights instead of the individual rights of all Kosovars, irrespective of their ethnic background.[49]

Janjić's analysis is correct, but neglects one important factor. The Albanian Kosovars' election boycott reflected not only their desire for independence, but also a correct reading of international public opinion at the time. As Miranda Vickers explains:

> In reality, however, the million Albanian votes could undoubtedly have ousted Milošević [in 1992], but as the Kosovar leadership admitted at the time, they did not want him to go. Unless Serbia continued to be labelled as profoundly evil – and they themselves, by virtue of being anti-Serb, as the good guys – they were unlikely to achieve their goals. It would have been a disaster for them if a peace-monger like Panić [then Yugoslav Prime Minister and Milošević's opponent at the elections] had restored human rights, since this would have left them with nothing but a bare political agenda to change borders.[50]

In 1992, instead of making common cause with Serbian opposition parties against Milošević, Kosovar Albanians opted (indirectly) to support him. In return, despite continuing policies of harassment, Milošević's regime seems to have tolerated a mushrooming of Kosovar Albanian parallel institutions. By the mid-1990s a status quo had emerged in which both sides were living side-by-side, believing in their ultimate victory: the Serbs because of their effective control of all the territory, the Albanians because they had recreated all the autonomous institutions taken over by the regime in 1989–92.

Henceforth, given the LDK's popularity and its pre-eminence over other Kosovar Albanian parties, it assumed a rather ambiguous role, being both a Kosovar Albanian movement and the legitimate representative of an underground Kosova state. It was organized more as a government than as a party. For example, various LDK advisory committees took on the functions of state ministries: foreign affairs, education, health care, economy, sports, culture, etc. The committees had subgroups reaching into the remotest Kosova municipalities, allowing the LDK full control over Kosovar Albanian society.[51]

The very success of the LDK in overseeing a Kosova shadow state eventually became one of the sources of Rugova's loss of political influence in the late 1990s. Establishing an underground state in Kosova had invigorated Kosovar Albanians. A sort of inverted apartheid had developed in which the oppressed, rather than the 'master', refused to cooperate with the other side. Many then wished to convert this accomplishment into a fully sovereign state, which had been part of the programme from the beginning. Thus, in 1994, the first signs of Kosovar Albanian weariness with Rugova's status quo politics emerged. This led to a split in the LDK (and in other Kosovar parties) between moderates who had not completely closed off the option of Kosova being a third federal unit within Yugoslavia, and hardliners who started to challenge Rugova's politics of non-violence.[52]

The turning point was the 1995 Dayton Peace Accord that ended the war in Bosnia and Herzegovina. By then it was obvious that whatever principles prevailed in the accord would be applied to the status of the Kosovar Albanians. Dayton represented a political compromise between the ethnicized version of the right to national self-determination and the right of the sovereign state to protect its territorial integrity. Bosnian Serbs were denied the right to outright secession, but given their own entity with extensive privileges within the federalized Bosnia and Herzegovina. Thus although the Dayton agreement did not deal with Kosovo, it implied that Kosovo could at best be elevated to the status of a constitutive part of Yugoslavia.[53]

After the initial shock of being once again ignored by the international community, Kosovar Albanians seem to have agreed that, in the words of Maliqi, 'all diplomatic games are a farce obscuring the fundamental axiom of freedom and sovereignty – one must fight for freedom and sovereignty and they can be won only by making an enormous sacrifice and by waging a war'.[54] Two diametrically opposed responses then emerged in the Kosovar Albanian community. One side was ready to accept reorganizing Yugoslavia into a loose federation (or confederation) between Montenegro, Serbia and the Republic of Kosova, as an interim solution on the way to the ultimate political goal of parting from Serbia. This approach would allow recognition of Kosovar Albanians as a constitutive nation with de facto if not *de jure* territorial sovereignty.[55] However, in the post-Dayton period, an increasing number of younger Kosovar Albanians rejected both Rugova's gradualist approach towards creating an independent Kosova and the sanctity of Yugoslavian (Serbia–Montenegro) territorial borders. These hardliners saw the international community's continuing acceptance of the borders as pushing Kosova back to Serbia. Seeing no room for compromise, they opted for active opposition to the Serbian domination. Thus already in the mid-1990s, the Kosovar Albanians were facing a choice between peace and war.[56]

The precarious balance between the two sides was upset in 1997 by three interrelated events. First, the Albanian political and security system collapsed in the spring, and military barracks were pillaged. A black market then developed in light weaponry (particularly kalashnikovs), much of which ended up in neighbouring Kosova in the hands of increasingly dissatisfied young Kosovar Albanians, who formed militant underground groups. Finally, in an effort to restore law and order in Kosovo, the Serbian regime responded in a terrorist manner, galvanizing the resolve of Kosovar Albanians to break with Rugova's principles of non-violence.

The relatively peaceful co-existence of the parallel worlds in Kosovo was totally destroyed in 1998. The previous year, the Kosovar Albanian insurgency, known as the Kosova Liberation Army – KLA (UÇK, or Ushtria Çlimtare e Kosovë) – had orchestrated a series of guerrilla actions that destabilized the province. These included taking civilian hostages and the summary execution of Serbian police officers and Albanians suspected of collaborating with the Serbian authorities. In February and March 1998, special Serbian police units, supported by the Yugoslav military, attacked a KLA stronghold in the Drenica region in an openly terrorist fashion, destroying three villages with artillery, helicopters and armed vehicles. More than 80 people were killed, including 24 women and children.[57]

The Drenica massacre backfired on the regime. Far from pacifying the insurgency, it undermined the remaining influence of those in Rugova's LDK who still hoped for a non-violent solution. Milošević's use of force only inflamed the Kosovar insurgency and transformed the KLA from a relatively obscure terrorist organization in late 1996 into a full-fledged national liberation army in 1998. Finally, in October 1998, the international community recognized the KLA as a political factor to be reckoned with. The KLA, not Rugova's LDK, was increasingly accepted as the legitimate representative of Kosovar Albanians in any possible peace talks between Serbian and Kosovar representatives. Despite (or perhaps because of) all the destruction and human losses, 1998 ended in victory for hardliners on both sides.

In 1999, after the period covered here, the situation further deteriorated.

After the failure of the Rambouillet peace talks, the United States and the EU, as the sponsors of the talks between the two sides, finally decided to take sides and NATO military intervention against Serbia followed on 25 March 1999. It lasted less than three months and ended in complete withdrawal of Serbian government forces from Kosovo. The final outcome of this military intervention is still hard to predict. At the time of writing, a sort of UN protectorate had been formed, but a political solution to the Kosovo crisis remains elusive.

In some ways, the NATO victory recreated the old catch 22 situation. On one side, Kosovar Albanians are increasingly in control of the province, while on the other, the legal basis for the UN administration of Kosovo is the UN resolution referring to the 'sovereignty and territorial integrity of the Federal Republic of Yugoslavia'. This would imply that the UN's vision of the future Kosovo is to grant it republic status within Yugoslavia; however, anything short of full independence is a non-starter for various Albanian political parties. They may disagree about anything else, but about their ultimate goal – Kosova independence – they are all united.[58]

CONCLUSION

This brief analysis of majority–minority relationships in Kosovo spotlights several ambiguities in contemporary theorizing about the rights to self-determination and secession. In societies like Serbia with more than one ethnic community, and yet regulated by the principles of a nation-state, tension between individual and collective rights can completely blur the boundaries between the two. For any organized human rights abuse in such a state will necessarily involve, or lead to, violation of rights to language, culture, free expression of religion, self-rule and the like. In other words, the target of such violations will not be some abstract individual, but an individual that is a member of a distinct national community. In many cases his or her only crime may be that s/he belongs to the 'wrong' ethnic group (Serbian, Albanian or whatever). So what may start as a case of violation of individual human rights can, and indeed quite often does, end up as a case of violation of collective rights.

Under such conditions, as Kosovo shows, national self-determination ceases simply to be a question of the character of the political system and whether individuals have equal rights to political participation. Instead, the issue becomes the extent to which the majority in a multination state is ready to recognize national minorities' claims to nationhood, and thus their status as peoples with distinct languages, cultures, religions and so on. Accordingly, consideration of the principle of nationhood in multination states almost inevitably raises questions about social unity and territorial integrity of such states.

The ethnic monism adopted by the Serbian state, particularly in the case of Kosovo, clearly shows how increasing majority pressure against minorities can undermine and destroy the social unity of the state. The Kosovo crisis was further sharpened by the fact that Kosovo Albanian de facto autonomy from 1968 to 1981 had imbued the Albanian movement with the feeling that nothing short of republican status in a new Yugoslavia could be accepted. Any Serbian suggestion that did not recognize Albanians on equal terms was viewed as yet another Serbian plot to squeeze Kosovar Albanians into the Procrustean bed reserved for minorities.

Liberal democratic principles based on the notion of equality would require the Serbian state to address the self-perception of the Albanian political community as a sovereign nation in a completely new way. The debate that never took place between the two sides should have explored various models of a decentralized Serbia and Yugoslavia in which Kosovo was either offered a special, asymmetrical status compared with other provinces in Serbia, or elevated to the status of one of Yugoslavia's constitutive republics. Nor should the option of an independent Republic of Kosova have been excluded, particularly if it was the outcome of mutual consent and democratic negotiations. Paradoxically, all these options were seriously debated among independent non-nationalist Serbian and Albanian intellectuals; but these discussions were totally marginalized by the maximalist acts of both Serbian officials and the leaders of the Kosova shadow state.

NOTES

1. Julie A. Mertus, *Kosovo: How Myths and Truths Started a War* (Berkeley: University of California Press, 1999), p. 5.
2. Recently, however, several historical and sociological monographs and lengthy essays on Kosovo have been published that challenge both the Western myth of Balkan primordialism and the overtly mythical and nationalistic representations of the region. See Christine von Kohl and Wolfgang Libal, 'Kosovo, the Gordian Knot of the Balkans', in Robert Elsie (ed.), *Kosovo in the Heart of the Powder Keg* (Boulder, CO: Columbia University Press, East European Monographs, 1997), pp. 3–104; Dušan Janjić, 'Nacionalni identitet, pokret i nacionalizam Srba i Albanaca', in Dušan Janjić and Škeljzen Malići (eds), *Sukob ili dijalog: Srpsko-albanski odnosi i integracija na Balkanu* (Subotica: Evropski građanski centar za rešavanje konflikata, 1994), pp. 111–64; Noel Malcolm, *Kosovo: A Short History* (New York: New York University Press, 1998); Miranda Vickers, *Between Serb and Albanian: History of Kosovo* (New York: Columbia University Press, 1998); and Petrit Imami, *Srbi i Albanci kroz vekove* (Belgrade: Samizdat 92, 2000).
3. Or, to put it differently, people do not kill each other for something that happened two hundred years ago, but because of something that is currently taking place.
4. The region had also been officially called Kosovo–Metohija between 1945 and 1968. However, with the constitutional amendments in 1968 granting a greater

autonomy to the region, the Albanian communist leaders requested the name to be changed to Kosovo.

5. The Belgrade Center for Human Rights, *Human Rights in Yugoslavia 1998* (Belgrade, 1999), pp. 356–7.

6. Hugh Poulton and Miranda Vickers, 'Kosovo Albanians: Ethnic Confrontation with the Slavic State', in Hugh Poulton and Suha Taji-Farouki (eds), *Muslim Identity and the Balkan State* (London: Hurst & Company, 1997), pp. 139–44.

7. Andrew March and Rudra Sil, *The 'Republic of Kosova' (1989–1998) and the Resolution of Ethno-Separatist Conflict: Rethinking 'Sovereignty' in the Post-Cold War Era* (University Park, PA: University of Pennsylvania, photocopy, 1999), p. 3.

8. A good overview of Serbia's position in regard to the 1974 constitution can be found in Miodrag Zečević's *Jugoslavia 1918–1992* (Belgrade: Prosveta, 1994), pp. 223–6; and Audrey Helfant Budding, 'Serb Intellectuals and the National Question, 1961–1991', Ph.D. dissertation (Cambridge, MA: Harvard University, 1998).

9. Bernard Zeneli, 'Albanian Nationalism Revisited', paper presented at the Fourth Annual Convention of the Association for the Study of Nationalities (New York, April 1998), p. 12.

10. See Mertus, *Kosovo*, p. 17. This scenario might seem fanciful today. Yet other nations had already been granted such status. Between the two world wars Yugoslavia had officially been a state of Serbs, Croats and Slovenes. In 1945 Macedonians and Montenegrins were recognized as constitutive nations, and in 1971 Bosnian Muslims (Bosniaks) were also recognized as a nation. So Kosovar Albanians had good reasons to believe that eventually they would be recognized as a sovereign nation with a right to their own republic (state).

11. Hivzi Islami, 'Demografska stvarnost Kosova', in Dušan Janjić and Škeljezen Malići (eds), *Sukob ili dijalog: Srpsko-albanski odnosi i integracija Balkana* (Subotica: Evropski gradjanski centar za rešavanje konflikata, 1994), pp. 30–1.

12. Hugh Poulton, *The Balkans: Minorities and States in Conflict* (London: Minority Rights Group, 1991), p. 61. Kosovo's ratio of students was 274.7 per 1,000 inhabitants, while the Yugoslav national average was 195 per 1,000. For a detailed picture of the Kosovo educational system, see A. Pipa and S. Repihsti, *Studies on Kosova* (New York: East European Monographs, 1984), pp. 111–14, 144.

13. See Mertus, *Kosovo*, p. 29.

14. Helen Lindhold, 'Kosovo – Intifada Tomorrow?', *Republika*, Special Issue no. 9 (Belgrade: 1994), p. 14.

15. Shkëlzen Maliqi, 'The Albanian Movement in Kosova', in *Kosova, Separate Worlds: Reflections and Analyses 1989–1998* (Priština: Dukagjini PH, 1998), p. 20.

16. Ibid., p. 20.

17. See Mertus, *Kosovo*, p. 43.

18. See Nada Raduški, *'Demografska slika Kosova'* (Belgrade: Institut društvenih nauka, 1998), p. 3. The Albanian population boycotted the 1991 census, but the Federal Bureau of Statistics estimated that the trend continued in the 1980s. According to their 1991 estimates, the population was 82% Albanian (1,596,072) and 10% Serb (194,190). Albanian scholars put the number of Albanians even higher, at about two million (90% of the total). For an excellent statistical overview of Serbo-Albanian Relations, see Srđan Bogosavljević, 'A Statistical Picture of Serbo-Albanian Relations', *Republika*, Special Issue no. 9 (Belgrade, February 1994), pp. 18–20.

19. Typical examples of genocidal rhetoric can be found in articles in the most

influential daily in the country, *Politika*. In 1990 its journalists habitually presented the Albanian population as 'wild', 'enemies of all colours', 'separatists and terrorists', 'fanatics', 'rapists of Serbian women', 'selfish and egotistical' and endowed with the 'virus of insanity'. See Izveštaj nezavisne komisije (Independent Commission Report), *Kosovski čvor: drešiti ili seći?* (Belgrade: Chronos, 1990), pp. 113–26.

20. The Independent Commission Report was written for the first non-communist political groups in Yugoslavia, the Union for Yugoslav Democratic Initiative and the Yugoslav Forum for Human Rights. Its members were from all parts of Yugoslavia, including Kosovo. However, they were treated with suspicion throughout the country, for their political aim was to preserve Yugoslavia as a democratic federation.

21. See *Kosovski čvor*, p. 8.

22. Ibid., pp. 15–18. Also, see Dušan Janjić, 'Nacionalni identitet', pp. 128–33.

23. Branko Horvat, *Kosovsko pitanje* (Zagreb: Globus, 1988), p. 109.

24. See *Kosovski čvor*, p. 26. Also, see an incisive article by Marina Blagojević, 'Iseljavanje Srba sa Kosova: trauma i/li katarza', in *Srpska strana rata: trauma i katarza u istorijskom pamćenju* (Belgrade: Republika, 1996), pp. 232–64.

25. See *Kosovski čvor*, pp. 37–47, 143–7.

26. Ibid., p. 156.

27. A. March and R. Sil, *The 'Republic of Kosova'*, p. 3.

28. Muhamedin Kulaši, 'Kosovo i raspad Jugoslavije', in Dušan Janjić (ed.), *Sukob ili dijalog*, p. 171.

29. See D. Janjić, *Report on the Juridical, Sociological and Political Aspects of the Nationality Politics and Minority Protection in the Federal Republic of Yugoslavia* (Belgrade: Forum for Ethnic Relations) pp. 39–40.

30. Helsinški odbor za ljudska prava u Srbiji, *'Izveštaj o ljudskim pravima u Srbiji'* (Belgrade: Helsinški odbor za ljudska prava u Srbiji, 1997), p. 52.

31. Humanitarian Law Center, *Spotlight Report* no. 24 (Belgrade, February 1998), pp. 2–3.

32. See Helsinški odbor, *Izveštaj o ljudskim pravima*, pp. 52–3.

33. See *Spotlight Report* no. 24, p. 3. The report is almost entirely dedicated to the problem of education of Kosovar Albanians.

34. See *Spotlight Report* no. 24, p. 4.

35. A full text of the declaration is published in Dušan Janjić, *Report*, pp. 88–94.

36. See Janjić, *Report*, pp. 90–1.

37. Djerdj Rrapi, *'Kosovo danas'* (Pristina, photocopy, November 1997), p. 8. Bajram Keljmendi also makes a similar point in 'Institutcionalizovana diskriminacija', *Srpsko-albanski dijalog* (Belgrade: Helsinški komitet za ljudksa prava u Srbiji, 1997), pp. 91–4.

38. See Rrapi, *Kosovo*, p. 10. One must also recognize the negative role played by the central Serbian opposition parties in nurturing a superior attitude towards the Albanian population. They never understood that their civic activities in Belgrade and other cities were simply insufficient to ensure the survival of Serbian democracy in the 1990s. The frontline of the defence of human rights and liberal democratic principles was always in Kosovo, because this was the site of the grossest violations of both human and national minority rights in the country. And yet, they never tried publicly to raise the question of the human rights abuses in Kosovo. Instead, the Serbian opposition party leaders' implicit acceptance of the regime's systemic oppression of Kosovar Albanians effectively legitimized the apartheid-like rule of Milošević's regime.

39. See Maliqi, *Kosova, Separate Worlds*, p. 26.

40. Ibid., p. 34. Civic groups emerged out of the Association of Philosophers and Sociologists. Their main representatives were Veton Surroi, Muhamedin Kullashi and Shkëlzen Maliqi. Supporters of the nationalist political platform came mainly from the Kosova Association of Writers. Ibrahim Rugova headed this current and he soon emerged as the most important Kosova Albanian politician.

41. Fehmi Agani, 'Nacija, nacionalna manjina i samoopredeljenje', *Sukob ili dijalog* (Subotica: Evropski građanski centar za rešavanje konflikata), p. 209.

42. See Maliqi, *Kosova, Separate Worlds*, p. 30.

43. Predrag Simić, *The Kosovo and Metohija Problem and Regional Security in the Balkans* (Belgrade: Institute for International Politics, 1996), p. 13.

44. Zoran Lutovac, 'The Participation of Minorities in Political Life', in V. Goati (ed.), *Elections to the Federal and Republican Parliaments of Yugoslavia* (Berlin: Edition Stigma, 1998), p. 126.

45. Many analysts classify Serbian policies in Kosovo as apartheid. However, although they were based on the formal legal inferiority of Kosovar Albanians, once they were implemented, Kosovar Albanians did not challenge them. Instead they opted to break all ties with a regime they perceived as colonizing and oppressive. So in a somewhat paradoxical fashion, Kosovar Albanians turned Serbian policies to their own advantage, cutting off contacts with the Kosovar Serbs. The Kosovar Albanian parties were guided not by an ideal of political equality, but by the ethnicized version of the principle of national self-determination, including secession.

46. M. Vickers, *Between Serb and Albanian*, p. 259.

47. Slobodanka Kovačević and Putnik Dajić, *Chronology of the Yugoslav Crisis 1942–1993* (Belgrade: Institute for European Studies, 1994), p. 72. Non-Albanian parties were also invited to participate at the elections. Only the Democratic Party (a Muslim party) and the Turkish People's Party accepted it.

48. See Vladimir Cvetković, 'Bermudski trougao moderne politike: demokratija, multukulturalizam, nacionalizam', in *Nova srpska politička misao* vol. IV, 3–4 (1997), p. 9.

49. See Janjić, 'Nacionalni identitet', pp. 153–5.

50. See Vickers, *Between Serb and Albanian*, p. 268. In addition, Kosovar Albanians could have responded to charges of fanatical boycotting of Serbian and Yugoslav elections by pointing to equally fanatical Serbian opposition party programmes which rejected any negotiations to change the minority status of Kosovar Albanians.

51. See March and Sil *The 'Republic of Kosova'*, pp. 7–13.

52. See Vickers, *Between Serb and Albanian*, p. 281.

53. See Denisa Kostovičová, *Parallel Worlds: Response of Kosovo Albanians to Loss of Autonomy in Serbia, 1986–1996* (Keele: Keele University European Research Center, 1997), pp. 56–7.

54. See Maliqi, *Kosova, Separate Worlds*, p. 141.

55. See Gazmend Pulja, 'Republika u refederalizovanoj SRJ', in *Srpsko-albanski dijalog*, pp. 132–8; and Adem Demaçi, 'Albanci moraju biti priznati kao nezavisni subjekat', in *Srpsko-albanski dijalog*, pp. 114–19. Demaçi, known as the Albanian Mandela, is the most famous Albanian political prisoner. By 1991 he had spent 28 years in Yugoslav socialist prisons. Well known for his hardline attitudes, he was nevertheless ready to accept a confederation between Montenegro, Serbia and Kosova that would also be open to other Balkan nation-states. He termed this would-be multination confederation 'Balkania'.

56. See Maliqi, *Kosova, Separate Worlds*, p. 141.

57. See The Belgrade Center for Human Rights, *Human Rights in Yugoslavia in 1998* (Belgrade).

58. The NATO bombing campaign against Serbia and the unresolved question of the Kosovo final status have raised many controversies, at the heart of which are the mutually contradictory rights to state protection, national self-determination and just war (or, in a new terminology, humanitarian intervention). The following books offer an exploration of the rhetoric of each of these rights from mutually contradictory perspectives: Robert Jackson, *The Global Covenant: Human Conduct in a World of States* (Oxford: Oxford University Press, 2000); Noam Chomsky, *The New Military Humanism: Lessons from Kosovo* (Monroe: Common Courage Press, 1999); Michael Ignatieff, *Virtual War, Kosovo and Beyond* (Toronto: Viking, 2000); and *The UN Independent Commission's Report on Kosovo* (Oxford: Oxford University Press, 2000).

REFERENCES

Agani, F., 'Nacija, nacionalna manjina i samoopredeljenje', in D. Janjić and Š. Maljići (eds), *Sukob ili dijalog* (Subotica: Evropski građanski centar za rešavanje konflikata, 1994), pp. 191–209.

Ash, T. G., 'Plači raskomadana zemljo', *Danas*, 1–12 February 1999.

Bakić-Hayden, M., 'Devastating Victory and Glorious Defeat: the Mahabharata and Kosovo in National Imaginings', Ph.D. dissertation (Chicago: University of Chicago, 1997).

The Belgrade Center for Human Rights, *Human Rights in Yugoslavia 1998* (Belgrade, 1999).

Blagojević, M., 'Iseljavanje Srba sa Kosova: trauma i/li katarza', in N. Popov (ed.), *Srpska strana rata: trauma i katarza u istorijskom pamćenju* (Belgrade: Republika, 1996), pp. 232–64.

Bogosavljević, S., 'A Statistical Picture of Serbo-Albanian Relations', *Republika*, Special Issue no. 9 (Belgrade, February 1994), pp. 18–21.

Chomsky, N., *The New Military Humanism: Lessons from Kosovo* (Monroe: Common Courage Press, 1999).

Cvetković, V., 'Bermudski trougao moderne politike: demokratija, multukulturalizam, nacionalizam', in *Nova srpska politička misao* vol. IV, 3–4 (1997), p. 5–22.

Demači, A., 'Albanci moraju biti priznati kao nezavisni subjekat', *Srpsko-albanski dijalog* (Belgrade: Helsinški odbor za ljudska prava, 1997), pp. 114–19.

Emmert, T. A., *Serbian Golgotha: Kosovo, 1389* (New York: Columbia University Press, East European Monographs, 1990).

Helfant Budding, A., 'Serb Intellectuals and the National Question, 1961–1991', Ph.D. dissertation (Cambridge, MA: Harvard University, 1998).

Helsinški odbor za ljudska prava u Srbiji, *Izveštaj o ljudskim pravima u Srbiji za 1997* (Belgrade: Helsinški odbor za ljudska prava u Srbiji, 1998).

Horvat, B., *Kosovsko pitanje* (Zagreb: Globus, 1988).

Humanitarian Law Center, 'Repression and Discrimination of Albanians', *Spotlight Report* no. 6 (Belgrade, August 1993).

Humanitarian Law Center, 'Crackdown on Kosovo Albanians', *Spotlight Report* no. 16 (Belgrade, February 1995).

Humanitarian Law Center, 'Education in Kosovo', *Spotlight Report* no. 24 (Belgrade, February 1998).

Human Rights Watch, *Humanitarian Law Violations in Kosovo* (New York, October 1998).

Humanitarian Law Center, 'Human Rights in F R Yugoslavia, 1998 Annual Report', *Spotlight Report* no. 28 (Belgrade, 1999).

Ignatieff, M., *Virtual War, Kosovo and Beyond* (Toronto: Viking, 2000).

Imami, P., *Srbi i Albanci kroz vekove* (Belgrade: Samizdat 92, 2000).

Islami, H., 'Demografska stvarnost Kosova', in Dušan Janjić and Škeljezen Malići (eds), *Sukob ili dijalog: Srpsko-albanski odnosi i integracija Balkana* (Subotica: Evropski gradjanski centar za rešavanje konflikata, 1994), pp. 29–51.

Izveštaj nezavisne komisije, *Kosovski čvor: drešiti ili seći?* (Belgrade: Chronos, 1990).

Jackson, R., *The Global Covenant: Human Conduct in a World of States* (Oxford: Oxford University Press, 2000).

Janjić, D., *Report on the Juridical, Sociological and Political Aspects of the Nationality Politics and Minority Protection in the Federal Republic of Yugoslavia* (Belgrade: Forum for Ethnic Relations, 1993).

Janjić, D., 'Nacionalni identitet, pokret i nacionalizam Srba i Albanaca', in D. Janjić and Š. Malići (eds), *Sukob ili dijalog: Srpsko-albanski odnosi i integracija na Balkanu* (Subotica: Evropski građanski centar za rešavanje konflikata, 1994), pp. 111–64.

Keljmendi, B., 'Institutcionalizovana diskriminacija', in *Srpsko-albanski dijalog* (Belgrade: Helsinški komitet za ljudksa prava u Srbiji, 1997), pp. 91–4.

Kostovičová, D., *Parallel Worlds: Response of Kosovo Albanians to Loss of Autonomy in Serbia, 1986–1996* (Keele: Keele University European Research Center, 1997).

Kovačević, S. and Dajić, P., *Chronology of the Yugoslav Crisis 1942–1993* (Belgrade: Institute for European Studies, 1994).

Kulaši, M., 'Kosovo i raspad Jugoslavije', in D. Janjić and Š. Malići (eds), *Sukob ili dijalog: Srpsko-albanski odnosi i integracija na Balkanu* (Subotica: Evropski građanski centar za rešavanje konflikata, 1994), pp. 166–75.

Lindhold, H., 'Kosovo – Intifada Tomorrow?', *Republika*, Special Issue no. 9 (Belgrade: 1994), pp. 13–17.

Lutovac, Z., 'The Participation of Minorities in Political Life', in V. Goati (ed.), *Elections to the Federal and Republican Parliaments of Yugoslavia* (Berlin: Edition Sigma, 1998), pp. 126–39.

Malcolm, N., *Kosovo: A Short History* (New York: New York University Press, 1998).

Maliqi, S., *Kosova, Separate Worlds: Reflections and Analyses 1989–1998* (Pristina: Dukagjini PH, 1998).

March, A. and Sil, R., *The 'Republic of Kosova' (1989–1998) and the Resolution of Ethno-Separatist Conflict: Rethinking 'Sovereignty' in the Post-Cold War Era* (University Park, PA: University of Pennsylvania, photocopy, 1999).

Mertus, J. A., *Kosovo: How Myths and Truths Started a War* (Berkeley: University of California Press, 1999).

Nushi, P., *Koliko se danas na Kosovu i Metohiji poštuju individualna ljudska prava* (Pristina, photocopy, 1997).

Pipa, A. and Repihsti, S., *Studies on Kosova* (New York: Columbia University Press, 1984).

Popović, M., *Vidovdan i časni krst* (Belgrade: Biblioteka XX vek, 1998).

Poulton, H., *The Balkans: Minorities and States in Conflict* (London: Minority Rights Group, 1991).

Poulton, H. and Vickers, M., 'Kosovo Albanians: Ethnic Confrontation with the Slavic State', in H. Poulton and S. Taji-Farouki (eds), *Muslim Identity and the Balkan State* (London: Hurst & Company, 1997), pp. 139–69.

Pulja, G., 'Republika u refederalizovanoj SRJ', in *Srpsko-albanski dijalog* (Belgrade: Helsinški odbor za ljudska prava, 1997), pp. 132–8.

Raduški, N., *Demografska slika Kosova* (Belgrade: Institut društvenih nauka, 1998).

Rrapi, Dj., *Kosovo danas* (Pristina, photocopy, November 1997).

Simić, P., *The Kosovo and Metohija Problem and Regional Security in the Balkans*

(Belgrade: Institute for International Politics, 1996).

Vickers, M., *Between Serb and Albanian: History of Kosovo* (New York: Columbia University Press, 1998).

von Kohl, C. and Libal, W., 'Kosovo, the Gordian Knot of the Balkans', in R. Elsie (ed.), *Kosovo in the Heart of the Powder Keg* (Boulder, CO: Columbia University Press, East European Monographs, 1997), pp. 3–104.

Zečević, M., *Jugoslavia 1918–1992* (Belgrade: Prosveta, 1994).

Zeneli, B., 'Albanian Nationalism Revisited', paper presented at the Fourth Annual Convention of the Association for the Study of Nationalities (New York: April 1998).

3

Ethnic Prejudices and Discrimination: The Case of Kosovo

Lazar Nikolić

The most recent example of the impact of increased prejudice has been in Kosovo between Kosovo Albanians and Serbs. In this chapter I intend to present the role of ethnic prejudices and negative stereotypes in everyday life of the Kosovo Albanian and Serbian ethnic groups. One of the important facts concerning Serbian–Albanian relationships deals with mutual perceptions and public opinion polls in Kosovo. From the beginning of the 1960s to the late 1990s a series of empirical studies of national stereotypes was carried out. This analysis is based on seven sociological research surveys made between 1966 and 1999 by scientists, mostly sociologists, from former Yugoslavia (Socialist Federal Republic of Yugoslavia, SFRY) as well as from the Federal Republic of Yugoslavia (FRY).

Prejudice, as indeed discrimination itself, produces changes which can be analyzed on several levels. In this work practical consequences of different forms of stereotyping are analyzed: firstly, at the *micro* level (the level of the individual as actor in everyday life); secondly, at the *middle* level (the level of social institutions and group memberships) and thirdly, at the *macro* level (the level of society). All these levels include different examples of relationships, actions and ways of thinking between Albanians and Serbs in individual, group and community settings. Examples that follow specify different strategies of self-perception and its interpretation, perception of the 'other' and perception of relationships.

In addition, my intention is to reconstruct different phases of relations between Albanians and Serbs in Kosovo in the second part of the nineteenth century and in the twentieth century. The concluding section summarizes the main research results and indicates practical limitations as well as perspectives for improving the relationship between Kosovo Albanians and Serbs.

While the prevailing discourse on Kosovo is a political one, sociological discourse is based on the sociological assumption that states consist of people. In a sociological approach, society is differentiated from the 'state' as a representative of the interests of political elites, which is especially the case with weak democracies.[1] In the political approach, however, states or nations, are personified, while the social realities are often neglected.[2]

One of the basic characteristics of Kosovo's social reality is a complete division of the Albanian and Serbian public opinions, resulting in different perceptions of the situational conflict. It is interesting that the two contrasting public opinions reflect each other like reality and image in a mirror. The prevailing image of self ('we-ness'), in both the Albanian and Serbian cases is that of 'being the victim'.[3]

The Albanian collective consciousness, as well as the Serbian one, sees itself as a total victim, antagonized by the opposite side. There is a total asymmetry of interpretation of any social or historical fact. History and memory are selective, coloured by the portrait of 'victim-image'. The greatest divergences are contained in views dealing with the far off past, best illustrated in both groups' collective memory of Kosovo as 'holy land'. Even the demographic structure is a subject of immense dispute. Some demographic phenomena, such as women's social immobility, are used as weapons to win legitimacy over the other.[4]

Albanians and Serbs do not live only in segmented territories, but in segmented realities and segmented time, claiming the monopoly in the victim-status.[5] An apparent absence of dialogue between Albanians and Serbs exists. Sociological research studied in this chapter shows that both societies, Albanian and Serbian, want ethnically pure and separate societies, and both groups claim to have suffered during the communist regime.

The Albanian perspective
For example, Albanians claim that ethnic cleansing has long been present in the Serbian tradition. Albanians claim that Kosovo has always been merely Serbia's colony.[6] For Albanians the Serbian oppression is an argument for secession.

The Serbian perspective
Serbs point to the forced migrations of Serbs from Kosovo from the 1960s to the 1980s. For Serbs the dominant argument for oppression of Albanians in Kosovo was the need to protect the remaining Serbs there. Serbs claim they have invested in Kosovo financially, but high birth rates among Albanians, wrong investment policy and the whims of local leaders made those investments useless.

There is less controversy regarding the observation that Kosovo is economically undeveloped, with a very high illiteracy rate and a traditional, patriarchal structure that creates mutually closed ethnic communities (a 'closed society').[7]

STEREOTYPING AT THE LEVEL OF INDIVIDUAL, SOCIAL INSTITUTION AND GROUP MEMBERSHIP

A generation of research on ethnic distance performed before the breakup of the SFRY demonstrated that levels of rejection of other nationalities expressed in surveys were consistently very low indeed.[8] Indeed, ethnic distance was 'smaller than in many other more developed countries of the world'.[9] Numerous studies of ethnic distance undertaken in SFRY, from 1960 to 1990, show that ethnic distance remained consistently low, even less than among the populations of much more developed countries.[10] The findings on many specific questions do show a lesser degree of ethnic distance in SFRY than findings for similar questions asked in the same year in the United States.[11]

Former Yugoslav heterogamy was lowest among people of Albanian, Slovenian, Muslim and Macedonian nationalities,[12] for example, 69 per cent of Albanians and 65 per cent of Slovenians, in research conducted between 1966 and 1990, illustrate that these groups maintained the greatest ethnic distance in former Yugoslavia. Slovenians represent the highest standard of living in former Yugoslavia while Albanians the lowest.

During the 1970s, social distance became the highest between Albanians and all other ethnic/national groups in the country. Most research on ethnic distance in former Yugoslavia showed consistently that Albanians were treated by others, and considered themselves, to be alien in Yugoslavia. In research conducted in 1990 it was found that Albanians expressed the strongest ethnic distance, relating to inter-ethnic marriages. Interestingly, younger respondents expressed a stronger desire for ethnic distance than older participants. Varying levels of education among Albanians had no impact on the exclusive ethnocentric position.[13] In 1990, half of the Albanians in Kosovo felt ethnic diversity was a problem, not an advantage, in Yugoslavia. Research based on a multiethnic sample of young people demonstrated that Albanians, in comparison with the other ethnic groups, were most separated. Other surveys indicate that social tension between other nationalities in former Yugoslavia was not nearly as great.[14]

In a survey conducted in Kosovo,[15] published in June 1997, on a sample of 816 Albanians and 404 Serbs it was found that Albanians were creating a completely black-and-white image of Serbs. The character traits that Albanians most frequently ascribed to Serbs were the following: dislike of other nations (81 per cent), sly (52 per cent), pushers (39 per cent), selfish (27 per cent) and rough mannered (26 per cent). Research conducted in 1993 in Serbia, 'Social Character and Social Change in Light of National Conflicts' confirmed deeply rooted stereotypes that Serbs have in respect to Albanians. More than 50 per cent of respondents accepted the stereotype that 'all Albanians are primitive and uncivilized'.

Ethnic stereotypes that Serbs held toward nations of the former

Yugoslavia have changed radically under the influence of the disintegration of SFRY and preceding conflicts, as well as a number of destructive subsequent events (war in Croatia and Bosnia-Herzegovina, sanctions against Serbia and Montenegro, economic collapse, hyperinflation, inflow of refugees, etc.). The previous relatively balanced and positive stereotypes held by Serbs toward other nations (except toward Albanians which were already saturated with negative contents) became highly negatively charged.[16]

In a 1987 survey[17] a smaller percentage of young people accepted the possibility of marriage with Albanians than with Turks, Arabs, Romanies or black people. From a representative sample of the young people in Serbia, excluding Kosovo, it was confirmed that Albanians were viewed most negatively: dislike of other nations (54 per cent), underdeveloped (51 per cent), deceitful (34 per cent), reserved (33 per cent), rough mannered and homogeneous (20 per cent each) and rash (16 per cent).[18]

One of the surveys from 1994 again showed that Albanians were the least accepted by Serbs. Only 33 per cent of citizens of Serbian nationality said they would agree to socialize with Albanians, 52 per cent accepted Albanians living in the same country, 48 per cent as co-workers, 40 per cent as friends, 22 per cent as leaders to be in high decision-making positions in the state and 22 per cent as a relative.[19]

A 1997 survey[20] conducted in Kosovo showed that Serbs described Albanians as united (62 per cent), hating other peoples (55 per cent), sly (46 per cent), backward (37 per cent) and rough mannered (20 per cent). The number of respondents judging Albanians as being cultured, civilized, clean or liking other peoples, did not amount to 10 per cent. Less educated individuals tended to hold considerably more negative stereotypes. As for age, older respondents had a more negative image of Albanians.[21] The stereotype held by Serbs of Albanians encompass almost all negative traits, to a very marked degree. In any pair of traits the negative trait is ascribed to Albanians much more frequently than the positive one. Albanians are described by Serbs as primitive, not liking other peoples, dirty, uncultured, insolent, dishonest, quarrelsome, selfish, stupid, cold and cowardly. Their other ascribed traits are also on the negative pole, but less markedly so: laziness and inhospitability. Sensibility, generosity, kindness and honesty are similarly infrequent traits recognized in Albanians by Serbs.[22]

A high correlation was found between the strength of these stereotypes and nationalistic attitude, authoritarianism, traditional orientation and an inclination toward étatism. Strict state measures regarding the Kosovo problem were supported by 41.3 per cent of Serbian respondents. However, in the Serbs' favour, 1.9 per cent of Serbs favoured autonomy for the Kosovo province, 4.7 per cent of Serbs preferred self-determination for the province and 41.1 per cent wanted compromise with the existing Albanian leaders. There was a high correlation between the Serbian negative stereotypes of Albanians and the desire to use 'strict state measures'.[23]

One of the surveys of Kosovo public opinion (although not a representative one[24]) throughout central Serbia and Vojvodina, showed that 40 per cent of the sample said that it was not possible for Serbs and Albanians to live without conflicts in the same country. However, 54.5 per cent said that it was possible.

Other interesting examples of how Albanians and Serbs perceive other ethnic groups are: 75 per cent of Albanians looked to Germany as an ally whereas 46 per cent of Serbs saw Germany as their worst enemy. Most Serbs trusted Greece as an ally but Albanians saw them as their worst enemy. Serbs and Albanians were divided fifty/fifty regarding how they viewed Russia.[25]

One of the recent surveys conducted on the territory of FRY, excluding Kosovo, was by Laslo Sekelj,[26] which showed that in 1999 the population of FRY considered particular states as enemies (Albania, Germany, US); or as friends (Greece, Russia, China) in accordance with the official propaganda. The degree of xenophobia is highly determined by the level of the international isolation of FRY.

PENDULUM OF DOMINATION

Sociological and psychological research of prejudice confirms a direct relation between holding beliefs determined by prejudice and discriminatory behaviour towards members of the targeted group. Clearly, the relations between prejudice and discrimination are very complex.

Of the possible models to organize relations between peoples (co-existence, assimilation and domination), the domination model has been used in Kosovo. This model is also used by victors in wars, which makes it even more rigid. When the Turkish army was victorious, it set up a political regime; when the occupying forces were victorious (Italy and Germany), they set up their own regime.[27] In Kosovo, for at least two centuries, two different standards have been used to judge the same occurrences. Relations between Serbs and Albanians can best be described as a 'pendulum of domination'.[28] There is a big difference between the one who defines the standards and the one who makes a judgement: a pendulum of domination keeps moving to one and then to the other side. At the moment, the position of the one who makes judgements and sets up their criteria is obtained by force. Neither side in the Kosovo conflict deals with the real issue, which surely is not the hegemony of one or the other, but a civil co-existence, democratic society and good-neighbourly relations. Roles have changed between Albanians and Serbs, switching the role of the victim between the mid-nineteenth century and the beginning of the twenty-first century. If we were to limit our consideration to the Serbian–Albanian relations in the province in the last 150 years, it would be possible to define nine specific periods.

Ottoman Rule of Kosovo

The period between the mid-nineteenth century and 1912 was marked by the domination of the Albanian group and discrimination against Serbs.

It was the period of Ottoman domination in this area. Thanks to the privileges they enjoyed, Albanians were Ottoman allies with favourable social positions. The Serbian population that survived the Ottoman pogroms suffered, unless it continued to move to northern parts of Serbia or to Austria. The Ottoman Empire sought to suppress Serbian spiritual heritage and the memory of Kosovo as the focal point of the Serbian medieval civilization. Discussing the problem of Balkan migrations, Jovan Cvijic, a renowned geoanthropologist from the first half of the twentieth century, pointed out three major aspects of migrations in this period: the historical/political aspect – migration as a consequence of the Ottoman system of government, as well as of numerous rebellions and wars against the Ottomans; the socio-psychological aspect – which included reactions of the local population against the Ottoman system of *timar-chiflik* feudal structure (forced labour, continuously increasing peasants' obligations, expropriation of land, etc.); and the geographic or natural aspect – migrations as a result of lack of fertile land and high birth rate.[29]

From the mid-nineteenth century, the Kosovo issue aroused the interest of the Great Powers since the outcome of the opposition against the Ottomans would have an impact on the future of the Balkans.[30] In 1878 the constituent assembly for the League of Prizren was held, which provided the germinating Albanian movement with a political organization. This occasion usually marks the birth of the Albanian nation, as Albanians, for the first time, assembled across clan and religious borders. The league was violently crushed by the Ottoman Empire, although peasant uprisings continued.[31]

Kosovo as part of Serbia

The period between 1912 and 1914 was marked by an attempt to establish domination of the Serbian group and discrimination against Albanians.

This period includes the Balkan wars and their aftermath. The first Balkan war was fought by the member states of the Balkan Alliance – Serbia, Bulgaria, Greece and Montenegro – against the Ottoman Empire, with the aim of driving out the Ottoman Empire from the Balkans. After the defeat, the Empire ceded this territory (to the west from the Enos-Midia line) to the Balkan Alliance. Greater Albania was formed, while Serbia sought to establish the institutions of the system in Kosovo (the judiciary, local administration, etc.). While some have interpreted this war as liberation from Turkish rule (Serbs, Montenegrins, Bulgarians and Greeks), for Albanians it was Serbian occupation. The state of Albania was declared in

November 1912, whereas the destiny of the Kosovo Albanians was determined a year later. Kosovo became a part of Serbia and Montenegro.[32] Victories obtained by the Balkan allies in the 1912 and 1913 wars triggered the process of migration. Some 20,000 Albanians moved from Kosovo to the newly established Albanian State.[33] The Serbian desire to create a southern Slav realm in the north-west of the Balkans was to become one of the cornerstones in the founding of Yugoslavia.[34]

The First World War and Kosovo

The period between 1914 and 1918 was characterized by the domination of the Albanian group and discrimination against Serbs.

This was the time of the First World War. Migratory movements continued during this period, when the Balkans became a battlefield of the great powers and the polarized Balkan states. The institutions of the Serbian state did not function, the king and the government were in exile. The Serbian Army was withdrawing to the south, pushed by the Austro-Hungarian forces, and crossed Kosovo and Albania. After the invasion of the country in 1915 the Serbian army, accompanied by civilian refugees, crossed the Albanian mountains on the way to the Adriatic Sea.[35] The period of open revanchism against Serbs began. In the course of the Serbian Army's two-month retreat across Albania, in the autumn of 1915, 150,000 Serbian soldiers died from starvation, and as a result of attacks by local people on exhausted stragglers.[36] Previous migrations in the nineteenth century had been sporadic, disorganized and spontaneous reactions of the population to abuses and pressures coming from foreign authorities. In the twentieth century they were triggered, organized and conducted by Balkan states' authorities and resulted from the issues of the 1912–1922 wars. In 1912 people affected by the migratory movements made 10.4 per cent of the Balkan population, and almost 6 per cent of the post-First World War Balkan states. If one adds approximately 2 million people killed, wounded or dead from epidemics, the toll of the Balkan migrations, casualties and people affected by the wars number 4.5 million which was over 19.4 per cent of the total population in 1912 and 10.8 per cent of the population in 1923.[37]

Kosovo in the first Yugoslavia

The period between 1918 and 1941 was characterized by the domination of the Serbian group and discrimination against Albanians.

After the victory of Serbia and the Allies in the First World War, the Kingdom of Serbs, Croats and Slovenes – later the Kingdom of Yugoslavia – was constituted. As the name of the country itself shows, Albanians were not considered a constitutive nation, but rather an ethnic minority. The discrimination of Albanians was to be expected if previously held rights and privileges under Ottoman rule are taken into consideration. Between the two World Wars, the Yugoslav authorities tried to change the ethnic composition of Kosovo, mainly through a colonization programme. In the 1920s and 1930s, land belonging to Albanians was confiscated. The aim was to break Albanian dominance within Kosovo. Furthermore, some Albanians were deported to Turkey.[38]

> Some 35,000 people emigrated, but these were mainly rich landowners, Turkish feudal lords and others with close economic and emotional ties with the former Turkish Imperial system. The land was divided up between the Serbian and Albanian former serfs. Although there was some discrimination against Albanians. The division of land in this area deviated only marginally from the exceptionally egalitarian land policy of the new state.[39]

Albanian demographers claim that in the period between 1919 and 1930 some 300,000 Albanians moved out,[40] which would amount to about 40 per cent of the total Albanian population of Kosovo. But here we have ventured onto the slippery terrain of historical demography, where the actual state of affairs in times past is notoriously difficult to establish. Like the Turkish state before, so the Serbian state encountered difficulties in establishing state institutions in the form of a specific organization of private and public life (tribal organization). The so-called *Kacac* emerged – groups of Albanians resisting the Serbian rule.

Second World War Kosovo

The period between 1941 and 1945 was marked by the domination of the Albanian group and discrimination against Serbs.

Albanian nationalism rose in the 1940s and the National Liberation Movement (NLM) was founded. The goal of the NLM was the reunion of Kosovo with Albania. In order to achieve this, the NLM joined the communist partisans under the leadership of Josip Broz Tito during the Second World War. In return Kosovo was to be granted equal status with other regions in a future federation. Most Kosovo Albanians, however, greeted the Italian rule from 1941, since they now achieved greater liberty. Thus, Kosovo Albanian organizations collaborated with the Axis powers and persecuted Serbs and Montenegrins who were settled in Kosovo. Following the Second League of Prizren in 1943, the Albanians rebelled against Tito's troops.[41]

This was also the period of the fascist state of Greater Albania (including western Macedonia, Kosovo and Metohija, except for the Trepca mines that were occupied by the Germans, Podujevo county, Vucitrn and Kosovska Mitrovica). A part of Kosovo belonged to the Nazi Greater Bulgaria. It is estimated that 70,000 Albanian colonists came to Kosovo from Albania, and that the same number of Serbs were moved out.[42]

Post-Second-World-War Kosovo

The period between 1945 and 1966 was marked by the domination of the Serbian communist group and discrimination against Albanians and a part of Serbs that had been moved out of Kosovo during the war and then prevented from returning by the SFRY Communist Party.

Following partisan victory against the Axis, the Yugoslav phenomenon was brought into being. In Yugoslavia, immediately after the war and new disturbances, martial law was imposed in Kosovo. At that time there was an authoritarian order with the ruling Communist Party at the centre, as in other parts of the country.[43]

The Yugoslav constitution of 1946 declared that Yugoslavia was

> a federal state having the form of a republic of equal nations consisting of six sovereign states – people's republics wherein the Autonomous Province of Vojvodina and the Autonomous Province of Kosovo-Metohija regions are constituent parts of the People's Republic of Serbia.

Whereas the republics consist of 'nations', the provinces were at that time labelled 'national minorities'; this was changed to 'nationalities' in 1963. Serbia was still, however, the political core of Yugoslavia. The idea of Tito's creation was thus to bridge the national cleavages. The republics were given extensive rights to self-management, in accordance with Tito's approach to communism.[44]

Following economic reforms in 1965, which further emphasized regional differences between the industrialized, developed economies of the north (Croatia and Slovenia) and the underdeveloped south (Macedonia, Kosovo and to a certain extent Serbia), national feelings were triggered as was the cracking of Yugoslav cohesion. In Kosovo, Aleksandar Rankovic, the Vice-President of Yugoslavia, pursued a heavily repressive policy, carried out by the secret police. A split emerged in the Albanian society between the leaders of the local Communist Party and the masses who resented the police brutality. Thus, national identity remained stronger than class feelings.[45] In the period after the Second World War, Yugoslav Albanians differed from other Yugoslav and European populations by having the highest birth rate, and lowest geographic mobility.[46]

The Era of Autonomy

The period from 1966 to the late 1980s was characterized by the domination of the Albanian group and discrimination against Serbs.

When the 'Rankovic case' was opened in 1966, it was not followed by a debate on the type of commanding hierarchy and the political police's place in it, rather the matter was shifted to the otherwise slippery ground of ethnic relations. Thus the entire affair was mostly presented as an offshoot of 'Greater Serbian hegemony'. Along with this wave came changes in the personal composition of the regime, but not in the actual nature of the regime.

The dismissal of Rankovic in 1966 led to greater liberty for the Albanians. New demands were eventually presented by the Albanian movement, which now called for the status of a republic of Kosovo within the Yugoslav federation. The idea of a republic was rejected by the Central Committee of the League of Communists of Yugoslavia (LCY). The Albanian demands led eventually, however, to amendments to the constitution in 1969 and 1971, increasing the rights of Kosovo and Vojvodina.

In late 1974 a new constitution was instituted, designed by Edvard Kardelj, a Slovenian close to president Tito. The Kosovo Provincial Assembly could veto any decision made by the Serbian Republic Parliament, although Kosovo was still a province within Serbia. The Serbian Parliament did not have the same rights over decisions made in Kosovo. The unique Yugoslav patchwork seemed to function satisfactorily as the republics and provinces enhanced their influence vis-à-vis the federal government. Following the constitutional changes of 1974, however, Kosovo witnessed a process of 'Albanization'. Serbs and Montenegrins lost their privileged status in the administration. Federal resources were used to purchase Serbian agricultural land, and Serbian villages were disintegrated.[47]

In this period 237 university professors and schoolteachers from Albania taught in Kosovo schools and at Pristina University. One of them was Rexhep Mejdani, later the president of Albania. One hundred and eighty-three researchers obtained their Ph.D. degrees at the University of Pristina. Over 20 per cent of all the books (particularly in the humanities) were imported from Enver Hoxha's Albania. In the 1960s and 1970s the federal government engaged in efforts to accelerate industrialization and to achieve a general process of modernization. The share of the Kosovo population engaged in agriculture declined from 80 per cent in 1948 to 25 per cent in 1981. From 1981 onwards Kosovo was treated as an 'extremely economically underdeveloped province'. In that period (1981–88) Kosovo was receiving 12 times as much federal Yugoslav funds as the other regions. This meant that Kosovo was essentially a privileged province in that period and not a colony as has been claimed.

Major social upheavals caused an uprooting of traditional society. Ties with the family, the community and the clan were weakened, although the clan structures are still valid. This is expressed for example in the *Besa* – an archaic patriarchal legal and moral code, based on a solemn oath, a given word which is of importance even today. Another feature of the clan structures is the blood feud,[48] which still exists in Albanian society. A medieval collection of laws, 'Canon Leka Dukadjini', has been used in parallel with contemporary Yugoslav laws.[49]

During the 1960s, a number of illegal groups were formed, headed by the Revolutionary Committee for the Liberation of Albanians. In 1974 another group, the Kosovo National Liberation Front, became active. Investigation into their activities revealed eight additional secessionist groups that employed or were planning to employ terrorism to drive non-Albanians from Kosovo. During the 1980s the Kosovo National Movement came about through the merger of four political organizations: the National Liberation Movement of Kosovo and Other Parts of Albanian Yugoslavia, the Kosovo Marxist–Leninist Organization, the Communist–Marxist–Leninist Party of Albanians in Yugoslavia and the Red National Front. This organization transformed itself into the Kosovo Liberation Army (KLA) in the 1990s.[50]

During this period of extremely high autonomy (1974–91) Kosovo Albanians established a pattern of discrimination over Serbs, pushing them to leave. As many as 100,000 Serbs left Kosovo in the 20–25 year period, among which 75–85 per cent did so under pressure. The number of 100,000 Serbian emigrants assumes even greater significance when compared with the total population of Serbs in Kosovo (1948 – 171,911; 1953 – 189,869; 1961 – 227,016; 1981 – 209,498; 1991 – 194,190).[51] Thus Serbs who emigrated accounted for almost a half of the whole Serbian population in Kosovo. Similar data are cited by the Albanian demographer Islami: 'It is estimated that ... from 1966 to 1981 about 52,000, and since 1981 about 20,000 Serbs left Kosovo through direct migrations'. During the 1980s the *New York Times* did speak about 'Albanian terror against Kosovo Serbs'. Thousands of Serbs from the late 1960s until the mid-1980s were leaving Kosovo under Albanian pressure and without any legal or political protection. Had the migrations of Serbs and Montenegrins from Kosovo been only economically conditioned, as is often pointed out in the predominant Albanian discourse, they would have been individual. Predominantly, the active population would have moved, and not entire households.[52] Reports on the burning of Serbian property, harassments, beatings and rapes directed against the Serbian population of Kosovo stirred Serbian nationalist feelings as well as fear.[53] Emigration of Serbs and Montenegrins from Kosovo continued into the 1980s and 1990s, albeit with less intensity.

The Milošević Era

The period since the late 1980s to the summer of 1999 was marked by the dominance of the Serbian group, complete parallelism, and discrimination against Albanians.

Emigration of Serbs from Kosovo is the key moral argument that Serbs developed in this phase – both for ongoing oppression of Kosovo Albanians, as well as for denying them the right to self-determination and secession. The moral background during the Serbs' oppression toward Albanians in Kosovo was found in the need to protect 'the rest of Serbs', who actually were under the highest pressure during the period of Albanian administration in Kosovo. In Serbia this period is usually described as a long-overdue correction to an unjust political arrangement which gave Kosovo power over the Serbian state as a whole.

To the Kosovo Albanians the final blow came in March 1989, when amendments to the Serbian constitution deprived the provinces of their autonomous status within the republic. The Changes 'effectively put an end to the autonomy of Kosovo'.[54] On 2 July 1990, Kosovo (as well as Slovenia) proclaimed their sovereignty based on the principle of the right to self-determination. Kosovo declared itself to be an 'independent unit in the Yugoslav community, equal to other republics' which made the Serbian National Assembly dissolve the government of Kosovo. Two months later Serbia once again adopted a new constitution which gave Serbia greater control over the provinces. The Serbian National Assembly was further granted the right to 'suspend any branch of the provincial government if its policies appear to be in conflict with Serbia's constitution and laws'. The constitution was widely debated before its adoption and the government of Kosovo adopted on 7 September a separate constitution, which proclaimed independence of Kosovo and declared Kosovo a republic.[55]

During this period, 'the factual majority in Kosovo felt as the functional minority, while the factual minority sought the position of a functional majority'.[56] Many political prisoners, including prisoners of conscience, were convicted by courts in proceedings which failed to meet international standards of fairness. The Serbian authorities denied many ethnic Albanians the right to work. This was particularly the case for members of the ethnic Albanian community who were professionals trained to work in the field of criminal justice. Most ethnic Albanian judges, prosecutors and police officers were dismissed (or put in situations where they had little choice other than to resign) by the Serbian authorities who replaced them with Serbs.[57] Over 85,000 Albanians were fired during this period.[58] A detailed review of information from numerous sources makes clear that the majority of accusations against Albanians were politically or ethnically motivated, involving searches, arrests, detentions, trials, physical violence and other illegal coercive measures.[59]

In 1998 Amnesty International witnessed an increase in human rights violations perpetrated by FRY security forces and paramilitaries in Kosovo.[60] Armed conflict erupted between members of the Kosovo Liberation Army, which had formed to fight for an independent Kosovo, and FRY forces, Serb police and paramilitary groups operating in the region. The vast majority of victims in Kosovo during the period of the armed conflict were ethnic Albanian. However, Serbs also suffered human rights abuses, such as abductions, beatings and executions, at the hands of armed ethnic Albanian groups such as the KLA.[61] There were 1,126 terrorist attacks by the KLA in Kosovo and Metohija between 1 January 1998 and 30 August 1998. Police forces were targets in 616 cases and civilians in 510. In the attacks on police forces 74 policemen were killed and 282 wounded. Albanian armed groups also killed 81 civilians, 30 Serbs and Montenegrins, 47 Albanians loyal to Yugoslavia, three Roma and one unidentified person, while 95 civilians were wounded. In this same period 208 civilians were kidnapped, 157 Serbs and Montenegrins, 42 Albanians, six Roma, one Macedonian, one Muslim and one Bulgarian. Of these 29 were women and nine were children. James Rubin, Spokesman of the US Department of State confirmed:

> The United States is deeply concerned about the safety of the civilian population in Kosovo, both Albanian and Serb. We are concerned about attacks against Serbian civilians in Kosovo by Albanian extremist groups, including the KLA. In recent weeks a number of Serb civilians have reportedly been kidnapped by armed Albanian groups.

When President Clinton announced the NATO air attacks, on 24 March 1999, he said that he was doing so because Serbian forces were 'moving from village to village, shelling civilians, and torching their houses'. Thus NATO supposedly was attacking to 'protect thousands of people in Kosovo from a mounting military offensive'.[62] It is clear, however, that the wide Serbian offensive against Kosovo Albanians began only after NATO attacks began. As the US State Department itself admits, 'In late March 1999, Serbian forces dramatically increased the scope and pace of their efforts, moving away from selective targeting of towns and regions suspected of Kosovo Liberation Army (KLA) sympathies'.[63] As the Organization for Security and Cooperation in Europe (OSCE) report confirms,[64] violence in Kosovo escalated dramatically when NATO air strikes began on 24 March. If NATO had indeed begun its attacks to 'prevent a greater catastrophe',[65] than what the US State Department acknowledges to have been 'selective targeting' of places suspected of KLA activities, it clearly failed: the attacks provoked a wider Serbian offensive against ethnic Albanians. Various ways of discriminating against Kosovo Albanians grew and culminated in ethnic cleansing during the NATO bombing. This result was hardly unpredictable, and was in fact predicted by military and Central Intelligence Agency (CIA) analysts, but these predictions were ignored. After NATO attacks began, Serb forces began the massive expulsion of ethnic Albanians from Kosovo. This process was also developed by the actions of the KLA, who saw their chance to rob and expel both uncooperative and cooperative Albanians and Serbs under the cover of NATO bombing and Serbian police, military and paramilitary actions. The goal of the NATO action supposedly switched to returning the refugees. However, the few reporters from the Western media who were on the ground in Kosovo in April and May 1999 reported that Albanians were by then leaving mainly because of NATO bombing.[66] With each passing day, as NATO increased the destruction of Kosovo, more Albanians left, and there were fewer possibilities for return: although Serb (para) military forces burned Albanian houses, it was NATO that destroyed the infrastructure. It can be argued that NATO's action provoked a humanitarian disaster.[67]

Kosovo Today

The period following the signing of the peace settlement after 78 days of NATO bombing was marked by domination of the Albanian group and discrimination against Serbs and other non-Albanians.

With the withdrawal of Serbian police and the Yugoslav Army, ten years of human rights violations perpetrated by these forces against ethnic Albanians came to an end in June 1999. However, more than six months after the deployment of a peacekeeping force, KFOR, led by NATO, and the establishment of the United Nations Interim Administration Mission in Kosovo (UNMIK) serious crimes and human rights abuses continue to be committed against Serbs and other non-Albanians.[68] Subsequently, in this last period those Serbs and other non-Albanian civilians who were involved in atrocities against Albanians left Kosovo (together with members of the Serbian police force, the Yugoslav Army and their families, Serb reservists and paramilitary groups). Serbs and other non-Albanians who believed they had no reason to fear retaliation by the returning ethnic Albanians, stayed in Kosovo. However, they became the targets of revenge and violence by the KLA, armed Albanian civilians and criminal gangs from Albania. The goal of these attacks is to arouse fear, create general insecurity and make life unbearable so that the non-Albanian population emigrates from Kosovo and thereby contributes to creating an ethnically pure Kosovo. The target of attacks by Albanian armed groups also include ethnic Albanians who are not willing to accept separatist politics, but who are loyal citizens of Yugoslavia.

The logic of 'who isn't with us is against us' puts ethnic Albanians on notice that they will be treated as enemies if they do not accept the declared national aspirations, police, and government buildings, because they represent the state, which the majority of Kosovo Albanians do not recognize.[69] UNMIK and KFOR have been unable to prevent violent attacks, including human rights abuses, often motivated by a desire for retribution, against non-Albanians (mainly Serbs, Roma and Muslim Slavs), ethnic Albanians accused of collaboration, or against ethnic Albanians of moderate political views.[70] Recent Albanian extremist violence against Serbs and other non-Albanians is reported with understanding, presented as justifiable revenge for what Serbian police, military and paramilitary units did. But the media that told the story this way, never explained that Serb ethnic cleansing after NATO started bombing could be 'understood' as anger at what they saw as the destruction of their entire country commissioned or demanded – as it was – by moderate as well as extremist Kosovo Albanians. Jiri Dienstbier, special informer to the UN, for human rights stated:

> It is not a revenge of Albanian extremists against Serbs and other non-Albanian extremists. It is a very well established politics of ethnic cleansing which is organized by Albanian extremists, and it is confirmed in fact that there are no non-Albanian inhabitants in Kosovo, except in Kosovska Mitrovica.

One year after the end of the war the political circumstances in Kosovo have become even more complex by the presence of international military forces. A year-long activity of the new factor has stirred up existing passions and has contributed to the elimination of the prospect of coexistence of different ethnic groups. It is completely opposite to the proclaimed goal of the international community. Insufficient competence of their representatives to neutralize the conflict, and the obvious intention of the international community to satisfy partial interests of the Albanians, does not motivate the sides in conflict to improve their relations and reconstruct everyday life of all ethnic groups in Kosovo.

Today Kosovo is the scene of continuing violence and intimidation, particularly by Albanian nationalist extremists. The spiral of exclusion continues, as one 'national' set of civilian victims has been replaced by another. After having been expelled by Serbian (para) military forces, masses of Albanian refugees have now returned to the province, which has caused the exodus of an overwhelming majority of Kosovo Serbs, Roma and other non-Albanian citizens, with little prospect for return. The large international military and diplomatic presence hovers between helplessness, arrogance, misinterpretation and incompetence.[71]

Dominance of one ethnic group over another has many consequences. One of those is immigration into and emigration from Kosovo. Another consequence of the shifts of dominance is related to the strengthening of revenge, leaving smaller and smaller territories for compromise. Since 1999 Kosovo has reached the nationalistic ideal: i.e. local and international forces have maintained a status quo, that is today one of the ethnically most homogeneous parts of Europe.

In the presence of international forces and under the rule of the UN over 200,000 Serbs and other non-Albanian people have been expelled from Kosovo. Almost 1,000 Serbs have been killed and 1,200 have been kidnapped.[72] The Albanian forces have burned down, plundered and illegally occupied tens of thousands of Serbian houses. More than 100

Orthodox churches were destroyed and blown up at Kosovo and Metohija. The destruction of Albanian villages in the Serbian police offensives grabbed the international media spotlights, but the plight of the rural Serbian peasantry was often ignored and dozens of villagers and farmers were abducted, tortured and left in mass graves. Three of the areas under investigations for mass graves of Serbs are thought to be the villages of Klecka and Glodjane and the town of Orahovac.[73] This process of violence in Kosovo is still going on while the 'anniversary of peace' is being celebrated.[74]

Today in Kosovo the international community's attempt to create a multiethnic province seems unrealistic. Ethnic identity motivates discrimination that non-Albanians face regularly.

The fact that the presence of the UN did not bring expected peace for all ethnic groups after a year can be interpreted as the inability of the international community to deal with complex realities in Kosovo. To the majority of Serbs the UN only confirmed the feeling of guilt for their troubles as well as the troubles of others. To Albanian nationalists it has created the appearance that they can enjoy the victory on account of the misery of others. Paradoxically the UN presence failed to weaken extremists on both sides, threatening the average citizens of Albanian, Serbian or other nationalities.

Frequent attacks by Albanian extremists on Serbs living in enclaves indicate that a soution for creating a democratic and multiethnic Kosovo remains to be found. Just as the unwarranted oppression of Serbian police in Kosovo deepened hostilities between Serbs and Albanians before the war, now, under the auspices of the authorities of the UN, the newly created Albanian police force fails to protect non-Albanians. The absurdity of the situation in Kosovo is that even if the biggest overseas US military base was built here, it cannot control the level of crime and provide a basic level of security to all the citizens of Kosovo.

NATO destruction was explained to the world as an emergency protection of vulnerable Albanian victims. Actual everyday destruction of the Serbian infrastructure, including the murdering and kidnapping of non-Albanian people is not considered as dangerous. It appears that the suffering of the non-Albanian population is not considered human loss. It does not matter if it is enlarged and if it happens in the full presence of international forces. It is not perceived as a proper reason to plan any protective measure for the victims of violence. The international community appears unable to defend the principle of Human Rights. It would take a completely new approach in the paradigm of thinking to find a lasting solution for all people who live, and still have to return to live, in Kosovo. By placing emphasis on the reconstruction of the quality of daily life the chances for the reconstruction of normal life for all in Kosovo exist.

CONCLUSION

The existence of conflicts and conflicting interests proves to be a powerful and efficient generator of prejudices and stereotypes. Conflict as a clash of opposing interests is a generator of negative feelings toward the other side that have the potential to grow into hostility. Stereotypes are consequently important means whereby cognitive consistency is established. They manage to explain the cause of the conflict and the actions of the other side, as well as to explain and rationalize one's own hostile attitudes and actions. Besides, negative attitudes and stereotypes are systematically developed because they enhance the group's homogeneity, make it more resistant to the influence of the other side and help mobilize the membership.

Through extremely polarized evaluations, there has traditionally been a profound division between Albanians and Serbs regarding almost all vital components that constitute a relationship of trust: there is a high level of acceptance of force as means to resolve the conflict; there is extremely high ethnic distance between Albanians and Serbs; opposed desirable political solutions are envisioned by both groups.

Dominance of one ethnic group over another produced many consequences. One of those was immigration into and emigration from Kosovo. Another consequence of the shifts of dominance is related to the strengthening of revenge, leaving smaller and smaller 'territories' for compromise. In the past months Kosovo has became ethnically the most homogeneous part of the Balkans.

All these are threads of the Kosovo knot, in itself each is a complex enough problem that requires enormous patience and wisdom to unravel and untangle.[75] The negative image of Serbs held by Albanians and of Albanians held by Serbs is certainly a consequence of the long-standing unsolved ethnic conflict in Kosovo, but also a factor making its solution more difficult. We may assume with great certainty that the escalation of armed conflicts in Kosovo has made such negative stereotypes more negative and widespread. If we take into account that the solution sought for Kosovo by the international community necessarily implies coexistence within the same province, while at the same time the image of Serbs espoused by Albanians, and vice versa, suggests a multiethnic society to be improbable.

The main difficulty in changing stereotypes is that they persist even when the factors that have generated them cease to be active, because they influence behaviour and the process of information processing obstructing their change. They function as self-fulfilling prophecies. One puts the other in the role matching the stereotype and adapts his or her own behaviour accordingly; the other person, in turn, reacts most often in a way that confirms the expectations. Information confirming stereotypes is easier to remember and is felt to be more credible. There is a paradoxical phenomenon in studies of changing attitudes: presenting comprehensive information to people who shape mutually opposing attitudes does not result in a rapprochement between the attitudes but on the contrary, in their polarization.[76] This means that even when ethnic conflicts are resolved and factors which, deliberately or inadvertently, generated stereotypes and prejudices during the conflict cease to be active, stereotypes and prejudices will not disappear by themselves. Rather their change should be the object of organized social action. Instead of a new global policy of coexistence, old hot points of confrontation are being stirred up and new ones created. With considerable differences in political perceptions and ethnic ideologies, any sophisticated, constructive solution should start with respecting the differences. To ignore these differences, or to focus only on the argumentation of one side, heightens antagonism.

NOTES

I give special thanks to Dr Marta Frajnd (Institute for Literature and Arts, Belgrade) and Professor Vesna Jezerkić (Faculty of Dramatic Arts, Belgrade) for the generous suggestions and patient proofreading of this chapter. I wish to thank Professor Dr Marina Blagojević for the useful insights she provided during the many conversations we had about this topic. I also wish to thank Sanja Pesek for constructive input in finalizing the chapter.

1. See M. Billig, 'Prejudice', in A. Kuper (ed.), *The Social Science Encyclopedia* (London: Routledge and Kegan Paul, 1985); A. Giddens, *Sociologija* (Podgorica: CID, 1998), p. 152; N. Mićunović, 'Balkan u modi', *NSPM*, VI, 1–2 (1999), p. 79.
2. See M. Blagojević, 'Kosovo: In/Visible Civil War', in T. Veremis and E. Kofos (eds), *Kosovo: Avoiding Another Balkan War* (Athens: ELIAMEP and University of Athens, 1998), p. 240.
3. Ibid.
4. See N. Popov, 'Difficulties with Dialogue', *Republika*, Special Issue 9 (1994), p. 3.
5. Ibid.
6. See G. Pula and E. Beqiri, 'Kosova: Colonial Oppression of Albanians in Yugoslavia', in *Kosova Watch* 1, 1 (Pristina: Kosova Helsinki Committee, 1992); H. Islami, 'Demografska stvarnost Kosova', in D. Janjić and Š. Malići (eds), *Sukob ili dijalog: Srpsko-albanski odnosi i integracija Balkana* (Subotica: Evropski gradjanski centar za rešavanje konflikata, 1994), p. 31.
7. See Popov, 'Difficulties', p. 3.
8. See R. Petrović, *Etnicki mesoviti brakovi u Jugoslaviji* (Belgrade: ISIFF, 1985).
9. See M. Kandido-Jakšić, 'Ethnically-Mixed Marriages and Social Distance Towards Members of Some Ex-Jugoslav Nations', *Sociologija* XLI, 1 (1999), p. 104; R. Petrovic, *Etnicki*, p. 57; E. Gordy, *The Culture of Power in Serbia: Nationalism and the Destruction of Alternatives* (University Park, PA: The Pennsylvania State University Press), p. 4.
10. See B. Kuzmanović, 'Socijalna distanca prema pojedinim nacijama', in M. Lazić (ed.), *Razaranje drustva* (Belgrade: F. Višnjić, 1994), p. 228.
11. See A. Fiamengo, 'Studenti sarajevskog univerziteta-pitanje braka posmatrano iz

aspekta nacionalne i religiozne pripadnosti i stepena obrazovanja bračnih drugova', *Sociologija* 1 (1960); R. Supek, *Psihologija radne akcije* (Zagreb: Mladost, 1963); D. Pantić, 'Etnička distanca u SFRJ', in *Izvesaj i studije Centra za istrazivanje javnog mnjenja 2* (Belgrade: CIJM, 1967); N. Rot and N. Havelka, *Nacionalna vezanost i vrednosti kod srednjoskolske omladine* (Belgrade: Institut za psihologiju and IDN, 1973); D. Pantić, *Nacionalna svest mladih Srbije* (Belgrade: IICSSO, 1987); D. Pantić, 'Drustvena distanca', in V. Goati (ed.), *Jugosloveni o druaštvenoj krizi* (Belgrade: Izdavacki centar Komunist, 1989); L. Bacević, 'Nacionalna svest omladine', in Mihailović et al., *Deca krize* (Belgrade: IDN, 1999); H. Schuman, S. Charlotte and L. Bobo, *Racial Attitudes in America: Trends and Interpretations* (Cambridge, MA: Harvard University Press, 1998).

12. See Petrović, *Etnicki*, p. 63.
13. See D. Pantić, 'Nacionalna distanca gradjana Jugoslavije', in *Jugoslavija na kriznoj prekretnici* (Belgrade: IDN, 1991).
14. See Kuzmanović, 'Socijalna distanca'.
15. A poll of Kosovo–Metohija public opinion conducted by the Forum for Ethnic Relations from Belgrade in collaboration with the Institute for Philosophy and Sociology in Pristina. See S. Mihailović, 'Etnički stereotipi i heterostereotipi na Kosovu', *Sociologija* LX, 3 (1998), p. 411.
16. See D. Pantić, 'Changes in Ethnic Stereotypes of Serbs', *Sociologija* 4 (1996), p. 560.
17. See Pantić, *Nacionalna svest*.
18. See Pantić, 'Changes'.
19. See Kuzmanović, 'Socijalna distanca'.
20. See S. Mihailović, 'Etnički stereotipi'.
21. See D. Popadić and M. Biro, 'Autostereotipi i heterostereotipi Srba u Srbiji', *NSPM*, VI, 1–2 (1999), p. 95.
22. Ibid., p. 99; D. Pantić, 'Changes', p. 569.
23. See Z. Golubović, B. Kuzmanović and M. Vasović, *Društveni karakter i društvene promene u svetlu nacionalnih sukoba* (Belgrade: IFDP and F. Višnjić, 1995).
24. Agency for Applied Sociological and Political Research from Belgrade, "Argument', sample 200, phone poll.
25. See S. Branković, 'Political Views of Serbs and Albanians in Kosovo' (Belgrade: Institute for Political Studies; Public Opinion and Marketing Center 'Medium', DS – Demografska statistika, SZS, 1993).
26. See L. Sekelj, 'Etnička distanca, ksenofobija i etnonacionalisticka manipulacija', *Sociologija* LXII, 1 (2000), p. 5.
27. See Popov, 'Difficulties', p. 5.
28. The term 'pendulum of domination' was originally used by Marina Blagojević when analysing the relations between Serbs and Albanians during the second half of the twentieth century. See M. Blagojević, 'Moving Out of Kosovo'; M. Blagojević, 'Kosovo: In/Visible'.
29. See J. Cvijić, *Metanastazicka kretanja, njihovi uzroci i posledice. Naselja i poreklo stanovnistva* (Belgrade, 1922).
30. See M. Frajnd (ed.) M. *Jovanovic. Engleska bibliografija o istocnom pitanju u Evropi* (Belgrade: Institut za knjizevnost i umetnost, 1978); *Diplomatska prepiska o arbanaskim nasiljima u Staroj Srbiji 1898–1899* (Belgrade: Ministrastvo inostranih dela, 1899); M. Rakić, *Konzulska pisma 1905–1911* (Belgrade: Prosveta, 1985).
31. H. Lindholm, 'Kosovo – Intifada of Tomorrow', *Republika*, Special Issue 9 (1994), p. 13; See also 'Dokumenti XVII – XIX vek', in A. Jeftic, *Zaduzbine Kosova* (Belgrade, Prizren: Bogoslovski fakultet and Eparhija Rasko-prizrenska, 1987), pp. 607–27.

32. Lindholm, 'Kosovo'.
33. See *DSPKS*, vol. VI, 3 (1913), Doc. 194, Report from Salonica 23, VII/5, VIII (1913), quoted after D. Djordjević, 'Migrations During the 1912–13, Balkan Wars and World War One', in *Migrations in Balkan History* (Santa Barbara: University of California, and Belgrade: SANU, Prosveta, 1998).
34. See Lindholm, 'Kosovo', p. 13.
35. See D. Djordjević, 'Migrations', pp. 115–31.
36. V. Djuretić, 'The Exodus of the Serbs from Kosovo in the Twentieth Century and Its Political Background', in I. Ninić (ed.), *Migrations in Balkan History*, pp. 131–47.
37. See Djordjević, 'Exodus', p. 125.
38. See Lindholm, 'Kosovo', p. 13.
39. Ibid.
40. See Islami, 'Demografska stvarnost', p. 43.
41. Ibid.
42. See also '*Dokumenti 1941–1945*. Statements of the Serbian Refugees from Kosovo and Metohija', in Jeftic, *Zaduzbine*, pp. 783–93.
43. See Popov, 'Difficulties', p. 5.
44. See Lindholm, 'Kosovo', p. 13.
45. Ibid.
46. See M. Blagojević, 'Kosovo: In/Visible Civil War'.
47. O. Sturesjo, *Kosovo Ett Jugoslaviskt Dilemma*, Karlospolitikens Dagsfragor (Stockholm: The Swedish Institute of International Affairs, 1990), quoted after Lindholm, 'Kosovo', p. 9.
48. See S. Djurić, *Osveta i kazna – Sociolosko istrazivanje krvne osvete na Kosovu i Metohiji* (Nis: Prosveta, 1998).
49. See W. Graff, 'Hintergründe des Kosovo-Konflikts', in Friedens-Forum, Heft 2, March 1990, OIF, quoted after Lindholm, 'Kosovo', p. 9.
50. The main target of the Albanian terrorist organizations was the Yugoslav Army.
51. See M. Blagojević, 'Serbian Migrations'; Blagojević, *Seobe Srba*.
52. See R. Petrović and M. Blagojević, *Kosovo*; M. Blagojević, *Seobe Srba i Crnogoraca sa Kosova i iz Metohije. Rezultati ankete sprovedene 1985–1986. godine* (Belgrade: SANU, 1989); M. Blagojević, 'Serbian Migrations from Kosovo from the End of the 1960s: Social Factors', in A. Mitrović (ed.), *Serbs and the Albanians in the Twentieth Century* (Belgrade: SANU, 1990).
53. See Lindholm, 'Kosovo', p. 9; Blagojević, 'Serbian Migrations'; R. Petrović and M. Blagojević, *Seobe Srba*; '*Dokumenti 1945–1986*', in A. Jeftić, *Zaduzbine*, pp. 793–846 ('*Napadi na crkve, nasrtaji na vernike, preotimanja manastirske imovine, sece suma, zlostavljanja monahinja. Pogorsanje stanja, pritisci, iseljavanja. Paljevina konaka Pecke patrijarsije*', etc.).
54. *Financial Times*, 1 February 1990.
55. See *Report on Eastern Europe* 1, 44, quoted after Lindholm, 'Kosovo', p. 9.
56. See S. Maliqi, 'Kosovo kao katalizator jugoslovenske krize', in *Kosovo-Srbija-Jugoslavija*.
57. See Amnesty International, 'Federal Republic of Yugoslavia (Kosovo). Amnesty International's Recommendations to UNMIK on the Judicial System', *Report*, EUR 70/06/00 (February 2000), at www.amnesty.org/ailib/aipub/2000/EUR/47000600.htm.
58. See Pula and Beqiri, 'Kosova'.
59. See *Human Rights in Yugoslavia 1998* (Belgrade: Belgrade Center for Human Rights, 1999); *Human Rights Violation in the Territory of former Yugoslavia 1991–1995* (Belgrade: HLC, 1997).

60. See Amnesty International, 'Kosovo: A Decade of Unheeded Warnings', Volume II, AI-Index: EUR70/40/99 (April 1999).
61. See Amnesty International, 'Federal', Report, EUR70/06/00 (February 2000).
62. See 'President Clinton. First Statement on NATO Attacks', *New York Times*, 24 March 1999.
63. See US Department of State, *Erasing History: Ethnic Cleansing in Kosovo* (1999).
64. See *As Seen, As Told*, Part II (June to October 1999), Report on Human Rights Findings of the OSCE Mission in Kosovo, at www.osce.org/kosovo/reports/hr/part2/index.htm; see also (in this Report) Annex II: Human Rights Violations by Category – Right to Life, Right to Physical Integrity, at www.osce.org/kosovo/reports/hr/part2/09-annex2.htm.
65. See 'President Clinton', *New York Times*, 24 March 1999.
66. See 'Dispatch From Kosovo: Serbs Steer Many Refugees Toward Home', *Los Angeles Times*, 26 April 1999; 'Kosovo's Ravaged Capital Staggers Back to Life', *New York Times*, 5 May 1999; 'Fleeing Kosovars Dread Dangers of NATO Above, Serbs Below', *New York Times*, 4 May 1999; *BBC Online Network*, 'World – Europe – The Refugees Who Remained' (1999).
67. See R. Hayden, 'Humanitarian Hypocrisy', *East European Constitutional Review* 8, 3 (1999), p. 92.
68. See Amnesty International, 'Federal', *Report*, EUR 70/06/00 (February 2000).
69. See 'Kosovo Roma: Targets of Abuse and Violence – 24 March–1 September 1999', *HLC*, Report.
70. See Amnesty International, 'Federal', *Report*, EUR 70/06/00 (February 2000).
71. See S. Jansen and I. Spasić, Introduction in Special Section: 'Belgrade, After the Bombing', *Intergraph* I, 2 (May 2000), University of Hull, at www.intergraphjournal.com.
72. See I. Torov, 'Poligon nasilja i nemoci', *Danas*, 10–11 June 2000.
73. See T. Walker, 'KLA Faces Trials for War Crimes on Serbs', *The Times*, 3 September 2000.
74. See *Crucified Kosovo* (Serbian Orthodox Church, 2000).
75. See Popov, 'Difficulties', p. 5.
76. See Popadic and Biro, '*Autostereotipi*', p. 110.

REFERENCES

Agani, F., 'Kriticki osvrt na politicki diskurs o Kosovu i Albancima', in *Kosovo, Srbija, Yugoslavija* (Ljubljana: KRT ZSMS, 1989).

Amnesty International, 'Kosovo: a Decade of Unheaded Warnings', 2, *AI Index*, EUR 70/40/99 (April 1999).

Amnesty International, 'Federal Republic of Yugoslavia (Kosovo). Amnesty International's Recommendations to UNMIK on the Judicial System', *Report*, EUR 70/06/00 (February 2000), at www.amnesty.org/ailib/aipub/2000/EUR/47000 600.htm.

As Seen, As Told, Part II (June–October 1999), Report on Human Rights Findings of the OSCE Mission in Kosovo,www.osce.org/kosovo/reports/hr/part2/index.htm.

Bacević, L. 'Nacionalna svest omladine', in S. Mihailović et al., *Deca krize* [Children of Crisis] (Belgrade: IDN, 1990).

Billig, M., 'Prejudice', in Kuper, A. (ed.), *The Social Science Encyclopedia* (London: Routledge and Kegan Paul, 1985).

Blagojević, M., 'Serbian Migrations From Kosovo From the End of the 1960s: Social Factors', in A. Mitrović (ed.), *Serbs and the Albanians in the Twentieth Century*

(Belgrade: SANU, 1991).

Blagojević, M., 'Iseljavanje sa Kosova', in N. Popov (ed.), *Srpska strana rata* (Belgrade: Republika, 1996), pp. 232–67.

Blagojević, M., 'Kosovo: In/Visible Civil War', in T. Veremis and E. Kofos (eds), *Kosovo: Avoiding Another Balkan War* (Athens: ELIAMEP and University of Athens, 1998), pp. 238–310.

Branković, S., 'Political Views of Serbs and Albanians in Kosovo'(Belgrade: Institute for Political Studies; Public Opinion and Marketing Center 'Medium', DS – Demografska statistika, Savezni zavod za statistiku, 1993).

Crucified Kosovo (Belgrade: Srpska pravoslavna crkva, 2000).

Cvijić, J., *Metanastazicka kretanja, njihovi uzroci i posledice. Naselja i poreklo stanovnistva* (Belgrade: Cvijić, J., 1922).

Diplomatska prepiska o arbanaskim nasiljima u Staroj Srbiji 1898–1899 (Belgrade: Ministarstvo inostranih dela, 1899).

'Dispatch From Kosovo: Serbs Steer Many Refugees Toward Home', *Los Angeles Times*, 21 April 1999.

Djordjević, D., 'Migrations During the 1912–1913, Balkan Wars and World War One', in I. Ninić (ed.), *Migrations in Balkan History* (Santa Barbara: University of California and Belgrade: SANU, Prosveta, 1989), pp. 115–30.

Djuretić, V., 'The Exodus of the Serbs from Kosovo in the Twentieth Century and Its Political Background', in I. Ninić (ed.), *Migrations in Balkan History* (Santa Barbara: University of California, and Belgrade: SANU, Prosveta, 1989), pp. 131–46.

Djurić, Dj., *Psiholoska struktura etnickih stavova omaldine OS 'Jovan Vukanovic'* (Novi Sad: Univerzitet u Novom Sadu, 1980).

Djurić, S., *Osveta i kazna – Sociolosko istrazivanje krvne osvete na Kosovu i Metohiji* (Niš: Prosveta, 1998).

Djuričić, M., *Cuvari bese* (Belgrade: SANU, 1979).

Dučić, J., *Sporna pitanja Kraljevine* (Belgrade: Knjizarnica Obradovic, 1990).

Fiamengo, A., 'Studenti sarajevskog univerziteta – pitanje braka posmatrano iz aspekta nacionalne i religiozne pripadnosti i stepena obrazovanja bracnih drugova', *Sociologija* no. 1 (1960).

Frajnd, M. (ed.), M. Jovanovic. *Engleska bibliografija o istocnom pitanju u Evropi* (Belgrade: Institut za knjizevnost i umetnost, 1978).

Giddens, A., *Sociologija* (Podgorica: CID, 1998).

Golubović, Z., Kuzmanović, B. and Vasović, M., *Društveni karakter i društvene promene u svetlu nacionalnih sukoba* (Belgrade: Institut za filozofiju i drustvenu teoriju and Filip Višnjić, 1995).

Gordy, E., *The Culture of Power in Serbia: Nationalism and the Destruction of Alternatives* (University Park, PA: The Pennsylvania State University Press, 1999).

Graham, P., 'Drug wars: Kosovo's New Battle', *National Post*, 13 April 2000, p. A14.

Hayden, R., *Blueprints for a House Divided: The Constitutional Logic of the Yugoslav Conflicts* (Michigan, MI: University of Michigan Press, 1999).

Hayden, R., 'Humanitarian Hypocrisy', *East European Constitutional Review* 8, 3 (1999), pp. 91–6.

Human Rights in Yugoslavia 1998 (Belgrade: Belgrade Center for Human Rights, 1999).

Human Rights Violation in the Territory of Former Yugoslavia 1991–1995 (Belgrade: Humanitarian Law Center, 1997).

Islami, H., 'Demografska stvarnost Kosova', in D. Janjić and Š. Malići (eds), *Sukob ili dijalog: Srpsko–albanski odnosi i integracija Balkana* (Subotica: Evropski gradjanski centar za rešavanje konflikata, 1994), pp. 29–51.

Jansen, S. and Spasić, I., Introduction in Special Section: 'Belgrade, After the Bombing', *Intergraph* I, 2 (May 2000), University of Hull, at www.intergraphjournal. com.

Jeftic, A. (ed.), *Zaduzbine Kosova. Spomenici i znamenja srpskog naroda* (Belgrade, Prizren: Bogoslovski fakultet i Eparhija Rasko-prizrenska, 1987), pp. 1–876.

Jirecek, K., *Istorija Srba* (Belgrade: Naucna knjiga, 1952).

Kandido-Jakšić, M., 'Ethnically-Mixed Marriages and Social Distance Towards Members of Some Ex-Jugoslav Nations', *Sociologija* XLI, 1 (1999), pp. 103–24.

'Kosovo Roma: Targets of Abuse and Violence – 24 March–1 September 1999', *Humanitarian Law Center Report* (1999).

Kuzmanović, B., 'Socijalna distanca prema pojedinim nacijama', in M. Lazić (ed.), *Razaranje društva* (Belgrade: Filip Višnjić, 1994).

Lindholm, H., 'Kosovo – Intifada of Tomorrow', *Republika*, Special Issue 9 (1994), pp. 13–17.

Maliqi, S., 'Kosovo kao katalizator jugoslovenske krize', in *Kosovo–Srbija–Jugoslavija* (Ljubljana: Univerzitetna Konferenca ZSMS and Knjižnica Revolutionarne Teorije, 1989).

Mićunović, N., 'Balkan u modi', *Nova srpska policika misao* VI, 1–2 (1999), pp. 79–89.

Mihailović, S., 'Etnicki stereotipi i heterostereotipi na Kosovu', *Sociologija* LX, 3 (1998), pp. 411–26.

Mitrović, A., 'Albanians in the Policy of Austria-Hungary towards Serbia 1914–1918', in A. Mitrović (ed.), *Serbs and the Albanians in the Twentieth Century* (Belgrade: SANU, 1990).

Mitrović, A., 'Yugoslavia, the Albanian Question and Italy 1919–1939', in A. Mitrović (ed.), *Serbs and the Albanians in the Twentieth Century* (Belgrade: SANU, 1990).

Nušić, B., *Kosovo* (Belgrade: Prosveta, 1986; published by Matica Srpska in 1902).

Pantić, D., 'Etnicka distanca u SFRJ', in *Izvesaj i studije Centra za istrazivanje javnog mnjenja*, 2 (Belgrade: Centar za istrazivanje javnog mnjenja, 1967).

Pantić, D., *Nacionalna svest mladih Srbije* (Belgrade: IIC SSO, 1987).

Pantić, D., 'Drustvena distanca', in V. Goati (ed.), *Jugosloveni o drustvenoj krizi* (Belgrade: Izdavacki centar Komunist, 1989).

Pantić, D., 'Nacionalna distanca gradjana Jugoslavije', in *Jugoslavija na kriznoj prekretnici* (Belgrade: IDN, 1991).

Pantić, D., 'Changes in Ethnic Stereotypes of Serbs', *Sociologija* 4 (1996), pp. 561–83.

Petrović, R., *Etnicki mesoviti brakovi u Jugoslaviji* (Belgrade: ISIFF, 1985).

Petrović, R. and Blagojević, M., *Migrations of Serbs and Montenegrins from Kosovo and Metohija* (Belgrade: SANU, 1989).

Petrović, R., 'Demographic Characteristics in the Development of Kosovo and Ethnic Circumstances', in A. Mitrović (ed.), *Serbs and the Albanians in the Twentieth Century* (Belgrade: SANU, 1990).

Popadić, D. and Biro, M., 'Autostereotipi i heterostereotipi Srba u Srbiji', *Nova srpska politicka misao*, VI, 1–2 (1999), pp. 89–111.

Popov, N., 'Difficulties with Dialogue', *Republika*, Special Issue 9 (1994), pp. 3–7.

'President Clinton. First statement on NATO attacks', *New York Times*, 24 March 1999.

Pula, G. and Beqiri, E., 'Kosova: Colonial Oppression of Albanians in Yugoslavia', in *Kosova Watch* 1, 1 (Pristina: Kosova Helsinki Committee, 1992).

Rakić, M., *Konzulska pisma 1905–1911* (Belgrade: Prosveta, 1985).

Rot, N. and Havelka, N., *Nacionalna vezanost i vrednosti kod srednjoskolske omladine* (Belgrade: Institut za psihologiju and IDN, 1973).

Samardžić, R., 'Migrations in Serbian History', in I. Ninić (ed.), *Migrations in Balkan History* (Santa Barbara: University of California, and Belgrade: SANU, Prosveta, 1989), pp. 83–90.

Samardžić, R. et al., *Le Kosovo Metohija dans l'histoire Serbe* (Lausanne: L'Age d'Homme, 1990).

Schuman, H., Charlotte, S. and Bobo, L., *Racial Attitudes in America: Trends and Interpretations* (Cambridge, MA: Harvard University Press, 1985).

Sekelj, L., 'Etnicka distanca, ksenofobija i etnonacionalisticka manipulacija', *Sociologija* LXII, 1 (2000), pp. 1–24.

'Selected Correspondence Concerning the NATO Aggression on the FR Yugoslavia', *Sociology* LXI, 3 (1999), pp. 273–380.

Stojančević, V. (ed.), *Serbia and the Albanians in the Nineteenth and Early Twentieth Centuries* (Belgrade: SANU, 1990).

Supek, R., *Psihologija radne akcije* (Zagreb: Mladost, 1963).

Torov, I., 'Poligon nasilja i nemoci', *Danas*, 10–11 June 2000.

US Department of State, *Erasing History: Ethnic Cleansing in Kosovo* (1999).

Walker, T., 'KLA Faces Trials for War Crimes on Serbs', *The Times*, 3 September 2000.

PART II
INTERNATIONAL
INTERVENTION PRIOR TO
THE WAR

4

The Limits of Non-Military International Intervention: A Case Study of the Kosovo Conflict

Stefan Wolff

The conflict in Kosovo is an ethnic conflict with strong territorial and cross-border/international dimensions. Its implications reach beyond Kosovo into Serbia, the Federal Republic of Yugoslavia (FRY) and the neighbouring states of Albania and Macedonia. The conflict also had (and still has) an impact on the stability of the entire Balkans.

Driven by concerns about the human rights situation in Kosovo and the implications of a further escalation of the latent conflict there, a number of international governmental organizations began to adopt various strategies of intervention from 1990, starting with the European Parliament's first resolution on Kosovo.[1] The intervention strategies adopted prior to NATO's air campaign ranged from declarations of concern and the funding of Non-Governmental Organizations (NGO) to Conference on Security and Cooperation in Europe (CSCE/OSCE) monitoring missions in Kosovo, and to concrete proposals of how to address the Kosovo crisis. The organizations involved were, on the global level, the United Nations and the International Conference on the Former Yugoslavia and its successor organizations; on the transatlantic level NATO, the CSCE/OSCE and the Contact Group on Bosnia-Herzegovina and, on the European level, the EU, the WEU, the European Parliament and the Parliamentary Assembly of the Council of Europe. Apart from these, there have been a number of bilateral and regional initiatives, such as the Kinkel–Védrine Initiative of November 1997[2] and the Turkey-inspired initiative to create a multinational rapid intervention force which was joined by Albania, Bulgaria, the Former Yugoslav Republic of Macedonia (FYROM), and Romania.[3] Individually, the governments of Russia, the United States, and, to a lesser degree, Germany, Italy and Greece have played a part in the international community's response to the evolving and subsequently escalating conflict in Kosovo.

The difficulties the international community was experiencing in formulating and implementing a consistent and effective policy approach towards the conflict in Kosovo had their sources within Kosovo, within the Federal Republic of Yugoslavia, within the wider region and within the complex framework of relations between the main actors in the international arena. Together these factors have, from the outset, limited the range of possible policies, resulting in international governmental actors failing, individually and collectively, to prevent and thus far to settle the conflict.

This broad picture needs to be transformed into a framework of distinct, yet interrelated, categories that allow an analysis of the conflict and the management and settlement strategies that were tried. Under the specific circumstances of the Kosovo conflict, such an analysis has to include the inter-ethnic situation in Kosovo, that is the sociodemographic structure of the area, including settlement patterns, and power and numerical balances, the level and nature of intergroup conflict and intergroup alliances, and the nature of cleavages between the various ethnic groups. It is further necessary to extend the analysis to the inside of the ethnic groups concerned in order to determine what the dominant political agendas were and if any intra-group rivalries existed. Beyond Kosovo, the situation in Serbia/FRY and the neighbouring states played a major role in the calculations both of decision makers in the region and of those in the relevant international bodies. These calculations included an assessment of the likelihood and consequences of conflict spillover, the impact of the ongoing conflict on regional stability in general and, in turn, the effect of the situation in other states of the region on the development of the conflict in Kosovo. These included the diverse policy agendas of major national and transnational players in relation to the conflict, cross-border ethnic alliances and the interest structures of the states concerned. Similarly significant were factors that can be located in the international context, such as the geopolitical significance of Kosovo, the existing interest structures and alliances in the international bodies involved and the availability and commitment of resources by international organizations. The individual factors in each of these five categories are summarized in Table 1.

THE CONSTRAINTS OF CONFLICT CONTAINMENT

Various policy initiatives by the international community had sought to prevent the violent escalation of the conflict in Kosovo, which occurred after years of inter-ethnic tensions in February 1998. Thereafter, the major objective of the international community was to prevent a spillover of the conflict into neighbouring countries, while simultaneously calming the situation in Kosovo and searching for an acceptable settlement. These efforts were frustrated by a variety of factors which, at the same time,

Table 1
Factors Influencing the Development of the Kosovo Conflict

Kosovo's Inter-Ethnic Situation	Kosovo's Intra-Ethnic Situation	Situation in Serbia	Regional Context	International Context
Socio-demographic structure	Dominant policy agenda	Political and economic importance of the conflict and the territory of Kosovo	Impact of the conflict: 1. stability of democratic institutions and ethnic balances	Geopolitical significance of the territory
Level and nature of inter-group conflict and alliances	Strength of leadership Existence of factions	Policy agendas of major parties	2. spill-over potential	Interest structures and alliances
Nature of cleavages	Availability of resources	Availability and commitment of resources	3. refugee flows Impact on the conflict:	Availability and commitment of resources by international organizations
Power and numerical balance		Perceived impact of the conflict on potential or actual other conflicts	1. policy agendas of major players in relation to the conflict	
			2. regional interest structures	
			3. cross-border ethnic alliances	

Source: Stefan Wolff

formed the background for subsequent efforts to find an interim solution at the Rambouillet negotiations. I will give a brief overview of these factors before turning to a more detailed analysis of the failure of the Rambouillet process.

The Inter-Ethnic Situation in Kosovo

The relationships between Albanians, Serbs and members of other ethnic groups in Kosovo have rarely been harmonious. Culturally the territory was significant for Serbs and Albanians alike, playing an important role in identity-shaping collective myths. With the creation of socialist Yugoslavia after the Second World War, hopes for the continuation of a greater Albania, created under Italian occupation, vanished into thin air. Several constitutional reforms between 1946 and 1974 increased the autonomy of the region, but failed to address the inter-ethnic unease. After 1974, the Serb population found itself to be increasingly victimized by the Albanian majority in the province. From about 1980 onwards, Albanians pressed ever harder for republican status for Kosovo, which in the Yugoslav constitution brought with it a conditional right to secession. Tensions between Serbs and Albanians in Kosovo and between the ethnic Albanian minority and the central government in Belgrade increased simultaneously to the rise of nationalism among all ethnic groups in Yugoslavia and culminated in the abolition of Kosovo's autonomy in 1989. Policies of segregation pursued by Serbs in Kosovo and Belgrade resulted in the creation of two parallel societies – Serb and Albanian. Albanians, after being forced out of the public sector, set up their own institutions, and proclaimed the Republic of Kosovo after a secret referendum and parliamentary and presidential elections in 1991 and 1992.

The marginalization of the Kosovo issue in international politics over the following years facilitated the radicalization of both Serbs and Albanians and, consequently, inter-ethnic relations deteriorated further. The two major problems which the international community had to confront with respect to the ethnic Albanian population in Kosovo were their demands for an independent state and the fact that otherwise no unified political platform among ethnic Albanians existed; and that all attempts to create one were frustrated by personal and political rivalries.

Until the mid-1990s, Ibrahim Rugova was the unchallenged leader of the ethnic Albanians' peaceful resistance to Serbia. There seemed to be a widespread determination among the existing political parties of Kosovo Albanians not to let party-political differences come in the way of a joint political agenda. Initially, this aimed at a restoration of the *status quo ante* plus, that is, the return to the 1974 constitutional regulations with a simultaneous upgrading of Kosovo to a republic and of ethnic Albanians to one of the constituent peoples of the Yugoslav state. Subsequently, however, continued Serbian repression made Rugova and his party demand independence.[4] Two presidential and parliamentary elections administered by the Kosovo Albanians confirmed his claim to the presidency of the self-proclaimed Republic of Kosovo. While Rugova thus possessed a certain degree of democratic legitimacy, even though the elections were organized under very difficult conditions, he had hardly any real power. At an internal level, this became apparent by the rejection of his authority by the KLA. Externally, in his relations with Serbia and the FRY, Rugova was not able to secure any substantial concessions from Yugoslav President Slobodan Milošević, apart from a March 1998 agreement to reopen Albanian language schools. Another severe blow to his strategy of non-violent resistance and of engaging the international community for the cause of an independent Kosovo was dealt by the European Union's official recognition of the FRY in 1996, before any resolution of the already obvious conflict in Kosovo. However, to some extent, blame also rested with Rugova himself. Insisting on the necessity and possibility of achieving Kosovo's independence from Serbia, he raised the hopes of ethnic Albanians even at a time when the international community had long made it clear that it did not support a unilateral change of borders.

The four main political rivals of Rugova's LDK were the Independent Union of Albanian Students, which was the first political organization to defy Rugova openly in 1997; Adem Demaçi's Parliamentary Party of Kosovo, who for some time also represented the KLA; the Social Democratic Party of Kosovo, which joined the former two in the boycott of the March 1998 Kosovo elections, and the Albanian Democratic Movement, which was formed at the end of June 1998 recruiting its members and leadership partly from dissatisfied former Rugova allies. Yet, while Rugova could claim some democratic legitimacy in relation to these political organizations, the major, and eventually successful, challenge to his leadership came from the KLA, who became increasingly popular among Kosovo's Albanian population and were well funded by the Albanian diaspora in western Europe and the United States and by proceeds from drugs and weapons trafficking.[5]

To prevent Kosovo's independence at all cost was the foremost objective of a large majority of the ethnic Serb population in the province. In this effort they had the overall backing of the Serbian government in Belgrade and the protection of the Serbian security forces. However, despite this active endorsement by the central government, ethnic Serbs in Kosovo were not in a particularly easy position. Their numbers shrank from just under one-third in 1961 to less than one-tenth in the 1990s.[6] This decrease was partly to do with emigration, motivated by the much lower standard of living in Kosovo compared with any other part of Yugoslavia, during the years before the breakup of the state. In addition, the Serbian perception of the post-1974 period in Kosovo had also been shaped by the experience of the 'national key' – a system that ensured proportional representation of ethnic groups in the public sector which, as Yugoslavia had a more or less completely nationalized economy, included almost all sectors of the job market as well. Consequently, Serbs saw themselves (and indeed occasionally they were) at a disadvantage in Kosovo in a variety of ways, especially in comparison with their pre-1974 position, and chose to emigrate in significant numbers.[7] From the mid-1980s onwards, ethnic Serbs in Kosovo began to organize themselves in order to lobby the central government in Belgrade. In January 1986, prominent Belgrade intellectuals sent a petition to Serbian and Yugoslav authorities claiming an anti-Serb genocide in Kosovo and demanding decisive constitutional and other steps be taken to reverse the fate of the Slav population in the province.[8] The Serb Resistance Movement, a political party of Kosovo Serbs, however, began to recognize that the main obstacle for a solution of the conflict was the lack of a democratic political process in Serbia, but its efforts to remedy this situation and promote dialogue between Serbs and Albanians were not very successful, mostly because of the lack of trust between these two groups.

In addition it must be noted that the Serb population of Kosovo was far from homogeneous, and this affected political developments quite strongly. Several thousand Serbs who had been forced out of Croatia were resettled in Kosovo, many of them against their will. When, in addition to the traditionally desperate economic conditions in the area, the security situation worsened as well (resulting in some 2,000 registered Serb and Montenegrin refugees by mid-July 1998[9]), this section of the Serb population in Kosovo became particularly radicalized, providing an electoral stronghold for the Serbian Radical Party and its leader Vojislav Šešelj.

The increased KLA targeting of Serbs and the continued instrumentalization of Kosovo in Serbian and Yugoslav politics diminished the chances of moderate forces among Serbs in Kosovo. Serb armament, 'retaliation', and cooperation with the security forces, in turn, contributed to the hardening of positions on the Albanian side, thus diminishing the already slim chances of an inter-ethnic accord as part of an agreement on the future of Kosovo.

The Situation in Serbia

The importance of Kosovo for Serbia or, more precisely, for the Serbian and Yugoslav governments, was primarily a political one. Yugoslav President Milošević began to be an essential player in the region in 1986/87 on a platform of Serbian nationalism focusing on Kosovo. Since 1998 his grip on power became ever more dependent on his ability to instrumentalize the Kosovo crisis. Throughout the period before NATO's intervention, that is, when a political rather than military solution still seemed possible, Milošević succeeded in rallying Serbian nationalist support behind him. By incorporating the Serbian Radial Party and the Serbian Renewal Movement into his government, Milošević managed to make two possible major critics share the responsibility for domestic and international consequences of government policy in Kosovo.[10] Against this background of growing influence of extreme nationalists, Milošević was also able to present himself as an indispensable guarantor of stability to the international community because of his influence in the region and because of the apparently undesirable alternatives after his departure. More importantly, he managed, internally, to prevent a democratization of the political process in Serbia and the FRY by keeping some one million Albanian voters away from the polls and by keeping inner Serbian and inner Yugoslav democratic opposition parties split.[11] Ironically, the electoral boycott of ethnic Albanians enabled the Socialist Party of Serbia (SPS) to increase its representation in parliament, as the seats not contested by Albanians went automatically to the SPS.

With Milošević gaining politically on several fronts from an ongoing conflict in Kosovo, initiatives aimed at a permanent settlement were unlikely to succeed without stronger international pressure. Without it, the odds were that Milošević would pursue a policy of moderate de-escalation (to avoid the risk of international intervention) and continuing tension in Kosovo (to maintain the conflict at a low intensity and manageable level).

Beyond Kosovo: The Regional Context of the Conflict

Historically, the Balkans have been a region of great instability for over a century. The demise of the Ottoman and Habsburg empires and the withdrawal of Russia from the region for most of the inter-war period left a power vacuum behind that was filled insufficiently by the new states that emerged on the ruins of these empires. The territorial arrangements adopted after the first and second Balkan wars and after the First and Second World Wars did not resolve many of the historical border and nationality disputes. These disputes, merely suppressed by the realities of the Cold War, came again to the forefront of international politics after 1989.

One of the central problems was the so-called Albanian question, i.e., the presence of large Albanian minorities in Macedonia, Montenegro, Greece and Kosovo and some smaller areas of southern Serbia. In the 1990s, the worsening situation in Kosovo had its most direct impact on Albania, Macedonia and Montenegro, where domestic developments and responses to the crisis in turn had consequences for Kosovo.

In Albania, communism began to crumble at the beginning of the 1990s. Multi-party elections in 1992 and 1996 resulted in Sali Berisha's Democratic Party winning overwhelming victories. As early as 1990, this party had reintroduced the issue of Kosovo into the emerging democratic political process in Albania. In 1992 the Kosovo Albanian shadow state was de facto recognized by a decision of the Albanian parliament asking the Democratic Party government of the day to recognize the Republic of Kosovo. Although the government did not act upon this resolution of the parliament,[12] it still remodelled the concept of Albanian citizenship along *jus sanguinis* lines to include all ethnic Albanians regardless of their country of residence.[13] Official support for Kosovo's independence from the Albanian government, however, did not extend far beyond verbal declarations, and even these stopped after the government recognized the existing borders with the FRY in the wake of the escalating war in the neighbouring country in 1994. In early 1997, Albanian society was at the brink of collapse and only narrowly escaped civil war when pyramid investment schemes collapsed taking with them the savings of a majority of the already poor Albanian population. The situation was blamed largely on the government in office, which was defeated in early elections in 1997.

The incoming government of Albania, preoccupied with the country's internal problems of a collapsed economy and increasing crime rates, tried not to get involved too deeply in the ongoing Kosovo conflict and, above all, not to lose critical western support in the rebuilding of Albanian society. Facing an increasing influx of refugees, it pursued a policy of de-escalation and of recognition of the existing borders of the FRY, favouring a solution within Yugoslavia giving Kosovo equal status with Serbia and Montenegro. This seemingly prudent approach taken by the new government in 1997 did not coincidentally fall together with the radicalization of the political spectrum in Kosovo and the increasing influence of forces determined to realize the goal of independence by all means possible, including the use of violence. Statements by government officials in Tirana accusing the KLA of terrorism and rejecting the idea of an independent Kosovo were not popular among any of the ethnic Albanian political factions in Kosovo.[14]

Albania's internal weakness, and in particular its almost complete lack of an effective defence force, increased the country's dependence on western military support. The Partnership for Peace agreement between NATO and Albania provided the Albanian government with some assistance in handling the evolving crisis in Kosovo.[15] However, even if NATO or the UN had been planning a border control mission in Albania similar to the one in Macedonia, the lack of infrastructure in Albania would have seriously delayed any such operation, probably beyond the point of its usefulness in conflict prevention policy.[16] The inability to protect effectively its northern borders, together with the ongoing feud among Albania's political parties and the response to it from the ethnic Albanian parties in Kosovo, once more increased the potential of a spillover of the conflict into Albania.

Similar to Albania, Macedonia was among the countries most affected by the Kosovo conflict, and at the same time also had a significant impact on the development of the conflict and its future solution. Although Macedonia's independence from Yugoslavia was peaceful, the country has experienced serious ethnic tensions. In particular, the government's relationship with the Albanian national minority remained difficult.[17]

Albanians in Macedonia are politically split between two important ethnic Albanian parties whose demands, however, are not fundamentally different. An unofficial referendum organized in 1992 showed that, at a turnout of 90 per cent of the ethnic Albanian electorate in Macedonia, roughly three-quarters supported the idea of their own political and territorial autonomous structures.[18] On this basis, ethnic Albanian parties argued for changes in Macedonia's constitution to elevate the ethnic Albanian population to the status of a constituent people of Macedonia, for improvements of the Albanian language situation, the establishment of an Albanian university and the inclusion of ethnic Albanians in the administration.[19]

In addition to this internal dimension, the complex nature of the relationships between Macedonia and Albania and Greece further added to the danger of Macedonia turning into a source of grave instability in a volatile region, especially in the light of existing ties between Kosovo and western Macedonia, which were already being used for the smuggling of weapons, the provision of support bases and funds, and the recruitment of militarily experienced fighters for the KLA.[20]

The impact of and on Montenegro had to be considered primarily from a Yugoslav perspective. At the same time when Milošević was able to rally nationalist support behind him in Serbia, he did not manage to secure a victory for his candidate for the Montenegrin presidency, Bulatović. The fear that pursuing a confrontational course vis-à-vis Montenegro and its president elect, Djukanović, could trigger the secession of Montenegro, and thus the end of the FRY, led Milošević to acknowledge Djukanović's victory. Although the Montenegrin president had to concede earlier than planned parliamentary elections, Milošević could not capitalize on this, as Bulatović's Socialist People's Party won only 29 out of 78 seats in the Montenegrin parliament, being defeated into second place by a three party coalition of Djukanović supporters who won an absolute majority.

By September 1998, Montenegro had accommodated around 40,000 refugees from Kosovo. Its resources to attend even to their most basic needs being stretched to the limits, the Montenegrin government decided to seal off the border to Kosovo and to turn away any further refugees. Moreover, the sheer number of refugees in Montenegro and their provisional accommodation relatively close to the border was likely to draw Montenegro directly into the conflict once KLA fighters established bases in the republic.

The International Context: United Nations, NATO and Russia

Another major problem that inhibited the international community's ability to devise and implement effective conflict prevention, management and resolution policies resulted from the fact that there was no unified approach to the Kosovo crisis. Not only was there a multitude of individual and collective players on the scene, with different mandates and capabilities, but there was also the problem of different allegiances, degrees of influence on the adversaries and strategic interests. The rift between the western powers and Russia in the contact group was the most obvious example of this. Since the idea of a potential NATO military intervention to restore peace in Kosovo had been born, Russia had fundamentally opposed it and constantly reiterated its conviction that there could be no military, but only a political, solution to the conflict. Russia's refusal in the UN Security Council to support a NATO strike in Kosovo was also accompanied by the implicit threat that such a move would be to the detriment of other strategic western interests, as it would alienate Russia from NATO and other Western-dominated international organizations. On the other hand, Russia also feared that it was losing even more influence on the developments in the Balkans[21] and therefore sought to remain involved in the international mediation efforts in Kosovo.

Russia's policy towards the Kosovo conflict included both the refusal to recognize the KLA as a partner in negotiations over a settlement, and a Russian engagement to broker a peaceful solution. After a meeting between President Milošević and President Yeltsin on 16 June 1998, Milošević agreed to begin talks with ethnic Albanians led by Ibrahim Rugova, who the Russians saw as the only legitimate representative of Kosovo Albanians, and to allow a Diplomatic Observer Mission unrestricted access to Kosovo. Russia also closely cooperated with the United States and other Contact Group members in the Diplomatic Observer Mission. In a joint statement in September 1998, President Yeltsin and President Clinton demanded an end of violence, the withdrawal of Serbian forces to their permanent locations, the immediate beginning of negotiations, possibilities for refugees to return to their homes and increased international monitoring of the situation in Kosovo. Russia also participated in the NATO Partnership for Peace exercise in Albania in August 1998 and supported an extension of the UNPREDEP mandate in the Macedonia. However, while Russia's involvement in international efforts to resolve the Kosovo crisis may have increased the international community's leverage over Serbia/FRY, it also made it more difficult to find consensus within the international community because of the increased diversity of interest structures.

Further difficulties arose for NATO from the pending admission of three new members – Hungary, Poland and the Czech Republic. Hungary, in particular, had its own specific national interests in the conflict because of the large Hungarian minority in the northern Serbian province of Vojvodina. During 1998, Hungary intervened several times on behalf of its kin-group, achieving, among other things, agreement that ethnic Hungarians were not to be drafted for military service in Kosovo.[22] In addition, public opinion in most NATO member countries was severely divided over the threat and use of force, and even the alliance's political leaders were far from united over this issue.

In September and October 1998, NATO leaders made it clear that a military strike had not been completely ruled out.[23] The willingness to deploy up to 50,000 troops for the enforcing of a negotiated cease-fire had been indicated, and a three-stage engagement programme had been made public to express a clear warning to President Milošević. Stage one of this programme – underpinning of neighbouring countries – was already under way in summer 1998 with NATO Partnership for Peace agreements and exercises in Albania and the Macedonia. Stage two was described as a phased escalation programme to punish continuous offensive actions, while stage three was full commitment of troops.[24] With the deteriorating refugee situation and no sign of an end to the violence in the conflict, international impatience grew. A letter sent by the UN Secretary-General to President Milošević on 1 September 1998, although it stopped short of threatening military action, demanded immediate steps to end violence and destruction in Kosovo, and could, in its directness, have been taken as an indication that the international community was edging towards action. Eventually the UN Security Council passed a resolution on 23 September 1998. Reaffirming its commitment to support a peaceful resolution of the Kosovo problem by means of an enhanced status for the province within the existing borders of the FRY, the security council also stated that the situation in Kosovo was a threat to peace and security in the region and would therefore require the action of the international community according to Chapter VII of the UN Charter.[25] In the resolution, the Security Council demanded, from both warring parties, that they put an end to violence and engage in a constructive dialogue. More specifically, the authorities of the FRY were asked, among other things, to stop all actions against the civilian population in Kosovo; to allow international monitoring, the return of refugees, and humanitarian assistance, and to commit to a timetable for negotiations and confidence building. Kosovo Albanians were requested to pursue their political goals exclusively by peaceful means and their leadership was urged to condemn all terrorist acts. Most significantly, however, the Security Council reserved for itself the right 'to consider further action and additional measures to maintain or restore peace and stability in the region' in case either one or both parties should not comply with the demands of the two resolutions.[26] This was a much tougher stance than the one adopted in the previous resolution on Kosovo, where the Security Council merely emphasized 'that failure to make constructive progress towards the peaceful resolution of the situation in Kosovo will lead to the consideration of additional measures'.[27] Eventually, NATO's obvious determination to act even without UN approval, and despite Russian objections, was the essential catalyst to force Serbia to back down for the time being and agree to withdrawing its troops from Kosovo.

SETTLING FOR AN INTERIM ARRANGEMENT

The complexity of a situation involving such a variety of local, regional and global actors with distinct interest structures, competing goals and different motivations for their involvement, made it a foremost challenge for the international community to initiate an inclusive, meaningful negotiation process that would be likely to result in a settlement. The difficulties with this were twofold. First, it had to be made clear to all parties involved that, in the absence of easy solutions, a preparedness to compromise and a willingness to settle for less than their maximum demands was the essential prerequisite for any stable long-term solution not only of the Kosovo conflict, but also of some of the region's other political problems. Second, it was necessary to bring the representatives of Kosovo Albanians and the Serbian/Yugoslav government together. With the Rambouillet talks, an environment for such a negotiation process was created.

Intrinsic Problems with an Interim Arrangement

Obviously the prospects for a solution of the Kosovo conflict in the short term were not too good, and there was no guarantee that a political settlement would be achieved in Rambouillet and subsequently successfully implemented. Yet with the ceasefire established in mid-October and the presence of international observers, there was an obvious need for an interim arrangement to provide for conditions in which the ceasefire could stabilize and a foundation be built upon which a permanent settlement for Kosovo could have been agreed. Such an interim settlement would have required the fulfilment of essential conditions, including an end of ethnic cleansing, the safe return of all refugees and displaced persons and Serbian/ FRY permission for international humanitarian relief efforts and monitoring of the situation to commence. A pre-condition of such an interim settlement, therefore, would have been a rather pragmatic approach by both sides, based on the realization that neither continuing violence nor insisting on maximum demands would benefit anyone. Even if the political elites, or parts of them, had taken such an approach, the decades-long cultivation of inter-ethnic mistrust and hatred would have made it difficult for them to find the necessary popular support to endorse such a change in strategy.

However, an interim arrangement, even if it had been found in Rambouillet, would have been far from an ideal solution. Among the most important disadvantages is the fact that there is no long-term security for either party, as the problem of negotiating and accommodating key demands remains. At the same time, a temporary solution establishes a false sense of calm, especially if a (permanent) ceasefire is part of it, when actually the danger of re-escalating violence remains if negotiations (with or without a timeframe) do not result in a substantial improvement of the situation for both parties. The threat of violence by extremists on either side gives the negotiating elites only very limited space for manoeuvre and concessions. A hardening of their positions in the negotiation process can very well prevent any constructive outcome, thus leading to a breakdown of the temporary settlement and a violent re-escalation of the conflict, probably on an even more intense level.

Another difficulty arises from the extent of an interim settlement. On the one hand, it must go beyond a ceasefire and the opening of negotiations. On the other hand, the more comprehensive an agreement is sought to be established in order to satisfy both sides, the more complicated and time consuming is the process of reaching it.

Lack of Ripeness: The Failure of the Rambouillet Talks

Like any other conflict, an ethnic conflict requires for its settlement the presence of a number of conditions. In the specific context of the Kosovo conflict, these conditions existed in each of the five dimensions initially established as a conceptual framework to guide this analysis. They are summarized in Table 2.

Table 2
'Ripeness' Conditions for the Settlement of the Kosovo Conflict

Inter-Ethnic Situation	Intra-Ethnic Situation	Situation in Serbia	Regional Context	International Context
Ability and preparedness of political elites to compromise on central issues	Strong leadership with a broad popular mandate to end the conflict	Strong leadership with a broad popular mandate to end the conflict	Limited chance of domestic instrumentalization of the conflict	Joint and flexible policy with sufficient room for manoeuvre and leverage on each of the parties
	Marginalization of extremists	Limited chance of out-flanking by anti-settlement parties		Availability and commitment of resources to facilitate negotiation and implementation/ operation of settlement
		Greater political benefits from settlement compared to continuation of conflict		

Source: Stefan Wolff

On a general level, it is important to note that, individually, these conditions were necessary to make the settlement of the Kosovo conflict possible, yet only in their entirety would they have been sufficient to do so. Their joint presence would have indicated that the conflict was ripe for a settlement, that is, that a window of opportunity existed for decision makers to achieve a settlement. In general, the simultaneous presence of these conditions does not say anything about whether this opportunity will be taken, what kind of settlement will be agreed or whether an adopted settlement will be stable, it merely points to the fact that the strategies of the conflict parties towards the conflict are no longer incompatible. Once this has been recognized, and there is no guarantee that every such opportunity will be recognized, the overall success of the settlement process depends upon the flexibility, determination and skill of those involved to design an institutional framework that fits the variety of contextual circumstances of their particular conflict situation, so as to provide for opportunities to resolve differences by peaceful and democratic means.[28]

The previous analysis of the various context factors has already indicated the severe difficulties encountered by the international community in the search for a political rather than military solution of the Kosovo conflict. In this final section, I will now examine what factors accounted for the failure of the Rambouillet negotiations and the follow-on conference in Paris.

With regard to the inter-ethnic situation in Kosovo, by the time the negotiations in Rambouillet began, the conflict was very much one between the central government in Belgrade and the KLA and ethnic Albanian population in Kosovo. Although the Serbian security forces used local Serbs as auxiliary forces, the conflict was primarily not an ethnic conflict between two local populations. All other ethnic groups in the area had been sidelined a long time ago and suffered the consequences of the conflict, rather than being active players in it. As a token gesture, the Serbian delegation in Rambouillet initially included representatives from other ethnic groups in Kosovo (to emphasize that the Albanian delegation did not represent Kosovo as a whole), but the more the Serbian delegation engaged with sincerity in the negotiations, the more these became replaced by specialists.[29] This meant that the influence of the situation in Serbia, as well as the political constellations within the Albanian population in Kosovo, became more significant for the course of the negotiations.

Before the negotiations began, the main point of contact for the international community had been Kosovo's elected government and president. Since the escalation of the conflict in February 1998, their influence on the ground in Kosovo had dwindled in favour of the KLA and a broad coalition of political parties opposed to President Rugova. This and international pressure resulted in a Kosovo delegation in Rambouillet that consisted in equal parts of these three groupings, with the KLA playing a dominant role, which was reflected in one of its members being elected head of the tripartite presidency of the negotiation team.[30] This made the position of the international community more difficult, as the KLA's commitment to achieve independent statehood for Kosovo clashed with international determination to preserve existing borders and to find a solution within them.[31] The compromise found in Rambouillet that brought the KLA on board was one of far-reaching self-government for ethnic Albanians in Kosovo with a mechanism for a final settlement (considering, among other things, the will of the people) to be adopted after further international discussions. While this reflected the changed situation in Kosovo more than anything else, international pressure as well as some concessions to the Kosovo negotiation team ensured that the delegation eventually agreed to sign the interim agreement.

While the international community thus possessed at least some leverage over the Kosovo delegation, this was not the case with the Serbian delegation. There were several reasons for this. Even though President Milošević had retained, if not increased, his political strength, there were very few incentives for him to utilize this strength for securing a successful outcome of the negotiations. Taking an accommodative stance in Rambouillet and Paris, and negotiating within the parameters set by the international community, could have easily cost him and his party their dominant position in Yugoslav and Serbian politics. A political radicalization in Serbia and a shift of power to the extreme nationalists in the Serbian Radical Party, together with the perceived weakness of the institution of the Yugoslav President, would have led almost certainly to renewed pressure for independence from Montenegro, and thus to the likely end of the FRY. Similarly, it was quite obvious that Milošević was playing for time to prepare a final assault on Kosovo, including massive troop deployments and forced population displacements in the border zones with Macedonia and Albania.[32] This would have enabled Milošević to claim a national victory, while the acceptance of the Rambouillet Agreement, with its mechanism for a final settlement after three years would, in all likelihood, have led to the secession of Kosovo. In addition, Milošević made his own judgement of the ability and willingness of NATO to act unilaterally against the will of Russia and for long enough to bring Serbia, which would rely on Russian support, to its knees.[33] In the same vein, Milošević was apparently calculating that consensus within NATO would break apart over civilian casualties and that there would be no majority to engage in a ground war.

Compared to the problems generated by the situation in Serbia, the regional context was far less troublesome. Obviously the international community could not encourage developments in Kosovo that would pose an immediate threat to the precarious stability of the Balkans. From this perspective, the outlining of the non-negotiable principles of a framework, within which Serbs and Albanians had to find a mutually acceptable interim settlement, was as much a result of taking the positions of the conflict parties on board as it was a sign of international awareness of the wider implications of the Kosovo conflict.[34]

The two most difficult challenges faced by the international community were the refugee problem and the situation in Bosnia. Data collected by the UN High Commission for Refugees (UNHCR) indicated as early as September 1998 that the Serbian military campaign and policy of ethnic cleansing had led to more than 250,000 Kosovo Albanians being internally displaced or seeking refuge in Albania, Macedonia, Montenegro and Serbia.[35] This number increased to over 300,000 by the beginning of March 1999, before the start of the NATO air campaign.[36] The largest number of those uprooted, about 250,000, were internally displaced in Kosovo, many of them trying to survive in the open. Another 55,000 had been displaced within Montenegro and Serbia. About 10,000 people fled to each Albania and Macedonia. In connection with the policy of the Serbs to destroy systematically the homes of ethnic Albanians, the international community saw it as its primary objective not only to put a stop to ethnic cleansing, but also to establish conditions that would allow the displaced to return to their towns and villages as quickly as possibly. Given the experience of ethnic Albanians with Serbia over the past decade, this meant in reality the deployment of an armed peacekeeping force, under NATO control, to instil those that had been forced to flee from their homes with enough confidence to return. The Bosnian dimension, on the other hand, was again much more closely related to the situation in Serbia. Milošević had been instrumental in reaching the Dayton Accords, and it was not inconceivable that he could use the growing dissatisfaction and radicalization among the population in the Republika Srpska (the Serb entity of Bosnia) to increase his leverage over the international community.[37] In addition, the implementation process of the Dayton agreement tied up considerable international resources and, for a significant period before the beginning of the Rambouillet negotiations, seemed to take priority in international strategic considerations. This, however, changed rapidly with the deterioration of the humanitarian situation in Kosovo. Ironically, it could be argued that the focus on Bosnia brought home to the international community its own tragic failure to prevent war crimes on a scale not seen in Europe since the Second World War, and facilitated the determination to prevent the same in Kosovo by taking decisive actions early enough.

Beyond a general commitment to humanitarian goals, consensus within the international community was thin. The Contact Group had agreed to seek a temporary settlement without territorial revisions, but had to concede to the Kosovo Albanians that some mechanism would be put in place after three years of operating an expected interim agreement that would also reflect the wish of the population in Kosovo.[38] The fact that such a mechanism was to be found at another international conference particularly served the interests of Russia as it assured the country's continued influence in the Balkans. It also relieved the Western members of the contact group of reconciling, at the time, the fundamental difference between Serbs and Albanians on the status of Kosovo. The major problem, however, that remained for the international community was the issue of the threat, and actual use, of force to obtain the consent of Serbia on the Rambouillet Agreement. While Russia was opposed to such action in principle, consensus within NATO was for humanitarian intervention, yet the strength with which each alliance member backed this differed. In the end, Serbia's refusal to sign must also be seen in the light of the open international disagreement about what to do in the event of a failure of the negotiations.

In conclusion, it can be argued that conditions of ripeness were not fulfilled at two levels – within Serbia and within the international community. The overall interpretation of the conflict by Serbia made it seem more beneficial for the Serbian and Yugoslav leadership to seek its continuation, rather than to settle for an accommodation along the lines proposed in Rambouillet. It is important to realize that the Serbian delegation, until the last minute of the reconvened conference, tried to renegotiate the entire agreement in its favour,[39] and that their refusal to sign was not a matter of the 'mysterious' Appendix B on the deployment of the NATO-led implementation force.[40] However, it must also be noted that the increasingly obvious rift between members of the Contact Group strengthened the Serbian–Yugoslav perspective on the costs and benefits of agreeing (or not) to the proposed settlement.

At the same time, the international community overestimated its leverage over the Serbian delegation in Rambouillet and Paris and over President Milošević in Belgrade. The Serbian delegation in Rambouillet was not susceptible to an offer by the European Union to lift all sanctions and allow the FRY to be reintegrated into European and international structures within two years in exchange for a greater preparedness to compromise at the negotiation table.[41] Likewise, increasingly credible threats of the use of force left Milošević and his negotiators unimpressed.

On the other hand, an extension of the negotiations in Rambouillet and Paris may have changed things in the short term. Yet further concessions to the Serbian delegation would then have been necessary, effectively meaning a renegotiation of the agreement to which the Albanian delegation had already given its consent. Given the Serbian demands in the final stages of the Paris follow-on talks,[42] such a re-opening of the negotiations was neither in the international community's interest nor was there much of a chance of the Kosovo Albanians making any concessions of the magnitude demanded by the Serbian delegation. Even if Milošević had agreed to a proposal made (unilaterally) by the Russian chief negotiator Majorski to reopen talks on all aspects of the Rambouillet Agreement,[43] and if some time could have been bought through this, it is doubtful whether this would have made any difference in the long term, as a fundamental change of the situation in Serbia/FRY or in the interest structure of its leadership were most unlikely to occur.

NOTES

1. The involvement of non-governmental organizations in Kosovo goes back to the 1980s, when Amnesty International and other human rights organizations began to monitor, and report on, the situation in Kosovo. See, for example, Amnesty International, *Yugoslavia: Recent Events in the Autonomous Province of Kosovo* (1989).

2. This initiative is summarized in a letter by the two foreign ministers to Slobodan Milošević, dated 19 November 1997. The official German and French versions are reprinted in Stefan Troebst, *Conflict in Kosovo: Failure of Prevention? An Analytical Documentation, 1992–1998*, ECMI Working Paper no. 1 (Flensburg: ECMI, 1998).

3. On details regarding the latter see, Defence Committee of the Western European Union, *Europe and the Evolving Situation in the Balkans*, WEU Document 1608, 13 May 1998 (Paris: 1998).

4. For the early political platform of the LDK, see the political declaration of 5 May 1991, reprinted (in a German translation) in 'The President of Schleswig-Holstein Parliament', *Minorities in Europe* (Kiel, 1991), pp. 119–20. On the future of Yugoslavia, the declaration states: 'A Yugoslavia constituted without the approval of the Albanians cannot be their state. In this case, Albanians would be forced to seek their independence and equality outside of it and in accordance with the principles of self-determination of peoples and in the spirit of the CSCE documents.'

5. See United Nations Economic and Social Council, Commission on Crime Prevention and Criminal Justice, Fifth Session, 21–31 May 1996 (Doc. E/CN. 15/1996/2) and US Department of Justice, Drug Enforcement Administration, *NNICC Report 1996*, at www.usdoj.gov/dea/pubs/intel/nnicc97.htm (July 1998), and US Department of Justice, Drug Enforcement Administration, *NNICC Report 1997*, at www.usdoj.gov/dea/pubs/intel/nnicc98.pdf (July 2000), p.72.

6. For the years 1961, 1971 and 1981, there are more or less reliable Yugoslav census data. As ethnic Albanians boycotted the 1991 census, all figures for the 1990s are estimates, but there seems to be consensus that there is about a 10% non-Albanian population in Kosovo, of which Serbs are the most numerous. See, for example, Herbert Büschenfeld, 'Ergebnisse der Volkszählung 1991 in Jugoslawien', *Osteuropa*, vol. 42, no. 12 (December 1992), pp. 1095–1101.

7. As early as 1993, there were also reports by independent human rights organizations that Serbs were subjected to intense ethnic discrimination and intimidation on the part of Albanians in Kosovo. See, for example, International Helsinki Federation for Human Rights, *From Autonomy to Colonization: Human Rights in Kosovo, 1989–1993* (Helsinki: IHFHR, 1993).

8. An English translation of the petition is reprinted in Branka Magaš, *The Destruction of Yugoslavia* (London, New York: Verso, 1993), p. 49.

9. Yugoslav Helsinki Committee, *Report on Refugees from Kosovo Situated in Montenegro* (Belgrade, 1998).

10. International Crisis Group, *Again, the Visible Hand: Slobodan Milošević's Manipulation of the Kosovo Dispute* (Brussels: ICG, 1998).

11. See United States Institute of Peace, *Serbia – Democratic Alternatives*, Special Report, June 1998, at www.usip.org/oc/sr/SerbiaDemocratic.html (July 1998).

12. Fabian Schmidt, 'Generationskonflikte in Albaniens großen Parteien', *Südosteuropa*, 49, 1–2 (2000), pp. 32–52, here p. 37f.

13. See International Crisis Group, *The View from Tirana: The Albanian Dimension of the Kosovo Crisis* (Brussels: ICG, 1998).

14. See for example, ATA News Agency, 10 September 1998; *AFP*, 11 September 1998.
15. On details of the PFP with Albania see NATO Press Release (98) 69 (29 May 1998) and George Katsirdakis, 'Albania: A Case Study in the Practical Implementation of Partnership for Peace', *NATO Review* web edition vol. 46, no. 2 (Summer 1998), at www.nato.int/docu/review/1998/9802–07.htm (September 1998).
16. See International Crisis Group, *The View form Tirana*.
17. One of the most contentious issues at the time was that of an Albanian language university in Tetovo. The handling of this dispute also led to disagreement among ethnic Albanians in the country. In May, more than 3,000 of them publicly protested against plans to establish a multilingual (rather than monolingual Albanian) university in the town and branded the Albanian Democratic Party (PDSH), a member of 'the government coalition, as collaborators, accusing them of siding with ethnic Macedonian parties in attempts to replace the currently private Albanian university. See Željko Bajić, 'Macedonian Language Dispute', *IWPR Crisis Report* no. 142 (23 May 2000).
18. International Crisis Group, *The Albanian Question in Macedonia: Implications of the Kosovo Conflict on Inter-Ethnic Relations in Macedonia* (Brussels: ICG, 1998).
19. See, Anthony Georgieff, 'Macedonia: Local Albanian Leader Complains of Discrimination', *RFE/RL Feature*, 23 February 1998.
20. See International Crisis Group, *The Albanian Question in Macedonia*.
21. One example for this trend was the formation of the south-eastern European Defence Ministerial on 26 September 1998, consisting of three NATO members (Italy, Greece and Turkey) and Albania, Bulgaria, Macedonia and Romania, with the United States and Slovenia acting as observers.
22. For an overview of the impact of the Kosovo conflict on Hungary, see Gusztav Kosztolanyi, 'Hungary, NATO and the Kosovo Crisis', *Central Europe Review*, vol. 20, nos. 28–34 and no. 37, all accessible via www.ce-review.org/authorarchives/csardas_archive/csardas37old.html, July 2000.
23. US Department of Defence, Bosnia Task Force, Briefing, 9 September 1998, and Pentagon Briefing, 10 September 1998.
24. US Department of Defence, Bosnia Task Force, Briefing, 9 September 1998.
25. Chapter VII is entitled 'Action With Respect to Threats to the Peace, Breaches of the Peace, and Acts of Aggression' and details the mandate of the UN in such cases.
26. United Nations Security Council resolution 1199 (1998).
27. United Nations Security Council resolution 1160 (1998).
28. For a more detailed exploration, see Stefan Wolff, *Disputed Territories: The Transnational Dynamics of Ethnic Conflict Settlement* (New York and Oxford: Berghahn, 2002).
29. See Marc Weller, 'The Rambouillet Conference on Kosovo', *International Affairs* 75, 2 (1999), pp. 163–203, here, p. 178f. Petritsch et al. note this, too, but also refer to the fact that, in a last minute attempt to delay the negotiation process in Paris, the Serbian delegation demanded extra time so that representatives of other ethnic groups in Kosovo could review the agreement which, by then, had already been approved by the Kosovo Albanian delegation. See Wolfgang Petritsch et al., *Kosovo/Kosova. Mythen, Daten, Fakten* (Klagenfurt: Wieser Verlag, 1999), pp. 279 and 341.
30. See Weller, 'Rambouillet Conference on Kosovo', p. 179.
31. See, for example, European Council, *Policy Paper on Former Yugoslavia* (EU

Bulletin 10–96), at europa.eu.int/abc/doc/off/bull/en/9610/p203001.htm; European Parliament, 'Resolution on the Situation in Kosovo of 12 March 1998', *Official Journal of the European Communities* C 104, 6 April 1998, pp. 216–17; Contact Group Statements on Kosovo of 24 September 1997, 8 January 1998, 25 February 1998, 9 March 1998, 25 March 1998 and 8 July 1998; NATO Press Releases M-NAC-1(98)61 (28 May 1998 Ministerial Meeting of the North Atlantic Council), M-NAC-D 1(98)77 (11 June 1998 Meeting of the Defence Ministers of the North Atlantic Council); US Department of State, 'Press Statement on Meeting between Secretary Albright and Ibrahim Rugova' (30 May 1998); and UN Security Council resolution 1160 (1998) of 31 March 1998.

32. See Petritsch et al., 'Rambouillet Conference on Kosovo', pp. 325, 344.
33. Marko notes in this context that there is a possibility that the 'implicit pro-Serbian bias of all the Hill-papers' led Milošević to believe that 'NATO threats ... were not to be taken seriously'. Joseph Marko, 'Kosovo/a – A Gordian Knot?', in Joseph Marko (ed.), *Gordischer Knoten Kosovo/a: Durchschlagen oder entwirren?* (Baden-Baden: Nomos Verlagsgesellschaft, 1999), pp. 261–80, here pp. 274–5.
34. For a list of the non-negotiable principles, see Weller, 'Rambouillet Conference on Kosovo', 177f.
35. The UNHCR reported 241,700 refugees by 1 September 1998. See UN Inter-Agency Report no. 59, YUGBE/MSC/HCR/1341. The UN Secretary-General's Report of 3 October 1998 gives the number of refugees and displaced persons at 280,000 people. See UN Secretary-General, 'Report of the Secretary-General Prepared Pursuant to Resolutions 1160 (1998) and 1199 (1998) of the Security Council'.
36. See UNHCR, 'Kosovo Update', 18 March 1999.
37. After some considerable delay, the OSCE had to concede in September 1998 that the radical Nikola Poplašen had defeated the OSCE-backed 'moderate' candidate for the Republika Srpska presidency, Plavšić, who was prepared to cooperate with the OSCE. Poplašen was dismissed by the OHR in March 1999.
38. See Weller, 'Rambouillet Conference on Kosovo', p. 197.
39. See Weller, 'Rambouillet Conference on Kosovo', pp. 186–8, and Petritsch et al., pp. 333, 337.
40. This was all the more the case as Milošević had once already agreed to the free movement of NATO troops across the territory of the FRY and to their immunity from prosecution, namely in the 1995 Dayton Accords. See Petritsch et al., *Kosovo/Kosova*, pp. 316–17.
41. See Petritsch et al., *Kosovo/Kosova*, p. 298.
42. These included, among others, the formal subordination of Kosovo to Serbia, unrestricted exercise of federal functions in the province, and an abolition of the office of the President of Kosovo. See Weller, 'Rambouillet Conference on Kosovo', p. 186f. See also Petritsch et al., *Kosovo/Kosova*, pp. 333–4.
43. See Petritsch et al., *Kosovo/Kosova*, p. 349.

REFERENCES

Amnesty International, *Yugoslavia: Recent Events in the Autonomous Province of Kosovo* (London: 1989).
Bajić, Z., 'Macedonian Language Dispute', *IWPR Crisis Report*, no. 142 (23 May 2000).
Büschenfeld, H., 'Ergebnisse der Volkszählung 1991 in Jugoslawien', *Osteuropa*, vol. 42, no. 12 (December 1992), pp. 1095–101.

Contact Group Statements on Kosovo of 24 September 1997, 8 January 1998, 25 February 1998, 9 March 1998, 25 March 1998 and 8 July 1998.

Defence Committee of the Western European Union, *Europe and the Evolving Situation in the Balkans*, WEU Document 1608, 13 May 1998 (Paris: Assembly of the Western European Union, 1998).

European Council, *Council Conclusions and Policy Paper on Former Yugoslavia* (EU Bulletin 10-96), at europa.eu.int/abc/doc/off/bull/en/9610/p203001.htm (July 1998).

European Parliament, 'Resolution on the Situation in Kosovo of 12 March 1998', *Official Journal of the European Communities* C 104 (6 April 1998), pp. 216–17.

Georgieff, A., 'Macedonia: Local Albanian Leader Complains of Discrimination', *RFE/RL Feature*, 23 February 1998.

International Crisis Group, *Again, the Visible Hand. Slobodan Milošević's Manipulation of the Kosovo Dispute* (Brussels: ICG, 1998).

International Crisis Group, *The View from Tirana: The Albanian Dimension of the Kosovo Crisis* (Brussels: ICG, 1998).

International Crisis Group, *The Albanian Question in Macedonia: Implications of the Kosovo Conflict on Inter-Ethnic Relations in Macedonia* (Brussels: ICG, 1998).

International Helsinki Federation for Human Rights, *From Autonomy to Colonization: Human Rights in Kosovo, 1989–1993* (Helsinki: IHFHR, 1993).

Katsirdakis, G., 'Albania: A Case Study in the Practical Implementation of Partnership for Peace', *NATO Review*, web edition, vol. 46, no. 2 (Summer 1998), at www.nato.int/docu/review/1998/9802-07.htm (September 1998).

Magaš, B., *The Destruction of Yugoslavia* (London, New York: Verso, 1993).

Marko, J., 'Kosovo/a – A Gordian Knot?', in J. Marko (ed.), *Gordischer Knoten Kosovo/a: Durchschlagen oder Entwirren* (Baden-Baden: Nomos Verlagsgesellschaft, 1999).

NATO Press Release (98) 69 (29 May 1998).

NATO Press Release M-NAC-1(98)61 'Ministerial Meeting of the North Atlantic Council' (28 May 1998).

NATO Press Release M-NAC-D 1(98)77 'Meeting of the Defence Ministers of the North Atlantic Council' (11 June 1998).

Pentagon Briefing, 10 September 1998.

Petritsch, W., Kaser, K. and Pichler, R., *Kosovo/Kosova. Mythen, Daten, Fakten* (Klagenfurt: Wieser Verlag, 1999).

Schmidt, F., 'Generationskonflikte in Albaniens großen Parteien', *Südosteuropa*, vol. 49, nos. 1–2 (2000), pp. 32–52.

The President of Schleswig-Holstein Parliament (ed.), *Minorities in Europe* (Kiel 1991), pp. 119–20.

Troebst, S., *Conflict in Kosovo: Failure of Prevention? An Analytical Documentation, 1992–1998*, ECMI Working Paper no. 1 (Flensburg: ECMI, 1998).

UN Inter-Agency Report no. 59, YUGBE/MSC/HCR/1341.

UN Secretary-General, 'Report of the Secretary-General on the United Nations Preventive Deployment of Force' (14 July 1998), S/1998/644.

UN Secretary-General, 'Report of the Secretary-General Prepared Pursuant to Resolution 1160 (1998) of the Security Council' (4 June 1998), S/1998/470.

UNHCR, 'Kosovo Update', 18 March 1999.

United Nations Economic and Social Council, Commission on Crime Prevention and Criminal Justice, Fifth Session (21–31 May 1996) (Doc. E/CN.15/1996/2).

United Nations Security Council resolution 1160 (1998), S/RES/1160 (1998).

United Nations Security Council resolution 1186 (1998), S/RES/1186 (1998).

United Nations Security Council resolution 1199 (1998), S/RES/1199 (1998).

United States Institute of Peace Special Report, June 1998, *Serbia – Democratic*

Alternatives, at www.usip.org/oc/sr/SerbiaDemocratic.html (July 1998).

US Department of Defence, Bosnia Task Force, Briefing (9 September 1998).

US Department of Justice, Drug Enforcement Administration, *NNICC Report 1996*, at www.usdoj.gov/dea/pubs/intel/nnicc97.htm (July 1998).

US Department of Justice, Drug Enforcement Administration, *NNICC Report 1997*, at www.usdoj.gov/dea/pubs/intel/nnicc98.pdf (July 2000).

US Department of State, 'Press Statement on Meeting between Secretary Albright and Ibrahim Rugova' (30 May 1998).

Weller, M., 'The Rambouillet Conference on Kosovo', *International Affairs* 75, 2 (1999), pp. 163–203.

Wolff, S., *Disputed Territories*.

Yugoslav Helsinki Committee, *Report on Refugees from Kosovo Situated in Montenegro* (Belgrade, 1998).

5

Rambouillet: A Critical (Re)Assessment

Elizabeth Allen Dauphinee

NATO's air war over Yugoslavia has the potential to fundamentally alter the way we view the relationship between humanitarianism, intra-state conflict and conflict management at the dawn of the new millennium. Operation Allied Force, as the air campaign came to be known, was ostensibly executed in defence of human rights on the premise that ethnic Albanians in Kosovo were suffering massive displacement, ethnic cleansing and even genocide at the hands of Serbian security and paramilitary forces. Central to the novelty of this particular operation was the assertion that the inviolability of human rights constitutes a fundamental value in the post-Cold War world. Czech President Vaclav Havel stated that NATO's attack on Yugoslavia was 'probably the first war [in history] that has not been waged in the name of "national interests", but rather in the name of principles and values'.[1] As such, the action has drawn a fair amount of scholarly interest and has fuelled the debate between the proponents of intervention and the defenders of sovereignty. Little attention, however, has been devoted to the Rambouillet process that led up to NATO's decision to engage in air strikes, and there has followed even less analysis concerning the ability of the agreement to facilitate peace in Kosovo.[2]

This chapter will therefore focus on four interrelated aspects of the Kosovo crisis and its aftermath. Firstly, a brief assessment of events leading up to the Rambouillet process which culminated in the Rambouillet Draft Interim Agreement. Secondly, an assessment of the alterations to the Rambouillet text following the air war. Thirdly, although the Rambouillet agreement is not currently undergoing implementation as foreseen by its drafters, an investigation of some of the problems inherent in the text which have the capacity to give rise to significant barriers to the peacebuilding process in Kosovo. Finally, an analysis of the discursive constructions that have characterized the response of the international community to the Kosovo crisis.

VIOLENCE AND CONDEMNATION

The Rambouillet process is the culmination of more than a year of so-called resolutions adopted by the United Nations (UN) and others condemning the violence in Kosovo. Open and active clashes between Yugoslav authorities and the secessionist Kosovo Liberation Army (KLA) began in early March 1998, when a Yugoslav attack on several villages in the Drenica valley left dozens of ethnic Albanians, including a prominent KLA leader, dead. The intensity and scope of the conflict grew predictably upon the arrival of warmer spring weather. As violence in Kosovo escalated, the UN Security Council enacted Resolution 1160, which called on all member states to join in an arms embargo against Yugoslavia, including against the KLA operating in Kosovo. SCR 1160 further called on the conflicting parties to institute 'meaningful dialogue on political status issues' for Kosovo. The Security Council called on Yugoslav authorities to cease and desist from 'excessive' military operations against the ethnic Albanian population in Kosovo, while simultaneously condemning 'all terrorist action' on the part of the KLA and its supporters. The resolution also stated that 'the way to defeat violence and terrorism in Kosovo is for the authorities in Belgrade to offer the Kosovar Albanian community a genuine political process'. Aside from some references to the willingness of the Contact Group (comprised of representatives from the US, UK, France, Italy and Russia) to assist in facilitating such a dialogue, there were no practicable solutions offered towards a possible political settlement. SCR 1160 was committed, however, to some kind of settlement within the framework of existing Yugoslav borders.

Regardless of the inability of SCR 1160 to offer any substantive or definitive means through which the escalating fighting might be stemmed and a full-scale war averted, Yugoslav authorities in Belgrade and the representatives of the Kosovo Albanian community did meet several times in an effort to forge a settlement to the crisis. At this time, the representatives of Kosovo were comprised mainly of members of the Democratic League of Kosovo (LDK), a grassroots political party committed to non-violent political resistance. The LDK acted as something of a shadow government for Kosovo's nearly two million Albanians, with Dr Ibrahim Rugova serving as its elected head.[3] Discussions between the LDK and Belgrade authorities broke down in the last weeks of May 1998, however, for two related reasons. Primarily, a rapid escalation in the fighting in Kosovo dampened the possibilities of a settlement and stalled the continuation of the talks. Furthermore, while Yugoslav leader Slobodan Milošević was likely firmly in control of the actions of his army and security units operating in Kosovo, Dr Rugova was not in any position of authority over the KLA, whose leaders and members were willing to engage in violence as a means of securing independence for the province.

SCR 1199, concluded on 30 September 1998, was generally a reiteration of the points contained in SCR 1160, with the exception that prescribed negotiations were now a demand rather than a suggestion, that international involvement in such a process would be mandatory and that these negotiations would be held to a strict (though unspecified) timetable. The Yugoslav authorities were condemned again for their use of excessive violence, and again the KLA was condemned for its use of terrorism. Nevertheless, in October, some positive developments took place. Milošević agreed to a cease-fire and withdrawal of security forces from Kosovo under the Holbrooke Agreement and the threat of NATO air strikes. After the cease-fire was in place, US Ambassador to Macedonia, Christopher Hill, was employed to help draft a political settlement. The most important agreement concluded involved the acceptance by Yugoslav authorities of the presence of an Organization for Security and Cooperation in Europe (OSCE) mission to be instituted in Kosovo. The Kosovo Verification Mission (KVM) was responsible for monitoring the compliance of Yugoslav pledges to withdraw troops from the province and to garrison all special police units. The KVM was complemented by a NATO air verification mission to patrol Kosovo and a deployment of NATO troops in neighbouring Macedonia, which could be used as an extraction force if the situation deteriorated further.

These developments were praised in SCR 1203 on 24 October 1998. But beyond reminding the Yugoslav authorities of their responsibilities to ensure the protection of the KVM, 1203 said little else. The UN's commitment to a political resolution for the crisis that included some form of self-governance for Kosovo's Albanians within the existing Yugoslav boundaries was reaffirmed. The need for an internationally brokered peace agreement was reaffirmed. The requirement that such an agreement be reached within a strict timetable was reaffirmed. The assistance of the Contact Group in reaching such a resolution was reaffirmed. How the parties might achieve their mutually exclusive and extreme goals in a peaceful manner and how the demobilization of one party to the conflict could occur without a guarantee of reciprocation was not addressed. In addition, Christopher Hill's proposal failed to convince either the KLA or the Yugoslavs to alter their chosen course of action.

The failure of the Hill proposal rendered the obstacles facing Kosovo more transparent than perhaps they had originally appeared to observers. While the proposal attempted to allocate varying degrees of authority to different levels of government in Kosovo, it fell short of independence for Kosovo. In fact, it did not purport to define any legal status at all for the province. Since the issue of legal status was central to the armed conflict that was raging on the ground, such a process had no choice but to fail conclusively. The KLA leadership would not accept an agreement that 'locked' the province into Serbia and Yugoslavia,[4] and the Yugoslavs would not accept an agreement that limited their authority in Kosovo.

A Yugoslav attack on the village of Racak in mid-January 1999 left more than 40 ethnic Albanians dead and is widely regarded as the turning point for NATO intervention. Photographs and eyewitness accounts from those who had escaped were relayed via satellite to the world, and public opinion was galvanized behind NATO's subsequent resolve. On 28 January 1999, NATO Secretary-General Javier Solana issued a statement on the decision to authorize NATO air strikes against Yugoslavia if the conflicting parties did not immediately comply with the demands of the international community. He continued to stress that 'all parties must end violence and pursue their goals by peaceful means only.' US Secretary of State Madeleine Albright praised the decision, stating that, '[t]he choice is truly up to the leadership on both sides, especially the authorities in Belgrade. Either they cease fighting and agree upon a peaceful interim settlement, or they will face the consequences NATO has spelled out today.'[5] On 6 February 1999, the Rambouillet conference on Kosovo was convened.

UNRAVELLING RAMBOUILLET

Although widely acclaimed by policymakers and negotiators alike as a viable and equitable solution to the conflict, Rambouillet, like the Hill proposal before it, left the legal status of Kosovo veiled in ambiguity. It was, perhaps, the very ambiguity of the agreement that helped to maintain the veneer of equity and balance that its drafters hoped to achieve, and which had been so characteristic of the earlier (failed) attempts to reach a settlement.[6] Nevertheless, many of the problems with the Rambouillet agreement can be traced to the process of the Rambouillet negotiations themselves in February 1999. One of the most glaring questions that remains is the composition of the Kosovo Albanian delegation to Rambouillet. Although Dr Rugova's LDK has dominated Kosovo Albanian politics in the recent past, and has done so as the result of an electoral process, the Kosovo delegation reflected a very different political situation. Marc Weller notes that:

> [t]he [LDK] government which had been elected by an overwhelming majority of the population of Kosovo constituted only a minority – one-third – of the delegation. Oddly, the negotiators [of the Contact Group] who may have helped to construct the delegation were somewhat taken aback when the delegation voted to appoint 29-year-old Hashim Thaçi from the KLA, rather than President Rugova, to head the tripartite presidency of the Kosovo team.

The remaining seats were apportioned between the KLA, the LBD (United Democratic Movement), and two independent representatives. This decision provided the KLA with de facto superiority at Rambouillet, as the LBD was perceived as being 'closer' to the KLA than the elected government.[7] Although it may be reasonable to suggest that, since the KLA was the group involved in clashes with the FRY, its representation was essential to securing an agreement for peace, it cannot be said that the KLA represented a clearly defined will of the majority of people in Kosovo.

The structure and process of the conference itself centred on Contact Group negotiators shuttling back and forth between the Albanian and Yugoslav delegations, who were expected to comment 'constructively' in writing on the principles which had already been drafted by the negotiators. Eleven of the principles were non-negotiable. Two of the eleven were irreconcilable. An international commitment to uphold the territorial integrity of Yugoslavia was juxtaposed inexplicably beside a clause that mandated an initially ill-defined 'mechanism' for a final political settlement following a three-year transition period. Nevertheless, the Albanian delegation engaged fully with the draft agreement, providing suggestions for governmental and legislative structures and various aspects of more practicable implementation. The written comments and suggestions pro-vided by the Albanian delegation were framed within the non-negotiable principles, and although Thaçi's team was not prepared to accept the agree-ment without qualifications, it did exhibit commitment and willingness to acknowledge the Rambouillet draft as a starting point for the interim agreement.

The Yugoslav delegation has been soundly criticized for its inactivity throughout the Rambouillet talks, and has shouldered the blame for their eventual deterioration and collapse. There was a great deal of speculation as the talks were progressing that the Yugoslav delegation had not been given the authority from Belgrade to sign any binding agreement or to comment on any proposals. Such speculation became even more plausible when, immediately after US Ambassador Christopher Hill returned from a hastily conceived meeting with President Milošević in Belgrade, the Yugoslav delegation produced a counterproposal of its own.[8] Empowered or not, the Yugoslav delegation and authorities in Belgrade easily concurred on two vital issues set forth by the Contact Group, which could not, even under the threat of air strikes, be accepted. First, the transitional occupation of Kosovo by NATO-led forces included the free use of all of Yugoslav territory and resources. This amounted to impunity for NATO troop and supply movement throughout Yugoslavia.[9]

The second obstacle to Yugoslav acceptance of the agreement was language later added that intimated a future independence referendum as the resolution mechanism following the three-year transition period. Towards the end of the talks, the Albanian delegation was able to clarify the initially vague references to the final legal solution for the Kosovo crisis. With the direct support of US Secretary of State Madeleine Albright, language was added to the agreement that referred to the 'will of the people' of Kosovo. Both delegations read this addition as the guarantee of a future independence referendum, which, it was believed, would clearly lead to an independent Kosovo after the three-year transition period. Following the inclusion of the future referendum on independence, the outcome of the talks appeared to be quite clear. Although it was plausible that some limited form of federal Yugoslav and/or republican Serbian authority might still be exercised in Kosovo, the Yugoslavs could now look forward only to a modification of their boundaries and the eventual secession of a significant percentage of their territory after the three-year transition period had passed.

It is important at this point to note that the Rambouillet talks were not as straightforward as they may have appeared. And although, as noted, the draft agreement was presented as a balanced and equitable mechanism for solution to the crisis, there appears to have been an outright dismissal of many of the political interests the two delegations were supposed to have come to Rambouillet to represent. In addition to the pending dissolution of Yugoslav sovereignty in Kosovo, the Rambouillet framework, for instance, called for the demobilization of the KLA; a virtual death sentence for the very organization that was effectively in control of the Albanian delegation.[10] Additionally, the military and civilian annexes concerning implementation of the agreement were not even presented to the delegations at Rambouillet until the day before the deadline for acceptance of the agreement. Marc Weller speculates that the Contact Group 'may have [felt that it was] unnecessary to acquaint the parties with the content of a document which they were expected simply to accept'.[11] On 20 February, just hours before the noon deadline that was to conclude the conference, the delegations were invited to accept the agreement that had been based on discussions over the previous 11 days. However, Weller notes that neither delegation had even been presented with an updated text of the agreement.[12] Both delegations thereupon declined to accept the agreement. The deadline for acceptance was then extended for three days in an effort to prolong negotiations. The Albanian delegation indicated willingness to accept the agreement only after the inclusion of the language pertaining to a final resolution based on the 'will of the people' of Kosovo.[13] Although the Yugoslav delegation agreed to sign the non-negotiable principles, an agreement that provided for the free use of Yugoslav territory for NATO forces could not be accepted, nor could the inclusion of the future referendum – the very addition that had won the assent of the Kosovo delegation.

Michael Mandelbaum characterized the diplomatic process thus:

> [NATO] summoned the Serbs and the KLA to the French chateau of Rambouillet, presented them with a detailed plan for political autonomy in Kosovo under NATO auspices, demanded that both agree to

it, and threatened military reprisals if either refused. Both did refuse. The Americans thereupon negotiated with the KLA, acquired its assent to the Rambouillet plan, and, when the Serbs persisted in their refusal, waited for the withdrawal of the OSCE monitors and then began to bomb.[14]

Such a stark view on the proceedings is not to be dismissed out of hand. Mandelbaum's assertion is lent some credence by the glaring fact that the two delegations never actually met to discuss either a ceasefire, or the possibilities for a representative political settlement for the province. It is important to keep in mind that earlier bilateral discussions between Belgrade and Kosovo's Albanian community had involved the LDK as representative of the Kosovo Albanian population. Negotiations between the KLA and Yugoslavia had not been attempted before the parties found themselves at Rambouillet. This had been in part because of the Yugoslav refusal to negotiate with what had been deemed a terrorist organization. Nevertheless, the Yugoslav delegation (as well as Russia's Contact Group representative, Boris Mayorski, who later refused to witness the assenting signature of the Kosovo delegation) attempted to press for direct negotiations at Rambouillet, and it is the case that had the parties been encouraged to meet, it would have been the first opportunity for bilateral negotiations. NATO Secretary-General Javier Solana would later write, however, that 'when NATO brought the Serbs and the [KLA] together at Rambouillet, France, in February 1999, it was clear to everyone concerned that this would be the last opportunity for a comprehensive settlement'.[15] The Serbs, he contended, chose not to take it.[16] It is not at all clear, however, that Rambouillet represented the last chance for a negotiated settlement. Neither is it clear that Rambouillet presented a coherent plan for achieving a negotiated settlement. The non-negotiable principles were irreconcilable, the civilian and military annexes on implementation were not presented to the parties until the last moment, the parties did not engage in any direct negotiations, and the Albanian delegation was provided with concessions amounting to the guarantee of an independence referendum. These points, at the very least, should give pause to any discussion of the manner in which the Rambouillet agreement was presented.

Why were the non-negotiable principles formulated as a paradox? Why did Rambouillet provide for a future independence referendum while still grounding its most basic principles in the maintenance of Yugoslav territorial integrity? Christopher Ryan writes that,

> [i]ndividual states have international legal obligations to protect human rights on their territories, [but] international society has had difficulty enforcing these obligations on violating states, since

international law, by upholding the concept of sovereignty, has generally recognized state autonomy of action in 'internal' matters.[17]

The dilemma outlined here as it pertains to the Kosovo conflict and the possible resolutions of it throughout the pre-Rambouillet crisis period is apparent. Kosovo, as a province of Serbia (not a constituent republic of Yugoslavia) does not have the constitutional right of secession. The governments of both Serbia and Yugoslavia have pointed to the constitutionally limited status of Kosovo in an effort to claim that the escalating conflict constituted an internal issue between separatist guerrillas and legitimate state authorities attempting to restore order, and thus was exempt from scrutiny on the part of other states or international bodies.

In the realm of international law, the right of interference in intrastate affairs is murky at best. Interpretations of conventional and customary legal norms range from strict non-interference to interference or intervention in exceptional cases of moral or political collapse and wide-scale human rights violations.[18] Stephen Garrett points out that,

> there has been a wide range of [international] agreements that have fleshed out the notion of the internationalization of human rights: from the famous Universal Declaration of Human Rights adopted by the UN General Assembly in 1948 to a number of subsequent UN covenants on civil, political, economic, social, and cultural rights, including specific issues such as genocide, racial discrimination, torture, and even matters as specific as freedom of association and collective bargaining.[19]

Such developments, of course, suggest that the possibilities for response to the Kosovo crisis were as wide-ranging or as narrowly defined as the international bodies which undertook to address the situation perceived them to be. The series of interventions undertaken in the 1990s[20] coupled with a range of recent literature sanctioning limited forms of intervention, or even codifying criteria under which intervention would become an international obligation, has helped to strengthen the notion that international law is moving away from 'the structures of sovereignty'.[21]

Yet in the local contexts of individual situations, 'broad claims' concerning the legitimacy and helpfulness of armed intervention such as took place in Kosovo is questionable at best. There is a range of regional and otherwise specific issues and implications that proponents of NATO action have so far failed to address, foremost among them the dilemma posed by attempting to employ a legal paradox as a solution to an armed conflict. As the following sections of this paper will demonstrate, the manner in which NATO undertook to resolve the conflict escalated human rights abuses and actually served various national causes, even while marginalizing the actors that promulgated them.[22]

OPERATION ALLIED FORCE AND REVISIONS TO RAMBOUILLET

There has been a variety of compelling critiques concerning the intent of NATO intervention in Kosovo.[23] For the sake of coherence, however, this study will move forward from the premise that NATO leaders acted for the reasons they publicized, and that the 78-day air war against the roads, train tracks, bridges, power plants, factories, processing plants, water pumping stations, heating and electrical plants, television studios, relay antennas, oil refineries, airports, gas stations, ski resorts, maternity hospitals and chemical plants of Yugoslavia was aimed at preventing a human catastrophe. Nevertheless, the manner in which intervention was undertaken and solutions conceived must be assessed with the goal of determining both short-term and long-term implications of the operation.

It is not at all clear that NATO's military operation alleviated the situation of Kosovo's Albanians, and there is irrefutable evidence that the humanitarian situation deteriorated drastically as a direct result of the bombing campaign. Even a preliminary investigation of the immediate results of the campaign serves to raise serious questions about the manner in which this intervention was conceived and carried out. One has only to look as far as the desperate state of the refugee camps in Albania and Macedonia during the air strikes, the shortage of medical and other humanitarian supplies and, above all perhaps, the clear lack of willingness to accommodate significant numbers (even temporarily) of Albanian refugees in (liberal democratic) host countries, where their safety and access to substantive nutrition and shelter could have been assured.[24] In contrast to the vast resources allocated for the military mission,[25] Kosovo Albanian refugees in Albania and Macedonia '[were] living in the open without any sanitation, camping in makeshift shelters or the trucks and tractor-drawn trailers that brought them from Kosovo'.[26] After ten days of NATO air strikes, the UN High Commissioner for Refugees (UNHCR) estimated that at least 100,000 refugees near the Kukes area were in urgent need of assistance, but that relief agencies could provide supplies for only a fraction of these. This was compounded by the puzzling fact that NATO would not allow the airstrip near Kukes to be utilized for humanitarian supply shipments.[27] At the Stenkovac refugee camp in Macedonia, Kosovo Albanians stood in lines for seven hours waiting for food rations as Macedonian Prime Minister, Ljupco Georgijevski, criticized NATO for having had the resolve to attack Yugoslavia, but not to provide adequate assistance for the refugees crossing out of Yugoslavia. 'The people in Brussels started this war and left for Easter holidays', he charged.[28]

In an effort to prevent losses of NATO planes to Yugoslav air defence systems, military strikes were carried out from heights in excess of 15,000 feet. The result was a series of horrendous errors in targeting that resulted in the deaths of hundreds of civilians. The misidentification of a refugee convoy on the Djakovica–Prizren road in western Kosovo on 7 April resulted in the deaths of more than 80 Kosovo Albanians. On 13 May, a deliberate attack against what was described as a 'military target with military vehicles with antennae' left 87 Kosovo civilians dead and wounded 100 others in the town of Korisa.[29] Another ten civilians were killed when a NATO pilot targeted a passenger train on the Grdelica crossing over the Juzna Morava river on 12 April. On 6 April, a high altitude attack on the small mining town of Aleksinac left 12 civilians, including several children, dead. At the conclusion of the bombing campaign, nearly one million people had fled Kosovo for the comparative safety of neighbouring countries. Nevertheless, on day 78 of the bombing campaign, 'with no casualties of its own, NATO had prevailed. A humanitarian disaster', wrote Javier Solana, 'had been averted'.[30]

Most important for the purposes of this study is the fact that the agreement which ended the bombing campaign in June 1999 included some relatively major conceptual changes to the future of Kosovo envisaged at Rambouillet. After 78 days of military strikes, NATO and the Contact Group were now prepared to negotiate a number of the principles that had been the most problematic for the Yugoslav delegation at Rambouillet. The post-bombing agreement allowed international troops to deploy only in Kosovo as opposed to the original agreement, which had allowed NATO freedom of movement throughout Yugoslavia. However, while the Rambouillet agreement expressed, and continues to express, the 'commitment of the international community to the sovereignty and territorial integrity of the Federal Republic of Yugoslavia', Belgrade's authority in Kosovo has been effectively foreclosed by the criteria established by NATO as conditional for the cessation of the bombing campaign.[31] These conditions stipulated that all organized forces under the control and command of Belgrade withdraw from Kosovo with no qualifications.[32] Although Rambouillet continues to mandate a limited return of Yugoslav security forces to carry out tasks allocated to the authority of the Yugoslav Federation (such as border control and customs services), none have been given permission to return. When pressed to comment on the status of the limited Yugoslav security re-entry, NATO Supreme Allied Commander (Europe), Wesley Clark, stated that, 'the Yugoslav army will not be permitted to return to Kosovo. If, by chance, it tries, it will be prevented'.[33]

Crucially, the language of Rambouillet pointing to a future independence referendum was removed. The international community no longer appeared to endorse a resolution based on the will of the people of Kosovo, as it had so openly at the Rambouillet conference in February.[34] The implications of these alterations should be explored in some detail, because it appears as though the post-bombing resolution has only compounded the ambiguity inherent in the Rambouillet agreement.

IMPLEMENTATIONAL PERPLEXITIES

Rambouillet and its revisions appear to have created a confused atmosphere characterized by a mixture of both support and dissent for the aims of local actors. The February 1999 Rambouillet agreement coupled with the bombing campaign provided clear support (whether intended or not) to the secessionist cause of the KLA. In effect, the members of the international community had condoned and supported the tactics and goals of the KLA with the manner of their response. This response made clear that the tactics and goals of Yugoslavia with respect to Kosovo were considered unacceptable, and Belgrade was dealt with using the ultimate coercion – overwhelming military force. However, the conclusion of the air campaign and the conditions under which agreement was reached represented a significant amount of backtracking on the part of NATO and the Contact Group. No longer was an independence referendum for Kosovo the intimated outcome of the three-year transition period.[35]

As a result, it appears as though the goals of both parties were (and continue to be) effectively nurtured and nullified simultaneously. The goal of Yugoslavia to maintain control over Kosovo was dismissed by the original support of Rambouillet for the future independence referendum. The goal of the KLA, to create an independent Kosovo, was dismissed by the post-bombing agreement in a *de jure* manner, and the goal of Yugoslavia was again dismissed in a *de facto* manner by the prohibitions placed on Yugoslav jurisdiction after the entry of KFOR. Nevertheless, de facto acts, like the reconstitution of the KLA as opposed to its mandated demobilization, have served to quietly nurture secessionist aims, even while the textual agreement guaranteeing Yugoslav integrity appears to support the eventual return of Yugoslav authority. In this way, the structure of the agreement has apparently served the mutually incompatible aims of both parties to the conflict. Bernard Kouchner of UNMIK suggested a full nine months after the entry of KFOR that the UN Security Council must define what the Rambouillet-sanctioned 'substantial autonomy' means, and although he remains staunchly opposed to independence, he has been forced to acknowledge that 'the majority of ethnic Albanians still want the province to break away from Yugoslavia'.[36] One editor of a prominent Kosovo Albanian journal noted that, 'as long as such uncertainty remains [concerning the legal and political future of Kosovo] the situation isn't about to improve'.[37] UN Secretary-General Kofi Annan expressed his growing concern that UNMIK is operating in 'limbo', because the future of the province has not been clearly defined. He also referred to the Rambouillet-imposed peace as 'a very ambiguous situation'.[38]

The inherent legal ambiguity of the future of Kosovo, perpetuated by the Contact Group, NATO, the UN and others creates a serious operational problem for the international peacekeeping force: it serves as a foundation for the continuation of conflict when and if a declaration of independence occurs, and it provides a framework for indefinite occupation by KFOR (either to enforce Yugoslav integrity or to guarantee independence). In this way, while the Rambouillet agreement may have halted conflict between the KLA and Serbian security forces, by removing the latter physically from the territory, the uncertainty surrounding the intent of the agreement continues to engender conflict on an intercommunal level in Kosovo, and has arguably contributed to ongoing insecurity in the region. The *Washington Post* reported in early March 2000 that 'international officials ostensibly in charge of pacifying and rebuilding Kosovo are lurching from one crisis to another without a clear vision of where they are going'.[39] An indication of this is apparent in a report of February 2000 which asserts that, since the entry of KFOR into Kosovo, the peacekeeping force has documented more than 615 incidents of hostile fire, 15 mortar attacks, 20 crowd-control conflicts and 129 grenade attacks, some of which have been directed against the peacekeepers themselves.[40]

Even if the legal and political ambiguities presented by Rambouillet could be momentarily left aside, the prescriptions for social reintegration are murky at best. In the civil sphere, the Rambouillet framework fosters public education in ethnic matters, specifically sanctioning curricula including education in national culture and history, to be controlled by 'communes' or local/municipal councils.[41] This creates an enormously paradoxical situation if the goal of the agreement is to foster ethnic pluralism. With the contestation of events (both current and historical) in Kosovo, and the particular national narratives that inform the respective communities, such provisions will likely lead to isolated enclaves in which classrooms are ethnically homogeneous; at least in part because the contents of educational curricula will be tailored to fit one or the other national community.[42] Further, Rambouillet sanctions the display and promulgation of nationalist symbols, and encourages the right to establish cultural and religious organizations and associations, for which (unspecified) relevant authorities will provide financial assistance.[43] Again, this is more likely to lead to continued polarization of ethnic/national communities into more homogenized enclaves, rather than to promote the ethnic conciliation that the drafters of Rambouillet ostensibly promulgated. Furthermore, Rambouillet has dictated all terms of economic engagement for Kosovo. These include a prescription for rapid transition to liberal democracy and market capitalism, which is not devoid of major implementational obstacles. Charles Philippe-David notes that:

> [d]emocratization within the context of a peacebuilding operation is not a neutral process. It entails a redistribution of power and competition for political control, which in a country devastated by war has an impact quite different from the case in countries free of

[widespread] violence. The transition period between the state of violence and democracy represents, in this sense, a twilight zone.[44]

What this means for Kosovo is that, in its very instability, the potential for inaugurating a new, essentialist, nationalist, exclusionary administration in a perfectly democratic manner is always present. Not only is this the case because political groups are informed by nationalism and remain highly polarized, but also because, where the Rambouillet agreement could have attempted to foster resolution to the political and legal ambiguities (thus helping to clarify the foundation upon which the future of Kosovo will be built), it did not do so.

PERCEPTIONAL PERPLEXITIES

Almost without exception, the wars of the former Yugoslavia have been presented through western discourses to reflect the 'primitive nature' of their actors and protagonists.[45] During the bombing of Yugoslavia (and arguably well before), the Balkans and Balkan peoples acquired what Edward Said has referred to with respect to other eastern peoples as 'a [Western constructed] library or archive of information commonly and, in some aspects, unanimously held'. This body of knowledge or information 'explained the behaviour of [Balkan peoples]; they supplied [Balkan peoples] with a mentality, a genealogy, an atmosphere; most important, they allowed Europeans to deal with and even to see [Balkan peoples] as a phenomenon possessing regular characteristics'.[46] The ability to cast roles – to reify both individual actors and whole peoples into particular, knowable, immutable categories – is crucial to the conclusion of the collection of 'truths' which inform observers about the Balkan peninsula and the character or nature and capacity of its peoples. An integral aspect of the creation of the Balkans in the western lexicon has included the deployment of descriptions such as 'primeval hatreds', 'centuries of conflict' and 'ethnic paranoia' (among innumerable others). Such discursive phrases capture and package a particular presentation – an 'essence' – of the Balkans that culminates in a clear, comprehensible and commodifiable product that is subsequently deployed as a ready-made example of why 'solutions' such as those offered by Rambouillet must be externally imposed.

Such discourses are underpinned by a hierarchic perception that serves overall to reinforce the superiority of liberal democratic claims to legitimacy and which allows the external imposition of solutions to conflict that are not necessarily viable, and may even create more problems than they solve. The legitimacy accorded to the Western liberal tradition allows for those engaged in the liberal democratic project to situate themselves at the pinnacle of a conceptual hierarchical chain that is characterized by the backwardness of others.[47] In this way, the (well articulated) political interests expressed by both the KLA and Yugoslav authorities can be scratched off (or added onto) a document such as Rambouillet with virtual impunity. Conversely, opposition to either the intent or the implementation of, for example, 'non-negotiable principles' can be summarily dismissed as the (backward) ravings of 'pre-European' peoples who do not know either how to govern themselves or what is appropriate for their respective societies.[48] Consider, for example, NATO Secretary-General George Robertson's comment on the assertion by Belgrade that Yugoslav forces, as permitted by the Rambouillet framework, should return to Kosovo: '[t]here may be quite a lot of very stupid people in Belgrade, but I don't think there are people stupid enough to think that they can come back into Kosovo again.'[49]

It is important to note that western narratives, which locate the Kosovo conflict in terms of historical and ethnic hatreds, served to inform the manner in which the international community sought to enact resolution to the conflict. The ascription of conflict to a reified history and subsequent assertions surrounding ethnic conflict also allows for the depoliticization of the particular goals or aims of the actors involved in the present, and their subsequent relegation to non-western worlds of primevalism. Best-selling author Michael Ignatieff, in his 'search for the new nationalism' observed that the former Yugoslavia was loaded with 'paramilitaries, drunk on plum brandy and ethnic paranoia, trading shots at each other across a wasteland'.[50] Commentaries such as these (and they are not in short supply) allow for a quick dismissal of the political interests of conflicting parties by reifying specific notions of conflict that are perceived by western observers in particular ways. What is crucial about this discourse is that it delegitimates the specific legal, political, or otherwise well-defined goals of the conflicting parties. Delegitimization is possible because such reification presents specific types of conflict as natural, normal and immutable (for certain types of peoples) and concludes an entire, compact collection of knowledge about the irrational, immoral, immaterial and timeless nature of certain societies. Consider US Secretary of State Madeleine Albright's historically-oriented explanation of the Kosovo conflict: 'The Balkans ... has always been a difficult area. World War I started in it, World War II was fought there. All you have to do is look at the map and understand the ethnic composition of these countries.'[51] In other words, western observers, if they simply looked at the maps, would (presumably) see immediately that the reason for the current conflict lies in ethnicity and in ethnically-defined historical perceptions. As a result of the reification of ethnic conflict in a discourse of historical inevitability, the specific political goals that give rise to that conflict in the present can be subsumed and marginalized with relative ease. This is particularly true with respect to non-democratic states with specific systems of governance that are perceived by democratic polities as illegitimate, and is reflected in the failure of the Rambouillet agreement (as well as in all the resolutions and negotiation initiatives that came before Rambouillet) to address the legal status of Kosovo in a substantive way.

The often cited SCR 1160, previously discussed, emphasized the need for the conflicting parties to 'pursue their goals by peaceful means only'. Such a statement highlights the astounding naivete with which the UN Security Council approached and perceived the Kosovo crisis. By the time SCR 1160 was drafted, violence in Kosovo had already reached an alarming level of ferocity. In the effort to protect international norms of upholding human rights and sovereignty simultaneously, the UN, NATO and Contact Group delegates iterated admonitions and statements that were absolutely useless as a template upon which political settlement could be reached. The paradox inherent in the expression of these two international values were reflected in the Rambouillet agreement and in the UN resolutions alike, which culminated arguably into an even more serious dilemma when long-term implications are taken into account. Instead of offering an atmosphere in which a viable political solution to the conflict might be located, the international community simply entrenched the paradox it was trying to uphold by locking Kosovo into an arrangement that is impossible to maintain over the long term precisely because it does not adequately address the conflictual issues.

In lieu of offering a viable legal settlement, the international community's intervention sought simply to patch over the legal conflict by offering the possibility of a 'legitimate' (i.e., liberal democratic) system of governance. Additionally, intervention with the goal of superimposing liberal democratic structures suggests, either implicitly or explicitly, that western actors have the capacity to conceive and implement legitimate forms of governance and economic systems, in states and among peoples, that are perceived through this discourse to occupy primitive political spaces. This becomes more evident if we recall Michael Mandelbaum's characterization of the Rambouillet conference: 'NATO summoned the KLA and the Serbs ... presented them with a detailed plan ... and threatened military reprisals if either refused'. In this way, the goals and political aims of local actors enjoy legitimacy only sporadically, and only in so far as they dovetail with the perceptions of Western leaders. This particular discourse is accompanied by the intimation that the recipients of western aid and/or punishment (whether economic, political or military) must concomitantly recognize that this aid and/or punishment is proper, legitimate and above all, helpful or instructive. The hierarchical discourse, then, places local actors engaged in 'ethnic conflict' in a more or less powerless position vis-à-vis the moral, legal, military and economic superiority of the intervening body.[52]

The ability of Western leaders to impose vastly ambiguous solutions in a conflict such as Kosovo is possible precisely because their own perceptions suggest that the superiority of western state structures takes legitimate precedence over all local possibilities. This is evident in, for example, KFOR commanders' dismay that some ethnic Albanians in Kosovo are firing upon the peacekeeping force. International officials were reportedly shocked by the violence in the city of Kosovska Mitrovica in February 2000, wondering 'how the very people whom the [NATO] troops intervened to protect ... could turn their guns on their protectors'.[53] A brief analysis of such a statement serves to highlight the interplay between the hierarchical under-standings that elevate the expectations and actions of Western institutions over and above the articulated interests of local actors (in this case Kosovo Albanians). As brief as it is, the statement says a great deal about perception in the Western narrative.

The NATO discourse has cast local actors in subordinate and immobile roles. When the parameters set by the discourse are violated by those actors, NATO has responded with perplexed, if muted, outrage. For example, Kosovo Albanians have been relegated to the role of victims, an ascription, of course, that is largely immobile and immutable. We are therefore greeted by shock and disbelief when members of this group step out of their assigned role and begin sniping at those who *should* be viewed as their protectors. In this hierarchical 'protector-protected' narrative, it is implicit in the discourse that Albanians recognize that they require KFOR protection, and that they must respect the rules laid down vis-à-vis this narrative in order for the operation to work (and for the discourse to make sense). Robertson, speaking in response to the violence in Kosovska Mitrovica in which 39 Albanians were detained by KFOR, reinscribed the framework of the NATO discourse by reminding Kosovo Albanians of both their own role and that of NATO, when he said

> I would remind all parties in Kosovo that it was NATO that put an end to organized ethnic cleansing and, through KFOR, has worked to restore peace and stability for all ethnic groups in the province. KFOR will not be deterred from this mission.[54]

The fact that neither peace nor stability has been achieved notwithstanding, such a statement reflects an unequivocal parental admonition that the Western-dominated international community is the only competent body to conclude decisions concerning the structure and process of peacebuilding in Kosovo. It is apparently inconceivable that perhaps the NATO presence has not created an atmosphere of confidence in its relations with Kosovars.[55] It is apparently inconceivable that Rambouillet has not facilitated dialogue and negotiation, but has rather, in effect, ended all negotiations between the actors and imposed an immobile, incontestable and non-representative peace.[56]

CONCLUSION

It is the contention of this chapter that the legal, structural and implementational ambiguities contained within the Rambouillet agreement have not contributed in a positive way to a clear, comprehensive understanding of the future of Kosovo. This is the result of a combination of factors, including the attempts of the international community to uphold the two contradictory principles of sovereignty and human rights simultaneously, and the perceptions of western policymakers with respect to certain types of conflict and the inevitable behaviour of particular peoples. Although the Rambouillet agreement was ostensibly aimed at negotiating a political settlement to the Kosovo conflict, the perceptional confines within which the Contact Group and others were operating and their unwillingness to deal with the central issue of legality has resulted in a host of problems which will only intensify if they are not addressed.

It appears, then, that the entire process through which the international community attempted to resolve the Kosovo conflict was seriously fundamentally flawed from the outset. Additionally, while the prescriptions for peace fail to address the core issues surrounding the conflict, they also contribute to an entirely new set of issues that are likely to proscribe the very peace that the implementers allegedly advocated. Not only will the Kosovo peace be lost, but renewed violence, when and if it occurs, will have as its basis the deep and divisive ambiguity that lies at the heart of the international community's response to Balkan conflict – again.

NOTES

Funding for the presentation of this study at the conference *Kosovo: Understanding the Past – Looking Ahead*, at Central European University in Budapest (31 March–2 April 2000) was made possible by the generous support of the Centre for International and Security Studies at York University in Toronto, Canada. The author would like to express her gratitude to Drs Sergei Plekhanov, David Mutimer and David Dewitt for their unwavering support and encouragement, including their willingness to provide invaluable comments and suggestions on previous drafts of this chapter. In its published form, this chapter also benefited greatly from the helpful insights of Florian Bieber.

1. Text of Vaclav Havel's speech to the Canadian parliament, cited in Noam Chomsky, *The New Military Humanism: Lessons from Kosovo* (Vancouver: New Star Books, 1999), p. 88.
2. At the time of this writing, the only comprehensive English language publication that deals with the Rambouillet talks in depth is Marc Weller, 'The Rambouillet Conference on Kosovo', *International Affairs*, vol. 75, no. 2 (1999). However, Weller, a legal advisor to the Kosovo Albanian delegation at Rambouillet, does not offer an analysis of the viability of the agreement. See also Wolfgang Petritsch, Karl Kaser and Robert Pichler, *Kosovo, Kosova: Mythen, Daten, Fakten*

(Klagenfurt: Wieser Verlag, 1999).

3. The elections that elevated Dr Rugova to the position of President of Kosovo were not recognized by Yugoslav authorities.

4. See Weller, 'The Rambouillet Conference', p. 220.

5. 'Albright on NATO Final Warning on Kosovo', State Department Press Release (30 January 1999).

6. Tim Judah has referred to the Rambouillet talks as having been aimed at an 'equitable' settlement for Kosovo. See 'Kosovo's Road to War', *Survival*, vol. 41, no. 2 (Summer 1999), p. 5.

7. See Weller, 'The Rambouillet Conference', p. 227.

8. Ibid., p. 229.

9. This stipulation was amended at the end of the bombing campaign, allowing NATO impunity in Kosovo, but restricting the peacekeeping force from the rest of the territory of Yugoslavia. See Institute for Public Accuracy, 'Was This Was Necessary?', Press Release, 9 June 1999.

10. See Weller, 'The Rambouillet Conference', p. 231.

11. Ibid.

12. Ibid., p. 232.

13. Ibid., pp. 232–3.

14. Michael Mandelbaum, 'A Perfect Failure', *Foreign Affairs*, vol. 78, no. 5 (September/October 1999), p. 10.

15. Javier Solana, 'NATO's Success in Kosovo', *Foreign Affairs*, vol. 76, no. 6 (November/December 1999), p. 116.

16. Ibid., p. 117.

17. Christopher M. Ryan, 'Sovereignty, Intervention, and the Law: A Tenuous Relationship of Competing Principles', *Millennium*, vol. 26, no. 1 (1997), p. 80.

18. For an overview of the legal bases for these positions, see Stephen A. Garrett, *Doing Good and Doing Well: An Examination of Humanitarian Intervention* (Westport, CT: Praeger Publishers, 1999), especially Chapter 3, 'The Realm of Law'.

19. Ibid., pp. 66–7.

20. Ostensibly humanitarian intervention in Iraq in 1991 kicked off a decade that seems to have been characterized by forceful interventions or the threat thereof, among them Somalia, Bosnia, Haiti and East Timor.

21. See Garrett, *Doing Good*; Amir Pasic and Thomas G. Weiss, 'Yugoslavia's Wars and the Humanitarian Impulse', *Ethics and International Affairs*, vol. 2 (1997); and Catherine Guicherd, 'International Law and the War in Kosovo', *Survival*, vol. 41, no. 2 (Summer 1999).

22. David Campbell discusses internationalist support for nationalism and nationalist paradigms with respect to the response of the international community to the Bosnian conflict in *National Deconstruction: Violence, Identity, and Justice in Bosnia* (Minneapolis, MN: University of Minnesota Press, 1998). For further discussion, see below.

23. There have been a variety of allegations put forth by scholars and commentators alike that NATO action against Yugoslavia was not a response to humanitarian crisis, but rather reflects more neocolonial or neo-imperialist intentions. Such analyses generally have their bases in macro views of the breakup of Yugoslavia since the early 1980s. Some interesting and relevant works include Michel Chossudovsky, *The Globalisation of Poverty* (London: Pluto Press, 1998); Chomsky, *Military Humanism*; and Paul Phillips, 'Why Were We Bombing Yugoslavia?', *Studies in Political Economy*, no. 60 (Autumn 1999).

24. The United States, for example, agreed to give temporary sanctuary to 20,000

refugees, planning to house them at military bases in Guam and Guantanamo Bay. Canada agreed to take 5,000. See 'Pitiful to Take Just 5,000', *Toronto Star*, Op. Ed., 8 April 1999. In total, the number of refugees that NATO countries agreed to shelter on a temporary basis amounted to 105,000 out of an estimated 900,000 Albanian refugees outside Kosovo. However, these noble plans were not, in the end, carried out as originally intended. UN High Commissioner for Refugees, Sadako Ogata, decided that the woefully overcrowded and under-supplied temporary shelters in Macedonia, Albania and Montenegro were sufficient. See 'UN Agency Rethinks Issue', *Toronto Star*, 9 April 1999. Critics suggested that 'the airlift was cancelled because of fears of a backlash in Europe, where immigration is politically sensitive'. See 'UN Calls Halt to NATO Airlift as Borders Set to Reopen', *National Post*, 10 April 1999.

25. The Federation of American Scientists estimated that the first 24 hours of bombing totalled more than $100 million, and would cost between $10 and $30 million per day after that. The Centre for Strategic and Budgetary Assessments suggested that the total cost of the campaign would fall between $2 and $4 billion. See 'The Cost of Kosovo', *ABC News*, 26 March 1999.

26. 'Doctors Fight to Control Disease Among Refugees', *National Post*, 10 April 1999.

27. 'Intolerable Conditions for Kosovo Refugees On Albanian Border', *Human Rights Watch*, 2 April 1999.

28. 'Refugees for Canada: Now Plan is in Doubt', *Toronto Star*, 9 April 1999, and 'Deportations Grim Reminder', *Toronto Star*, 9 April 1999.

29. Canadian Brigadier-General David Jurkowski defended the attack, saying that the antennae at the site 'showed it was a command post'. See 'NATO Admits Bombing Refugees', *Toronto Star*, 16 May 1999.

30. See Solana, 'NATO's Success', p. 118.

31. Rambouillet, Constitution, Article 1: Preamble.

32. Interview with George Robertson, UK Secretary of Defence, BBC One, 6 June 1999.

33. 'Russia and Yugoslavia Prepare to Test NATO,' *Stratfor Global Intelligence Update*, 4 January 2000.

34. See Institute for Public Accuracy, 'Was This War Necessary?'.

35. The February agreement was also committed to the territorial integrity of Yugoslavia, but that guarantee appeared to be valid for only the term of the three-year transition period.

36. 'UN Head: Define Autonomy for Kosovo,' *Washington Post*, 7 March 2000.

37. Ibid.

38. Ibid.

39. 'Uncertainty Hampers Kosovo Mission,' *Washington Post*, 5 March 2000.

40. 'Trouble Brewing in Kosovo,' *ABC News*, 7 February 2000.

41. Rambouillet, Article VII: National Communities, Section 4a (iii).

42. For an analysis on this problem in Bosnia, see Ermin Cengic, 'The Historic Divide: Bosnia and Herzegovina's Story Changes Depending on Where You Live', Transitions, vol. 6, no.1 (January 1999). The situations are not, however, identical. There is, at the very least, a linguistic difference in Kosovo that would have to be addressed before any educational setting could be broad based.

43. Rambouillet, Article VII: National Communities, Section 5f.

44. Charles Philippe-David, 'Does Peacebuilding Build Peace? Liberal (Mis)steps in the Peace Process', *Security Dialogue*, vol. 30, no. 1 (March 1999).

45. The assertion that Balkan conflicts are characterized by 'primitive' urges and 'centuries of hatred' has been central to western discourse on Balkan conflicts.

For example, Daniel Goldhagen, writing for the *New York Times* asserted that Serbia 'clearly consists of individuals with damaged faculties of moral judgement and has sunk into a moral abyss from which it is unlikely to emerge ... unaided'. See 'A New Serbia', *New York Times*, 29 May 1999.

46. Edward Said, *Orientalism* (London and New York: Vintage Books, 1979), pp. 41–2.

47. I am aware of the difficulties of treating 'the west' as a homogenized whole. However, due to the limited space offered by this chapter, I will adopt the view of Biljana Vankovska, who notes that 'NATO countries no doubt hold a set of identical values (such as [the] free market, the rule of law, human rights and freedoms) which are also included in the codex of the alliance they have established'. See 'NATO's War Over Yugoslavia: Civilian Control in Focus', at www.transnational.org. Catherine Guicherd also provides a basis for such a discussion when she writes that 'NATO regards itself as an alliance of democratic nations, whose political system is based on the rule of law'. See 'International Law', p. 19. For a critical analysis of western self-perceptions, see Jacques Derrida, *The Other Heading: Reflections on Today's Europe* (Bloomington, IN: Indiana University Press, 1992).

48. I have borrowed the notion of the 'pre-European' from John Caputo in *Deconstruction in a Nutshell* (New York: Fordham University Press, 1997). He writes that particular forms of the internationalization of western European Enlightenment values seeks 'to paint the whole world European, and to treat what is not European as "pre-European", which means pre-rational ...', p. 69.

49. 'Kosovo Is Out of Bounds: NATO Warns Belgrade', *Guardian*, 19 February 2000.

50. Michael Ignatieff, *Blood and Belonging: Journeys into the New Nationalism* (Toronto: Penguin Books, 1993), p. 4.

51. Secretary Albright, Press Conference on Kosovo (Washington DC, 25 March 1999).

52. The work of post-colonialism is extremely valuable in this kind of analysis. See Roxanne Lynn Doty, *Imperial Encounters* (Minneapolis, MN: University of Minnesota Press, 1996); Maria Todorova, *Imagining the Balkans* (New York: Oxford University Press, 1997); and Said, *Orientalism*.

53. 'Killers and Victims', *Guardian*, 18 February 2000.

54. 'NATO Peacekeepers to Handle Kosovo Attacks Toughly', *ABC News*, 14 February 2000.

55. Kosovars of all ethnic groups are included here. One of the more problematic contributions of the international community to perceptions of Kosovo is the conflation of the term 'Kosovar' with 'Albanian'. The conflict in Kosovo has often been characterized as one of 'Serbs' versus 'Kosovars'. Not only does this politicize conflict in a particular way, but it suggests that those non-Albanians living in Kosovo are not legitimately 'Kosovar', lending unwitting support to monoethnicity in the province. A similar problem is extant in Bosnia, where the term 'Bosnian' was conflated with 'Bosnian Muslim', thereby leading some Serbs and Croats to reject the term altogether as even a marker of citizenship. Settled western understandings of the conflict often describe 'Serbs' versus 'Bosnians', which results in something of a discursive erasure of Bosnian Serbs.

56. Similar observations concerning the nature of international peacekeeping in Bosnia have been expressed by Chantal de Jonge Oudraat in her chapter on Bosnia in Donald C. F. Daniel et al. (eds), *Coercive Inducement and the Containment of International Crisis* (Washington DC: US Institute of Peace Press, 1999). De Jonge Oudraat notes that '[t]he consent of the local parties [to SFOR occupation] was obtained through coercive diplomacy and forceful persuasion. Hence, once the

force is withdrawn, it is likely that the consent and co-operation of the parties will evaporate ... Without any clear choices, international troops will likely need to remain in Bosnia indefinitely.' Pp. 75–6.

REFERENCES

Campbell, D., *National Deconstruction: Violence, Identity, and Justice in Bosnia* (Minneapolis, MN: University of Minnesota Press, 1998).

Caputo, J., *Deconstruction in a Nutshell* (New York: Fordham University Press, 1997).

Cengic, E., 'The Historic Divide: Bosnia and Herzegovina's Story Changes Depending on Where You Live', *Transitions*, vol. 6, no. 1 (January 1999).

Chomsky, N., *The New Military Humanism: Lessons from Kosovo* (Vancouver: New Star Books, 1999).

Chossudovsky, M., *The Globalisation of Poverty* (London: Pluto Press, 1998).

Daniel, D. C. F. et al. (eds), *Coercive Inducement and the Containment of International Crisis* (Washington DC: US Institute of Peace Press, 1999).

Derrida, J., *The Other Heading: Reflections on Today's Europe* (Bloomington, IN: Indiana University Press, 1992).

Doty, R. L., *Imperial Encounters* (Minneapolis, MN: University of Minnesota Press, 1996).

Garrett, S. A., *Doing Good and Doing Well: An Examination of Humanitarian Intervention* (Westport, CT: Praeger Publishers, 1999).

Guicherd, C., 'International Law and the War in Kosovo', *Survival*, vol. 41, no. 2 (Summer 1999).

Ignatieff, M., *Blood and Belonging: Journeys into the New Nationalism* (Toronto: Penguin Books, 1993).

Judah, T., 'Kosovo's Road to War', *Survival*, vol. 41, no. 2 (Summer 1999).

Mandelbaum, M., 'A Perfect Failure', *Foreign Affairs*, vol. 78, no. 5 (September/October 1999).

Pasic, A. and Weiss, T. G., 'Yugoslavia's Wars and the Humanitarian Impulse', *Ethics and International Affairs*, vol. 2 (1997).

Petritsch, W., Kaser, K. and Pichler, R., *Kosovo, Kosova: Mythen, Daten, Fakten* (Klagenfurt: Wieser Verlag, 1999).

Philippe-David, C., 'Does Peacebuilding Build Peace? Liberal (Mis)steps in the Peace Process', *Security Dialogue*, vol. 30, no. 1 (March 1999).

Phillips, P., 'Why Were We Bombing Yugoslavia?', *Studies in Political Economy*, no. 60 (Autumn 1999).

Ryan, C. M., 'Sovereignty, Intervention, and the Law: A Tenuous Relationship of Competing Principles', *Millennium*, vol. 26, no. 1 (1997).

Said, E., *Orientalism* (London and New York: Vintage Books: 1979).

Solana, J., 'NATO's Success in Kosovo', *Foreign Affairs*, vol. 76, no. 6.

Todorova, M., *Imagining the Balkans* (New York: Oxford University Press, 1997).

Walter, B. F., and Snyder, J. (eds), *Civil Wars, Insecurity, and Intervention* (New York: Columbia University Press: 1999).

Weller, M., 'The Rambouillet Conference on Kosovo', *International Affairs*, vol. 75, no. 2 (1999).

PART III
THE NATO INTERVENTION IN YUGOSLAVIA AND THE WAR IN KOSOVO

6

When Doves Support War and Hawks Oppose It: An Analysis of Humanitarian Intervention in Kosova

Leon Malazogu

Meaningful humanitarian intervention does not threaten world order. Rather, it vindicates the fundamental principles for which the United Nations was created.[1]

The whole array of humanitarian action deserves great attention. This chapter, however, focuses on the use of force by the international community in a sovereign country when the latter fails to protect its citizens, either by tolerating ethnic cleansing on its territory or by embarking on such an operation itself. The chapter further differentiates between a legal and moral entity to authorize and conduct intervention and therefore focuses on the type of operations that do not receive the green light from all the permanent members of the Security Council, but do receive widespread moral support on the righteousness of intervention. One may correctly interpret that the essence of the moral dilemma lies in prioritizing widespread moral norms at the expense of concerns of individual members of the Security Council. The theoretical object of this study has at least one ideal archetype, the NATO intervention in former Yugoslavia in 1999. The chapter is thus based on the case of Kosova primarily because it has crystallized hitherto unsaid principles at the expense of the ones previously taken for granted, more specifically an absolute understanding of sovereignty.

'Humanitarian intervention' requires clarification of both components of the term. To start from the latter, there is no broad consensus among scholars on what intervention is. I concur with Hopkins and Donnelly that the defining characteristic of intervention is the presence of coerciveness, defined as the lack of consent by warring parties rather than the employment of forceful means.[2] 'Consent and coercion are mutually exclusive: by definition, one cannot agree to be coerced.'[3] Hence, any external action installed with the consent of local warring parties, such as peacekeeping operations, cannot be considered intervention. Regarding the first component of the term, 'humanitarian', it is important to recognize the inappropriateness of interpreting a comprehensive multifunctional operation through a single factor. While the operation in Kosova is viewed as humanitarian, it is widely held that no operation has ever originated out of a single motive, be that humanitarianism. This study follows a broad distinction made by Cooper and Berdal and analyzes operations that are coercive but primarily peace-keeping or humanitarian in nature.[4]

Trying to build a coherent argument on the use of force that oppose legal norms for peaceful goals is thus the challenge of this work. Fixdal and Smith claim that 'as an object of analysis, it [humanitarian intervention] sits at the intersection of the realist and idealist traditions in the study of international relations'.[5] Since the idealist tradition is widely identified with the use of peaceful means, the use of force to bring about peace has largely been viewed as hypocritical and contradictory. Humanitarian intervention thus attempts to combine humanitarian and human rights norms typically associated with the idealist tradition and the use of force usually associated with the realist tradition. A recent debate, whether respect for human rights can be enforced upon a party, has blurred the borderline between realpolitik and moralpolitik types of intervention. A working hypothesis claims that the international community can enforce universal values upon a defiant party and, under particular circumstances, military intervention may indeed be the only effective response to save a nation from its demise.

Humanitarian intervention arises from the tension between international deference for state sovereignty and rights of individuals against oppressive states. As Cassese states,

> In the current framework of the international community, three sets of values underpin the overarching system of inter-state relations: peace, human rights and self-determination. However, any time that conflict or tension arises between two or more of these values, peace must always constitute the ultimate and prevailing factor.[6]

It must also be noted that negative peace, or the mere absence of international wars is not the ultimate goal. One ought to strive for positive peace that entails wider reaching justice, safety and rights for individuals and sub-state groups as well.

More than anything, this chapter conducts an ethical analysis of humanitarian intervention, concluding that of all options available in the case of Kosova, intervention was ethically justified as a lesser evil. This analysis is made through two lines of reasoning: through consequentalist ethics where the criteria is an optimal overall outcome and through 'just war' theory. The third part complements the chapter by Gábor Sulyok, by taking a more positivistic debate on the flaws of our understanding of sovereignty.

This chapter in no case attempts to glorify the use of force in internal wars. On the contrary, wanting to see peace and justice at any cost, it does not preclude any way of reaching it. The argument is rather that the use of force ought not to be excluded a priori from the list of viable options, for under specific circumstances it may be the only way to prevent human disasters.

THE ETHICAL ARGUMENT FOR HUMANITARIAN INTERVENTION IN KOSOVA: A LESSER EVIL

I would like to ponder briefly on what it would take, or what needs to happen, for anyone to want her or his own country to be bombed. Out of 800,000 refugees coming out of Kosova in the spring of 1999, virtually none of them declared that the NATO intervention should not have occurred. Most of them thought that a ground attack was necessary in addition to the bombing. Kosovars would not want to see bombs destroying their country, but the military campaign of regular and irregular Serbian forces were seen as the greater evil which had to be stopped.

Many wars seem to occur quite quickly. At least that is what many tend to believe due to a lack of an early warning system or insufficient attention to previous escalation. Most analysts at least somewhat familiar with the situation in Kosova had been expecting violence to break out for over a decade. There were plenty of early warnings. Various remedies were indeed tried: humanitarian aid, observer missions, diplomatic pressure, support for the Serbian opposition and economic sanctions. As Väyrynen claims,

> ... for conflict prevention Kosovo is a hard case. The recalcitrance of the Milošević government, the headstrong policies of the KLA (Kosova Liberation Army), and the deep divisions in the Kosovo society rendered practically all preventive strategies ineffective. Milošević had few incentives to change his mind.[7]

Non-violence was a widely appealing principle in Kosova throughout the 1990s, nevertheless, despite widespread sympathies for the non-violent movement of Ibrahim Rugova, many Kosovars started to doubt the success of it. Kosova intrigued many into questioning whether pacifist principles are universally valid – everywhere at all times. Solving conflict through non-violent means is the most desirable method. However, there are circumstances under which one is ethically bound to use force as the last resort to stop a greater evil. Clearly, the ethical criterion followed throughout the rest of the chapter is consequentalist, where the overall benefit of any action must outweigh the overall cost incurred, and the option taken must be the optimal from all the available ones, including inaction.

Non-violent means can only be successful as a preventive measure, not to contain the vertical escalation of a conflict.[8] Väyrynen claims that as a rule, 'conflict prevention is thought to focus on the phase preceding the active resort to violence'.[9] It is thus important to note the chronological order of the events prior to the intervention. As noted by a Serbian international lawyer, Obradović, one can speak of armed warfare, and not merely incidents of violence, since January 1998.[10] The war in Kosova had, in effect, started a year earlier than is often considered as the beginning of the conflict, the NATO bombing. In this respect one should note that the KLA was an organization with all levels of hierarchy that had a built-in civil structure alongside a military one and active rules and courts that also kept contact with international diplomats and observers.[11] Obradović even compares the KLA with Tito's early national liberation movement, concluding that it could not be legally termed terrorist. Keeping in mind the highly organized structure, tacit international recognition, regular military and the parallel civilian structure, the KLA can be considered a well organized army.

In a fight between two well organized armies that consistently disregard humanitarian law (depending on their capacity and interest to do so), it becomes too late to solve the conflict by non-violent means as non-interventionists around the world were prophesying. Due to terrifying conditions of hundreds of thousands of internally displaced persons (IDPs) and constant physical threat by regular Serbian security forces and irregular paramilitary formations, thought to be under direct rule of President Milošević, the priorities of the international community change. No matter how important the principle of non-violence may be, it is more pressing to stop civilian mass execution as an immediate threat to humanity and humanitarian principles altogether and to try to contain both the horizontal and vertical escalation of the conflict. It is thus important to make the distinction between long-term goals and strategies and short-term imperatives. While it is a long-term goal to nourish peaceful methods of conflict resolution, it is a short-term necessity to put an end to a disaster or, ideally, prevent it from occurring. Alternative methods cease to exist as viable options when long-term goals present only extravagant ideas to a nation facing an immediate catastrophe. As Hoffman argues, alternative means may not save the lives of those that the humanitarian intervention initially seeks to.[12] Economic sanctions did not impede concentration camps and massacres in Bosnia, while a military intervention may as well have, as it subsequently did in Kosova.

The cost of action (sins of commission) should be measured against the cost of inaction (sins of omission). If one is to judge an operation by the criteria of human cost only, the NATO air strikes named Operation Allied

Force cannot be compared with the ten-year-long Serbian rule in Kosova. While the death toll incurred by NATO varies between 500 and 2,000, mainly Serbian military personnel, the toll of the last year of the Serbian rule in Kosova is expected to amount to over 10,000 victims, the vast majority of them civilians. The comparison between the two is further bolstered by what was expected to happen in the following weeks and months had NATO not attacked. Hundreds of thousands of refugees remained in the mountains of Kosova without any food, sick, and being chased by the Yugoslav Army and paramilitaries. The last 200 refugees who fled Kosova, just one day before Milošević signed the accord, were in the worst condition of all the refugees who had crossed the border until then. Needless to say, around 300,000 IDPs faced rapidly deteriorating circumstances, facing death not only from the Yugoslav Army but also from starvation, exhaustion and various diseases. By mid-2000, over 4,000 bodies had been recovered from the war and, judging from the lists of missing people, at least 6,000 could not be unaccounted for.

O'Hanlon presents a set of criteria by which the utility of a humanitarian mission can be measured. 'Since all human lives have equal value, the United States and other countries should use their military and political resources where they can save the greatest number of individuals.'[13] The drawback of this is that 'early action is founded on foreknowledge'.[14] Some aspects of the debate can only be made clear retrospectively. Predicting the sins of commission and the sins of omission before the intervention can only be conducted in a counter-factual manner that inevitably leads to speculative estimations. Despite the drawbacks of incomplete information, it was clear that intervention was a race against time. It was the rapid pace of the Yugoslav plan of ethnic cleansing in Kosova, Operation Horseshoe (as found by the German Ministry of Defence), that allowed no room for hesitation and brought the last resort of extreme measures earlier than many had expected.

Bell, Keeney and Raiffa illustrate well what the process of decision making with limited options goes through:

> Almost all of the issues that decision makers face in actuality involve multiple objectives that conflict in some measure with each other. In such issues, decisions that serve some objectives well will generally satisfy other objectives less well than alternative decisions, which, however, would not be so satisfactory for the first group. The decision maker then must select from among the possible decisions the one that somehow establishes the best mix of outcomes for his multiple conflicting objectives.[15]

The task of a morally concerned decision maker is to weigh conflicting moral claims. As a result, intervention cannot be prescribed as a universal remedy even if the Security Council allows it, and by the same token it cannot be excluded even if the Security Council prohibits it. The results must be weighed before hand, on a case by case basis, and one cannot formulate universal rules.

How does one deal with the paradox of using non-violent means when people may be suffering as a result of that? It is very frustrating when, for inflexible principles and lack of better options, pacifism becomes associated with passivism. A true pacifist in this scenario prioritizes not to violate his or her principles at the expense of allowing a war to burn out. Once violence erupts to the level that it did in the conflicts of Kosova and Bosnia options shrink significantly: intervene militarily and stop the conflict or allow the 'Darwinian peace' to set the stage for all small nations around the world. If the international community had chosen the latter, there would be up to two million Kosovar refugees around the world. As Gray points out, '[i]ndividuals in society and within a system of law would be at least morally in error were they to observe a crime taking place that they might be able to prevent or arrest, yet choose to do nothing'.[16] It can be extrapolated that it is morally unacceptable to sacrifice human lives to an abstract realist doctrine of non-intervention. However wretched a war may be, not only in Kosova, but others such as the Gulf War, there are 'pro-war doves' like Havel and Shevardnadze, who hold peaceful reasons for supporting it.[17]

There is no doubt that Operation Allied Force was at the very least imperfect. It is a moral imperative to save innocent civilians on whatever side they are found – and NATO could have done more to protect Serbian and Albanian civilians. The next section analyzes the way that the intervention was conducted and the fact that a number of Serbian and Albanian innocent civilians could have been saved if different strategies had been used. However, as discussed earlier on, the overall human damage that NATO prevented from occurring certainly outweighs the damage that it incurred. 'The damage to civilians and to neutral states which resulted from such problems do not begin to compare, in any grim comparison of losses, with the effects of the ethnic cleansing in Kosovo.'[18]

The cost of inaction is both internally and externally risky. Aside from measurements in solely human terms, outlaw nations like Serbia produce negative externalities such as violence, crime, smuggling, drug trafficking, illegal arms trade and refugees, setting a very bad example throughout Europe. As Schopflin points out in the case of Bosnia:

> The war impacted on Europe in a variety of unexpected and unpredicted ways. It showed the highly costly relationship with non-democracies in the immediate geographical vicinity of democracy and carried the implication that democracies have an interest in extending democratic norms. The costs of instability and of non-intervention to the West's self-image and self-esteem could well have been higher than

> military action. After all, non-intervention in Bosnia-Herzegovina
> exacted a very high price in both moral and material terms.[19]

Or as Brown argues, the costs of inaction are very difficult to measure and
'are usually realized only in the long term: they include damage to core
political values, international norms of behaviour, international law and
order, and regional and international stability'.[20]

Early humanitarian intervention (coercive or not) also has the effect of
averting local use of force which typically triggers a chain effect of violence.
For nine years of peaceful resistance, Rugova had trouble convincing
Kosovars that the world was 'watching closely'. When the KLA emerged,
outside intervention suddenly appeared more probable. Sadly enough, a
large majority of the Kosovar population easily deduced the obvious –
violence attracted the attention of the international community much more
than non-violence did. In order not to encourage self-defence or freedom-
fighting by force and to decrease local incentives to use force, the
international community should instead support non-violent freedom
movements, be they secessionist or not.

In post-war Kosova, there was a high level of violence against the Serbian
community mainly out of revenge or due to criminal motivations. The
conditions for violence were auspicious: there was tremendous hatred,
numerous legal and property disputes and virtually non-existent police or
judicial authorities. Despite great differences in the nature and the extent
of the violence in post-war Kosova, such acts cannot be justified.

JUS AD BELLUM AND *JUS IN BELLO*: A JUST WAR

Analyzing the moral properness of such a large military operation requires
more than a single ethical criterion. The second part of this chapter evalu-
ates whether the war was 'just' according to Just War theory. The Christian
tradition claims that even when wars are necessary for survival, vital
interests or values of a civilization, they ought to be fought according to
standards and rules for war making. Hence, a war is 'just' only when its
purpose is just and when the means employed are appropriate. Fixdal and
Smith categorize the just war doctrine in two widely agreed upon terms: *jus
ad bellum* 'concerns when we may justly resort to war', and *jus in bello*
'looks at the way that a war may be legitimately fought'.[21]

The two are analyzed separately in this chapter. However, many scholars
question whether *jus ad bellum* can be separated from *jus in bello*. One can
defend the NATO intervention as a just war arguably well, however, there
are serious claims that it violated standards for 'decent war making' in
several respects. Since the argument in this chapter is primarily based in
consequentialist principle of ethics, I place greater priority on the final

outcome of a humanitarian intervention, therefore prioritizing the overall effect over the means used. Many scholars disagree with this type of prioritization referring to possible manipulations and abuse of a greater 'just' goal. That is certainly possible. Many leaders have justified harsh measures against their own people with promises of a greater future vision. On the other hand, the danger lies in victimizing a long-term vision for a non-essential short-term principle. The reasoning behind is therefore not whether one can be prioritized over the other, because it can, but its cautious employment to avoid any manipulations for a wrong cause. Sometimes the need to deal with an immediate problem takes priority and puts the justice of the goal over the justice of the action. In order to have human rights and democracy later, one needs to protect a nation from its demise in the short term. Those to whom democracy is promised ought to be saved from being wiped out in the first place, for democracy would not have any utility for those who have been exterminated.

As do most just war theorists, Phillips argues that for a war to qualify as 'just', it has to fulfil six conditions.[22] The first condition requires a 'just cause' in order to produce a just war. According to realist principles, only self-help qualifies as legitimate use of force. As alternative theoretical discourses increasingly render realism less relevant, 'the law is not just which allows a traveller to kill a robber in order to avoid being killed by him. Helping one's neighbour is a repeatedly stated and easily understood duty.'[23] As concluded above, in a world driven by universal human principles, the moral imperative of saving lives, and allowing the use of force to help others, is prioritized over the traditional principle of non-interventionism.

A second condition is that only a legitimate authority may make the decision to go to war. Because the UN Security Council is viewed as the ultimate authority on security matters, it may be potentially problematic to argue about the right authority of NATO to act in Kosova. On the other hand, a moral argument can be made on the righteousness of the Security Council to decide on all global security matters. This chapter makes no attempt to strip the world its only authority on security and bring back an anarchic state of the world. However, in order to improve current institutions or replace them with better ones, a comparison between the Security Council and NATO can be useful to understand better where the world ought to be headed.

NATO is comprised of more countries than the Security Council, and every NATO member has the right to veto any decision, which, morally speaking, warrants greater justice than the Security Council does. For the Security Council to agree on an action it is sufficient for none of the permanent members to be against it. Resolutions that do not pass are mostly because a permanent member opposes them and rarely because the proponent behind a draft resolution cannot gather enough non-permanent supporters to back it up. On the other hand, it is much harder for NATO to enter an operation because all 19 members have the right to veto and all, to varying degrees, have internal democratic structures with active civic societies involved in foreign affairs. It is thus much harder for NATO to be manipulated into a wrong operation. True, NATO is an exclusive organization, but effectively speaking so is the Security Council. The importance of non-permanent members is more nominal than effective, and they rarely play an important role.

The only aspect on which the Security Council is morally superior to NATO is that it is more global and reflects better global military-might than NATO does. If Yugoslavia was anywhere besides Europe, that argument would hold. On the contrary, the country attacked more or less belonged, or aspired to, the same political and cultural tradition as most current and future NATO members do.[24] On the other hand, the fact that Russia and China would oppose the intervention does not add any moral credibility to a decision taken by the Security Council. Russia and China in that respect are similar to France and the UK at the end of the Second World War. They still hold colonies, hence their decision is based on vested interests not to allow any precedent in supporting indigenous, colonized or minority populations.

The UN Charter itself needs to solve some contradictions that now appear blatantly obvious. As Cooper and Berdal claim, '[a]lthough the advantages of the United Nations in terms of universality and impartiality are significant, the organization has not yet addressed the broader implications of its role in intrastate conflict'.[25] This inevitably relates to the discussion on sovereignty. In order for the charter contradictions to be solved, one needs to adopt a rather internationalist, or even cosmopolitan-ist, understanding of sovereignty versus a statist one, as categorized by Donnelly, where sovereignty is no longer an absolute principle but a relative one, derived to the state by its own citizens.[26]

The third condition claims that groups going to war may do so only with the right intention, that is to bring peace, never intending revenge, harm or self-interest. 'The purpose is not to kill the murderer, but to stop aggression', argues Phillips.[27] The fact that the UN was immediately given the role of administering Kosova, to decide on its political future, prepare a pluralistic society able to democratically govern itself, shows NATO's intentions to some extent.

The fourth condition is that war may be undertaken only as a last resort. The situation in Kosova was escalating to the point of resembling Bosnia, which was an obvious indication that diplomacy was not leading anywhere. The concept of 'race against time' was first witnessed in Bosnia. UN peacekeepers eyewitnessed the death of thousands of people while waiting for a concrete idea to solve the conflict. As accepted by the UN itself, the UN holds partial responsibility for the Srebrenica massacre where 8,000 Bosnian Muslims were killed by Serbian security forces. While Bosnians were begging for NATO intervention, it was the UN that gave false hope to people by promising safe havens and not being able to protect them.[28] The over-ambitious mission of the UN also delayed Operation Deliberate Force that eventually ended the conflict in a matter of weeks. One can always claim that there were more diplomatic possibilities available in Kosova and cite 'unreasonable requests' in Rambouillet as an example. This argument is valid unless it is extended to tolerate the annihilation of a nation on grounds that diplomacy is still being tried. Certainly one might claim that if Serbia had been offered a better deal at Rambouillet it might have accepted the proposal and averted war. Serbia had been offered many options prior to Rambouillet, however, it accepted none.

The fifth condition for a 'just war' asserts that the goal must be a likely emergent peace, which is obvious due to the great military difference between the Yugoslav Army and NATO's ability to win large-scale conflicts. The post-war presence of ethnically motivated crime does not refute this point because it is a sign of failure in other sectors of peacebuilding, such as policing and the judiciary, and not of the intervention itself.

Finally, the war may not be disproportionate, that is, the total evil may not outweigh the total good achieved by a just war. This condition is slightly ambiguous. In terms of the armament used, the intervention was no doubt disproportionate. However, in terms of the overall results, the total evil seems to be far lower than the total good achieved by the war, as established earlier on by measuring action against inaction.[29]

Normally in the just war doctrine, the main driving principles are those of balance of local forces and that of self-help, however, one cannot exclude the possibility of self-help coming from outside.

> If the dominant forces within a state are engaged in massive violations of human rights, the appeal to self-determination in the Millian sense of self-help is not very attractive. That appeal has to do with the freedom of the community taken as a whole; it has no force when what is at stake is the bare survival or the minimal liberty of (some substantial number of) its members. Against the enslavement or massacre of political opponents, national minorities, and religious sects, there may well be no help unless help comes from outside. And when a government turns savagely upon its own people, we must doubt the very existence of a political community to which the idea of self-determination might apply.[30]

NATO has also been criticized for collective punishment. Despite widespread outrage over the bombing of certain dual-use targets such as the Serbian TV station and bridges, the collateral damage was far lower than, let's say, Chechnya or Vietnam. While there was no collective punishment, one has to recognize the existence of collective responsibility. This is not to say that every single Serbian citizen is to blame, but rather that a public apology to the Kosovar nation would somewhat improve relations. Conversely, many Serbs today blame Milošević not for waging four wars and killing around 300,000 people, but for losing them. This may be a result of long-term media indoctrination, nevertheless it does not render the damage done any the less. Serbs have regularly criticized Milošević for isolation and poor economic conditions, but rarely for thousands of Kosovars killed. This is not to say that collective punishment is logical, but rather to instil a sense of moral responsibility over the actions of people's representatives, and the need for all the people to be alert to what their government and armed forces do. Milošević may have exhibited features of a dictator at later stages in the Kosova conflict, but certainly not during the war in Croatia and Bosnia.

Another criticism of humanitarian intervention doctrine is its selectiveness; intervention not carried out whenever needed. According to Halliday, since humanitarian reasons do not suffice, selectivity is inevitable as a result of the overlap between self-interest and humanitarian action (but also because of logistical, strategic reasons and expectations for success).[31] In addition to the humanitarian motives outlined earlier, 'the NATO states were united by a sense of shame that, in the first four years of atrocious wars in the former Yugoslavia (1991–95), they had failed, individually and collectively, to devise coherent policies and to engage in decisive actions'.[32] NATO's credibility was at stake as well. External interventions in general are more successful if, in addition to altruistic intention, they are combined with a clear national interest and a clear goal.

The selective application of a principle does not necessarily render it illegitimate. As Phillips claims, 'the fact that any moral argument, including pacifism, can be corrupted is not a good reason for abandoning such perspectives. The ever-present possibility of misuse should, however, cause us to be keenly aware of inconsistency.'[33] Rejecting the principle of forceful humanitarian intervention on the ground of its selective employment does no justice to its occasional right use. The answer is not then to discard the principle, but to try to eliminate the corrupt elements within it, to whatever extent feasible, as long as they do not outweigh the overall benefit of the operation. In any case, even some self-interest in a humanitarian operation does not necessarily render it ineffective or unjust. As a matter of fact, the most successful operations are usually those that the main actors have high stakes in.

> Self-interest, as construed by politicians and, not least, their electorates, will dictate the limits of those interventions and other humanitarian action that do take place. This will also mean that selectivity will continue to operate, justified on grounds of practicality and by the lame but not invalid argument that it is better to try to do some good than none at all.[34]

Going back to the principle of pacifism, it is very interesting to juxtapose it with the 'just war' doctrine. Extreme pacifism that outlaws every type of violence is apparently useless because it outlaws self-defence as well, which would be rejected by every nation that has ever been attacked. In any case, pragmatic pacifism that allows proactive defence seems not too far from a carefully applied 'just war' doctrine.

COSMOPOLITAN SOVEREIGNTY, PERHAPS?

> Far from heralding a new age of humanitarian interventionism, the war in Kosovo highlights the difficulty of pursuing such a course.[35]

There are obvious disagreements about what is understood by sovereignty. The analysis of the term is beyond the scope of this study, however, it is useful to recognize different aspects of sovereignty made by Krasner. He makes the distinction among Westphalian sovereignty, international legal sovereignty, interdependence sovereignty and domestic sovereignty.[36] The focus here is on the last category, where a state uses its recognized supremacy to exert its authority primarily internally to quell challenges by any means available.

Sovereignty was initially recognized as a principle that guarantees certain rights to the people and prevents external states from violating them. Sovereignty is therefore assured to countries with the purpose of protecting,

> ... fundamental advantages to the people ... thus enhancing the safety or people's lives and property from 'foreign' interference ... it presumes a single authoritative body or procedural code for establishing rule over the people and territory. It is expected to protect against crime, enforce, secure the rights of individuals and groups (family, religious associations, ethnic groups) ...[37]

However, if the state becomes an 'outlaw nation' as Mertus[38] calls it, and instead of guaranteeing those rights to its citizens it becomes the primary institution that denies them on regular basis, one can reasonably conclude that the state in place has lost its moral authority to govern that population, or at least a part of it. Hopkins argues that,

> [t]he rise of counterclaims within 'sovereign' states from groups claiming discrimination and seeking relief may lead to the division of a territory into two or more distinct sovereign entities, as for example the division of Czechoslovakia into two states in 1992.[39]

Or as Johansen claims,

[i]n this historical era, states derive legitimacy, in part, from their citizens. As a result, if a state denies many of its citizens their fundamental rights, the traditional constraint against external intervention in the domestic jurisdiction of a state's sovereignty no longer applies with its previous strength.'[40]

Therefore, recognizing external sovereignty is a function of the government's respect for human rights of its own citizens. Once the latter is violated, there are reasons not to respect the former.

An unambiguous way a state loses its legitimacy is to conduct genocide, or according to the Genocide Convention, 'take steps to destroy any ethnic, religious or national groups'.[41] Not only is it forbidden by the Genocide Convention, but it is also a breach of social contract between the suppressed portion of the population and the state. Thus, the present state can no longer be considered a proper governing authority. The scale and the pace of ethnic cleansing in Kosova clearly speak of the loss of legitimate authority to run the region. More than 800,000 Albanians were refugees outside of Kosova and over 300,000 were internally displaced. Judging from the estimated 1.5 million Albanian Kosovars right after war, it seems that few Albanians had not moved from their homes. As much as this speaks for Kosovar independence, it speaks even louder for international interference. As Fixdal and Smith summarize the opinions of half a dozen other authors regarding Bosnia, 'neither inaction nor neutrality can be justified in the face of such egregious crimes'.[42]

A pragmatic starting point is to change the way we understand sovereignty. As long as sovereignty is understood as an absolute term (a state is either sovereign or not) one is neglecting the increasing interdependence in the world. When sovereignty is seen as an absolute source of power, it also provides a greater incentive for internal forces to fight for independence or secession. Horowitz claims that sovereignty should rather be looked on as a continuum, with individual human rights at one end and state rights at the other.[43] 'Because the principle of sovereignty is qualitative – sovereignty is possessed or not – that principle becomes an obstacle to inter-ethnic accommodation.'[44] This may eventually have the result of allowing more sets of sovereign authorities to co-exist in the same area, paving the way for various power-sharing and federal arrangements which may provide the basis for seeking legal solutions for numerous ethnic conflicts around the world. With such an understanding of human rights and sovereignty, the conclusion is that 'the right to determine their own destinies' as an essential human right outweighs 'the rights of states to conduct their own affairs'.[45] Except for economic interdependence, sovereignty has also been challenged by the ideological delegitimization of colonialism leading 'to an erosion of traditional sovereignty'.[46]

The argument in this section may be too positivist or too flexible for those who seek true or false answers in international law. Law ought not to be static. It ought to change in order to reflect the changing nature of our world society. As there is a desperate need to reform international law, and despite calls on Kosova's unique circumstances, Kosova needs to be viewed in the larger context with consideration of where international law is headed. As much as this paper tries to justify Kosova, it tries even more to prevent future heavy tolls on weak nations around the world arising from legal loopholes.

The UN charter itself (in the Preamble and in Article 13) upholds general human rights principles – 'the UN Charter itself allows for action by member-states that override sovereignty, not only where international peace and security are threatened but also where serious violations of humani-tarian law occur.'[47] The charter has increasingly been loosely interpreted as placing human rights higher on the agenda of the UN. According to Halliday, serious humanitarian violations today are sufficient enough to override sovereignty.[48] As a result, there is a great disagreement over the importance and definition of sovereignty today that stems directly from the UN charter. Various interpretations point out serious contradictions between Article 2, Article 51 and Chapter VII – where does sovereignty end, and where do human rights and self-determination start?

Absence of wars among states, in peace studies referred to as inter-national or negative peace, was the primary principle which dictated the original formation of the UN Charter in 1945. International war was the main fear of the international community at the outset of the Second World War. One ought to look around and recognize the changes that the world has experienced since then. There are few inter-state wars today. The upward trend is in citizens fighting states and each other. Internal wars are the main threat to humanity today and as such, the international community should devise strategies to deal with them, and protect small nations from demise.

> In 1945 the Charter's system of collective security was constructed in light of breaches in peace that were experienced at that time, which mostly consisted of trans-border armed attacks by armed forces of another state. In the course of fifty years this scenario has become exceptional.[49]

While sovereignty may have guaranteed international peace for decades, in the post-cold war era when international wars have largely been absent, sovereignty guarantees to autocratic states a free hand in consolidating their power at the expense of freedom and democracy of their own citizens. While decades ago the main fear was strong states undermining small states 'in order to expand or preserve their ideology and power positions, the world is now faced with different manifestations of what might be called 'people power' revolting against the existing states'.[50]

There are several ways that a 'community cause' as Hoffman terms humanitarian intervention, can be legitimate: licensed by the UN Charter or the Security Council under Chapter VII, or by the OSCE; when the cost of promoting a community cause is lower than refusing any international involvement, or 'if the UN has been incapable of dealing with such an issue, and demonstrated its paralysis or impotence – as in the cases of Tanzania's removal of Idi Amin from Uganda, and of Vietnam's interventions against Pol Pot'.[51]

As rationalized above, there are inherent contradictions in international law in general and the UN Charter in particular. The right of states to their sovereignty is in direct opposition to the right of individuals and groups within states to international protection.[52] On broader terms, the overriding dilemma is that current international law does not reflect realities on the ground. In order for law to be effective it must not detach from reality because, if it does, it will not be viewed as law that has evolved from everyday practice but rather as an unreasonable standard that no one is expected to follow closely. It must also be 'better' than the reality in order to serve as a model and encourage change. Currently, one may conclude that the UN Charter is state centric and thus distanced from a human rights culture that has been increasingly embraced throughout the world. 'The moral and the strategic are intimately connected: what is required is a framework of argument that embraces both'.[53]

Can one point to an emerging doctrine in international law that allows 'the use of forcible countermeasures to impede a state from committing large-scale atrocities on its own territory' when the Security Council is incapable of responding to a crisis properly?[54] A rule, legalizing humanitarian intervention without the participation of the Security Council may be evolving. The present legal system rules out such efforts to stop slaughter. This does not speak on the behalf of the system, it accentuates the need to revise the present paradigm.[55] This is a critique against NATO as a violator of the rule, but it even better reflects the state of international law and the need to affect change.

It is also very important to note the massive non-opposition, if not endorsement, of UN member states. There was only one draft resolution put forward at the Security Council which asked to condemn NATO intervention, and that was rejected by twelve votes to three. 'A group of states ought to decide to halt the atrocities, with the support or at least the non-opposition of the majority of Member States of the UN', Cassese claims, and argues further, that 'It should also be noted that no state or group of states has taken the step that would have been obvious in case of strong opposition to NATO armed intervention: to request an immediate meeting of the General Assembly'.[56]

Despite the UN's obvious deficiencies in some respects, NATO intervention and subsequent events show extensive respect towards the UN as the central global body.

> Did NATO's action set a precedent – that a UN imprimatur on intervention for humanitarian ends is nice but not necessary? Perhaps. But Kosovo ultimately says more about the UN's continued strength than its weakness. The United Nations proved to be a central character in the intricate diplomatic minuet danced by the Americans, the Europeans, and the Russians in the weeks leading up to Belgrade's surrender. Once Belgrade gave in, the UN was given political control over Kosovo. Moreover, the United Nations will have the decisive role in determining the territory's political future.[57]

Kosova types of intervention should be put firmly under the roof of the UN, and this ought to be done not by illegalizing them, but by enlarging the 'roof' of the UN to accommodate humanitarian intervention doctrine as a vital component of contemporary international relations. The UN faces the danger of getting sidelined if it proves inflexible in adapting to dynamic contours of transnational ethnic politics and conflict patterns, as delineated above. By the same token, the UN needs to change in several directions in order to diffuse the monopoly of decision making on security issues.[58]

In a contemporary understanding of a single human race, we need to recognize that borders are not sacrosanct in front of human suffering.[59] The link between present global institutions with the prevailing view on the primacy of human rights has to be made. The institutions established in a largely chaotic world need to reflect the changes that have occurred in the world during the last 50 years. We ought not lose the momentum. If we want to keep the institutions that we have created, they have to reflect the unity of the human race.

> The operation was announced at the start as based on the idea (closely related to the one advanced in the Pinochet decision) that there are some crimes so extreme that a state responsible for them, despite the principle of sovereignty, may properly by the subject of military intervention.[60]

Several conditions need to be fulfilled to justify an intervention on a human rights or humanitarian basis:

1. Flagrant human rights abuses amounting to ethnic cleansing or genocide either directly conducted or tolerated by the state, or due to its inability to prevent it.
2. If the Security Council is unable to respond properly to a crisis it should condemn massacres and term the situation a threat to peace and international security; therefore allowing those willing and able to give help. If serious disagreement among any permanent members leads to a decision making deadlock, security matters are then handled either by a regional organization or by the General Assembly.

3. All diplomatic means must be exhausted prior to any coercive intervention, taking into account the local power dynamics and the pace of events. The expectation of success can also be added both when considering various diplomatic strategies and military options. As carrots do not work without sticks, diplomacy need not be employed separately from military deterrence.
4. As Cassese claims, 'a group of states ought to decide to halt atrocities, with the support or at least the non-opposition of the majority of Member States of the UN'.[61] It should not be up to the Security Council to veto a decision, but the majority of the Member States. This is biased as well, however far less than the Security Council.
5. Force should be exclusively used to stop atrocities and restore respect for human rights. The air raids against Serbia stopped as soon as the agreement was reached.

Or as Halliday astutely observes,

> The question Kosovo poses is not, therefore, whether a legal case can be made for the NATO action. It can. Nor is it whether an element of self-interest, and selectivity, operates. It does. It is rather whether, in the circumstances, this was the most prudent policy to pursue, in the light of what Serbia's response might be, and in the light of the constraints which, in the name of the very self interest that the critics denounce, operate on the NATO operation.[62]

NOTES

For extensive remarks and suggestions on literature, I thank professor Raimo Väyrynen from the Kroc Institute for International Peace Studies, my colleague Zeynep Bülütgil and my good friend, Židas Daskalovski, from Oxford University. For any stylistic coherence that the paper may have, I thank my colleague Cecily Nicholson, who generously offered to proofread it. For great moral support and patient listening to the original speech, I thank Marlise Richter.

1. Julie Mertus, 'Back to the Drawing Board: Human Rights Should Know No Boundaries', *Washington Post*, 11 April 1999, Outlook Section.
2. Jack Donnelly, 'The Past, the Present, and the Future Prospect', in Milton J. Esman and Shibley Telhamic (eds), *International Organizations and Ethnic Conflict* (Ithaca, NY: Cornell University Press, 1995), p. 49.
3. Michael E. Brown, 'Internal Conflict and International Action', in Michael E. Brown (ed.), *The International Dimensions of Internal Conflict* (Cambridge, MA: The MIT Press, 1996), p. 618.
4. Robert Cooper and Mats Berdal, 'Outside Intervention in Ethnic Conflicts', *Survival*, vol. 35, no. 1 (Spring 1993), p. 134.
5. Mona Fixdal and Dan Smith, 'Humanitarian Intervention and Just War', *Mershon International Studies Review*, vol. 42 (1998), p. 283.
6. Antonio Cassese, 'Ex iniuria ius oritur: Are We Moving Towards International

Legitimation of Forcible Humanitarian Countermeasures in the World Community?', *European Journal of International Law*, vol. 10, no. 1 (1999), p. 23.

7. Raimo Väyrynen, 'Challenges to Preventive Action: The cases of Kosovo and Macedonia', unpublished manuscript (2000).

8. Ibid. Väyrynen defines vertical escalation as deterioration of the extent of the conflict as opposed to horizontal escalation which means a spillover in neighouring countries.

9. Ibid.

10. Konstantin Obradović, 'Medjunarodno humanitarno pravo i Kosovska kriza' [International humanitarian law and Kosova crisis], *Medjunarodni problemi* year LI, no. 3–4 (August 1999), p. 270.

11. Ibid., pp. 270–1.

12. Stanley Hoffmann, 'Comments on Comments', in Stanley Hoffman (ed.), *The Ethics and Politics of Humanitarian Intervention* (Notre Dame, IN: University of Notre Dame Press, 1996), p. 98.

13. Michael O'Hanlon, 'Saving Lives with Force: When – and How – Should the United States Intervene to Stop Genocidal Wars?', *New Republic*, no. 4408 (12 July 1999), p. 21.

14. See Fixdal and Smith, 'Humanitarian Intervention and Just War', pp. 283–312.

15. David E. Bell, Ralph L. Keeney and Howard Raiffa (eds), *Conflicting Objectives in Decision* (New York: John Wiley & Sons, 1977), p. v.

16. Colin S. Gray, 'Force, Order, and Justice', *Current*, no. 357 (November 1993), p. 21.

17. Taking into account the attitude towards the use of force in general and regarding a specific conflict, Spencer categorizes policy makers in four categories: prowar doves, antiwar doves, prowar hawks and antiwar hawks. Metta Spencer, 'Antiwar Hawks and Prowar Doves in the Gulf War', *Peace & Change*, vol. 17, no. 2 (April 1992), p. 172.

18. Adam Roberts, 'NATO's "Humanitarian War" Over Kosovo', *Survival*, vol. 41, no. 3 (1999), p. 115.

19. George Schopflin, 'After the War', *Radio Free Europe/Radio Liberty*, 17 November 1999, Archive.

20. See Brown, 'Internal Conflict and International Action', p. 627.

21. See Fixdal and Smith, 'Humanitarian Intervention and Just War', p. 286.

22. Robert L. Phillips and Duane L. Cady, *Humanitarian Intervention: Just War vs. Pacifism* (Lanham, MD: Rowman & Littlefield Publishers, 1996), p. 37.

23. See Fixdal and Smith, 'Humanitarian Intervention and Just War', p. 296.

24. One may question Serbian association with NATO countries, however, Serbia's (or former Yugoslavia's) ties, before the crisis began, were mostly with European countries that either belong or aspire to join NATO. The Serbian cultural and political elite have traditionally looked towards Europe as a model and not towards Russia. Today, Serbia is completely encircled either with NATO members or NATO aspiring countries and, as such, it can be argued that Serbia is within the NATO sphere of interest.

25. See Cooper and Berdal, 'Outside Intervention in Ethnic Conflicts', p. 140.

26. Jack Donnelly, 'State Sovereignty and International Intervention: The Case of Human Rights', in Gene M. Lyons and Michael Mastanduno (eds), *Beyond Westphalia? State Sovereignty and International Intervention* (Baltimore, MD: Johns Hopkins University Press, 1995), pp. 120–3.

27. See Phillips and Cady, *Humanitarian Intervention*, p. 79.

28. United Nations, 'Report of the Secretary-General pursuant to General Assembly

Resolution 53/35 (1998): The Fall of Srebrenica', A/54/549 (15 November 1999).

29. See Phillips and Cady, *Humanitarian Intervention*, p. 37.
30. Michael Walzer, *Just and Unjust Wars: A Moral Argument with Historical Illustrations* (New York: Basic Books, 1977), p. 101.
31. Fred Halliday, 'Are NATO Actions Prudent and Are They Legal?', *Irish Times*, 1 April 1999.
32. See Roberts, 'NATO's "Humanitarian War" Over Kosovo', p. 104.
33. See Phillips and Cady, *Humanitarian Intervention*, p. 82.
34. See Halliday, 'Are NATO Actions Prudent and Are They Legal?'.
35. Ivo H. Daalder and Michael E. O'Hanlon, 'Unlearning the Lessons of Kosova', *Foreign Policy*, Autumn 1999, pp. 128–40.
36. Stephen D. Krasner, *Sovereignty: Organized Hypocrisy* (Princeton, NJ: Princeton University Press, 1999), pp. 3–4.
37. Raymond F. Hopkins, 'Anomie, System Reform, and Challenges to the UN System', in Milton J. Esman and Shibley Telhami (eds), *International Organizations and Ethnic Conflict* (Ithaca and London: Cornell University Press, 1995), p. 79.
38. See Mertus, 'Back to the Drawing Board'.
39. See Hopkins, 'Anomie, System Reform, and Challenges to the UN System', p. 80.
40. Robert C. Johansen, 'Limits and Opportunities in Humanitarian Intervention', in Stanley Hoffman (ed.), *The Ethics and Politics of Humanitarian Intervention* (Notre Dame, IN: University of Notre Dame Press, 1996), p. 68.
41. Ted Robert Gurr and Barbara Harff, *Ethnic Conflict in World Politics* (Boulder, CO: Westview Press, 1994), p. 147.
42. See Fixdal and Smith, 'Humanitarian Intervention and Just War', pp. 283–312.
43. Donald Horowitz, 'Making Moderation Pay: The Comparative Politics of Ethnic Conflict Management', in Joseph V. Montville (ed.), *Conflict and Peacemaking in Multiethnic Societies* (New York: Lexington Books, 1991), pp. 452–3.
44. Ibid., p. 452.
45. See Gurr and Harff, *Ethnic Conflict in World Politics*, p. 147.
46. Stanley Hoffmann, 'Sovereignty and the Ethics of Intervention', in Stanley Hoffmann (ed.), *The Ethics and Politics of Humanitarian Intervention* (Notre Dame, IN: University of Notre Dame Press, 1996), p. 15.
47. Halliday, 'Are NATO Actions Prudent and Are They Legal?'.
48. Ibid.
49. R. Gaiger, 'Humanitarian Intervention and the UN Charter – Some Remarks', *European Journal of International Law*, 19 May 1999.
50. Ibid.
51. See Hoffmann, 'Sovereignty and the Ethics of Intervention', p. 22.
52. See Halliday, 'Are NATO Actions Prudent and Are They Legal?'.
53. See Fixdal and Smith, 'Humanitarian Intervention and Just War', p. 284.
54. See Cassese, '*Ex iniuria ius oritur*', p. 23.
55. See Walzer, *Just and Unjust Wars*, p. 108.
56. See Cassese, '*Ex iniuria ius oritur*', pp. 28–9.
57. See Daalder and O'Hanlon, 'Unlearning the Lessons of Kosova', pp. 128–40.
58. For example, the veto power should be removed and the number of permanent members to the Security Council could be increased to include India, Japan, Germany, Brazil, Nigeria and, maybe, South Africa.
59. See Phillips and Cady, *Humanitarian Intervention*, pp. 85–6.
60. See Roberts, 'NATO's "Humanitarian War" Over Kosovo', p. 103.
61. See Cassese, '*Ex iniuria ius oritur*', p. 29.
62. See Halliday, 'Are NATO Actions Prudent and Are They Legal?'.

REFERENCES

Bell, D. E., Keeney, R. L. and Raiffa, H. (eds), *Conflicting Objectives In Decisions* (New York: John Wiley & Sons 1977).

Brown, M. E., 'Internal Conflict and International Action', in M. E. Brown (ed.), *The International Dimensions of Internal Conflict* (Cambridge, MA: The MIT Press 1996), pp. 603–27.

Cassese, A., '*Ex iniuria ius oritur*: Are We Moving Towards International Legitimation of Forcible Humanitarian Countermeasures in the World Community?', *European Journal of International Law*, vol. 10, no. 1 (1999), pp. 23–30.

Cooper, R. and Berdal, M., 'Outside Intervention in Ethnic Conflicts', *Survival*, vol. 35, no. 1 (Spring 1993), pp. 118–42.

Daalder, I. H. and O'Hanlon, M. E., 'Unlearning the Lessons of Kosova', *Foreign Policy*, Autumn 1999, at www.foreignpolicy.com/articles/Fall1999/kosovo.html.

Donnelly, J., 'The Past, the Present, and the Future Prospect', in M. J. Esman and S. Telhamic (eds), *International Organizations and Ethnic Conflict* (Ithaca, NY: Cornell University Press, 1995).

Donnelly, J., 'State Sovereignty and International Intervention: The Case of Human Rights', in G. M. Lyons and M. Mastanduno (eds), *Beyond Westphalia? State Sovereignty and International Intervention* (Baltimore, MD: Johns Hopkins University Press, 1995), pp. 115–46.

Fixdal, M. and Smith, D., 'Humanitarian Intervention and Just War', *Mershon International Studies Review*, vol. 42 (1998), pp. 283–312.

Gaiger, R., 'Humanitarian Intervention and the UN Charter – Some Remarks', *European Journal of International Law* (19 May 1999), at www.ejil.org/forum/messages/46.html.

Gray, C. S., 'Force, Order, and Justice', *Current*, no. 357 (November 1993), p. 21.

Gurr, T. R. and Harff, B., *Ethnic Conflict in World Politics* (Boulder, CO: Westview Press, 1994).

Halliday, F., 'Are NATO Actions Prudent and Are They Legal?', in *Irish Times* (1 April 1999), at www.ireland.com/newspaper/opinion/1999/0401/opt3.htm.

Hoffmann, S., 'Comments on Comments', in S. Hoffman (ed.), *The Ethics and Politics of Humanitarian Intervention* (Notre Dame, IN: University of Notre Dame Press, 1996), pp. 97–100.

Hoffmann, S., 'Sovereignty and the Ethics of Intervention', in S. Hoffman (ed.), *The Ethics and Politics of Humanitarian Intervention* (Notre Dame, IN: University of Notre Dame Press, 1996), pp.12–37.

Hopkins, R. F., 'Anomie, System Reform, and Challenges to the UN System', in M. J. Esman and S. Telhami (eds), *International Organizations and Ethnic Conflict* (Ithaca and London: Cornell University Press, 1995), pp. 72–97.

Horowitz, D., 'Making Moderation Pay: The Comparative Politics of Ethnic Conflict Management', in J. V. Montville (ed.), *Conflict and Peacemaking in Multiethnic Societies* (New York: Lexington Books, 1991), pp. 451–75.

Johansen, R. C., 'Limits and Opportunities in Humanitarian Intervention', in S. Hoffman (ed.), *The Ethics and Politics of Humanitarian Intervention* (Notre Dame, IN: University of Notre Dame Press, 1996), pp. 61–86.

Krasner, S. D., *Sovereignty: Organized Hypocrisy* (Princeton, NJ: Princeton University Press, 1999).

Mertus, J., 'Back to the Drawing Board: Human Rights Should Know No Boundaries', *Washington Post*, 11 April 1999, Outlook Section.

Obradović, K., 'Medjunarodno humanitarno pravo i Kosovska kriza', *Medjunarodni problemi* year LI, no. 3–4 (August 1999), pp. 257–94.

O'Hanlon, M., 'Saving Lives with Force: When – and How – Should the United States Intervene to Stop Genocidal Wars?', *New Republic*, no. 4408 (12 July 1999), p. 21.

Phillips, R. L. and Cady, D. L., *Humanitarian Intervention: Just War vs. Pacifism* (Lanham, MD: Rowman & Littlefield Publishers, 1996).

Raiffa, H., *The Art and Science of Negotiation: How to Resolve Conflicts and Get the Best Out of Bargaining* (Cambridge, MA: Harvard University Press, 1982).

Roberts, A., 'NATO's "Humanitarian War" Over Kosovo', *Survival*, vol. 41, no. 3 (1999), pp. 103–123.

Schopflin, G., 'After the War', *Radio Free Europe/Radio Liberty*, 17 November 1999, Archive, at www.rferl.org.

Simma, B., 'NATO, the UN and the Use of Force: Legal aspects', *European Journal of International Law*, vol. 10, no. 2 (1999), pp. 1–22.

Spencer, M., 'Antiwar Hawks and Prowar Doves in the Gulf War', *Peace & Change*, vol. 17, issue 2 (April 1992), p. 172.

United Nations, 'Report of the Secretary-General Pursuant to General Assembly Resolution 53/35 (1998); The Fall of Srebrenica', A/54/549 (15 November 1999).

Walzer, M., *Just and Unjust Wars: A Moral Argument with Historical Illustrations* (New York: Basic Books, 1977).

Väyrynen, R., 'Challenges to Preventive Action: The Cases of Kosovo and Macedonia', unpublished manuscript (2000).

7

The Theory of Humanitarian Intervention with Special Regard to NATO's Kosovo Mission

Gábor Sulyok

The aim of this chapter is to discuss certain aspects of the controversial Kosovo mission of the North Atlantic Treaty Organization (NATO), codenamed Operation Allied Force, through the lens of international law, as well as to examine briefly the factual circumstances of the air operation in order to answer the question whether or not the world was facing a humanitarian intervention in March–June 1999. Much has been said, but less is known, about humanitarian intervention, a hotly debated, very special legal phenomenon that has been setting international lawyers against one another for a long period of time. For this reason, I consider it essential to outline the notion of humanitarian intervention and also to enumerate its unique characteristics within the framework of this chapter. Once these features are introduced, they can be applied to the 1998/9 Kosovo realities, thus the determination of the above mentioned question becomes possible.

THE THEORY OF HUMANITARIAN INTERVENTION

The theory of humanitarian intervention is directly linked to the international acceptance of particular standards of humanity (i.e., in this case, international human rights), and is based upon two assumptions. On one hand, a state has certain international obligations in relation to its own nationals; it may not treat them at its discretion and must guarantee them certain fundamental rights. On the other hand, massive and grave violations of these fundamental rights of human persons by any state concern all states of the international community, even if those are committed by a state vis-à-vis its own nationals.[1]

Even though a number of international lawyers go as far as denying the very existence of humanitarian intervention and to claim that this category has no *raison d'être* in contemporary international law, several scholars believe that this legal phenomenon does exist, furthermore – in the light of the horrible abuses of human rights taking place all over the world – there appears to be a definite need for its existence.

One of the most frequently cited definitions on humanitarian intervention was formulated by Hersch Lauterpacht, an outstanding authority of international law, according to whom:

> There is general agreement that, by virtue of its personal and territorial supremacy, a State can treat its own nationals according to discretion. But there is a substantial body of opinion and of practice in support of the view that there are limits to that discretion and that when a State renders itself guilty of cruelties against and persecution of its nationals in such a way as to deny their fundamental human rights and to shock the conscience of mankind, intervention in the interest of humanity is legally permissible.[2]

Two brief explanatory remarks should be added to this definition. Firstly, it can be regarded only as a segment of a broader definition of the phrase 'humanitarian intervention', which – besides the actions of external actors – also embraces situations in which a state resorts to force in order to provide protection to its *own* nationals when fundamental human rights of these persons are gravely violated outside the borders of its territory by another state.[3] This view is, however, shared by only a few experts,[4] whereas most international lawyers claim that such an action is not a humanitarian intervention, but rather a manifestation of self-help, or – according to a legally somewhat incorrect position – self-defence on behalf of the intervening state. My second remark is that this theoretical, introductory part deals exclusively with the contemporary notion of humanitarian intervention. It should be borne in mind that the concept itself has undergone considerable changes in the past, an evolution that falls outside the scope of the present analysis which focuses on an event of the very recent past.

As for the ground of humanitarian intervention, various views are in existence. The common denominators of these are as follows. First, there have to be large-scale violations of extreme gravity of fundamental human rights. Secondly, these violations have to be committed by public authorities rather than by individuals. Notwithstanding, violations perpetrated by individuals may also serve as a ground in case the territorial state fails to fulfil its obligation to put a stop to atrocities. It must be stressed that the category of fundamental human rights is far from being precisely defined. It constitutes one of the most debated segments of the notion of humanitarian intervention, and any attempt to establish an exhaustive enumeration of these rights seems to be virtually impossible.

Humanitarian interventions are usually classified into three groups with respect to the number and quality of subjects carrying them out. Nowadays, humanitarian interventions can and should be carried out by an international organization of universal nature (i.e., the United Nations). Such interventions are generally recognized without any special conditions, in view of the fact that the required legality is provided by a resolution of the competent organ of the organization (i.e., UN Security Council), and – because of the universal cooperation of states within the framework of the organization – the risk of abuse of the right of intervention is negligible (e.g., UNOSOM II, Somalia, 1993/5). An ad hoc or a permanent group of states (i.e., international organizations other than the UN) can also carry out a humanitarian intervention which, for the time being, is legally acceptable exclusively on condition that the UN Security Council issues an authorization thereto, usually when the UN itself is not available for a particular action, and the aim of the involvement is merely to put an end to atrocities (e.g., Bosnia and Herzegovina, 1995). Intervention by one or more unauthorized state, even within the framework of an international organization – a so-called 'unilateral humanitarian intervention' – is generally looked at with extreme disfavour, and is unacceptable under contemporary international law. However, instances of such actions can be found in recent history (e.g., India in Pakistan, 1971).

To conclude the brief theoretical analysis of the doctrine of humanitarian intervention, as well as to summarize and complete the enumeration of the main features thereof, the following general characteristics can be listed:[5]

1. Only large-scale and grave violations of fundamental human rights committed or permitted by public authorities may serve as sufficient grounds for a humanitarian intervention. The atrocities have to reach a certain, yet clearly and universally indefinable gravity. A single international crime (e.g., genocide, torture, apartheid, etc.), or a blatant abuse of a particular human right (e.g., right to life, non-discrimination, etc.) cannot be declared as *the* ground for action. There is, however, a vague term used by several scholars (e.g., Lauterpacht and Manouchehr Ganji[6]) and international documents (e.g., the 1998 Rome Statute of the International Criminal Court[7]) that may serve as a scale for this purpose. According to this, the carnage must 'shock the conscience of mankind'.
2. At least a group of states, but desirably a universal international organization, should carry out the action in order to eliminate concerns of an abusive intervention. Unilateral interventions are, therefore, to be avoided. There being no customary right of humanitarian intervention, an authorization by the UN Security Council is essential for the legality of the action, a condition to be discussed in more detail later.

3. The primary aim of the intervention must be of humanitarian nature: it is the cornerstone of legitimacy, as opposed to legality provided by the Security Council. However, according to realistic views expressed by some observers, such as Fred Halliday,[8] intervening states may also have other motivations besides the primary humanitarian purposes, for having only humanitarian considerations would be a condition impossible to meet. With a bit of cynicism one may say that altruism has never been a particularly ordinary behaviour-pattern of states.

4. The intervention must be a response given to extreme necessities raised by a humanitarian catastrophe and proportional to the gravity and quality of atrocities to be halted. The requirement of proportionality is twofold. It contains both the proportionality of means (i.e., observation of international humanitarian law), and the proportionality of duration (i.e., once the goals are achieved, the action should be terminated).

5. During the intervention the right of self-determination of the people of the target state must be respected. Consequently, under the veil of an intervention the political, economic, social or cultural systems of a state may not be forcibly altered. When assessing this feature, theoretical problems may nevertheless arise due to the fact that the concept of self-determination is not absolutely clear in international law.

6. Prior to the use of force all other possible remedies to the situation, especially peaceful measures, have to be used in good faith and prove ineffective.

LEGAL CONCERNS REGARDING NATO'S OPERATION ALLIED FORCE

It might be seen as an irony of fate that some of the earliest humanitarian interventions also took place in the Balkans, with the aim of protecting religious minorities against the atrocities of the Ottoman Empire in the mid- and late-nineteenth century.[9] It is quite obvious though that the European great powers used the notion of humanitarian intervention to disguise their efforts to push the Ottoman Empire out of the Balkans, to expand their influence over the region, and to gain domestic public support for their goals. However, these actions of the 'European Concert' also served to improve conditions for the Christian minorities and the halting of atrocities committed against them, thus it is fair to say that they were humanitarian in nature. A little more than 150 years later, further humanitarian interventions took place in the Balkans: in Bosnia and Herzegovina in 1992/5 and in Kosovo, Federal Republic of Yugoslavia in 1999.

Since the time of the first humanitarian interventions, however, many factors have changed. Following the adoption of the United Nations Charter in 1945 a new era began in international law, in which the former principle of *ius ad bellum* ceased to exist and the relations within the international community were put on the basis of peace and friendship. Member states of the United Nations undertook such solemn obligations as not to use force or threat of force against, and not to interfere with the internal affairs of, any other state; they also obliged themselves to settle their disputes by peaceful means, as well as to respect one another's sovereign equality.

There are only two exceptions to the comprehensive obligation not to use force or threaten to use force enacted in the UN Charter. Firstly, according to Article 42 of the Charter:

> Should the Security Council consider that measures provided for in Article 41 would be inadequate or have proved to be inadequate, it may take such action by air, sea, or land forces as may be necessary to maintain or restore international peace and security. Such action may include demonstrations, blockade, and other operations by air, sea, or land forces of Members of the United Nations.[10]

Secondly, although it is somewhat beside the point of our topic, Article 51 provides for 'the inherent right of individual or collective self-defence if an armed attack occurs against a member of the United Nations'.[11] (Evidently, the FRY was in a state of self-defence vis-à-vis NATO, during the air operation.)

It is well known that in the case of Kosovo NATO had not been in possession of an authorization by the Security Council when it launched its air operation. This fact per se implies that NATO violated the most fundamental rules of international law, and bears international responsibility for its actions. On the other hand, international responsibility undeniably arose on the side of the FRY, and – in the form of international criminal responsibility – on the side of its leaders as well, for the campaign of atrocities against the Kosovo Albanians. Thus, it seems that neither of the parties of the conflict were blameless, and both of them violated international law.[12]

'Who is to blame then?' This oversimplified question is asked by people throughout the world. Given that the FRY filed several applications in the Court's Registry on 29 April 1999 concerning the legality of the use of force, coming to a decision on this extremely complex question is now the task of the International Court of Justice (ICJ). In its applications, the FRY claimed that Belgium, Canada, France, Germany, Italy, the Netherlands, Portugal, Spain, the United Kingdom and the United States had respectively committed the following acts:[13] violation of the obligation not to use force against another state (act of aggression); violation of the obligation not to intervene in the internal affairs of another state; violation of the obligation not to violate the sovereignty of another state; violation of the obligation to protect the civilian population and civilian objectives (as well as historical monuments, works of art or places of worship) in wartime; violation of the obligation to protect the environment; violation of the obligation relating to free navigation on international rivers; violation of the obligation regarding fundamental human rights and freedoms; violation of the obligation not to use prohibited weapons; violation of the obligation not to inflict conditions of life calculated to cause the physical destruction of a national group (crime of genocide).

One does not need to be a legal expert to understand how serious these charges are, although some of them – such as the crime of genocide – are manifestly ill-founded. In principle, the so-called 'Yugoslavia cases' seem to leave no room for defence and make it appear to be quite futile. However, coming to a decision condemning NATO is not simple at all – not in theory, but especially not in practice. For lack of prima facie jurisdiction the ICJ rejected the Yugoslav request for provisional measures and, for the same reason (i.e., lack of jurisdiction), it dismissed the cases against the United States and Spain.[14] As a matter of fact, it is very likely that a definitive decision will never be made in the rest of the cases. This suspicion is reinforced by the piece of information that, following the democratic changes in autumn 2000, the Minister for Foreign Affairs of the FRY, in a letter addressed to the ICJ, dated 18 January 2001, requested 'a stay of the proceedings or ... to extend the time limit for the submission of observations of Yugoslavia, for a period of twelve months'.[15] In possession of the defendant countries' consent, the Court admitted the request in 2001 and a further extension in 2002, suggesting that in the light of democratic changes in Yugoslavia the case is unlikely to be pursued.

Let us examine now, whether or not NATO's Kosovo involvement was really a legitimate humanitarian intervention in the light of the working definition of the phrase outlined above. (An interesting addendum is that only the Kingdom of Belgium used the concept of humanitarian intervention in its arguing before the ICJ,[16] as it evidently cannot establish international legality.) It is advisable to examine the characteristics of humanitarian intervention point by point, and observe if the factual circumstances of Operation Allied Force fit into the prerequisites thereof.

In Kosovo, large-scale and grave violations of fundamental human rights were, beyond any reasonable doubt, perpetrated by Serbian authorities (i.e., police and military forces), or encouraged thereby (see the activities of paramilitary forces). In support of this statement I would like to draw attention to the vast number of international reports and resolutions dealing with the Kosovo situation.[17] These documents, issued by a variety of intergovernmental organizations, such as various organs of the UN, the Organization for Security and Cooperation in Europe, the Council of Europe and by several non-governmental organizations, such as Amnesty International or the Human Rights Watch, painted a picture of a massive, constantly intensifying police and military campaign against Kosovo

Albanians, including *inter alia* summary executions, indiscriminate and widespread attacks on civilians, indiscriminate and widespread destruction of property (e.g., shelling and burning of Albanian dwellings), mass forced displacement of civilians, torture and other cruel, inhuman or degrading treatment. The violence seems even more revolting if one recalls that the former Yugoslavia used to be a 'prize state' regarding the number of ratifications and accessions to major international human rights treaties.

In proof of their objectivity, the rapporteurs had not failed to condemn the repugnant acts of violence (e.g., taking of hostages, raids against Serbian police and military forces and even against non-combatants) perpetrated by armed, ethnic Albanian groups, and qualified by Serbs as terrorist activities. Members of the UÇK (Kosova Liberation Army: KLA) are also indisputably responsible for a number of serious criminal acts, however, the gravity thereof is simply incomparable with those committed systematically – within the framework of the alleged Operation Horseshoe – by Yugoslav armed forces. Unspeakable acts of violence took place in numerous villages, towns and cities in Kosovo. Nevertheless, 'it is noteworthy that, apart from Racak, the date of perpetration of each criminal act fell after 24 March [1999]'.[18]

The extreme gravity of atrocities is also well illustrated by the fact that on 22 May 1999, Louise Arbour, former Prosecutor of the International Criminal Tribunal for the Former Yugoslavia (ICTY) indicted then President Slobodan Milošević and four other high-ranking political and military leaders for crimes against humanity and violations of the laws and customs of war.[19] For quite some time it had seemed that the indictment would never be followed by substantial trial. However, on 29 June 2001, the Serbian Government – causing a minor, domestic, legal and political turmoil – transferred the former president (arrested on 1 April 2001 by local authorities) to The Hague, thereby removing the only obstacle which had stood in the way of proceedings.

The most expedient way to illustrate the extreme gravity of human rights violations is to evoke statistical data from unbiased sources. Just weeks before the commencement of air strikes, in late January 1999, the number of internally displaced persons within Kosovo was around 180,000 to 200,000, whereas another 50,000 sought refuge in other parts of Serbia.[20] Unquestionable is the fact – although the parties to the conflict offer contradictory explanations thereto – that the flood of refugees intensified during NATO's intervention. Hence the humanitarian situation, by the end of May 1999, looked as follows: 230,000 refugees fled to the Former Yugoslav Republic of Macedonia (FYROM), 430,000 refugees sought refuge in Albania and about 64,000 in Montenegro. A further 21,500 people ran to Bosnia and Herzegovina and more than 61,000 were evacuated into other, non-neighbouring countries, including several western states. Roughly

580,000 people were internally displaced within Kosovo. In total, by the end of May, approximately 1.5 million people (i.e., 90 per cent of the overall population of the troubled province) were forced to leave their homes. After the cessation of hostilities, nearly 225,000 Kosovar were declared missing, while the number of casualties of killings was put at 5,000.[21] Additionally, an investigation carried out by humanitarian organizations, as early as late-1998, concluded that only 40 per cent of all houses in Kosovo were habitable, while 30 per cent were partially or totally destroyed[22] – percentages that constantly increased as time passed.

Testimonies of survivors and refugees have also confirmed that the gravity of atrocities – which were very similar to those that had been committed earlier in Bosnia and Herzegovina – reached the magnitude and quality of an ethnic cleansing, a policy generally regarded as a form of the abhorrent crime of genocide.[23] Whether Serbian activities amounted to one of the arch-crimes of international law, we still may not certainly know for a number of legal reasons. Some sources were and are convinced that the Serbian campaign in the province was indeed an ethnic cleansing (i.e., genocide),[24] while other commentators, such as the German Bruno Simma, doubt it.[25] Surprising as it may seem, the determination of whether the acts of Yugoslav authorities reached the gravity of genocide, or only constituted a lesser crime, is of no key importance in our case. The atrocities undoubtedly shocked the 'conscience of mankind', and therefore provided a satisfactory ground for a humanitarian intervention.

As is widely known, the United Nations was unavailable for the intervention, as the probable Russian and Chinese vetoes would have hampered any attempt of action under the UN Charter. The lack of prior Security Council authorization is the legal Achilles heel of Operation Allied Force, and suggests that the action commenced – but was not necessarily conducted – in breach of international law.

Operation Allied Force, if seen as a humanitarian intervention, was both an intervention by a group of states and a unilateral one, and as such, the requirements of absolute impartiality and proportionality need to be thoroughly examined. As for impartiality, one should recall the conditions set out by NATO for halting the air strikes: end of all military actions in Kosovo; withdrawal of military forces; acceptance of an international military presence in Kosovo; return of all refugees and displaced persons to their homes; humanitarian aid organizations to be allowed access to refugees and assurances given by the FRY of its willingness to achieve a political settlement of the crisis.[26] Suffice it to say that these goals and the pursuance thereof seem to be in support of NATO's impartiality, although the Alliance certainly had other motivations as well (e.g., security reasons, credibility, etc.). Nevertheless, it should be noted that the Alliance significantly contributed to the humanitarian relief activities (Operation Sustain Hope).

In light of the flagrant violations of human rights, and the massive flood of refugees, a state of extreme humanitarian necessity probably existed, however – in contrast to the opinion of Belgium presented to the ICJ[27] – it did not arise on the side of the NATO countries, but rather with respect to Albania and the FYROM. Kosovo Albanians, too, were definitely in a state of necessity, but in the ordinary and not technical, legal sense of the word, which in every case is related to states rather than peoples. Therefore, and especially taking into account the definition of necessity elaborated by the International Law Commission,[28] any referral to the doctrine of necessity in defence of NATO is, in this case, misleading and unfounded.

Answering the question whether Operation Allied Force was conducted in a lawful way is a difficult task. Throughout the air campaign NATO officials repeatedly claimed that the Alliance was attacking only military or military-related targets. However, some of the targets – and I am not referring to the so-called 'collateral damage' now but rather, for example, to Tornik ski resort on Mount Zlatibor, or to the city power plant in the town of Krusevac[29] – gave rise to legal concerns.

The charge concerning the use of prohibited weapons raises similar dilemmas. The use of certain means of warfare, such as cluster bombs, could readily be considered illegal. A number of international conventions, as well as the so-called 'Martens Clause' provide for the obligation not to use such indiscriminate weapons. The most serious concerns, however, are linked to the use of weapons containing depleted uranium which, at least to some extent, unquestionably damaged the environment. In March 2000, NATO confirmed that it had used approximately 31,000 rounds of such ammunition in over 100 bombing sorties throughout Kosovo. According to the Balkans Task Force (BTF) – an international body set up by the United Nations Environment Programme (UNEP) and the United Nations Centre for Human Settlements (UNCHS/Habitat) in May 1999 to evaluate the environmental aftermath of the Kosovo conflict – the pieces of information provided by the Alliance are insufficient for a proper assessment of the environmental and health consequences caused by the use of this kind of ammunition.[30]

It should be underlined that the destruction of certain chemical and other industrial facilities also polluted and damaged the environment and caused far-reaching, as yet not exactly known, harmful effects. A 1999 report prepared by the BTF concluded that the war over Kosovo had not caused an environmental catastrophe, however at four locations (Pancevo, Kragujevac, Novi Sad and Bor) the detected rate of pollution was significant and posed a threat to human health.[31]

Due to the public outcry surrounding the issue of alleged violations of international humanitarian law, a special committee was set up on 14 May 1999 by the Prosecutor of the ICTY to assess the allegations of war crimes, and determine if there was a basis to initiate an investigation. The committee concluded that

> NATO has admitted that mistakes did occur during the bombing campaign; errors of judgement may also have occurred. Selection of certain objectives for attack may be subject to legal debate. … On the basis of information available, the committee recommends that no investigation be commenced by the OTP [Office of the Prosecutor] in relation to the NATO bombing campaign or incidents during the campaign.[32]

The right to self-determination of the people of the FRY was generally respected throughout the air operation. The NATO involvement neither altered the political, economic, social or cultural systems of the FRY, nor was it carried out to provide support for the UÇK, or to forcibly overthrow the Milošević regime. However, misinterpretation of particular events that took place after Operation Allied Force, such as the democratic changes in autumn 2000, can lead to the opposite conclusion, despite that the intervention was probably not a *conditio sine qua non* thereof. NATO was obviously not militarily promoting the objectives of armed Albanian extremists either (that is, an independent Kosovo, that could have been a first step towards a Greater Albania), but pursued and observed its original, separate goals, which have been enumerated above. Accordingly, NATO was not an 'ally' of the UÇK, as it had been qualified by Serbs, and often even in the media during the bombings. If one recalls the policy of refusal that the Alliance adopted towards extremist Albanians in the evolving Macedonian crisis in early 2001, this statement gains credible confirmation.

Taking into account *inter alia* the numerous Security Council resolutions, the agreements of October 1998, the activity of the UN Secretary-General and of the G8 countries, as well as of the Contact Group, and in the light of the Rambouillet and the follow-on Paris talks, it is fair to say that all peaceful measures had been taken, and had proven to be ineffective prior to the use of force. Although a detailed examination of the diplomatic efforts preceding Operation Allied Force falls outside the scope of the present chapter, it should be mentioned that suspicions have been voiced concerning the conduct of the Contact Group and its good faith throughout the period of diplomatic negotiations. The relevant concerns point out that draft provisions of the Rambouillet Accords were formulated in such a way as to make them unacceptable for the FRY from the very beginning, and therefore paved the way for the air strikes.

To conclude the analysis focusing on the humanitarian nature of Operation Allied Force, I believe it can be declared that the action was indeed a legitimate humanitarian intervention, although – as the American scholar

Richard A. Falk wrote – it was a 'badly flawed' one.[33] This conclusion, however, does not dispel the legal concerns, especially the one related to the lack of Security Council authorization. Due to the absence thereof, further examinations are required in order to shed some more light on the issue of the legality and legitimacy of NATO's mission.

SELECTED LEGAL ARGUMENTS IN FAVOUR OF OPERATION ALLIED FORCE

Arguments with Respect to an Authorization by the UN Security Council

As I have mentioned, most of the legal concerns in connection with Operation Allied Force are directly linked to the absence of the Security Council's authorization issued under Chapter VII (Article 42) of the UN Charter. Although the Council did not adopt any resolutions in which it gave an *explicit* authorization to implement forcible enforcement actions against the FRY, it adopted several others that should be examined. The wording of these documents left room for certain assumptions that the Security Council did in fact give an authorization for the air strikes, but its approval was put in an *implicit* or, according to a different view, an *ex post facto* form.[34]

First, let us consider the idea of an implicit authorization. The Council was acting under Chapter VII of the UN Charter – entitled 'Action With Respect to Threats to the Peace, Breaches of the Peace, and Acts of Aggression' – as it adopted its resolutions with respect to the crisis in Kosovo. In its resolution 1160 it stated, 'that failure to make constructive progress towards the peaceful resolution of the situation in Kosovo will lead to the consideration of additional measures'.[35] The wording 'additional measures', according to a number of experts, might have been a reference to a future armed enforcement action under Chapter VII of the UN Charter. In its subsequent resolution 1199 the Council declared that the situation in Kosovo posed 'a threat to peace and security in the region'.[36] Further provisions of this resolution also prove that the UN and NATO shared the same concerns and held out the prospect of the use of force in case the crisis continued in Kosovo: 'should the concrete measures demanded ... not be taken, [the Security Council is] to consider further action and additional measures to maintain or restore international peace and stability in the region'.[37]

This provision, according to Klaus Kinkel, Germany's Foreign Minister in office at the time, made resolution 1199 a 'springboard resolution' (i.e., for NATO to intervene). Javier Solana, NATO Secretary-General at that time, seemed to share this view:

... I conclude that the Allies believe that in the particular circumstances with respect to the present crisis in Kosovo as described in UNSC resolution 1199, there are legitimate grounds for the Alliance to threaten, and if necessary, to use force.[38]

Note that Mr Solana used the word 'legitimate' instead of 'legal'.

Prior to Operation Allied Force the Security Council also adopted a third resolution, in which it *inter alia* repeated its previous demands and reaffirmed that the 'unresolved situation in Kosovo, Federal Republic of Yugoslavia, constitutes a continuing threat to peace and security in the region'.[39]

At a press conference in January, UN Secretary-General, Kofi Annan, when answering a question regarding the possibilities of use of force against the FRY said: 'Normally a UN Security Council resolution is required'.[40] The use of the word 'normally' indicates that the Secretary-General, having spoken on behalf of the UN, seemed to support a possible NATO action politically, although he must have been aware that the necessary Council resolution, due to a probable Russian and/or Chinese veto, was practically impossible to adopt.

Those, who advance arguments in favour of an *ex post facto* authorization claim that the Security Council expressed its approval of Operation Allied Force by remaining 'still' after the commencement of the air operation. There are particularly powerful arguments in favour of this view. On 26 March 1999, only two days after the air strikes had begun, Russia – along with Belarus and India – submitted to the Security Council a draft resolution condemning the NATO action.[41] An overwhelming majority of Council members rejected the proposal: the initiative failed by twelve votes to three (i.e., by four-fifths of the members of the Council).

In its resolution 1244 of 10 June 1999,[42] providing for the post-war settlement of the Kosovo crisis, the Council also refrained from condemning NATO's action. Moreover, resolution 1244 presents us with an interesting legal and logical dilemma. The principle of the obligation not to use or threaten to use force states that the results of aggression shall not, under any circumstances, be recognized as lawful. What the Security Council did by adopting this resolution was a clear recognition and exploitation of the outcome of Operation Allied Force, an action that was *prima facie* an act of aggression, since it lacked the necessary approval by the Council. If the air operation was indeed an act of aggression, then the Council adopted the resolution at issue in breach of international law. But if the Council acted lawfully, then Operation Allied Force – logically – had not been, could not have been, an act of aggression.

Finally, Article 2 of the UN General Assembly resolution 3314(XXIX) on the Definition of Aggression can also be cited in indirect support of an *ex post facto* authorization:

> The first use of armed force by a State in contravention of the Charter shall constitute *prima facie* evidence of an act of aggression although the Security Council may, in conformity with the Charter, *conclude that a determination that an act of aggression has been committed would not be justified* in the light of other relevant circumstances, including the fact that the acts concerned or their consequences are not of sufficient gravity.[43]

The question is whether or not the Council can, under this article, express such a conclusion by refraining from adopting a resolution that condemns a particular use of force, and qualifies it as an act of aggression.

UN General Assembly resolution 377A (v) – also and better known as the 'Uniting for Peace' resolution – could also have been used by NATO to obtain at least *some* legality for its Kosovo mission. According to the relevant provisions of this controversial resolution, the General Assembly:

> Resolves that if the Security Council, because of lack of unanimity of the permanent members, fails to exercise its primary responsibility for the maintenance of international peace and security in any case where there appears to be a threat to the peace, breach of the peace, or act of aggression, the General Assembly shall consider the matter immediately with a view to making appropriate recommendations to Members for collective measures, including in the case of a breach of the peace or act of aggression the use of armed force when necessary, to maintain or restore international peace and security.[44]

Being a resolution of the General Assembly, a recommendation under the 'Uniting for Peace' resolution is not legally binding, however, because it supposedly expresses the will of the international community, any action based upon it – although lacking the authorization of the Security Council – would raise far less serious legal concerns than Operation Allied Force did, the way it happened. The only problem concerning this resolution is that it requires a 'breach of the peace' or 'an act of aggression' for a recommendation to use force – situations that are incompatible with domestic violations of human rights, which seem to fit only in the category of 'threat to the peace'. Note, furthermore, that this resolution could have been resorted to not only by, but also vis-à-vis NATO. Suppose that the international community fiercely opposed the air operation, but was unable to condemn it in the Security Council due to the 'Allied veto'. Why did it fail then to convene an emergency special session of the General Assembly to seek condemnation of Operation Allied Force?

Resorting to the Theory of International Law in Support of NATO's Action

The aim of every humanitarian intervention is to provide protection for individuals whose fundamental human rights are gravely violated en masse. Although human rights constitute a relatively new category in international law, some segments thereof undoubtedly possess the characteristics of *ius cogens*. However, in cases like Kosovo, human rights seem to be in conflict with some of the traditional *ius cogens* norms of international law, such as the obligation not to use force, the principle of non-intervention or the obligation to respect the sovereign equality of states.

Whether or not human rights – on the basis of the principle *lex posteriori derogat lex priori* – prevail over these traditional, older *ius cogens* norms cannot be determined at present. It is extremely doubtful if there can even be a genuine conflict between these fundamental norms, since they all point towards the same goals. Many tend to celebrate the beginning of a new era in international law in which human rights constitute some kind of a 'supreme' law. I respectfully disagree with this idealistic view. I am convinced that human rights will gain more importance, but may never rise above other *ius cogens* norms of international law. State sovereignty will remain the hardcore of law, despite the fact that it is likely to be considerably restricted by human rights. This is why Operation Allied Force, as it was, will probably not constitute a precedent for further humanitarian actions to come.

Nevertheless, the definition of *ius cogens*, as contained in Article 53 of the Vienna Convention on the Law of Treaties, does not rule out future changes of these norms:

> ... [A] peremptory norm of general international law is a norm accepted and recognized by the international community of States as a whole as a norm from which no derogation is permitted and which can be modified only by a subsequent norm of general international law having the same character.[45]

The second argument is, in fact, a reference to a famous principle of law that is generally agreed upon and has existed since ancient times: *summum ius, summa iniuria*. The principle was established as a reply to a serious legal problem; an overly rigid application of a legal rule might result in unjust situations, a phenomenon which, of course, should be avoided. Thus, under certain unique circumstances, but especially when there is a 'gap' in law, justice may prevail over the rule of law. NATO's intervention in Kosovo could have been an example of justice prevailing over law.

CONCLUDING REMARKS

The aim of this chapter has been to outline the doctrine of humanitarian intervention, as well as to apply its special characteristics to NATO's Operation Allied Force in order to determine whether or not the circumstances of use of force can be fit therein. I believe, in the light of the working definition of the phrase outlined in the first part, it has become evident that NATO's Kosovo mission was basically a genuine humanitarian intervention; therefore it was a legitimate action. Nevertheless, with respect to international legality, one cannot make a similarly positive statement. The fact that the air operation commenced without prior authorization by the UN Security Council, and conducted in a 'badly flawed' (sometimes excessive) manner gave rise to extremely serious legal concerns, moreover it provided a legal ground for the FRY to file applications at the ICJ against certain NATO member states. This controversial action touched one of the most sensitive points of the present international system established upon the Charter of the United Nations. The general lesson of the crisis in and around Kosovo is, I think, as follows: the international community has to come to a consensus on humanitarian intervention.[46]

For the time being, a humanitarian intervention is lawful only if the Security Council has previously authorized it. Consequently – since legality is attributed to an appropriate resolution of the Council – it is more or less irrelevant how we characterize and describe a particular use of force: 'enforcement action' or 'humanitarian intervention'. In such an approach, humanitarian intervention is being dissolved in the comprehensive category of the prohibition of the use of force; in other words, it is unlawful if there is no Council authorization. However, the Security Council is frequently paralysed (usually in the worst cases like Kosovo) due to the lack of unanimity of its permanent members; a problem, which cannot be ignored as being insignificant in the future, not even in the short term. Current conditions leave unauthorized states willing to help an oppressed population with two options: either to stay idle or to override the disabled Council in breach of international law. What to do in a situation when the principle of the rule of law is in contradiction with the fundamental requirements of justice? Armed conflicts, such as the one under discussion, have shown the world that casting the contemporary system of international law in concrete, on the basis of the rule of law, may go to the opposite extreme compared with the benevolent effects it has been calculated to result in. However, it is not only a non-regulated, persistent 'Kosovo-like' state practice, but also an inadequate (hypothetical) legal regulation of humanitarian intervention, which is likely to undermine the fragile system of peaceful and friendly cooperation of states. Thus, even though changes are certainly essential in the field of the forcible protection – or rather enforcement – of human rights, these changes have to be very cautiously elaborated and introduced. As a result of this rationale, it is doubtful that Operation Allied Force will ever constitute a precedent: it should remain an isolated action, as it was meant to be.

Finally, for the particular case of Kosovo, it can be stated that NATO's controversial air operation paved the way for a lawful and legitimate international involvement in the settling of the crisis via KFOR and UNMIK. Paradoxical as it may sound, Operation Allied Force can be seen as a first step towards peace in the Balkans. Years after the cessation of hostilities, the international community has still the very same, complicated tasks ahead as it faced in June 1999: deterring renewed hostilities and preventing 'reverse ethnic cleansing'; establishing and maintaining a secure environment in and around the province; reintegrating former combatants into civilian life; improving the humanitarian conditions and helping the further return of refugees, as well as preparing Kosovo and the entire region for a peaceful future.

NOTES

1. See M. Ganji, *International Protection of Human Rights* (Geneva and Paris: Librairie E. Droz – Librairie Minard, 1962), p. 9.
2. L. Oppenheim, in H. Lauterpacht (ed.), *International Law: A Treatise* (London: Longmans Green & Co., 1955), p. 312. See also G. Sulyok, 'Humanitarian Intervention: A Historical and Theoretical Overview', *Acta Juridica Hungarica*, vol. 41, no. 1–2 (2000), pp. 79–109.
3. See, for instance, Israel's hostage rescue mission in Entebbe in 1976 (Operation Jonathan), or the United States' unsuccessful military action in Iran in 1980 (Operation Eagle Claw).
4. This broader view is more common to the American legal doctrine, whereas in Europe lawyers tend to treat the forceful protection of own nationals separately from humanitarian intervention. In the relevant literature see *inter alia* R. B. Lillich (ed.), *Humanitarian Intervention and the United Nations* (Charlottesville: University Press of Virginia, 1973), pp. 22–3; L. Henkin, R. C. Pugh, O. Schachter and H. Smit, *International Law: Cases and Materials* (St Paul, MN: West Publishing Co., 1980), pp. 922–4; U. Beyerlin, 'Humanitarian Intervention', in R. Bernhardt (ed.), *Encyclopedia of Public International Law* (Amsterdam: North-Holland Publishing Company, 1982), p. 212.
5. Concerning the characteristics of humanitarian intervention see, for instance, A. Cassese, '*Ex iniuria ius non oritur*: Are We Moving towards International Legitimation of Forcible Humanitarian Countermeasures in the World Community?', *European Journal of International Law*, vol. 10, no. 1 (1999), p. 27; J. I. Charney, 'Anticipatory Humanitarian Intervention in Kosovo', *American Journal of International Law*, vol. 93, no. 4 (October 1999), pp. 838–40; Danish Institute of International Affairs, *Humanitarian Intervention. Legal and Political Aspects* (Copenhagen: DUPI, 1999), pp. 103–11; Lillich, *Humanitarian Intervention and the United Nations*, e.g., pp. 49–50; T. Malanczuk, *Humanitarian Intervention and the Legitimacy to Use Force* (Amsterdam: Het Spinhuis Publishers, 1993), pp. 3–6; S. D. Murphy, *Humanitarian Intervention. The United*

Nations in an Evolving World Order (Philadelphia, PA: University of Pennsylvania Press, 1996), pp. 382–7.

6. See Oppenheim, *International Law: A Treatise*, p. 312; Ganji, *International Protection of Human Rights*, p. 13.

7. Rome Statute of the International Criminal Court, adopted by the UN Conference of Plenipotentiaries in Rome, 17 July 1998 (UN Doc. A/CONF.183/9, as corrected by the *procés-verbaux* of 10 November 1998 and 12 July 1999), preamble.

8. See N. Gordon and G. Wirick, 'Humanitarian Intervention as an Instrument of Human Rights', *The Agenda for Change Papers*, United Nations Association in Canada, at www.unac.org/unreform/gordon.html (March 1996), endnote 11.

9. For a detailed account of these interventions, see Ganji, *International Protection of Human Rights*, pp. 17–38.

10. Charter of the United Nations, Article 42.

11. Ibid., Article 51.

12. See Richard A. Falk's theory on 'double condemnation', in R. A. Falk, 'Kosovo, World Order and the Future of International Law', *American Journal of International Law*, vol. 93, no. 4 (October 1999), p. 848.

13. See ICJ, Case concerning the Legality of Use of Force (Yugoslavia vs. Belgium), (Yugoslavia vs. Canada), (Yugoslavia vs. France), (Yugoslavia vs. Germany), (Yugoslavia vs. Italy), (Yugoslavia vs. Netherlands), (Yugoslavia vs. Portugal), (Yugoslavia vs. Spain), (Yugoslavia vs. United Kingdom), (Yugoslavia vs. United States). Application Instituting Proceedings, 29 April 1999.

14. See ICJ, Case concerning the Legality of Use of Force (Yugoslavia vs. Spain), (Yugoslavia vs. United States). Request for the Indication of Provisional Measures, Order, 2 June 1999.

15. See ICJ, Case concerning the Legality of Use of Force (Yugoslavia vs. Belgium), (Yugoslavia vs. Canada), (Yugoslavia vs. France), (Yugoslavia vs. Germany), (Yugoslavia vs. Italy), (Yugoslavia vs. Netherlands), (Yugoslavia vs. Portugal), (Yugoslavia vs. United Kingdom). Order, 21 February 2001.

16. See ICJ, Case concerning the Legality of Use of Force (Yugoslavia vs. Belgium). Public sitting held on Monday 10 May 1999 at 3 p.m. at the Peace Palace, Verbatim Record, CR 99/15 (translation, uncorrected).

17. See *inter alia*, UN Secretary-General: Report of the Secretary-General, 4 December 1998, UN Doc. S/1998/1147; Report of the Secretary-General prepared pursuant to resolutions 1160 (1998), 1199 (1998) and 1203 (1998) of the Security Council, 24 December 1998, UN Doc. S/1998/1221; Report of the Secretary-General prepared pursuant to resolutions 1160 (1998), 1199 (1998) and 1203 (1998) of the Security Council, 30 January 1999, UN Doc. S/1999/99; Report of the Secretary-General prepared pursuant to resolutions 1160 (1998), 1199 (1998) and 1203 (1998) of the Security Council, 17 March 1999, UN Doc. S/1999/293; UN General Assembly: GA Res. 52/139, 1 December 1997, UN Doc. A/RES/52/139; GA Res. 53/164, 9 December 1998, UN Doc. A/RES/53/164; *Organization for Security and Cooperation in Europe*: reports are typically reprinted in the reports of the UN Secretary-General; *Council of Europe*: 'Crisis in Kosovo and the Situation in the Federal Republic of Yugoslavia', Doc. 8309 (Opinion), 26 January 1999; 'Crisis in Kosovo and Situation in the Federal Republic of Yugoslavia', Doc. 8364 (Report), 29 March 1999; *Amnesty International*: Ljubenic and Poklek: 'Extrajudicial Executions, Excessive Use of Force and "Disappearances": A Pattern Repeated', July 1998, AI-index: EUR 70/046/1998; 'Deaths in Custody, Torture and Ill-treatment', June 1998, AI-index: EUR 70/034/1998 (each at www.amnesty.org); *Human Rights Watch*: 'A

Week of Terror in Drenica', February 1999; Report on the Massacre in Racak, January 1999 (each at www.hrw.org).

18. J. Juhász, I. Magyar, L. Valki and P. Tálas, *Koszovó: Egy válság anatómiája* (Budapest: Osiris Kiadó, 2000), p. 341.

19. Originally see Milošević et al., Indictment, Case No. IT-99-37, 22 May 1999. Those indicted are: Slobodan Milošević, President of the FRY; Milan Milutinovic, President of Serbia; Nikola Sainovic, Deputy Prime Minister of the FRY; Col. Gen. Dragoljub Ojdanic, Chief of the General Staff of the Yugoslav Armed Forces (VJ); and Vlajko Stojiljkovic, Minister of Internal Affairs of Serbia. Since then substantial changes have been introduced to the proceedings. For instance, the charges against former President Slobodan Milošević have been extended in order to include atrocities having been previously perpetrated in Croatia, and Bosnia and Herzegovina, as well. At present, the case – currently referred to as the 'Milošević Case, Case No. IT-02-54, Kosovo, Croatia, Bosnia and Herzegovina' – is being tried by Trial Chamber III, with Judge Richard May (UK) presiding. See furthermore Milutinovic et al., Case No. IT-99-37, 'Kosovo'.

20. See UN Inter-Agency Update on Kosovo Situation, 25 January 1999, para. 5–6.

21. Source: www.kforonline.com/resources/facts.htm. Furthermore '[a]ccording to [ICTY's] Chief Prosecutor, Carla del Ponte, since June 1999, the Tribunal investigators have dug up about 4,000 bodies from mass graves in Kosovo. She believes that it will never be possible to establish the exact number of victims ...' Belgrade Centre for Human Rights: Human Rights in Yugoslavia, 2000. 'Legal Provisions, Practice and Legal Consciousness in the Federal Republic of Yugoslavia Compared to International Human Rights Standards' (Belgrade, 2001), p. 352.

22. See UN 'Inter-Agency Update on Kosovo Situation', 26 November 1998, para. 13.

23. See GA Res. 47/121, 18 December 1992, UN Doc. A/RES/47/121, preamble.

24. For instance, Mary Robinson, UN High Commissioner for Human Rights, spoke about 'a pattern of ethnic cleansing carried out with cold-blooded determination'. See UN Press Release of 30 April 1999, UN Doc. HR/99/34. The UN Commission on Human Rights also strongly condemned Belgrade's Kosovo ethnic cleansing. See UN Doc. E/CN.4/1999/L.3/Rev. 1; UN Press Release of 13 April 1999, UN Doc. HR/CN/99/34.

25. B. Simma, 'NATO, the UN and the Use of Force: Legal Aspects', *European Journal International Law*, vol. 10, no. 1 (1999), p. 2.

26. See Press Statement by Dr Javier Solana, Secretary-General of NATO, 23 March 1999; Lord G. Robertson, *Kosovo One Year On. Achievement and Challenge* (NATO, 2000), p. 11. US Department of Defense: 'Kosovo/Operation Allied Force: After-action Report'. Report to Congress, 31 January 2000, pp. 8–9.

27. See ICJ, Case concerning the Legality of Use of Force (Yugoslavia vs. Belgium), Public sitting held on Monday, 10 May 1999 at 3 p.m. at the Peace Palace, verbatim record, CR 99/15 (translation, uncorrected).

28. See 'Draft Articles on Responsibility of States for Internationally Wrongful Acts' adopted by the International Law Commission at its 53rd session (2001), Article 25. (For the previous version, having existed at the time of the NATO air operation, see 'Draft Articles on State Responsibility'. Text provisionally adopted by the International Law Commission on first reading (1996), Article 33.)

29. ICJ, Case concerning the Legality of Use of Force (Yugoslavia vs. Belgium), (Yugoslavia vs. Canada), (Yugoslavia vs. France), (Yugoslavia vs. Germany), (Yugoslavia vs. Italy), (Yugoslavia vs. Netherlands), (Yugoslavia vs. Portugal), (Yugoslavia vs. Spain), (Yugoslavia vs. United Kingdom), (Yugoslavia vs. United

States). 'Request for the Indication of Provisional Measures concerning the Application of the Federal Republic of Yugoslavia for Violation not to Use Force', Belgrade, 28 April 1999.
30. Complete UN Kosovo coverage at www.un.org/peace/kosovo/news/kosovo2.htm (21 March 2000).
31. Ibid.
32. International Criminal Tribunal for the Former Yugoslavia. Final report to the prosecutor by the committee established to review the NATO bombing campaign against the Federal Republic of Yugoslavia. 9 June 2000. 39 I.L.M. 1257 (2000), para. 90–1.
33. See Falk, 'Kosovo, World Order and the Future of International Law', p. 856. Extremely sharp criticism was formulated by, for example, Noam Chomsky. See N. Chomsky, *The New Military Humanism. Lessons from Kosovo* (London: Pluto Press, 1999).
34. See Simma, *NATO, the UN and the Use of Force: Legal Aspects*, p. 4.
35. SC Res. 1160, 31 March 1998, UN Doc. S/RES/1160 (1998), para.19.
36. SC Res. 1199, 23 September 1998, UN Doc. S/RES/1199 (1998), preamble.
37. Ibid., para. 16.
38. Quoted in Simma, *NATO, the UN and the Use of Force: Legal Aspects*, p. 7.
39. SC Res. 1203, 24 October 1998, UN Doc. S/RES/1203 (1998), preamble.
40. Quoted in Simma, *NATO, the UN and the Use of Force: Legal Aspects*, p. 8.
41. Sovet Bezopasnoti: Belarus, Indijai Rossijsakja Federacija: Proket Resoljuncii, 26 March 1999, UN Doc. S/1999/328. See also, including the English text of the document, UN Press Release of 26 March 1999, UN Doc. SC/6659.
42. SC Res. 1244, 10 June 1999, UN Doc. S/RES/1244 (1999).
43. GA Res. 3314, 14 December 1974, UN Doc. A/RES/3314 (xxix), Annex, Definition of Aggression, Article 2 (emphasis added).
44. GA Res. 377A, 3 November 1950, UN Doc. A/RES/377A (v), para. 1.
45. Vienna Convention on the Law of Treaties, 23 May 1969, Article 53.
46. Statement of Professor Ramesh Thakur, United Nations University. Complete UN Kosovo Coverage at www.un.org/peace/kosovo/news/kosovo2.htm (21 March 2000).

REFERENCES

Belgrade Centre for Human Rights, *Human Rights in Yugoslavia, 2000. Legal Provisions, Practice and Legal Consciousness in the Federal Republic of Yugoslavia Compared to International Human Rights Standards* (Belgrade, 2001).

Beyerlin, U., 'Humanitarian Intervention', in Bernhart, R. (ed.), *Encyclopedia of Public International Law* (Amsterdam, New York and Oxford: North-Holland Publishing Company, 1982), pp. 211–15.

Cassese, A., '*Ex iniuria ius non oritur*: Are We Moving towards International Legitimation of Forcible Humanitarian Countermeasures in the World Community?', *European Journal of International Law*, vol. 10, no. 1 (1999), pp. 23–30.

Charney, J. I., 'Anticipatory Humanitarian Intervention in Kosovo', *American Journal of International Law*, vol. 93, no. 4 (October 1999), pp. 834–41.

Chomsky, N., *The New Military Humanism. Lessons from Kosovo* (London: Pluto Press, 1999).

Danish Institute of International Affairs, *Humanitarian Intervention. Legal and Political Aspects* (Copenhagen: DUPI, 1999).

Falk, R. A., 'Kosovo, World Order and the Future of International Law', *American*

Journal of International Law, vol. 93, no.4 (October 1999), pp. 847–57.

Ganji, M., *International Protection of Human Rights* (Geneva and Paris: Librairie E. Droz, Librairie Minard, 1962).

Gordon, N. and Wirick, G., 'Humanitarian Intervention as an Instrument of Human Rights', *The Agenda for Change Papers*, United Nations Association in Canada, at www.unac.org/unreform/gordon.html (March 1996).

Henkin, L., Pugh, R. C., Schachter, O. and Smit, H., *International Law: Cases and Materials* (St Paul, MN: West Publishing Co., 1980).

Juhász, J., Magyar, I., Valki, L. and Tálas, P., *Koszovó: Egy válság anatómiája* (Budapest: Osiris Kiadó, 2000).

Lillich, R. B. (ed.), *Humanitarian Intervention and the United Nations* (Charlottesville: University Press of Virginia, 1973).

Malanczuk, T., *Humanitarian Intervention and the Legitimacy to Use Force* (Amsterdam: Het Spinhuis Publishers, 1993).

Murphy, S. D., *Humanitarian Intervention. The United Nations in an Evolving World Order* (Philadelphia, PA: University of Pennsylvania Press, 1996).

Oppenheim, L., in H. Lauterpacht (ed.), *International Law: A Treatise*, vol. 1: Peace. Edn 8 (London: Longmans Green & Co., 1955).

Robertson of Port Ellen, Lord, *Kosovo One Year On: Achievement and Challenge* (NATO, 2000).

Simma, B., 'NATO, the UN and the Use of Force: Legal Aspects', *European Journal of International Law*, vol. 10, no. 1 (1999), pp. 1–22.

Sulyok, G., 'Humanitarian Intervention: A Historical and Theoretical Overview', *Acta Juridica Hungarica*, vol. 41, no. 1–2 (2000), pp. 79–109.

Weller, M., 'The Crisis in Kosovo 1989–1999: From the Dissolution of Yugoslavia to Rambouillet and the Outbreak of Hostilities', *International Documents & Analysis*, vol. 1 (Cambridge: Documents & Analysis Publishing Ltd, 1999).

8

War on Kosovo: A Victory for the Media?

Marina Blagojević

STATES-TO-BE AGAINST SOCIETY

Coming from Belgrade, where I have lived almost all my life, including during the catastrophic 1990s, I have learned very clearly that war can be created almost anywhere, at almost any time. I have also learned another absurd but nevertheless true lesson – that the lower the probability of war the easier the possibility of manufacturing it, because of the absence of systemic and structural mechanisms to prevent it. This has, I believe, been the true situation in all of the wars involving former Yugoslavia. They happened exactly because they did not need to happen, in a vacuum of determinism which gave too much authority to the powerholders while, at the same time, producing disbelief, confusion and distrust on the part of those who were powerless and predominately victimized. Wars (one war or several?) in former Yugoslavia were the wars of 'states-to-be' against society. The problem was that there were too many 'states-to-be' and only one society which 'needed to be' ripped apart.

Post factum explanations of those tragic wars start with the self-validating assumption that they were logical, determined and therefore explicable. But for the vast majority of people living in former Yugoslavia, back in the late 1980s and early 1990s, wars were not expected, not logical and not justified. This perspective did not express the naïveté of the masses but stems from the fact that the wars of former Yugoslavia have been basically wars of states-to-be against society/societies. The winners are the states, small and caricatured, and the political elites and war-profiteers. The loser is society, artificially and painfully sacrificed for 'higher' national goals.

The greater the lack of a rationale for the wars to occur the greater has been the media activity in inventing one.[1] In fact, the media played an absolutely key role in preparing the population for war. They were feeding the collective consciousness with reasoning, explanations, justification of the necessity and inevitability of war, along with dubious ethical prevarication. The weaker the 'real' reasons were, the stronger was the war propaganda.

It would be logical to expect that real reasons for ethnic wars would be based on religious tensions and/or discrimination. Yet neither of these existed to any substantial degree in former Yugoslavia, certainly not in comparison with any western democracy. The population was primarily atheistic (in the 1970s, 1980s and early 1990s), and discrimination against minority ethnic groups, in each of the republics or provinces, was extremely weak (with the exception of Kosovo where, from the 1970s onward, the non-Albanian population was exposed to extensive discrimination by the Albanian administration and the Albanian population in general). In fact, data from the 1981 census demonstrated convincingly that almost nowhere in former Yugoslavia did individual upward mobility depend on ethnic origin.[2] For the majority of the population, regardless of ethnic origin, there was a high probability that an individual born after the Second World War could until the end of the 1980s live the whole of his/her life, without experiencing or feeling ethnic or religious discrimination or prejudice. This was especially true in urban settings, of which Sarajevo was a prime example.

While the society of former Yugoslavia was largely free of ethnic tensions the restructuring from federation to confederation, starting with the Constitution of 1974, led to the empowerment of ethnic/national elites. The economic crisis of the 1980s predictably added to ethnic tensions in a manner similar to societal patterns found in other cultures. As the size of the cake was shrinking competition for the pieces was growing. The pressures within former Yugoslavia were also substantially influenced from the outside, both by international monetary institutions and especially by the rapidly changing context of European integration. In the latter case the inclusion of some strongly emphasized the exclusion of others. In the context of former Yugoslavia nationalism was emerging as a synthesis of anti-communist fervour, on the one hand, and 'blame-the-victim' and 'scapegoat' ideologies, on the other.

The 'other' was virtually an overnight invention. It is not that such ideologies did not exist before, but no context had existed to support the wide acceptance and justification of animosity, discrimination and aggression towards 'otherness'. Although both the nationalists and other disappointed and nostalgic former Yugoslavs consider the slogan of 'brotherhood and unity' as a self-deceptive relic of communist ideology, the fact is that 'brotherhood and unity' were experienced, practised and believed in, and were at least as real then, as nationalism is now.

In the 1980s, according to many surveys, ethnic distancing was increasing, permeating mainly from above, from the level of the ethnic elites, but also reactivating some 'archaeological' buried layers of negative collective memories. The growth of ethnic distance was clearly demonstrated in the decline in the number of inter-ethnic marriages. At the same time the process was expressed by a kind of empty hatred; stereotypes and prejudices without content, but more a simple feeling of alienation. At the end of the 1980s hatred existed, prompted by harsh economic realities and the impoverishment of the population, but other justification was still absent. It was a difficult feat to invent, in a short period of time, these stereotypes and prejudices – against one's own neighbours, cousins and friends. Therefore, historical 'explanations' of eternal hatreds were activated and reinforced by a set of old and new narratives:

1. *of exclusive victimization* (we are the only victims);
2. *of hierarchization of victimization* (we are the greater victims);
3. *of justification of revenge* (we are giving back to them what they did to us);
4. *of preventive aggression* (if we do not do it to them they will do it to us).

Narratives based on hostilities which had lain dormant since the Second World War were reactivated, recycled and, through the media, regurgitated with the rubric of undeniable historical truths. They gradually superseded all other problems related to 'real life'; hunger, poor health, poor education, unemployment, housing ...

THE MEDIA CONSTRUCTION OF THE CONFLICT

There is a vague and porous boundary between the political manipulation of conflict in the specific interests of concrete social actors, the promotion of conflict by the media, and its justification by 'scientific' interpretation and prediction. The initiation and orchestration of conflict are two sides of a coin, which I would classify as 'ethnic hostility/conflict making'. While the instigation of conflict takes place at the level of real interests and a clear cost–benefit analysis and is undertaken by those who are major decision makers, the actualization of conflict relies on the prior preparation of the ground and its self-justification.

The media's role in encapsulating 'reality' at the end of the twentieth century, of necessity, includes an essential role in the promulgation of ethnic conflict and war, although by itself it does not create sufficient preconditions for war to occur. The media's key role in self-justification of conflict, lies in defining it as necessary, unavoidable, normal, predetermined and even justified and moral, thus creating a broad consensus through a wide range of pro-war arguments. Without this mobilization of propaganda through the media, ethnic conflict and/or war simply would not make sense for most of the social actors, who are almost always also the main losers. There would be no driving force, no logic, no inevitability without this media promotion of war, which exhorts a collective readiness to victimize (others) and to sacrifice (themselves).

In former Yugoslavia the media basically had two different roles, similar in nature, but with different consequences. The first was related to the slow but steady deconstruction of former Yugoslav commonalties and the promotion of divisive ethnic cultures. This fulfilled the necessary condition for defining difference, and later for justifying separation and antagonism. The second role was to add to that matrix of unnegotiable differences the seeds of hate and to create demands that 'something must be done' to justify concrete political acts and military actions.

Paradoxically this same pattern could be seen in analysing the approach of CNN (Cable News Network), for example; on one hand the creation of the same matrix, the 'otherness of the Balkans', and on the other hand, the creation of pressure that 'something must be done', with little consideration, even active disregard of the consequences. Both of these roles, one of creating a certain matrix, the other of exerting pressure, can be clearly demonstrated in any extensive analysis of media content.

One of the most puzzling questions in relation to the media's engage-ment in the war is who is controlling whom? Is the media independent in promoting war, according to its own interests, or is it in fact just one of the strings that the powerholders pull when they need to? It seems that both possibilities may be true. However, since the Gulf war, the media has become increasingly more independent and influential in pursuing their own interests of prestige and profitmaking. There is a profound change in the role of the media in relation to conflict which has not yet been sufficiently analysed or understood. In a dominant worldwide media the culture of violence, aggression and war itself is becoming an important profit source for the media.

In the Kosovo conflict three sides were clearly involved: the Serbs, the Kosovo Albanians and NATO. Though nominally representing different political, cultural and interest positions, there were striking similarities between the media of all three of them, which clearly suggests that the media can be considered as a single, specific, element of the conflict. The common-alities in media strategies of promoting the conflict demonstrate that 'conflict making' is an intrinsic component, representing the very nature of international media as it existed at the end of the twentieth century. Understanding how the media helps to prepare the preconditions for conflict, to make it possible and probable, and to orchestrate it, may lead us to seriously consider demanding a different role for the media in the future.

SERBIA: THE CLEAR CASE

The Serbian situation is the simplest to analyse because media control was absolute. Open attack on independent media in Serbia was an essential part of the Serbian regime's preparations for war in Kosovo. In the first half of 1998 three simultaneous actions by Milošević's regime took place: instigation of the Kosovo crisis, the introduction of new laws which effectively placed the university under the absolute control of the regime (thereby making the university an important centre of opposition to Milošević) and the introduction of other laws which annihilated the independent media. Both the university and the media became victims of complicated bureaucratic games leading to confusion and exhaustion, fear and coercion, in a way that was not visible to the majority of the population. At first glance it may seem strange, even coincidental, that attacks were mounted simultaneously on these three fronts; however, the creation of chaos was a favourite Milošević strategy which, over time, has proved 'successful'. It became necessary for the opposition to disperse its resources in different directions, thereby decreasing its power and effectiveness.

Within the Serbian public, immediately before the war started, an atmosphere was created which effectively neutralized any possibility of questioning, discussion or negotiation about the regime's policies towards Kosovo. Kosovo was never on the agenda as an issue capable of resolution in different ways. Moreover, since the mid-1990s it had been treated as a non-existent problem. A referendum at the onset of the war, instigated by Slobodan Milošević, resulted in a suspiciously high refusal of the population to countenance external mediation. However, the referendum, though a useful democratic tool, can in fact be easily subverted as a means to justify a totalitarian leader's decisions. The purpose of the referendum was less to exclude foreign influences, than to expose the public to the absolute will of the leader who overnight invents a referendum to confirm his 'patriotic' position. Paradoxically the referendum, far from encouraging free and open discussion of the painful and serious problem of Kosovo, created momentum for its suppression.

Pressure on the independent media was calibrated to the regime's strength. In all of the previous free elections in Serbia it was proved that the election results were closely linked with the sphere of influence of the independent media. However, the democratic opposition in Serbia made the catastrophic mistake of accepting free elections in combination with limited freedom of the media. In all of the protests against the regime, including the ongoing ones, the regime did everything in its power to block the free flow of information. In 1999 the Serbian opposition to the regime was thrown back to a communication and information stone age in which only informal communication channels can be relied on to counter the distortions of the official state media.

During the war with NATO the Serbian regime had the pleasure of introducing its full range of special control measures. However, when a country is in a state of war it is, in any case, unrealistic, even unfair, to expect objectivity. What is significant is that before, during and after the war, there exists strong continuity, expressed in discourse, narrative strategies, symbols and even visual elements. The war itself simply offered convincing justification for a further continuation of the Serbian regime's ongoing anti-western propaganda. Under NATO bombing it was easy to convince the people of Serbia that the West hated Serbs, and that the whole world was against us. It was extremely easy to perpetrate a credible conspiracy theory, to picture an 'upside-down world' created by 'the new world order'. In the NATO war against Serbia-Yugoslavia Serbian reality became the self-fulfilment of Western prophecy.

What is happening after the war is also déjà vu. The special regulation of media during the war, continued. As Milenko Vasović, a journalist from Belgrade, reported:

> Pumping out a steady diet of reports on reconstruction and war heroes and on opposition politicians as anti-Serbian traitors, Belgrade has allowed no opening for fresh debate after the Kosovo debacle. There is no information about the shortage of petrol, the absence of salaries and pensions, or prospects (as yet lacking) for rebuilding the destroyed bridges. Instead, State Radio Television Serbia (RTS) and the regime press appeal blindly for national unity. The demonstrations being held throughout the country are hardly covered, so that citizens sometimes find out about them only when going out in the streets.[3]

The state authorities were using a varied assortment of different strategies against the independent media. In some cases independent media were shut down during the war, some were exposed to absurd legal and bureaucratic regulation, some to financial pressure through taxation and some editors and journalists have been arrested. For those who regularly ask 'What is the Serbian opposition doing?' it might be interesting to know that, for example, Nebojša Ristić, editor of TV Soko from Sokobanja in Southern Serbia, was sentenced to a year in prison for hanging a 'Free Press – Made in Serbia' poster in the newsroom during the NATO bombing. There are many similar examples. However, most indicative of the cynicism of the regime is the example of Radio B92, symbol and core of the free-media movement in Serbia. From the first days of the war the staff of Radio B92 were replaced with 'patriotic staff' who 'converted this usually lively alternative culture and politics station into a standard government-run organ',[4] which in the case of Serbia means a combination of cheap propaganda and kitsch patriotism from neo-folk music.

Contrary to the fallacious invention of Western media, packaged as a

171

widespread oversimplified formula, for the Serbian public Kosovo has represented a problem for more than 15 years, pre-dating the Milošević regime. The Serbian population was already leaving Kosovo, under the pressure of Albanian nationalism, in the 1970s, and especially in the 1980s.[5] Up to one-third of the Serbian population left Kosovo after experiencing different kinds of discrimination and violation of human rights, while thousands of Serbian demonstrators were coming from Kosovo to Belgrade to demand protection from the republican and federal political leaders. However, within the context of the already strong centripetal forces of former Yugoslavia the Kosovo situation could not be resolved within the federation, which was already fragmenting. Instead the real issues of inter-ethnic relations in Kosovo were adopted by Slobodan Milošević as a platform to promote a resurgence of Serbian nationalism. According to M. Thompson, the Kosovo media campaign was a cornerstone of the Serbian Cultural Revolution 1986–1989. The 'war language' promoted by the media was invented long before the real war started.

The media on both sides of the conflict, Serbian and Albanian, was deeply involved in the radicalization of the conflict. Already in 1990 Svetlana Slapšak analysed the correspondence section of *Politika*, the most prominent Serbian daily newspaper, showing how a whole new rhetoric was invented to describe the Kosovo situation. From the late 1980s and espe-cially in the 1990s the Kosovo problem was treated in the Serbian media purely as an emotional and historical issue, thus resisting any possible realistic and rational, future-oriented solution. The atmosphere created around Kosovo prevented any part of the opposition to Milošević adopting a different stance because the risks of losing public sympathy were too high. On the other side there was a very weak, often unbalanced and incomplete critique of Serbian nationalism which completely ignored the fact of Albanian nationalism. Kosovo, for the Serbian public of the 1990s, became a dividing line between 'patriotism' (related to Serbian interests) and 'human rights advocacy' (related to Albanian interests). The truth was seen as belonging to either the Serbian or the Albanian side. These two mutually exclusive positions were each dealing with only one part of the truth, never both. Efforts to show both sides in the conflict in objective terms were marginal and sporadic, exemplified by the efforts of the independent weekly *Vreme* which, before the war, was giving accurate, objective, highly professional and anti-war information, warning of the escalation of the conflict leading to the war. However, the public influence of *Vreme* was limited to a narrow intellectual elite.

The content and influence of Albanian media remains largely under analysed. There are some studies showing that during the period of the Albanian administration (1974–1989) the Kosovo media played a key role in justifying discrimination against Serbs. During the communist regime there was nothing unusual in the manipulation of information according to the needs of the power holders and the Kosovo Albanian media was no exception to this rule. For example, large demonstrations for secession in 1981 were largely ignored by the media. Discrimination against Serbs also went unreported. To understand this phenomenon properly one needs to understand that ethnification of institutions which had already commenced in the 1970s with the Constitution of 1974, was also influencing the media. In former Yugoslavia this ethnification first took place actually in Kosovo, probably because the society was pre-modern, meaning that the role of ethnic/tribal collectivities was extremely significant. The media's role in defending ethnic interests was paralleled by similar processes in other spheres of social life (politics, economy, education, culture, etc.).

The Albanian Kosovo media, together with the Albanian educational system, through inventing Albanian history were responsible for the creation of 'ethnic truths', and 'ethnic argumentation'.[6] A paradox of media war can be illustrated in the phenomena of 'mirroring'. Serbian and Albanian media were frequently offering identical arguments for their opposite causes: that a certain ethnic group had a longer history in a given territory; that a certain ethnic group is the only one who had been discriminated against in prior history; that a certain ethnic group was forcefully divided (by the communist regime) into separate states and should be re-united. Even the terms 'Albanization' and 'Serbization' of Kosovo, which were supposedly neutral concepts of ethnic composition changes, were imbued with negative content by both sides.

The combination of media propaganda concerning the NATO attack on Serbia has resulted in absolute confusion amongst the Serbian public. The least confused were the Serbian nationalists, because everything was clear to them and accorded with their long-held beliefs. The most confused were Serbian democrats and the pro-Western urban middleclass, those who protested for several months in the winter of 1996/97 and whose cities were severely bombed. Missing is any common denominator for what had happened and why, as well as any new narrative strong enough to replace the old outdated ones. Although it might be conveniently simple to believe that the common denominator is President Slobodan Milošević, everybody in Serbia knew that the truth was much more complex. Nobody was innocent, inside or outside Serbia. Without cognitive and ethical acceptance of reality, with all its paradoxes and contradictions, it was hard to imagine how any way out could be found. At the same time it was also hard to believe that there could be any way out unless the 'Serbian part of the truth' was also acknowledged. So far this truth has been so fragmented that it seems that a necessary precondition for resolution must include the establishment of a discourse to identify and confront the main causes of the Serbian trauma.

WESTERN MEDIA: PROFESSIONAL INVENTION OF REALITY

For someone who was trying to protect herself from the polluting and destructive influence of state media in Serbia, experiencing the Western media interpretation of the Kosovo conflict and the NATO action, was a numbing and shocking experience. The very first night of the war I found myself in a totally confusing multiplicity of diverse roles: I was an observer watching a spectacle – which was what it was meant to be – of NATO bombing of my native city, Belgrade; I was a daughter talking with my mother on the phone at the same time that the bombing was taking place and, naturally, crying in panic; I was a sociologist–researcher, trying to analyse the course of a conflict which I had personally anticipated for several years;[7] I was also an activist in the feminist and peace movements, who felt defeated by the very first western bombs and was suddenly confronted with the 'other face' of Western democracy; I was a Fellow at Collegium Budapest, in a formerly friendly country which had become a NATO member just a few days before the war; finally, overnight, I also became 'an intellectual in exile', perhaps, with my daughter, even a refugee.

The confused shock in which I found myself was further heightened by the events of the following day, technically the first day of the war: I was to give my final lecture to the students of the Minority Studies Program at ELTE, with whom I discussed their projects on 'Media Construction of the Kosovo Conflict', and a few hours afterwards, an open lecture at the Central European University (CEU) with the title: 'Towards a Visible Women's History: The Women's Movement in Belgrade in the 1990s', explaining how developed the women's movement was and what kind of efforts were being made to create a civil society in Serbia. All those pieces of my personal reality, interwoven with the intense historical drama of the moment, made my own life almost unreal. I spent the next three weeks mostly watching CNN and EURONEWS, giving a number of interviews to different media and using the Internet to receive and forward information on 'the other side of the coin'. I felt personally and directly the consequences of the media's engagement in conflict making, while simultaneously I was myself trying to utilize the power of the media for purposes in which I passionately believed. As I never thought that 'my' truth excludes 'yours', I did not find it difficult or unethical to speak about the suffering of the other side. In fact, I firmly believed, and still do, that balance is needed. Balance is the only remedy for the radicalization which produced the conflict in the first place. The media should be held responsible for maintaining this healthy balance, instead of feeding extremism.

But, are the Western media balanced and objective? My answer is a clear and unequivocal 'NO!'. The Western media were deeply involved in the conduct of the conflicts in former Yugoslavia and bear considerable responsibility for the confusing, inconsistent and counterproductive measures of their respective governments in relation to the crisis in former Yugoslavia. Allocating sole blame to the media would be unjust; however, to fail to identify their devastating role and to ignore the manipulation employed in the promulgation of 'media truth', of media constructed 'para-reality', which was then accepted as a template for 'real' reality, would be immoral, short-sighted and dangerous. The Gulf war was the first post-modern war in which the role played by the media was an essential aspect of 'reality'; the Kosovo war was (so far) the most recent one.

The Western media's manipulation of the conflict relied on a series of mechanisms, not entirely original but deployed in a previously unprecedented pattern and intensity. None of those mechanisms in isolation would be capable of producing 'the wrong picture' but, in combination, they succeeded in creating an intensive justification of the NATO war against Yugoslavia. Similar strategies were widely employed by the Serbian media (and most probably the Albanian media), but in comparison with Western media, their lower level of professionalism made them less convincing. The seductive quasi-objectivity of Western media was far more dangerous than the blatant, crude, primitive propaganda of Serbian State television.

So, what mechanisms were used by the Western media in constructing ethnic conflict?

Fragmentation of the Truth

The Kosovo conflict was represented through fragments of the truth which justified the initial assumption of Serbian guilt. Important aspects such as the pre-war Serbian migration from Kosovo under Albanian pressure, of the high level of acceptance of secession by the Albanians, of the Albanian refusal to vote against Milošević, of aggressive actions by the KLA, which could have assisted in creating a more balanced view of the problem, were simply ignored.

Reduction and Simplification of the Explanation

Explanation of the conflict was largely reduced to the political aspect, very superficially treated, ignoring that the ethnic conflict involved a much wider social context. Ethnic conflict in Kosovo had occurred many times throughout history, under very different social conditions. The latest development of conflict is related to the process of ethnic-state development in former Yugoslavia, and also to the economic underdevelopment of Kosovo, exacerbated by explosive population growth (the highest in Europe, higher than in Albania). The Albanian community of Kosovo was, and still is, functioning according to a system of pre-modern, traditional regulation, which has very specific effects on social organization, including the range of individual

175

political choices. The power of collectivity has not been as strong anywhere in former Yugoslavia as it has in the Albanian community. Oversimplification, leading to the identification of 'good guys' and 'bad guys', finally resulted in the cynical promotion of the KLA as the legitimate 'representatives' of the Albanian population of Kosovo and their becoming the most important partner of NATO in resolving the Kosovo issue. The recognition now, after the war, of the relevance of economic factors was a kind of moral cynicism; what was regarded as normal and essential investment in the development of the region, and especially of Kosovo, after the devastation, was not imaginable as a preventive action prior to the conflict.

Dehistoricization or False Historicization of the Conflict

The complex, shifting ethnic conflict in Kosovo resembles the movement in historical time of a pendulum whose swing determines that a particular moment in time defines who is the victim and who the victimizer. Once President Milošević had been cast in the role of villain by the Western media, a veritable metaphor for ultimate evil (in exactly the same manner as Saddam Hussein), a black-and-white context was established within which it was easy to demonstrate the absolute guilt of the Serbs and the absolute innocence of the Albanians. The starting point most commonly used for this analysis was the elimination of widespread Albanian autonomy in Kosovo, a simplified view which is acceptable as long as it strategically ignores the expulsion of the non-Albanian population which had taken place during the period of autonomy. The selection of a starting point of explanation carried within itself the consequent judgement. False historicization was usually linked to Serbian 'historical claims' over Kosovo to the current situation, thereby representing the Serbs as completely irrational people, stuck in a six-century-old myth. The fact that Kosovo is a part of Serbian state territory, that it contains much Serbian investment, that many Serbs still were and are living in Kosovo and that it is the home of valuable monasteries, recognized as part of the world cultural heritage, was simply ignored, while non-Serbian rational interests were acknowledged and respected.[8]

Decontextualization or False Contextualization of the Conflict

Ethnic conflict always takes place within a specific context. Just as the selection of a starting point influences the judgement, the selected context influences the perspective. What in fact was the geographical context of the Kosovo conflict? Was it Serbia, Yugoslavia, the Balkans, the Mediterranean Region or Europe?

Maybe the context of the Kosovo conflict was former Yugoslavia with its individual, highly complex inter-ethnic dynamic, in which Albanian nationalism was strongly supported by some members of the former federation as a counterbalance to Serbian nationalism. This was the same former Yugoslavia where the protection of the minority rights of Albanians (who were a majority in Kosovo) had effectively created discrimination against the official Serb majority (in the state of Serbia as a whole), who remained numerically a minority group in Kosovo Province (together with Montenegrins, Roma and other non-Albanian nations). In fact, positive discrimination aimed at the protection of the Albanian population led to the counter effect of discrimination against the supposedly majority Serb population. How (deliberately?) confusing the chosen context could become was clearly illustrated in President Clinton's speech on the first night of the NATO attack, in which he explained that the purpose of NATO intervention was to bring stability to the entire region. What followed was exactly the opposite.

Preparing the Ground

Careful content analysis of Western media would indicate how profes-sionally, in the manner of a good thriller, a build-up of suspense was created, which could result in an average Western citizen experiencing some kind of moral catharsis with the release of the first NATO bombs. The intensity of pro-war propaganda was not in proportion to the real gravity of the existing problem, but rather to the internal political dynamics of the main players within NATO, and NATO's own quest to redefine its role as 'the world's policeman'.

Counting on Ignorance

The media did not only simplify issues, but also catered to the assumed ignorance of its consumers. Much research has demonstrated that the quantity of information presented on a given political topic bears little relationship to an increased public understanding of the issue. One can perhaps conclude that the hidden function of publishing information about a certain topic is to produce some other effect, for example to produce wide acceptance by the democratic public of a 'just war'. The Western media was playing with the emotions and the moral feelings of the public in the same manner as the Serbian media when the latter showed the bodies of Serbian citizens in Kosovo who had been killed by the KLA. In fact, both the Western media and the Serbian media were each focused on an individual (and opposite) side of the conflict, assuming that the Serbs, or the Albanians were the problem, not that ethnic conflict as such was the problem.

The Media's Use of Science and Expertise

To validate 'truths' and to demonstrate their own objectivity the media called on various authoritative experts to present scientific information. However, the rules of the game always favoured the chosen interpretative framework. Instead of offering a deeper and more analytical approach to the topic, the media spoon-fed expert and scientific knowledge in a form that was palatable and easy to swallow. This was achieved as much through the low quality of the questions posed by the journalists as it was by the cooperation of the tame experts.

Use of Public Opinion

Parallel with the exploitation of expert knowledge was the use of public opinion polls and interactive programmes. Western public opinion which was based on the media influences already described, was then quoted to justify the policies of both the media and the war. In fact this tautology would be almost comical were the subject not so tragic. What were sacrificed here were the high principles of Western civilization: rationality, objectivity and fairness. What was confirmed, however, was that modern Western civilization is based on reductionism, expediency and the principles of either/or and of rigid hierarchies.

Creating Victory

The more problematical a NATO 'victory' became, the more necessary it was to create a victorious image in the media. One technique employed was to create 'heroes', which is why so many Western leaders visited the refugee camps of Kosovo Albanians during the war, and Kosovo itself afterwards, where photo-opportunities were created to portray the joyous reception of NATO 'saviours'.

The Power of Victimization

The most pervasive technique employed by the media was the legitimization of military action by exploiting the scenario of victims and victimization. This even produced competition for the highest 'victim status'. Stage-managing events was certainly not a historical first but it was particularly blatant in the wars of former Yugoslavia, including Kosovo. This has yet to be fully documented. All sides were putting their victims on display, under-standing that this could be a powerful vehicle of persuasion. For example, in Serbia, during the bombing, employees were not allowed to leave certain places although they knew for certain that bombing would take place. They were forced to stay and anticipate their own destruction, to satisfy

Milošević's need of victims for his domestic public. In other instances, the international public was deeply moved by cases of victimization, which later proved to false or exaggerated. The 'victim game' was made possible by the media's adoption of an inappropriate role; rather than opposing the conflict as such, asking bold and searching questions about whose interests were being served, the media radicalized the conflict by taking sides.

Producing Stereotypes, Prejudices and Hatred

It is widely acknowledged that stereotypes and prejudices are the antecedents of discrimination. However, creating negative stereotypes against distant 'others' apparently becomes legitimate when these 'others' were victimizing their 'others'. This chain of 'otherness' has not been recognized. In the case of former Yugoslavia this becomes even more confusing. Convincing analysis by Sadkovich, for example, demonstrates the extent to which the orientation of the Western media was anti-Croatian and anti-Muslim.[9] In Serbia similar research proves the opposite – that the Western media was fundamentally anti-Serbian.[10] However, one does not necessarily exclude the other. The fact of the 'otherness' of the Balkans and of the people living there was demonstrated in both instances. Whoever is chosen as the 'other' from the Balkans he/she/they are effectively selected to represent the 'otherness' of the entire region. After a while it becomes less and less important for the average Western viewer to know 'who is doing what to whom' as it becomes clear that those being described are all savages obsessed by tribal hatreds. With this background narrative it became simple to legitimize any kind of intervention imposed on the Balkan 'savages'.

Destruction of Meaning

In the Kosovo conflict the media's capacity to subvert verbal meanings reached a new level of paradox with the constant use of concepts and phrases like 'humanitarian bombing' or 'collateral damage', the latter as a description of civilian victims. On CNN, bombing that lasted almost eighty days and nights, was not defined as war, but described as 'strikes against Yugoslavia'. So, war was not war and peace was certainly not peace but the situation was something in between, nameless, formless, out of control and with very visible consequences.

Factual Distortion

One of the simplest, but nonetheless powerful, means of creating conflict is through factual distortion. A good example, unfortunately, relates to the figures quoted of Albanian inhabitants of Kosovo and of Albanian refugees. At a certain point reports from identical sources were citing figures differing by 40 to 50 per cent. The 'phantom' figure of 90 per cent Albanians in the total population of Kosovo was officially maintained as the primary justification for the right of Albanians to an independent Kosovo. It consequently became necessary to demonstrate that the number of refugees, plus the number of people killed in Kosovo, plus those who remained in Kosovo, really did add up to 90 per cent of the total Kosovo population. Albanians had chosen not to participate in the census of 1991, so in fact the figure of 90 per cent is very likely highly exaggerated, as was the case in Macedonia, where they claimed to be 40 per cent of the population but, by an internationally controlled census, it was shown that they constituted 24 per cent of the Macedonian population.

Destruction of Empathy and Construction of New Moralism

As political leaders became increasingly aware of the potential for exploiting images of their nations being victimized to manipulate Western public opinion, deliberate victimization of their own populations became a viable strategy. It would be very interesting to compare how different victims were presented by the Western media. For example, in the case of both Iraq and Serbia, people were presented as almost used to bombing. The Western media presented a parallel of people in Belgrade singing, alongside footage of Albanian refugees leaving Kosovo; scenes which were shown without commentary but were clearly manipulative of viewer's emotions, creating prejudice against 'ruthless' and 'racist' Serbs on one hand, and 'pure victims' on the other hand. What could be a more convincing justification for the bombing? In fact the real situation was very different. Initially the people of Belgrade tried spontaneously to gain strength against their own fear and powerlessness by getting together and protesting in the centre of the city. Later these gatherings were co-opted by the regime, and people were forced to assemble under the threat of losing their jobs and through other forms of coercion.

The West was experiencing, rightly, shock at the images of thousands of Albanian refugees fleeing their homes in fear and hopelessness. However, showing human suffering day after day, probably resulted eventually in more apathy than empathy. Although these tragic pictures were very disturbing, not many Western countries opened their doors to the Albanian refugees, and especially not in large numbers. On the other hand, with the NATO war the West again imposed itself as 'guardian' of 'the values of the civilized world', despite the West's own history of barbaric actions, in the not so distant past. Recent wars, such as the Vietnam and the Gulf wars are riddled with examples of ethnic brutality and moral hypocrisy.

Empty Space

One of the most important techniques for producing ethnic conflict through the media was the omission of a great many relevant but inconvenient topics, for example the role of the arms industry, the profits of war, Mafia involvement, geo-strategic issues, ecological issues, censorship, peace initiatives and resistance to the war. The Western media ignored complex and controversial topics which could complicate or bring different perspectives to understanding the conflict. The ecological effects of the NATO bombing, which were carefully suppressed, in fact showed reckless disregard towards the whole of the region, and especially to Kosovo, which was exposed to the most intensive bombing.

Hierarchization of the Victims

Maybe the most powerful way of subverting moral and ethical public reactions in the West to the war was the application of double and triple standards towards the victims of the war. There was open racism in Western media, most clearly expressed in the exaggerated attention given to the fate of the three, captured, American soldiers. Meanwhile Albanian refugees were mostly treated en masse, not as individuals, and Serbian victims became 'collateral damage'.

CONCLUSION: WAR AS A SELF-FULFILLING PROPHECY

As social engineering can be used for conflict resolution or peacekeeping and peacemaking, it can equally, if not even more effectively, be used in conflict making. Instead of treating war and conflict as spontaneous and sporadic, it would be much more useful to treat them as structural, endemic and even 'rational', at least for those who are the winners or profit makers. This is where the media plays a highly significant role, both instrumental and strategic. I believe that the media radicalizes conflict when it takes sides. In the 1990s the media is succeeding in restructuring reality to fulfil its own interests. The media is definitely not only a mirror of reality; it is creating reality and it is extremely difficult to define the boundary between the two.

Retrospective analysis, based on a detailed review of content, would clearly demonstrate the extent to which political decisions, and even military decisions, followed certain media initiatives. The whole dynamic of the wars of former Yugoslavia, including the latest one of Kosovo, was very much related to media campaigns which preceded specific events. Of course, this kind of understanding comes, of necessity, *post factum*, when it is too late for any political initiative to abort the conflict. In certain instances events are created for media consumption, at a second level, in other instances, the media start to initiate events themselves, thereby starting even to form 'reality'. War is an extremely fertile and potent ground for this kind of manipulation. It appears that the world is entering a period in which the media threatens domination over societies. The vicious cycle of political decision making and media campaigns is still invisible to most of the public who still tend to reach their 'independent' judgements based on what they assume to be fair and objective reporting.

However, I maintain that in fact the power of the media definitely influenced the conflict in Kosovo: its initiation, its escalation and its outcome. It may still seem unclear who are the winners and the losers in this paradoxical war of NATO against Serbia but it seems that, whatever the eventual consequences, the real victory belongs to the media.

NOTES

This chapter was presented for the first time as a paper at a Collegium Budapest workshop: 'Kosovo in Media', organized in May 1999, by the author who was at that time senior fellow at the Collegium. I want to express my gratitude for the support, both professional and emotional, which I received from the Collegium Budapest staff and fellows during my stay there.

1. The operational definition of the notion of 'media' used in this text includes printed and electronic media.
2. See M. Blagojević, 'Društvene karakteristike etničkih grupa: kako meriti diskriminaciju?' in V. Stanovičić (ed.), *Položaj manjina u saveznoj republici Jugoslaviji* (Belgrade: SANU, 1996), pp. 653–66.
3. See M. Vasović, 'The Media War Continues', *Balkan Crisis Report* no. 57 (16 July 1999).
4. Ibid.
5. See R. Petrović and M. Blagojević, *Seobe Srba i Crnogoraca sa Kosova i iz Metohije* (Belgrade: SANU, 1989).
6. For more information on forceful migrations of Serbs and Montenegrins from Kosovo in the 1980s see: M. Blagojević and R. Petrović: *Seobe Srba i Crnogoraca sa Kosova i iz Metohije* (Belgrade: SANU, 1989). The estimated number of Serbs who left Kosovo after the NATO war is 230,000 (up to April 2002), with the number of returnees being insignificant. In addition, over 100 Serbian historical monuments have been destroyed since the entry of peacekeeping forces.
7. See M. Dogo, 'National Truths and Disinformation in Albanian-Kosovar Historiography', in G. Duijzings, D. Janjić and S. Maliqi (eds), *Kosovo – Kosova: Confrontation or Coexistence* (Nijmegen: Political Cultural Center 042 and Peace Research Center – University of Nijmegen, 1997), pp. 34–45.
8. See M. Blagojević, 'Migrations of Serbs from Kosovo during the 1970s and 1980s: Trauma and/or Catharsis', in Nebojša Popov (ed.), *The Road to War in Serbia: Trauma and Catharsis* (Budapest: CEU Press, 2000), pp. 212–43.
9. See J. Sadkovich, *The US Media and Yugoslavia, 1991–1995* (Westport: Preager Publishers, 1998).
10. See J. Bakić, 'Pisanje strane stampe o raspadu Jugoslavije i ratu vodjenom na njenom tlu (januar 1991–mart 1992)', *Sociologija* vol. 39, no. 3 (1997), pp. 401–23.

REFERENCES

Bakić, J., 'Pisanje strane štampe o raspadu Jugoslavije i ratu vodjenom na njenom tlu (januar 1991–mart 1992)', *Sociologija* vol. 39, no. 3 (1997), pp. 401–23.

Blagojević, M., 'Društvene karakteristike etničkih grupa: kako meriti diskriminaciju?' in V. Stanovičić (ed.), *Položaj manjina u saveznoj republici Jugoslaviji* (Belgrade: SANU, 1996), pp. 653–66.

Blagojević, M., 'Migrations of Serbs from Kosovo during the 1970s and 1980s: Trauma and/or Catharsis', in Nebojša Popov (ed.), *The Road to War in Serbia: Trauma and Catharsis* (Budapest: CEU Press, 2000), pp. 212–43.

Dogo, M., 'National Truths and Disinformation in Albanian-Kosovar Historiography', in G. Duijzings, D. Janjić and S. Maliqi (eds), *Kosovo – Kosova: Confrontation or Coexistence* (Nijmegen: Political Cultural Center 042 and Peace Research Center – University of Nijmegen, 1997), pp. 34–45.

Petrović, R. and Blagojević, M., *Seobe Srba i Crnogoraca sa Kosova i iz Metohije* (Belgrade: SANU, 1989).

Sadkovich, J., *The U.S. Media and Yugoslavia, 1991–1995* (Westport: Preager Publishers, 1998).

Vasović, M., 'The Media War Continues', *Balkan Crisis Report*, no. 57 (16 July 1999).

9

Religion in Kosovo and the Balkans – Blessing or Curse?

Laurie Johnston

After watching the former Yugoslavia endure a series of painful splits along religious lines, most recently in Kosovo, one might conclude that religion in that area of the world is nothing more than a divisive force, an instrument good for nothing except the justification of exclusion and ethnic cleansing. Even if one recognizes that the recent wars were not primarily religious in nature, there is still little that can be said about the role of the religious communities that is flattering. Nevertheless, it would be wrong to conclude that there is no potential for good in these faith communities, just as it would be wrong to conclude that the people of the former Yugoslavia are somehow genetically predestined to be forever at war. In examining the ways religion has helped cause violent conflict in Kosovo, it is hoped that this chapter will also illuminate some ways that religion has contributed, and can contribute in the future, to the resolution of conflict instead.

In an essay about the role of religious people in conflict resolution, David Steele describes a remarkable story which was told by a Bosnian imam during a conflict resolution seminar in Sarajevo in 1995:

> While living in Žepa at an earlier point in the war, he and his people had been literally starving. In the midst of such tragedy, he began to ask what could possibly bring healing to his people. He found himself, then, thinking about the Serbs surrounding the city and realized that they were afraid of the same thing – death! This realization made him examine the reasons for their survival anxiety. As he enumerated for us, in front of Serb participants, some of the historical reasons why Serbs might be afraid, the door was further opened for creative dialogue on the problems currently facing the ethnically mixed residents of Sarajevo.[1]

This imam was able to do something that is extremely difficult to do in the middle of a war: put himself in the shoes of his enemy. This basic ability to recognize that the other, the adversary, is also a human with basic needs and, in some ways, a victim as well, is essential for peace and co-existence ever to occur. But why is it that the imam was able to make that cognitive leap when so many, especially in the former Yugoslavia, are not able to? The reasons must ultimately remain a mystery. But the question remains whether his role as a religious leader had something to do with it, and if so, how?

For anyone who takes their religious tradition seriously, the relationship between religion and violence is a matter of great concern. When societies split along the fault lines of religion, adherents of those religions must, if they are honest with themselves, ask the following: does my religion lead people to be more just and loving, as it ought, or is it more often the cause, or at least one of the causes, of violent conflict? A few words first, then, about the role that religion generally plays in conflicted societies.

After studying a variety of religious groups ranging from violent terrorist groups to absolute pacifists, Professor Scott Appleby of the University of Notre Dame recently wrote a book about religion and conflict which he entitled *The Ambivalence of the Sacred*. This title sums up very well what seems to be the nature of religion. Whether or not one accepts the existence of God or other such religious truths, it is necessary to acknowledge that at times religion helps people to act in profoundly unselfish ways and to transcend their own limited circumstances. Yet it seems that far more often, religion simply helps people maintain their own narrow world views, and provides justification for violence in times of war. Nevertheless, it is quite clear that violence is not a core tenet of any of the world's major religions. When Christians in the Balkans claim that Islam basically teaches that all Christians should be killed, or when Muslims claim that Christianity approves of violent violations of the human rights of Muslims, this merely shows that both sides lack even a basic understanding of the other's theology. Further study reveals that both traditions have violent and non-violent strains. There are texts and saints in any religious tradition which can be mobilized to support a given political goal, and there are those that can be read as supporting pacifism. This is the ambivalent nature of religion: it can be used to support both positive and negative causes.

A similar ambivalence is also evident in the roles that individual religious leaders play. Whether an imam, priest or rabbi, the calling of a religious leader generally has two aspects, often referred to as the 'pastoral' and the 'prophetic'.[2] The word pastor is a Latin word which means shepherd, and thus the pastoral leader is, like a shepherd, concerned about preserving the physical safety of the flock and, in addition, its spiritual safety. The pastor is a nurturer who cares for his community and supports them, even if they are flawed and sinful. The pastor provides teaching, counsel and healing, and celebrates the major events of the community, such as births and marriages. Thus, the pastor is primarily focused inward on his or her own community and is acutely aware of any suffering that community members experience.

The prophetic role is a rather different one. Instead of being focused on nurturing a community, the prophet is focused on the core religious principles of that community. The prophet believes faithfulness to that tradition is far more important than the physical continuity of the community. The prophet often takes a critical role, stepping away from a situation to reproach the leaders which have drawn the community away from the foundation which gave it life in the first place. We see this clearly in the Hebrew scriptures: as soon as the office of king came into being among the Jewish community, the office of prophet came into being to hold the kings accountable. Rather than being focused on the needs of his own particular church or mosque, then, a prophetic leader may look outward, at politics or at other societies beyond the boundaries of his own community. The prophet speaks truth even when it hurts.

Obviously, these two roles are ideal types; in actuality religious leaders generally represent some aspects of each. Often, then, they find themselves pulled in two directions, especially in situations of conflict. On the one hand, the pastoral leader is extremely concerned with the ways that his own community is suffering in the war. He is the one holding all of the funerals, visiting the wounded, comforting all the widows and trying to provide for the newly homeless. Thus, if nationalist leaders are promising to protect the interests of one's own community, there is a natural resonance with the pastor's concerns. It is not surprising that the pastoral leader might be among the most strident nationalists in his community.

On the other hand, religious leaders also have a call to uphold the high ideals of their religions. The priest or minister is called to teach Christians to love their enemies. The imam is called to remind Muslims of the Prophet's commandment to protect the *dhimmi* – the people of the book, that is, the Christians and Jews around them. Furthermore, these monotheistic religions call their leaders to transcend the categories of race and nationality – if there is one God, it is a God for all people, not for just one tribe. They must recognize the universal humanity of all people. In addition, these religious leaders often have ties to their co-religionists in other countries. For instance, Catholic priests have a call not just to relate to the people of their own local community, but must also be in communion with the church around the world and with the Pope in Rome. Similarly, Serbian Orthodox leaders have ties to other Orthodox churches as well as the Ecumenical Patriarchate in Istanbul. Such links can broaden one's view.

Different religious leaders respond differently to this tension between the call to the particular community and the call to the universal. Where they fall in the spectrum has a great deal to do with whether or not they give in to the temptation to offer religious justification for violence. It is clear that in the Balkans, many religious leaders have given in to this temptation. Although this is a controversial point, it is obvious that religious leaders must bear a significant part of the blame for the recent wars in Bosnia and Kosovo. Some have supported them outright; others who did not support the violence nevertheless have not spoken out against it as much as they ought. In any case, the instrumentalization of religion for political and often violent goals has been clearly evident in many ways; among the most extreme examples is the fact that during the wars in Croatia and Bosnia, some members of the clergy from all sides blessed the troops and even participated in war, and it was not uncommon to hear religious slogans such as *Allahu Akbar* (God is great) and *Bože cuvaj Hrvatsku* (May God protect Croatia) used by soldiers.[3] This does not mean that these wars were primarily religious wars, although religion played a major part because it was the primary identity marker. Thus it is not surprising that an increase in ethnic division has to be accompanied by an increased emphasis on religious differences. But, as Paul Mojzes writes, the war was 'being fought largely by irreligious people who wear religion as a distinguishing badge but do not know what the badge stands for'.[4]

In Kosovo, religion has also played a major role, although in a very different way than in Bosnia and Croatia. For the Serbian Orthodox, Kosovo has such deep religious significance that it is seen as the 'Jerusalem' of the Serbian Orthodox Church. Regarded as the cradle of the Serb nation, Kosovo contains many important and historic religious sites. Most importantly, though, Kosovo was the site of the defeat of the Serbs and their allies at the hands of the Turks in 1389, and the death of the Serb martyr–hero Prince Lazar. As the tradition goes, Lazar was offered an earthly kingdom or a heavenly kingdom; he chose the latter and so met a martyr's death. He came to be seen as a Christ figure who epitomized the sufferings of all of the Serb people. Just as the Christ-like Lazar chose holy suffering and a heavenly kingdom, so the Serbs, by their sufferings at the hands of Ottomans, Hapsburgs, Nazis, communists and now NATO, earn a special reward from God and a kind of 'chosen people' status. This Kosovo myth has inspired generations of Serb fighters, including Gavrilo Princip, who sparked the First World War by assassinating Archduke Franz Ferdinand.[5]

In the 1980s, the Serbian Orthodox Church began to revive the Kosovo myth. Prince Lazar's body was carried in a procession around Serbia and Bosnia in 1988.[6] During this period, the Church began to issue calls for the protection of Serbs in Kosovo. It called attention to the threat of 'Muslim fundamentalism' and the danger which the clergy, and religious sites, faced from Albanian violence. This contributed to the sense of Serb victimhood and the growing force of Serbian nationalism. In so doing, the Orthodox Church was playing a role which it had held many times in the past: the natural protector of the Serbian nation. Orthodoxy was what had preserved Serb identity under the Ottomans; ever since, the interests of Serbian nationalism had been seen as identical with those of the Serbian Orthodox Church. Slobodan Milošević embraced this religion-fed nationalism with his infamous declaration to Kosovo Serbs in 1987 that 'nobody should dare to beat you'. This statement was highly ironic since it was the Albanians who had for years experienced oppression under the Yugoslav regime. It is an example of the abuse of religious myths for political gain that has played such a large part in fomenting the recent conflicts.

Among Albanians in Kosovo, religion has played a far less important role in forming a national identity. Albanian nationalism has been consistently secular in nature, as evidenced by the slogan, 'The faith of Albanians is Albanism'. As Duijzings points out, this has been necessary in part because Albanians represent a variety of religious traditions; attempts to appeal to any single one would be divisive and counterproductive for nationalists.[7] While the majority of Albanians are Sunni Muslim, there are significant Catholic, Orthodox and Sufi (Bektashi) populations. In Kosovo, there are virtually no Albanian Orthodox, but Catholic and Bektashi do exist. Islam in Kosovo has been relatively weak, however, and largely dominated by the more highly educated *ulema* of Sarajevo. In part because of the strongly atheistic regime in Albania, a specifically Albanian Muslim community has been slow to develop, as evidenced by the fact that an Albanian translation of the Koran became available only in the late 1980s.[8] The Bektashi sheiks represent a more independent form of Islam in Kosovo (as well as Albania), but have been strongly discouraged by the more orthodox Bosnian Muslim hierarchy. Thus, in the struggle for autonomy for Kosovo, Islam has had little relevance for the Albanians. This is borne out by evidence that Slavic and Roma Muslims in Kosovo have not been spared expulsion from Kosovo in recent months, but rather have been targeted for violence along with the Serbian Orthodox.

In describing the role of both Christianity and Islam in Kosovo, it is important to remember that as a border region, Kosovo has long been a place where ethnic and religious identities are fluid. Despite the recent polarization of religious and ethnic identity, many of the people of Kosovo have mixed backgrounds that belie current political constructions of identity. Both religious and ethnic 'conversions' and also 'reconversions' have occurred at various times in the past centuries. This has led to a degree of syncretism, as Ger Duijzings shows in his descriptions of 'mixed' pilgrimages of both Muslims and Christians to the same holy sites.[9] This complex history has contained periods of peaceful coexistence that suggest that religious enmity is far from inevitable in Kosovo. Nevertheless, the traumatic history of forced conversions also helps explain why religion has so easily become a source of tension and a tool for instrumentalization.

Paul Mojzes, in writing about the pastoral vs. prophetic role of religious leaders in light of the recent Balkan conflicts, said the following: 'In the Balkans the prophetic element in the community is rare, while the physical preservation of the community tends to be always paramount.'[10] Unfortunately, the events of recent years seem to prove the accuracy of this statement. Physical preservation of the community has been an issue of such difficulty for so long that the prophetic element of religious leadership has been stunted. All of the religious communities of the former Yugoslavia have suffered tremendous loss of life and property, particularly during the Second World War. For centuries religious leaders have been tormented by the fear that some change in the always-fragile political situation might lead to mass conversions and decimate their flock. Under communism, the mass conversions took place again, but this time to atheism. So once again, the religious leaders were on the defensive. Furthermore, any impulses that past religious leaders had towards ecumenism and interreligious dialogue have been discouraged by the communist regime's manipulation. Tito's government encouraged ecumenism as a way of emphasizing the inter-nationalism and unity of the Yugoslavs and thus suppressing nationalism. For instance, the communists took advantage of the history of Catholic Bishop Josip Strossmayer, glorifying his ecumenical efforts for their own agenda.[11] Indeed, Strossmayer was a brave figure who spoke out against religious division; yet after watching how he was manipulated by the communists, it is no wonder few wanted to follow in his footsteps. All of this history helps explain why religious leaders have recently been so easily manipulated by nationalist politicians. As nationalist parties gained support, they emphasized their alignment with the religious communities as a means of gaining power. Suddenly, instead of being marginalized, these leaders found themselves 'courted by politicians, the media and even by aca-demics'.[12] That must have been a rather heady experience for them. And since these politicians were advocating policies that had long been pastoral concerns of the religious leaders, it was not surprising that those leaders initially gave enthusiastic support to politicians like Tudjman and Milošević.

Still, it would be unfair to suggest that the prophetic element does not exist in the religious communities in the Balkans. At times, religious leaders in the former Yugoslavia have seen the situation with remarkable clarity. One of the most interesting figures is Serbian Orthodox Bishop Nikolaj Velimirovic. Although he was an ardent Serbian nationalist, his nationalism was not defined as enmity towards Croats and Muslims, as Serbian national-ism has been more recently. In fact, he often praised the Catholic clergy, and clearly envisioned a multi-ethnic Yugoslavia. The terms on which he sought this unified Yugoslavia were not entirely palatable to those other groups, of course. In any case, he was convinced that it was possible, and that religion (or at least Christianity) could be a unifying force in Yugoslavia, and expected that the 'future Yugoslav state will contain about fifty dioceses, half of them Catholic and the other Orthodox ... All future governments in Serbia will be, we confidently believe ... sincere and broad-minded in religious matters.'[13] Velimirovic certainly remains an ambiguous and contro-versial figure, but he had moments of clarity that are still striking today. Of particular interest is the following criticism of religious leaders throughout

Europe (including Serbia) for not playing a more prophetic role with regard to the First World War. He writes:

> When the Austrian government declared war on Serbia, the Church of Austria adopted the standpoint of the Austrian government as the right one. The Serbian Church adopted the standpoint of the Serbian government, of course, as the right one. So it happened that the Churches in Austria and Serbia prayed to the same God, and against each other.
>
> The Church of Germany stood up against the Church of Russia because the German government stood up against the Russian Government. Neither could the Church of Germany raise any protest against the warlike German government, nor could the Church of Russia say anything to cancel what the Russian government had already said. And so it happened that the Churches of Germany and Russia prayed to the same God for each other's destruction.
>
> The Churches of France, England, Belgium, and Italy have fully recognized the justice of the governments of France, England, Belgium, and Italy concerning the War of those countries against other countries, whose justice on the other hand has been fully recognized by their churches. And so it has happened that during the last three years the most contradictory prayers have been sent to God in Heaven from the 'one, holy, catholic church' on earth.[14]
>
> Future generations will be, I hope, more truly Christian than we have been – they will be shocked to read in the history of the greatest and bloodiest conflict in the world's history, that the worldly governments, and not the Christian Church, formulated the truth; in other words, that the politicians and soldiers were bearers and formulators of the truth, and that the Church was only a follower and support of that truth, [in] disobedience of all God's Ten Commandments.

Others have offered more recent criticism in this prophetic tradition: Orthodox Bishop Hrizostom of Bosnia criticized the Pale leadership for

> cheating you when they tell you that they have solved our problems by giving us burnt and looted homes which belong to others, who are refugees just as we are ... The Serb politicians have used our trust against the interests of their people.[15]

Patriarch Pavle has also made statements calling for an end to violence and demanding the resignation of Milošević, although it can certainly be argued that such statements came too little, too late. Most importantly, though, Bishop Artemije of Kosovo has, for some time now, been extremely direct in criticizing the Milošević regime's violent tactics against the Kosovo

Albanians. One of Bishop Artemije's advisers, Father Sava, recently said in an interview:

> The bombardment of Serbia was a great tragedy and a crime, but we have to keep in mind that it was provoked by the behaviour of the regime in Belgrade. A confrontation with the whole world with the goal of prolonging a dictatorship has been for years the style of Milošević's rule. He is aware that the bombardment has extended his political life. When his power gets endangered again he will provoke another clash and provoke NATO to again bomb our country.[16]

Bishop Artemije's criticism of the Milošević regime's actions have been so strong that they have exposed a serious split in the Serbian Orthodox hierarchy; he and other members of the Orthodox Church openly criticized Patriarch Pavle for attending a government function celebrating the 'Day of the Republic' in November 1999.[17]

There have been similarly prophetic statements from the Muslim and Catholic sides; the Orthodox ones are worth emphasis because in the West those have been rarely heard. Also worthy of mention, however, is a statement made by the Presidency of the Islamic Community of Kosovo on 25 August 1999. The statement clearly condemned the actions of the Milošević regime, but also condemned the acts of retribution being carried out against Serbs in Kosovo. Reconstruction, the statement affirmed,

> must be based on deep principles of justice that guarantee that all citizens regardless of religion, ethnicity, or language shall join together in common living ... Thus, the Presidency of the Islamic community of Kosovo rejects every violation of human rights and appeals to its believers to respect the rights and freedoms of all, regardless of their religion or ethnicity.[18]

There has also been a suggestion made recently by a member of the Islamic Faculty in Pristina to organize an interfaith conference for youth in Kosovo, including Serbs. Whether this will actually be possible is unclear, but nevertheless even the expression of a desire to hold such a conference is an important prophetic step.

In any case, it is important to conclude from all of this that we ought to give attention to the positive possibilities of religion in the former Yugoslavia as well as the negative. Some people in the United States dismiss those possibilities; they pay lip service to respecting local leadership and institutions, but become extremely uncomfortable if those local leaders happen to be religious figures. Instead, intervening organizations try to impose their own secular, individualistic notions of civil society whether they fit or not. This shows deep disrespect for the rich religious traditions in the former

Yugoslavia; a far more sensitive and realistic approach would be to try to draw from those traditions 'the moral norms and basic beliefs that are consistent with and reinforce a vision of society in which religious, ethnic, and national differences are less a source of conflict than a reason for coexistence'.[19]

On a practical level, religious leaders can play an extremely important role in civil society building, yet they are often ignored and mistrusted by secular Western organizations. To be sure, there is sometimes good reason for this mistrust. Nevertheless, it is crucial for the international community to recognize those leaders who do think more broadly about the concerns of people beyond their own religious communities. Provided these leaders have the confidence of their own religious communities, they can use their authority to lead the way to inter-ethnic cooperation. They are also part of organized networks in a society where few institutions remain, and so can help with the vital tasks of distributing aid and beginning reconstruction.

Religious leaders do best, it seems, when their pastoral and prophetic roles can be integrated. Neither one ought to be abandoned, and some of the most interesting results come when people like the imam from Žepa move from a focus on their own pastoral concerns to a recognition that there are also pastoral concerns on the other side. It was in part Žepa's deep, pastoral awareness of his own people's suffering that helped him make that leap. David Steele tells a story of how some local religious leaders in Bosnia were able to overcome an impasse in their relations with one another by sharing stories about the many funerals for which they were responsible. For many of them, holding funerals was their primary activity during the war, and this common pastoral concern helped them realize that suffering was truly happening on all sides. For others, the crucial concern was being able to minister to their people who were trapped across enemy lines. There are stories of one religious leader providing safe passage to another, of a different faith, in this type of situation where freedom of movement was limited. Some local leaders have been very helpful in acting as escorts to refugees who are returning as minorities in their communities. Other issues that religious leaders can unite around, no matter what their tradition, include the destruction of religious buildings and the necessity of providing counselling to the many people of their communities who are suffering from trauma.

Some of the most promising work that is being done at grass roots in Kosovo now is conflict resolution which is being carried out by World Vision, a religiously based NGO. They have been helping to set up local community councils to deal with practical questions such as the fair distribution of aid. Being religious people themselves, World Vision staff are not afraid to turn to the local religious leaders for help in this, and so the religious leaders have served as the backbone of these councils. These efforts have earned commendations from a wide range of observers, including UNMIK.[20]

On the level of the religious leadership, the World Conference on Religion and Peace (WCRP) has succeeded in bringing together religious leaders in Kosovo, both before the NATO bombing and later in Amman, Jordan in October 1999. During the bombing itself, they attempted to provide a continuing communications channel. Their efforts in Kosovo are modelled on what they have accomplished in Bosnia, where they helped create an Interreligious Council in Sarajevo that regularly brings together the major religious leaders for dialogue and joint public statements. The work for interreligious dialogue is seen as particularly crucial in Kosovo because, as a WCRP document notes:

> The religious communities represent perhaps the only social institutions that have made any kind of effort to bridge the divide and speak about the future of Kosovo as one that belongs to all who live there. The current environment makes this message even more important, and even more difficult to communicate. Therefore, the religious communities require strong support and assistance to be able to play a role in the social reconstruction of Kosovo.[21]

WCRP and other religious peacemaking organizations are well-poised to provide this assistance.

Finally, it is important to anticipate a common criticism of the suggestion that religious leaders can contribute to peacemaking in the former Yugoslavia. Because of communism, the argument goes, religious leaders have such little credibility, and certainly such little political power, that they can't be expected to do much of anything in this regard. While certainly they face many obstacles, nevertheless there is some power here. No matter how little people know or believe about their own religious traditions, the traditional reverence for religious authorities that has existed for centuries could not be so easily destroyed by communism. So when religious leaders of different sides appear together in public, there is an important symbolic value to that. Furthermore, if religious leaders and symbolism had not had a good deal of power, nationalist politicians would not have found them so useful in mobilizing support for the nationalist cause.

The challenge now is to alter the significance of religious symbolism. The power of religious symbols cannot be eliminated; it stems largely from the fact that they represent a history of resistance against oppression and so in the face of further oppression, they are not likely to die out. But perhaps they can be transformed, so that they mean something other than simply defiance of one's enemies. Can being Catholic mean being truly catholic in the sense of universal? Can being Orthodox mean being truly orthodox in the sense of holding fast to the original teachings of Christ, such as the commandment to love one's enemies? Can being Muslim mean being truly Muslim in the sense of submission to a God who demands protection and justice for all Christians, Jews and other people of the book? That is the challenge for the next generation of religious leaders in the former Yugoslavia and throughout the world.

NOTES

1. David Steele, 'Conflict Resolution Among Religious People in Bosnia and Croatia', in Paul Mojzes (ed.), *Religion and the War in Bosnia* (Atlanta, GA: American Academy of Religions, 1998), p. 250.
2. See Mojzes, 'The Camouflaged Role of Religion in the War in Bosnia and Herzegovina', in Paul Mojzes (ed.), *Religion and the War in Bosnia*, p. 77.
3. Ibid., p. 84.
4. Paul Mojzes, *Yugoslav Inferno* (New York: Continuum, 1995), p. 170.
5. Ger Duijzings, *Religion and the Politics of Identity in Kosovo* (New York: Columbia University Press, 2000), p. 191.
6. Ibid., p. 197.
7. Ibid., pp. 158–60.
8. Ibid., p. 128.
9. Ibid., pp. 65–85.
10. See Mojzes, 'The Camouflaged Role of Religion', p. 77.
11. Sabrina Petra Ramet, *Nihil Obstat* (Durham: Duke University Press, 1998), p. 154.
12. See Mojzes, 'The Camouflaged Role of Religion', p. 81.
13. Episkop Nikolaj Velimirović, *The Soul of Serbia* (London: Faith Press, 1916), pp. 70–1.
14. Velimirović, 'The Agony of the Church', in *The Collected Works of Episkop Nikolaj Velimirović 'Savrana Dela' III* (Himelstir, Serbian Orthodox Episcopacy of Western Europe, 1986).
15. Onasa, 21 February 1996, cited by Gerard F. Powers, 'Religion, Conflict and Prospects for Peace in Bosnia, Croatia, and Yugoslavia', in Mojzes (ed.), *Religion and the War in Bosnia*, p. 236.
16. Translation by Father Sava, at www.decani.eunet.yu, of an interview by Jelena Tasic, 'We Are Going to Suffer Even Worse Without Absolute Repentance', in *Danas*, Belgrade, 6 January 2000.
17. Florian Bieber, 'Some Considerations on Nationalism in Serbia after the Kosovo War', unpublished manuscript (April 2000), p. 5.
18. The text of the statement is available at www.wcrp.org/programs/kosovo 082599.html.
19. N. Gerald Shenk, 'Bosnia: A Case Study in Religious and Ethnic Conflict', in Mojzes (ed.), *Religion and the War in Bosnia*, p. 245.
20. Personal correspondence with David Robinson of World Vision, January 2000. Also, some information available at www.wvi.org.
21. At www.wcrp.org/programs/kosovo082599.html.

REFERENCES

The author gratefully acknowledges the assistance of the Center for the Study of World Religions at Harvard Divinity School.

Appleby, S., *The Ambivalence of the Sacred: Religion, Violence, and Reconciliation* (Lanham, MD: Rowman & Littlefield Publishers, 2000).

Bieber, F., 'Some Considerations on Nationalism in Serbia after the Kosovo War', unpublished manuscript (April 2000).

Cohen, L. J., 'Bosnia's "Tribal Gods": The Role of Religion in Nationalist Politics', in Paul Mojzes (ed.), *Religion and the War in Bosnia* (Atlanta, GA: American Academy of Religions, 1998), pp. 43–73.

Duijzings, G., *Religion and the Politics of Identity in Kosovo* (New York: Columbia University Press, 2000).

Kristo, J., 'The Catholic Church in a Time of Crisis', in S. P. Ramet and L. S. Adamovich (eds), *Beyond Yugoslavia: Politics, Economics and Culture in a Shattered Community* (Boulder, CO: Westview, 1995), pp. 431–50.

Malcolm, N., *Kosovo: A Short History* (New York: New York University Press, 2000).

Mojzes, P., *Yugoslav Inferno* (New York: Continuum, 1995).

Mojzes, P., *Religion and the War in Bosnia* (Atlanta, GA: American Academy of Religions, 1998), pp. 74–98.

Morozzo della Rocca, R., *Kosovo: La Guerra in Europa* (Milano: Guerini e Associati, 1999).

Powers, G. F., 'Religion, Conflict and Prospects for Peace in Bosnia, Croatia and Yugoslavia', in P. Mojzes (ed.), *Religion and the War in Bosnia* (Atlanta, GA: American Academy of Religions, 1998), pp. 218–45.

Ramet, P., 'The Catholic Church in Yugoslavia, 1945–1989', in P. Ramet (ed.), *Catholicism and Politics in Communist Societies* (Durham, NC: Duke University Press, 1990).

Ramet, S. P., 'The Serbian Church and the Serbian Nation', in S. P. Ramet and D. Treadgold (eds), *Render Unto Caesar: The Religious Sphere in World Politics* (Washington, DC: American University Press, 1995), pp. 301–23.

Ramet, S. P., *Nihil Obstat* (Durham: Duke University Press, 1998).

Ramet, S. P., *Balkan Babel* (Boulder, CO: Westview, 1999).

Reitan, R., 'The Kosovo Conflict and a Model for Peacebuilding', unpublished manuscript (January 2000).

Shenk, N. G., 'Bosnia: A Case Study in Religious and Ethnic Conflict', in P. Mojzes (ed.), *Religion and the War in Bosnia* (Atlanta, GA: American Academy of Religions, 1998), pp. 99–107.

Steele, D., 'Conflict Resolution Among Religious People in Bosnia and Croatia', in P. Mojzes (ed.), *Religion and the War in Bosnia* (Atlanta, GA: American Academy of Religions, 1998), pp. 246–53.

Sugar, P. F., *East European Nationalism, Politics, and Religion* (Brookfield, VT: Ashgate, 1999).

Velimirović, Episkop N., 'The Agony of the Church', in *The Collected Works of Episkop Nikolaj Velimirović 'Savrana Dela' III* (Himelstir, Serbian Orthodox Episcopacy of Western Europe, 1986).

Velimirović, Episkop N., *The Soul of Serbia* (London: Faith Press, 1916).

Vickers, M., *Between Serb and Albanian: A History of Kosovo* (New York: Columbia University Press, 1998).

PART IV
INTERNATIONAL ADMINISTRATION OF KOSOVO

10

The UN in Kosova:
Administering Democratization?

Besnik Pula

The United Nations (UN) has been handed the task of building institutions of democratic self-government in Kosova while administering the territory in the interim.[1] This is a novel task for the UN and, not unexpectedly, it has run into severe difficulties. The UN Interim Administration Mission in Kosova (UNMIK) is facing persistent problems in the areas of security, rule of law, ethnic and political polarization and economic reconstruction and reform. These problems stem from the trauma, inter-ethnic enmity and destruction caused by Belgrade's campaign of ethnically-based murder and expulsion in Kosova, NATO bombing of Yugoslavia and a decade of institutionalized apartheid and repression against Albanians countered by a mass-based Albanian secessionist movement; the legacy of a failed socialist economy with no serious efforts at genuine reform and an aggressive, authoritarian regime ruling Serbia. Faced with the daunting problems that have resulted as a consequence of these troubled legacies, UNMIK is putatively making efforts to build an interim administration to handle the day-to-day governing of Kosova while concurrently introducing measures to facilitate economic reconstruction, foster the growth of civil society and build institutions of self-government. However, as developments so far have shown, the path to achieving these goals is laden with a host of obstacles that have caused considerable frustrations among international actors and the Kosovar population.

Analysts and policymakers in the West are almost unanimous in the belief that the democratization of Kosova is the key to ensuring stability in Kosova and the region of south-eastern Europe. The institutions of self-government that UNMIK has been charged with building will, almost by definition, be of a democratic nature.[2] However, rhetorical declarations of Western leaders aside, students of democratization know that post-socialist transitions encompass a variety of complex processes laden with many political and economic hurdles, risks and uncertainty.[3] Given the legacies of economic failure, authoritarian rule, ethnic conflict and the lack of a political settlement regarding the legal status of the territory, the process of democratic transition in Kosova will necessarily face far greater difficulties than those encountered in established states that underwent similar transformations.[4] Nevertheless, with the presence of an unprecedented UN mission in the territory and with the decade-long experience of states that have undergone transitions to democracy, Kosova may have an advantage that policymakers can put to good use.

The purpose of this chapter is to examine whether UNMIK is capable of introducing democracy in Kosova. It will do this by examining UNMIK's mandate, by evaluating UNMIK's performance during its first year of operation, and by discussing some of the fundamental issues that may be obstacles to democratizing Kosova. I argue that UNMIK's performance has been hampered due to a variety of political problems, international and domestic, and that genuine democratization in Kosova is unlikely, if not outright impossible, until a series of fundamental issues, including the level of self-government, the rule of law, the minority problem, political polarization, and economic reform, are successfully resolved.

WHY THE UNITED NATIONS?

A variety of political factors have contributed to NATO member governments settling on the UN (as opposed to, for example, the Organization for Security and Cooperation in Europe (OSCE), Kosovar self-rule or some type of NATO occupational regime) to gain authority over Kosova after the end of the NATO bombing campaign against the Federal Republic of Yugoslavia (FRY). The four main reasons are:

1. NATO governments' eagerness to end the bombing campaign and the UN's general acceptability among its member states;
2. Belgrade's refusal to hand over Kosova to any foreign government or military alliance, and its willingness to transfer control of the territory to the UN;
3. Russia's (and, to a lesser extent, China's) interest to increase its influence over the developments in Kosova and the Balkans;
4. the unwillingness of Western governments and Russia to recognize an independent Kosova.

Since the air campaign against FRY did not immediately produce the desired outcome, at one juncture NATO governments were faced with the possibility of prolonged war, the initiation of ground operations against Yugoslav and Serbian security forces or failure.[5] Since the majority of NATO governments opposed a ground operation, the Yugoslav president's indications that he was interested in ending hostilities offered an opportunity to end the air campaign without involving a risky ground operation. Moreover, ending the war on NATO's terms – primarily, the full withdrawal of all Serbian–Yugoslav police, military and paramilitary forces – would achieve NATO's goal of ending Serbia's ethnic cleansing campaign in Kosova, which had created a tide of nearly one million refugees and threatened to destabilize fully the entire southern Balkans.

On the political side, however, things were trickier. Given the fact that the effort to negotiate a settlement between Belgrade and the Kosovars in Rambouillet, France, had failed, and since no government was prepared to recognize an independent Kosova – the demand of the majority of Kosovars – an interim solution had to be found. The UN seemed the optimal choice for all parties. For Western governments, the UN was considered a 'neutral' player, that is capable of facilitating a peace process, and one that could be handed the burden of resolving post-war problems such as repatriation of refugees and reconstruction. For Russia the UN was acceptable because, given Russia's authority in the Security Council, it is given the possibility to exert more influence over future developments and remain involved as an active player. For Belgrade, the reasons were twofold. In the best scenario, NATO bombing ends while the UN is permitted to administer Kosova temporarily, until the reestablishment of Serbian control. In the worst scenario, turning over Kosova to the UN is a face-saving device for the regime of Slobodan Milošević, since it is an easier political sell compared with 'losing' it to a foreign aggressor or to the Kosovar Albanians.

One obvious thing missing from this picture is the lack of consideration, on either the NATO side or other sides, for the capabilities of the UN to handle the task it was charged with. The UN has no prior experience with the type of mission it has been handed in Kosova. The most closely related mission that the UN has performed was the one in Cambodia, where the UN was charged with creating a 'neutral political atmosphere' and organizing and monitoring the country's first multiparty elections.[6] Furthermore, in most of the former Yugoslavia, especially with the disastrous performance of its UN Protection Force (UNPROFOR) mission in Croatia and Bosnia-Herzegovina, the UN has gained the reputation of a notoriously ineffective organization. One need not be reminded of the case of Srebrenica in July 1995, where at least 2,500 Muslims were slaughtered in a UN designated 'safe haven', as a sad reminder of one of the UN's most tragic failures.

UNMIK: SCOPE AND MISSION

UNMIK has been established under authorization from Resolution 1244 (1999) of the UN Security Council. It fits in the category of what William Durch has called a 'multidimensional peace operation',[7] and Steven Ratner has termed a 'second-generation' UN peacekeeping operation[8] – a distinct feature of post-Cold War UN involvement in intrastate or regional conflicts. UNMIK was given the unprecedented mandate to perform the full range of governing functions in an entire territory and build from scratch institutions of self-government.

Resolution 1244, being a result of a political compromise between members of UNSC wielding veto power – the United States, Great Britain and France representing NATO states on one side, and Russia and China on the other – is ambiguous on several key points. The resolution preserves FRY's (but not Serbia's) sovereignty over Kosova and authorizes the creation of a UN administration which will 'provide an interim administration for Kosovo under which the people of Kosovo can enjoy substantial autonomy within the (FRY), and which will provide transitional administration while establishing and overseeing the development of provisional democratic self-governing institutions'. The resolution states that Kosova will enjoy 'substantial autonomy', but its degree and nature are not defined. The resulting ambiguities over Kosova's political status have created a major problem from the outset.

While the UN is given a leading role in the mission, its components are divided between several other international institutions. The OSCE is charged with the task of institution building, the European Union (EU) with reconstruction, while humanitarian efforts were coordinated by the UN High Commission for Refugees (UNHCR).[9] Furthermore, in contrast with previous UN peacekeeping missions where the UN civilian head was in charge of both the civilian and military components, the military and civilian components of the international mission in Kosova are clearly separated. The military component, led by NATO and known as the Kosovo Force (KFOR), is charged with creating a secure environment in Kosova, mainly by ensuring compliance of Yugoslav and Serb forces with the Kumanovo withdrawal agreement. While there is coordination between UNMIK's civilian head and KFOR command, they are formally two separate but complementary operations. It should be noted that this chapter will evaluate the military and humanitarian components only as they directly relate to the success of the overall mission of the civilian component.

The most closely related mission that the UN has performed is the one in Cambodia.[10] The UN Transitional Authority in Cambodia (UNTAC) was established as a result of the 1991 Paris Accords between the warring Khmer factions. UNTAC, established in 1992, had a twofold military and civilian mandate. The military mandate included the monitoring of the ceasefire and the withdrawal of all foreign forces (armed forces of Vietnam, Thailand and Laos), and the demilitarization of all Khmer factions. The civilian mandate, which was the widest in scope that the UN had performed until that time, included the repatriation of refugees (handled by the UNHCR), the deployment of a 3,600-strong police force to supervise local law enforcement and full mandate to supervise the local civilian administration.

The latter component of the mission included the monitoring of all of Cambodia's administrative bodies to ensure the creation of a 'neutral political environment' for the conduct of elections, including the authority to reprimand or dismiss officials that did not comply with the UN's mission and the goals of the Paris Accords. Finally, UNTAC's mission was to organize and supervise Cambodia's first multiparty elections, after the successful conduct of which UNTAC would be dismantled.[11]

One of the most obvious differences between UNMIK and UNTAC is the manner in which the mandate came to exist. UNTAC was established as a result of a clearly formulated peace accord agreed upon by all conflicting parties, and was assigned the job of overseeing the conduct of free and fair elections. In contrast, UNMIK was established with the agreement of NATO, Russia and FRY, but not of the Kosovars – who, after all, were to become UNMIK's 'subjects' – to set up institutions of self-government and perform administrative functions until that is achieved. As it will be explained in the following section, this would cause considerable problems once UNMIK began its operation on the ground.

Furthermore, UNMIK's mandate is substantially wider in scope compared to UNTAC. While UNMIK is charged with the task of serving as an interim government for Kosova,

> [...] UNTAC's civil administrative supervision and control mechanisms were never designed as a way to 'run' Cambodia. UNTAC administrators were to have unrestricted access to administrative operations and information and authority to investigate noncompliance with the Paris Accords, to issue binding directives, and to require the removal or reassignment of personnel. But their fundamental objective was narrowly crafted: to 'ensure a neutral political environment conducive to free and fair general elections', by thwarting any overt political bias traceable to bureaucratic behaviour – actions such as the issuing of passports to some but not to others, selling off public assets to the benefit of certain constituencies, fomenting strife in opposition political parties, intimidating or harassing voters, authorizing public works projects in some villages but not others, or using public finance to underwrite political activities.[12]

Notwithstanding the fact that Kosova is over 16 times smaller than Cambodia in territory and has less than a sixth of its population – which should make the success of the mission easier to achieve – the physical damage resulting from the war, the need to build a bureaucracy from scratch due to the departure of Yugoslav personnel and the destruction or seizure of a large number of bureaucratic records by Yugoslav forces, and the irregular and insufficient financial and personnel support from donor countries thus far, make this a daunting task.

UNMIK ADMINISTRATION: EXPEDIENCY AND PROBLEMS OF LEGITIMACY

Immediately upon its establishment in Kosova, as any ruling authority, UNMIK faced the need to gain the voluntary submission and acceptance of the population over which it was to exercise its power – in other words, its authority had to be accepted by the local population as legitimate. Gaining legitimacy was an especially thorny problem with UNMIK since no single representative of the Kosovars had given any formal consent to the UN serving as a transitional government for Kosova.

So how does an international administration become legitimate in the eyes of the population it is ruling, especially when none of its political representatives are formally bound to agree to its establishment? There is little prior experience in these types of mission that may provide a theoretical guide to assist us in understanding this process. UNMIK may provide us with a case that can provide answers to that question. I propose that this is a multifaceted process that involves the following:

1. co-option of local elites;
2. economic co-option of the local population resulting from the immense economic power of the ruling organization;
3. a generally favourable view of international intervention by the local population;
4. strategically limited use of coercion.

Local elites represent the greatest challenge to an external structure being established to rule a certain territory, since the power captured by the new structures is, to a certain extent, power denied to them. If local elites are fragmented and do not enjoy mass support, resistance is likely to be limited. A fragmented local elite offers the external power the possibility of negotiating individually with its members and co-opting them, by giving them a limited share of power. This is what happened in Kosova, when UNMIK was challenged by the UÇK-led Provisional Government of Kosova (PGK),[13] which was attempting to establish its own authority. UNMIK's first and unsuccessful attempt at co-option was the creation of the Transitional Council (TC),[14] which contained individuals perceived as being politically influential and/or relevant.[15] As it became obvious that the TC would not suffice in eliminating the challenges to authority posed by the PGK,[16] a new structure was created after weeks of secret negotiations. The PGK leader Hashim Thaçi agreed in December 1999 to dissolve the PGK and integrate some of its members to an UNMIK-controlled structure termed the Joint Interim Administrative Structure (JIAS). UNMIK had gained leverage over Thaçi and the PGK especially after the transformation of the UÇK into a lightly armed civilian protection force, under KFOR supervision (which was treated as a separate issue), and the strengthening of its own administration with the continued arrival of more international personnel to fill its ranks.

The PGK, which had managed to establish a semblance of order in the initial chaotic weeks after the withdrawal of Serb forces,[17] was suffering a crisis of legitimacy of its own. Despite attempts at broad representation,[18] it lacked any participation from the LDK (Democratic League of Kosovo), the party whose elaborate local organization had served as the backbone for the parallel state that existed in Kosova during most of the 1990s, under Belgrade's rule.[19] The mobilizational basis of the pre-war, mass-based resistance in Kosova had disintegrated, and thus precluded the possibility of the continuation or the emergence of another successful parallel state.[20] A changing balance of forces on the ground combined with the disappearance of Belgrade's rule from Kosova, resulted in the almost immediate evaporation of the ostensive political homogenization of Kosovar Albanians. In addition, the PGK lacked effective means of coercion, since its Ministry of Interior was banned from operating by KFOR. It also faced a persisting cash-flow problem.[21]

The creation of the JIAS, which included the creation of an Interim Administration Council (IAC), the expansion of the TC, the creation of administrative departments (equivalents of ministries) co-headed by internationals and Kosovars, and the creation of local administration boards to co-opt municipal PGK leaders, had the effect of creating among Kosovars the impression that local politicians had been given 'more say' in UNMIK's administration of Kosova. The IAC is essentially a transplantation of the TC but expanded to include the heads of UNMIK's pillars and providing a symbolic, rotational co-chairman position for its Kosovar members.[22] It retains its consultative role for the SRSG, as does the TC, which was designated a lower position in the institutional hierarchy and given an open admissions policy for leaders of smaller political parties and individual NGO leaders purportedly representing 'civil society'.

Co-option of local leaders is not the only factor that has enabled UNMIK to gain domestic legitimacy. UNMIK's gradual monopolization of political power displaced all local structures from the authority to appoint individuals to positions of power, such as police officers, judges, prosecutors, teachers, managers of public enterprises and so on. This was especially helpful in attracting those segments of society that were excluded from the PGK, such as urban intellectuals and LDK members. UNMIK is also Kosova's principal economic power, spending hundreds of millions of dollars in donated funds for its operations and personnel. In a poor region such as Kosova, with a scarcity of jobs and currency, such a development has major economic impact. People employed directly by UNMIK for unskilled and semi-skilled labour such as guards, drivers and interpreters receive enormous sums in payment by Kosovar standards. Furthermore, the enormous spending power of international personnel with Western-level salaries has been the driving force behind the emergence of a plethora of service-oriented businesses, from housing to massage parlors.[23]

Kosovars' perception of 'the West' and, more specifically, NATO as an ally in the conflict against Serbian rule was an important factor that helped UNMIK in its quest for acceptance as a friendly force among the local population. During and after the war, NATO forces were held by most Kosovars as heroes, helping end the bloodshed and expel Serbian forces from Kosova.[24] Western leaders, especially those most supportive of the bombing campaign such as US President Bill Clinton and British Prime Minister Tony Blair, NATO leaders and spokespersons such as US General Wesley Clark, who led the bombing campaign, NATO Secretary-General Javier Solana and even NATO's ardent spokesman Jamie Shea, became immediate celebrities in Kosova and enjoyed levels of popularity far greater than in their home countries, or by any single Kosovar leader.[25] Among the contentions between the LDK and the former UÇK camp is the debate over which camp deserves the credit for 'bringing NATO', illustrating how important international intervention has become for local political groups attempting to legitimize themselves as bearers of national interest. UNMIK was able to benefit from this environment by mobilizing a discourse of democracy and Westernization – being an organization led by west Euro-peans and Americans, it is seen by many Kosovars as an organization that is capable of Westernizing Kosova.[26]

Direct coercion is a less prominent feature of UNMIK rule. While coercion itself is rarely an effective instrument for gaining legitimacy, it certainly is one of the best means for establishing authority. UNMIK's capability for coercion has been limited because of personnel and funding problems, especially with its police force, and the ineffectiveness of the legal system.[27] KFOR has acted in cases when major security matters were at stake, but since it is a military force it has generally shunned the role of a routine law enforcer. Thus, coercion has been applied selectively and usually in cases that do not provoke heavy political backlashes, either domestically or internationally. This is best illustrated by UNMIK's and KFOR's con-tinued tolerance of 'bridge watchers' in the ethnically divided city of Mitrovica – young Serbian men with walkie-talkies that constantly monitor traffic on the bridge dividing the city, and whom are reportedly linked with Mitrovica's Serb leader Oliver Ivanovic.[28] Concurrently, similar local groups run by Albanians claiming to fight crime have been quickly disbanded and its members arrested by KFOR and UNMIK police soon after their discovery. This is not to claim that UNMIK's and KFOR's acts are ethnically biased, but that coercive measures aimed at gaining compliance from the population are constrained by capabilities and by their perceived political repercussions or level of threat to security personnel.[29] Heavy reliance on coercion may at any rate be strategically unwise since it could provoke a backlash against international personnel or KFOR troops, a highly sensitive issue given the constant fear in NATO states of 'sons and daughters coming home in body bags'.

STRUCTURAL CHALLENGES TO DEMOCRATIZATION

While Kosova did not lag behind in the trends of liberalization and pluralism that captivated Yugoslavia in the late 1980s, the contention over Kosova's status, the subsequent institutionalized repression and the emergence of an autocratic regime in Serbia, derailed the process of fuller democratization of provincial institutions. Constrained by the developments, political struggle focused almost exclusively on secession, while issues of democratization took a back seat. Civil society groups that emerged, such as human rights groups, independent unions and media, were primarily concerned with exposing Belgrade's abuses and pressing for independence. The period after June 1999 thus marks the beginning of a renewed effort for democratization, although under substantially different conditions and led by an international civil administration.

Unsurprisingly, the aftermath of armed conflict, the recent (authoritarian) and more distant (socialist) past have left behind a series of structural problems that pose hurdles for the democratization of Kosova. These include: undefined legal status, security, establishing the rule of law, economic reconstruction and reform, inter-ethnic relations, political polarization and lack of governing experience.

The undefined legal status of Kosova poses one of the greatest obstacles to instituting democracy. The unclear legal position of Kosova vis-à-vis FRY and the contradictions between legal depiction and factual reality has long presented a problem for building autonomous governing institutions. First and foremost, the undefined 'substantial autonomy' that Resolution 1244 states that Kosova must enjoy until a final settlement is reached, has resulted in implementation problems for UNMIK, since there are no defined limits to the authority of the governing institutions to be built other than references in the Rambouillet document.[30] The UNSC (UN Security Council) gives little help in resolving disputes over interpretations of resolution 1244, due to the competing interests of Russia and Western members of the UNSC, although the Legal Office of the UN's Department of Peacekeeping Operations (DPKO) has increasingly assumed the role of final arbiter on disputes over interpretations of resolution 1244 and is the entity that gives final clearance to the adoption of UNMIK regulations. The greatest problem is that the undefined status issue creates political disputes in a range of other issues, from the serious to the seemingly mundane, such as the status of formerly socially owned enterprises and the acronym that is used on UNMIK-issued license plates. The unresolved status issue may have also been an important factor in UNMIK's decision to hold local-level elections before provincial-level ones, despite vehement demands by Kosovar politicians for the opposite order.

The presence of KFOR deters any possible attempt by Belgrade to reintegrate Kosova through the use of force, and thereby ensures province-wide and regional security. However, at another level, personal security is less stable due to ethnically motivated and other types of crime. On one hand, these illustrate the continuing social instability in Kosova, while on the other hand, they expose UNMIK's inability to build an effective legal system and properly institute the rule of law.

Instituting the rule of law will most likely continue to be a challenge for UNMIK. UNMIK's law enforcement has been most seriously hampered by the inadequate level of police. While UNMIK initially planned to create a police force of 3,100, Bernard Kouchner nearly doubled the number of requested officers, and the recruitment of international officers has proceeded at a significantly slow pace.[31] Furthermore, the training of local police has also proceeded at a slow pace, while deployed officers enjoy little authority to act independently. This has forced UNMIK to stretch its force thin and rely on KFOR for policing, which has drawn a series of complaints from NATO governments that their soldiers are not trained to be policemen. Furthermore, since soldiers do not perform services such as traffic control and criminal investigations, the situation has resulted in lawlessness. This was evident not only by the immediate post-war level of ethnic violence but also by the staggering crime rate and the growth in illicit activities.[32]

Law enforcement has also been hampered by the slow establishment of a judicial system and the adoption of a criminal code. The issue of the criminal code became a controversy when Kosovar lawyers and judges refused to apply Serbia's laws in Kosova. In December 1999 UNMIK settled for their demand, which was the reinstitution of Kosova's 1989 criminal code, which was in power prior to the abolition of Kosova's autonomy – with the exception of those provisions that run counter to international norms on human rights. In March 2000 the OSCE published a compilation of Kosova's criminal laws in force on 22 March 1989. UNMIK has announced plans to appoint 400 judges and prosecutors. However, the judicial system, faced with such mundane problems as the lack of bureaucratic records, office equipment and proper working space, as well as with more serious ones such as inadequate salaries and the inability to protect prosecutors and judges from threats, have rendered it ineffective in prosecuting criminals and keeping them in prison.[33] KFOR and UN police have frequently complained that arrested suspects have been quickly released due to the absence of a working court system. In addition there have reportedly been cases when judges have released suspects despite an overwhelming amount of incriminating evidence. The lack of adequate law enforcement and criminal conviction has also created an environment conducive to organized crime and other types of criminal activity.

Economic reconstruction and reform has been problematic and has sparked a variety of controversies. Kosova inherited an unevenly developed and staggering economy. Even in its heyday in the 1970s, Kosova's per capita income was 30 per cent of former Yugoslavia's average and one-seventh of that in the wealthiest republic, Slovenia.[34] After the Serbian takeover the situation worsened. From US $700 in 1989, per capita income fell to US $340 in 1995, turning Kosova into Europe's poorest region.[35] From 1989 to 1995 industrial output fell by over 80 per cent, while total investment, including investment in infrastructure, was reduced by nearly 70 per cent in the period 1990–94.[36] The 1999 conflict only added to the already dreary economic situation. While there has been some damage to infrastructure resulting from NATO bombing, Kosova's economy suffered the most from the systematic campaign of Serbian forces to loot and destroy houses and other private property, as well as goods and property belonging to a small but vibrant entrepreneurial class.

One of the most sensitive points in the post-war economic development of Kosova has been the issue of ownership, especially of the formerly 'socially owned' enterprises. In socialist Yugoslavia, ownership of enterprises was based on the Yugoslav economic system of self-management, which sought to devolve managerial authority to the local worker level. Hence, enterprises were 'socially owned', that is, owned by the workers, but as titular owners rather than shareholders. This rather abstract system of ownership was replaced after 1990, when the Assembly of Serbia adopted a new constitution and a series of subsequent laws that redefined ownership rights. The Law on the Assets Owned by the Republic of Serbia (1995) transformed the status of all formerly socially-owned property, including ownership of enterprises, into state-owned assets. Having abolished the Assembly of Kosova, which until 1989 served as the body that promulgated the laws governing property status and management, and having introduced so-called emergency measures in all enterprises through which local directors were replaced and a vast majority of the Albanian workforce laid off, Belgrade gained a free hand in managing and dealing with the status of enterprises.

Using this leverage, Belgrade undertook additional measures that transferred ownership of various enterprises either by seizing or selling off their assets, or by annexing them to enterprises based in Serbia. These manipulations, which were prevalent throughout Serbia but most blatant in Kosova and performed largely out of political considerations, combined with the lack of investments, resulted in continued economic decline. In the present situation it has resulted in a controversy over who is the rightful owner of the formerly socially-owned assets in Kosova. Kosovar economists, legal experts and former employees have argued strongly against the continuing application of Serbia's ownership laws and have proposed the restitution of all available assets to enterprises that have existed in 1989, after which a special UNMIK privatization agency would begin the process of privatizing ownership over these assets.[37] On the other hand, UNMIK officials, based on a supposedly strict reading of Resolution 1244 that recognizes the sovereignty of FRY in Kosova, have so far refused to initiate any transformation of the ownership status of these assets.[38]

The problem of ownership has greatly hampered the process of economic reform. Resolving this issue is crucial to starting a meaningful process of economic reform in Kosova, for without a process of privatization and without the creation of a new legal framework that is conducive to foreign investment, economic restructuring is impossible.

The post-war situation offers an ample opportunity for beginning a process of widespread economic reform and instituting a market economy. The shock-therapy versus gradual transformation-approach debate that took place among policymakers and scholars in former socialist states is meaningless in the Kosovar context since the economic and social shocks of the layoffs and impoverishment have been already felt in the early 1990s. What is now necessary is the therapy.

To date, UNMIK has established a Banking and Payment Authority (BPA), the equivalent of a central bank, has licensed one commercial bank, and is in the process of licensing a series of other lending institutions. These steps are vital in creating the basis of a market economy. However, without the revitalization of industry, which is nearly impossible without thorough economic restructuring, prospects for genuine and sustainable economic growth will be dim.

The issue of economic development is related to the issue of ongoing ethnic and political tensions and is crucial for the success of democratization. With joblessness and despair pervading society, ethnic and political tensions will be more difficult to contain. And without a growing economy, it will be harder to establish a sustainable democratic system in Kosova.

Inter-ethnic relations and political polarization are two other hurdles that challenge Kosova's democratization. While some progress has been achieved on the latter issue,[39] much more remains to be done on the former. The main problem remains the successful integration of Serbs,[40] as the largest and politically most relevant minority community, into Kosovar governing institutions. Thus far, the Serb community has been divided into two factions, one led by the Serbian Orthodox Bishop Artemije and his Serbian National Council (SNC) based in Graçanica, who have generally favoured participation of Serbs in UNMIK-sponsored institutions, and a hardline, nationalistic faction, which favours reintegration with Serbia and the shunning of UNMIK institutions.[41] One of the issues faced by local Serbs has been participation in local elections in Kosova. While all major Serb groups have proclaimed their intention to boycott the elections, the compromise reached between Kouchner and SNC has been that Kouchner will appoint individual Serb councillors to municipal councils where Serbs live. While this solution may be suitable for the current circumstances, in the long run, UNMIK must ensure the participation of Serbs in Kosovar institutions if democratization is to proceed successfully.

The other challenge that may be overcome more easily if proper policies are followed, is the lack of governing experience by Kosovar parties. As is evident from the predominance of the theme of Kosova's independence in campaigns for the local elections, Kosovar political groups are still undergoing the process of transformation from ideologically-oriented resistance movements to policy-oriented political parties. One of UNMIK's challenges in this regard is, therefore, to help provide policy training and guidance to parties at the local level.

CONCLUSION: DEMOCRACY OR CONTINUING CONFLICT?

The democratization of Balkan states is seen by many analysts and policy-makers as key to the long-term stabilization of the region after a decade of instability and conflict. The challenge to democratize Kosova includes a series of other challenges that must be overcome if UNMIK is to be successful in completing its mission of building democratic institutions of government in Kosova. It is evident that the process of the democratization of Kosova will take a considerable amount of time and is inevitably linked to the developments in FRY and how those will reflect on the final settlement of Kosova's political status. Nevertheless, the main challenge is to develop structures in Kosova that foster civic participation and political accountability. In this regard, a significant portion of the success will be determined by the extent to which Kosovars consider the new institutions their own and the faith they have in them. UNMIK's policy to exclude Kosovars from key debates and decisions and to continue holding back proper authority from them is detrimental in this respect, and if continued will have dire consequences for both democratization as well as stability in the region.

At the same time, the presence of UNMIK offers a unique opportunity for Kosovars. Kosova has benefited from the presence of experienced administrators and policymakers and the pouring in of hundreds of millions of dollars for reconstruction and development, something that makes any government envious. The territory has been given the opportunity to build an administration from scratch, with technical and financial assistance from Western governments. It has been given the opportunity to rebuild its infrastructure at a pace that would have been unimaginable without inter-national assistance. It has also been given a chance to redesign its institutions of governance in a way that best fits the needs of the society. Overall, the presence of UNMIK has given Kosova a fresh start, one that is rarely enjoyed by other countries.

Although this chapter has focused on UNMIK, I should note that in many respects, the struggle for democracy is primarily a Kosovar struggle, and not one of the UN. This must be understood by both the Kosovars and UNMIK. The democratization of Kosova will depend on the courage of the Kosovars, to take steps in resolving their society's problems, and on the ability of UNMIK to provide sufficient space for that to happen.

NOTES

I would like to thank Florian Bieber and Leon Malazogu for their helpful comments on earlier versions of this chapter.

1. See resolution 1244 of the Security Council of the UN, 10 June 1999, and 'Report of the Secretary-General pursuant to paragraph 10 of Security Council Resolution 1244 (1999)', 12 June 1999. 'Territory', rather than 'province', is the legal term the UN uses to refer to Kosova, and it is the term used here.

2. The terms 'democracy' and 'democratic' are here understood as a government in which there exists an 'accountability of rulers to citizens acting indirectly through the co-operation and competition of their representatives'. See Philippe C. Schmitter and Terry Karl, 'What Democracy Is ... and Is Not', *Journal of Democracy*, vol. II, no. 3 (Summer 1991), pp. 75–88.

3. For a view of post-socialist transitions in the democratic transition literature see Juan J. Linz and Alfred Stepan, *Problems of Democratic Transition and Consolidation: Southern Europe, South America, and Post-Communist Europe* (Baltimore: Johns Hopkins University Press, 1996). For a social anthropological approach on post-socialist transformations see Katherine Verdery, *What was Socialism, and What Comes Next?* (Princeton, NJ: Princeton University Press, 1996).

4. The analysis in this chapter is based on the argument that the conflict in Kosova is a direct consequence of the failure of political institutions in the former Yugoslavia and of the introduction of an authoritarian regime in Serbia and, hence, a development that must be viewed in the broader context of transformation and instability that followed the collapse of socialism in eastern Europe and Eurasia. As such, it positions itself against arguments that reduce the conflict in Kosova to a case of escalating ethnic violence, or of rising nationalist passions or a development linked to the allegedly endemic historic and cultural tendency in the Balkans to nationalist violence. For one argument that situates the Yugoslav conflict in this broader context see Susan Woodward, *Balkan Tragedy: Chaos and Dissolution after the Cold War* (Washington, DC: Brookings, 1995).

5. As the leaders of NATO and NATO governments frequently pointed out throughout the bombing campaign, the issue at stake was not only a victory in Kosova, but also the future of the Alliance and the international credibility of the West, especially that of the United States. This made it greatly more important for NATO to secure a victory in Kosova.

6. See James A. Schear, 'Riding the Tiger: the United Nations and Cambodia's Struggle for Peace', in William J. Durch (ed.), *UN Peacekeeping, American Politics, and the Uncivil Wars of the 1990s* (New York: St. Martin's Press, 1996), pp. 135–91.

7. William J. Durch, 'Keeping the Peace: Politics and Lessons of the 1990s', in

W. J. Durch (ed.), *UN Peacekeeping, American Policy, and the Uncivil Wars of the 1990s* (New York: St. Martin's Press, 1996).

8. Steven R. Ratner, *The New UN Peacekeeping* (New York: St. Martin's Press, 1995).

9. It should be noted that the UNHCR ceased to be a 'pillar' of UNMIK in June 2000 and has begun to roll back its operation.

10. Another similar mission that the UN has performed in the Balkans is the UN Transitional Administration for Eastern Slavonia (UNTAES). The goal of UNTAES was to oversee the transition of the local Serb administration in eastern Slavonia to Croatian authorities, while providing protection to the Serbs. The mission differs from UNMIK in that, like UNTAC, it was transitional and was meant to supervise the transition from one authority to another, and not to govern on its own.

11. For a summary of UNTAC's mission see Schear, 'Riding the Tiger', Table 5.1, pp. 146–7 and Table 5.2, pp. 148–9.

12. See Schear, 'Riding the Tiger', p. 147.

13. The Provisional Government of Kosova (PGK) was formed in April 1999 on the basis of a political agreement signed in February 1999 in Rambouillet, France, by the three Kosovar political representatives that led the Kosovar delegation to the peace talks: Hashim Thaçi (UÇK), Ibrahim Rugova (LDK) and Rexhep Qosja (LBD).

14. The Transitional Council (TC) was established in the initial months of UNMIK's mission. It was intended as a consultative body of locals that the SRSG could consult on issues of policy. The TC had no legislative authority.

15. The TC, among its 'Albanian representatives' included Hashim Thaçi, then prime minister of the PGK and political leader of the UÇK; Ibrahim Rugova, Kosova's erstwhile leader and head of the Democratic League of Kosova (LDK), Rexhep Qosja, a vocal intellectual and leader of the United Democratic Movement (LBD), and Veton Surroi, a media publisher and influential political figure who enjoys good standing in the West. These are the same individuals that signed the Rambouillet document in March 1999. In addition, the TC had two 'Serb representatives', Momcilo Trajkovic and Father Sava Janjic, indicating how political developments after the war changed the West's perception of who matters in Kosova.

16. The tactic employed by UNMIK was to consistently deny any recognition to the PGK, while continuing to cooperate with its leadership and selectively recognize its acts. For example, UNMIK worked with municipal leaders appointed by the PGK, as well as enterprise directors, most notably the *Korporata Energjetike e Kosovës* [Energy Corporation of Kosova] and *Posta dhe Telekomi i Kosovës* [Post and Telecom of Kosova].

17. This was done primarily through the establishment of local governments at the municipal level. The PGK appointed mayors in 27 out of the 29 municipalities (communes) of Kosova (exempted were the two northern-most municipalities that are demographically dominated by Serbs). These PGK-formed local governments continued to play a role even after the establishment of regional UNMIK administrations and its leaders were co-opted as co-heads in the JIAS municipal Boards after the dissolution of the PGK.

18. At one point the PGK included members from over ten political parties.

19. See note 13 for a background on the formation of the PGK.

20. The structural conditions that enabled the LDK's 'parallel state' to function, principally the repressive Serb state, were also gone. However, the PGK represented the final vestige of the Kosovar maintenance of a claim to sovereignty

through parallel institutions, with roots that trace back to Belgrade's forceful abolition of Kosova's self-governing institutions in 1989. On the origins of the Kosovar 'parallel state' see Besnik Pula, 'Contested Sovereignty and State Disintegration: Explaining the Albanian Secessionist Movement in Kosova', MA Thesis (Washington, DC: Georgetown University, 2001).

21. This may have been one of the factors pushing the PGK to insist on appointing its own directors in public enterprises. While most of the enterprises were inoperative or even non-existent, certain enterprises became operational, especially the 'Kosova' enterprise that ran most of Kosova's hotels, reaping enormous profits since it catered to international personnel. 'Taxes' from these enterprises reportedly served as sources of funding for the PGK.

22. The co-chairman position is symbolic since it wields no decision-making authority. The SRSG is the IAC's permanent chairman and final decision maker.

23. Rentals to international organizations and personnel of homes and apartments – already scarce due to large-scale wartime destruction – has turned into one of the most lucrative businesses in Kosova. For example, in the period 1999–2000, monthly rents in Pristina have ranged from 500 DEM for small apartments to over 10,000 DEM for larger houses (an average teacher is paid around 200 DEM a month). The political effect of this is that many Kosovars have benefited enormously from the presence of international organizations and thus have a vested interest in their continuation.

24. Immediately after the war, Pristina was awash in NATO flags and flags of NATO member states, especially the states with their own military sectors in Kosova: the US, UK, Germany, France and Italy. By comparison, with the exception of official buildings, UN flags were nowhere to be seen.

25. No local leader could draw either the crowds or the enthusiasm that prominent NATO and NATO member state officials drew during their post-war visits to Kosova.

26. It is striking how many Kosovars actually prefer being ruled by UNMIK than by any of the local parties. A typical response that I received in my discussions with local residents of Pristina in the summers of 1999 and 2000, especially those considering themselves to be more urbane and distrustful of any of the Kosovar parties (and therefore not affiliated with any political party), was 'thank God that these foreigners came to rule us. If any of the local guys were in power we'd be at each others' throats.' Local political groups and leaders were viewed as 'corrupt' and 'interested only in personal gain'. And while most of these individuals did not express unreserved faith in UNMIK, they indicated their certainty that at least with foreigners in control there is a lesser chance of power being abused.

27. See discussion below.

28. Such activity may have even been legalized and encouraged by the Memorandum signed by Bishop Artemije and Kouchner, with its provision on 'neighbourhood watch' groups. Although in the West, especially in the US, there is a tradition of neighbourhood watch groups, there is no analogous tradition in Kosova or elsewhere in the Balkans.

29. A similar argument may be made of the SFOR troops in Bosnia-Herzegovina and their continued reluctance to apprehend individuals indicted for war crimes by the UN-sponsored International Criminal Tribunal for the former Yugoslavia in The Hague, Netherlands.

30. More recent developments have rendered this statement untrue. The setting of Novermber 2001 as the date for Kosova-wide elections and the adoption of a so-called Constitutional Framework that defines Kosova's future self-governing

institutions – including an assembly, a government and a president – have provided some clarity to the status issue, although the success of the project for a joint UNMIK–Kosovar administration is yet to be seen. Under the new arrangements, Kosovars will be handed a greater share in day-to-day administration while UNMIK will continue to be responsible for security, policing and overall economic and fiscal policy, and retains the powers to supersede the authority of the Kosovar institutions.

31. By August 2000 there were nearly 4,000 international officers deployed.
32. UNMIK's own data illustrate the ineffectiveness of its police force. According to data from UNMIK police, released in June 2000, the number of serious crimes that have resulted in an arrest is a meagre 30%.
33. See Valbona Mehmeti, 'Pse nuk zbulohen krimet në Kosovë?' *Koha Ditore*, 11 October 2000.
34. Elez Biberaj, 'Kosovë: the Struggle for Recognition', in *The Albanian Problem in Yugoslavia: Two Views* (London: The Institute for the Study of Conflict, 1982), p. 33.
35. Muhamet Mustafa et al., *Aktivitetet ekonomike dhe zhvillimi demokratik i Kosovës: projekt studimor* (Pristina: Riinvest, 1998), p. 39.
36. Ibid.
37. See, for example, *Problem of Ownership and Property Rights in Kosova: Analyses and Recommendations* (Pristina: Kosova Action for Civic Initiatives, 1999).
38. According to reports in the Kosovar press, UNMIK has more recently given indications that it plans to take steps towards privatization. These measures emerge after the steps UNMIK has taken to lease a number of former Kosovar enterprises to foreign and domestic companies.
39. Tensions between Kosovar political factions have been considerably more manageable compared to the period prior to 1999. While divisions between the LDK and the former UÇK block are still prevalent, and sporadic incidents have occurred, political leaders have been able, through UNMIK institutions, to establish working relationships. Whether the faltering reconciliation is genuine or a result of domestic and international pressures is debatable, nevertheless, it has helped stabilize Kosovar politics.
40. Political parties representing the interests of other minorities, such as Turks, Bosniacs, and Ashkali will be participating in the coming local elections.
41. Apparently, the latter faction seems to dominate among Kosovar Serbs. According to UNMIK, nearly 45,000 Serbs in Kosova participated in Yugoslav elections held in September 2000, and according to Mitrovica Serb leader Oliver Ivanovic, most voted for the ousted Yugoslav president and indicted war criminal Slobodan Milošević.

REFERENCES

Biberaj, E., 'Kosovë: the Struggle for Recognition', in *The Albanian Problem in Yugoslavia: Two Views* (London: The Institute for the Study of Conflict, 1982), p. 33.
Durch, W. J. (ed.), *UN Peacekeeping, American Policy, and the Uncivil Wars of the 1990s* (New York: St. Martin's Press, 1996).
Kosova Action for Civic Initiatives, *Problem of Ownership and Property Rights in Kosova: Analyses and Recommendations* (Pristina, 1999).
Linz, J. J. and Stepan, A., *Problems of Democratic Transition and Consolidation: Southern Europe, South America, and Post-Communist Europe* (Baltimore: Johns Hopkins University Press, 1996).

Mehmeti, V., 'Pse nuk zbulohen krimet në Kosovë?', *Koha Ditore*, 11 October 2000.

Mustafa, M. et al., *Aktivitetet ekonomike dhe zhvillimi demokratik i Kosovës: projekt studimor* (Pristina: Riinvest, 1998), p. 39.

Pula, B., 'Contested Sovereignty and State Disintegration: Explaining the Albanian Secessionist Movement in Kosova', MA Thesis (Washington, DC: Georgetown University, 2001).

Ratner, S. R., *The New UN Peacekeeping* (New York: St. Martin's Press, 1995).

Report of the Secretary-General pursuant to paragraph 10 of Security Council Resolution 1244 (1999), 12 June 1999.

Resolution 1244 of the Security Council of the United Nations, 10 June 1999.

Schear, J. A., 'Riding the Tiger: the United Nations' and Cambodia's Struggle for Peace', in W. J. Durch (ed.), UN Peacekeeping, American Politics, and the Uncivil Wars of the 1990s (New York: St. Martin's Press, 1996), pp. 135–91.

Schmitter, P. C. and Karl, T., 'What Democracy Is ... and Is Not', *Journal of Democracy*, vol. II, no. 3 (Summer 1991), pp. 75–88.

Verdery, K., *What was Socialism, and What Comes Next?* (Princeton, NJ: Princeton University Press, 1996).

Woodward, S., *Balkan Tragedy: Chaos and Dissolution after the Cold War* (Washington, DC: Brookings, 1995).

11

Ethnic Borders to a Democratic Society in Kosova: The UN's Identity Card

Isa Blumi

The recent war in Kosova raises questions about the nature of inter-human exchange and the viability of certain operational institutions that are central to our concept of modern governance. As with other conflicts, the war in Kosova has produced responsive discourses that utilized foundational principles that prove to be highly problematic. Unfortunately, scholars have rarely sought to understand the structural politics set behind such principles. These discourses are at their core rendered operational through the evocation of essentialist representations of the conflict, resulting in crude sociological models that help both the media and the academic community explain human tragedy to an audience disinterested in detail.[1] While we should not lose touch with the operational value of reductionism in the production of knowledge, I want to use the case of the international administration of Kosova to demonstrate why citing such categories – especially 'ethnicity' – fail to properly criticize a number of pre-determined 'reforms' which were expected to bring peace and prosperity and as a consequence, 'democracy' to Kosova.[2] In the end, I suggest this process will fail because the indigenous civic mechanisms that constitute the very foundations of democracy have been actively destroyed by this international administration on the basis of the operational logic it adopts when using such categories.[3]

ETHNICITY AS THE RESURGENT NIGHTMARE

Ethnicity has been for many years the source of professional quibbling among anthropologists.[4] Ethnicity is also the ethnographic and sociological category that has been mobilized to characterize Kosova's crisis. The international community, represented by all the major non-governmental organizations (NGOs), the United Nations (UNMIK), NATO (KFOR) and the OSCE have used this filter of ethnicity to 'read' the conflict in Kosova in terms reducible for purposes of explanation. Ethnicity, therefore, has, as an 'immutable', 'primordial' identifying tool, animated all policy in Kosova today in ways that reflect conditions of analysis that have been soundly condemned by a number of theorists uncomfortable with the use of naturalizing essentialism. The problem is manifested in Kosova as ethnicity has glossed over the distinctive social structures that have developed over decades, if not centuries in a variety of contexts.[5] Ethnicity as used in the current context, has become a tool of explication and, in many poignant ways, extrication. It silences inherent complexities as it operates as a comprehensive tool of analysis. In particular, it is used to create identifiable units, often set in diametrically opposite sides of the political, social or cultural field of analysis. 'Albanians' and 'Serbs' in Kosova are thus analytical constructs used in a discourse of distinction that has powerful implications for how the international community has administered the region.

The process I am treating here has replicated similar methodologies of engagement in which individuals and the communities they form are constituted an identity on the basis of a variety of criteria that often determine the limits of both performative and theoretical self-articulation. As most clearly noted in relations between men and women, black people and white people, narrative values given to categories carry great socio-logical weight when they are interlaced with relations of power in any given context. The function of the category, not only ethnicity, but any category, is at once meant to fix identity of a given subject and to limit the terms of engagement. In the case of UNMIK's Kosova, 'Albanians and Serbs' must resolve their differences in institutional mechanisms that reduce the representative scope of the polity to one firmly in the control of UNMIK. Albanians are thus fixed within a very small space of expression, deviation beyond which would constitute grounds for repression. It is the boundary drawn around permissible mediums of self-expression that constitutes the functions of state-imposed identity, gender norms, racial myths and morality in the modern world and are the central problem of Kosova's current situation. It comes as no surprise that the discourse that frames these socially permissible spaces in which Albanians and Serbs can interact also have a way of reinforcing their 'objective reality' over time. This is especially important when hegemonic powers such as UNMIK seek to control potential rivals to legitimacy claims or economic control.

Judith Butler notes that it is the performative constitution of identity in the very 'reiterative and citational practice' of discourse that 'produces the effects that it names'.[6] To put it differently, the strategic or naïve application of terms that distinguish normative practices between a self-defined 'us' and 'them' in the form of racial, ethnic, ethical or cultural difference, while often 'innocently' constituted, nevertheless realizes a truism when reinforced by the violence in which they are situated to explain events. It is particu-larly the international community's blind faith with the idealist–materialist

218

dichotomy, often noted in academic and diplomatic applications of policy, that fails to address the internal assumptions driving these narratives. Identity, be it ethnic, racial or class is not a manifestation of a material truth, but is a function within a discourse that seeks to reinforce structures of power.

Within the same dynamic, evoking categories such as 'ethnic Albanians', as applied in the case of Kosova by every medium of analysis, inherently silences discursive or even extra-discursive alternatives. In Kosova, therefore, people identified as 'Albanian' have no means to move beyond all that the imposed category implies and are left bounded by associations often constructed well beyond an individual's reality. To the outside world, 'Once an "Albanian" always an "Albanian"'.

From the perspective of the international community 'Albanian-ness', in the context of a larger performative space called the Balkans, only makes sense in the discursive networks of the negatively marginal. Ethnic hatred, which is the *bête noire* of the international community and is targeted for elimination in all its operational literature, immediately implicates 'Albanians' for all manifestations of violence in the past and future. This had powerful consequences when UNMIK sought to establish administrative control over Kosova. One only need to look at how Bosnia's besieged population was directly implicated in the very acts of genocide perpetrated against them to see how similar no-win situations have materialized for Kosova's population. As far as the post-communist logic of the world goes, since the war between 'Albanians' and 'Serbs' was ethnic in nature, the mass murder perpetrated by a sovereign state (Serbia) implicated everyone, victim and aggressor, as 'equally guilty'. This has been reinforced by what has taken place since the cessation of NATO bombing in 1999. For strategic reasons discussed below, UNMIK and KFOR spin doctors encouraged the representation of the flight of more than half of Kosovar Serb-speakers from Kosova as a 'systematic attempt to realize ethnic cleansing in reverse'. What such statements, made in numerous press conferences, disguise is the fact that this exodus of Kosovar Serbs, loaded with refrigerators, washing machines and just about anything of value in Kosova, took place before 'Albanians' returned from the numerous camps in neighbouring countries.

This logic of levelling has found resonance in the world today as it did for the case of Bosnia, causing what I call the 'internalization of ethnicity' by the region's inhabitants. As human beings faced with a number of immediate needs – in Kosova today that means everything from finding shoes for the baby to wood for the stove – the conceptual boundaries set by discursive standards mean 'Albanians' have to interact with UNMIK, based in Pristina, on terms set beyond their control. This leads to self-regulation in ways antithetical to all the values a human being may hold dear because UNMIK controls access to much needed supplies, supervises the administration of the social services and, most importantly, holds the keys to political legitimacy. The most significant victim of this phenomenon which is spread throughout the world today, is the individual voice as articulated in its ability of collective mobilization. In today's Kosova, for instance, no longer can an individual make demands for supplies to help rebuild villages still in ruins after three years, for such a person is immediately identified as part of 'the Albanian mob' that has 'invaded' Pristina since 1999. In the same manner, the individual is rendered powerless in the search for justice. The individual can no longer address crimes committed during 70 years of occupation because of 'Albanians'' 'natural' hatred for 'Serbs'.[7] Characterizing Kosova's tragedy along lines of 'ethnicity' has thus reduced the capacity of individuals, and the communities they make, to act outside the conditions set by UNMIK which only recognizes its constituents in ethnic terms: Albanian, Serb, Roma or Goran.

The masking of all human activity in the discursive framework of ethnicity makes it impossible for individual communities, which never constituted a single 'Albanian' unit, to represent themselves outside the parameters of their assumed 'ethnic' identity. This is extremely important in Kosova for UNMIK has taken a position of institutional management that requires a rigid 'restructuring' of political life along these same 'communal' lines.[8] UNMIK and its first appointed administrative leader, Bernard Kouchner, mobilized a rhetoric of liberal democracy through institutions which operated on the grounds of these ethnic divisions.

The Interim Administrative Council (IAC), for instance, intuitively wanted to bring the 'two sides' to the same table. What such a performative gesture assumed however, was that the body, constituting four members of the 'Albanian' community, one from the 'Serb' and four from the 'interational' communities were representative of easily identifiable constituents. The notion that the IAC was a representative council only reconfirmed the immutable boundaries between each 'ethnic' group as opposed to creating any co-habitational spirit. The fundamental assertion made by UNMIK was that the IAC marked a new beginning, thus delegitimizing all structures that existed in Kosova prior to June 1999 as some archaic form belonging to the terrible years of 'ethnic conflict'. Both the networks of Yugoslav internal security (MUP) *and* 'Albanian' local councils not attached to UNMIK needed to be eradicated. The very institutionalization of 'ethnic' difference implicitly accepted the racist pretext that 'Albanians' and 'Serbs' are distinctive and must have, to use a cliché, separate but equal facilities to conduct daily life. This has been most clearly manifested in the enforced segregation of the northern city of Mitrovica, where UNMIK and KFOR authorities have even gone to the effort of constructing a wall along portions of the river that divides the city, separating the 'two' communities.

Importantly, UNMIK's imposed political mechanisms actively seeking to sidestep a dynamism within each 'community' that proved more diverse than unified, more varied than monolithic. The four leaders 'representing' the Kosovar Albanians in the IAC were expected to serve as liaison between Pristina and the community (note, singular) at large. Outside the parameters set in this 'coalition', there no longer remained the possibility to develop and articulate local solutions to local problems. What this meant was traditional local resources of problem solving were being appropriated by Pristina and distributed to pliable 'partners' who proved eager to maintain a good standing with UNMIK.[9] The inherent diversity of Kosova's political, cultural and economic life was reduced to fit manageable boundaries for administrative purposes.

What compounds the problem in 2002 is the general feeling that UNMIK is not doing its job. This sense of failure has deep roots, beginning with the very first months of UNMIK administration. On 18 August 1999, for example, I posed a question at the daily press conference that exposed how little UNMIK actually understood post-war Kosova. The spokesperson of then chief administrator Bernard Kouchner admitted that Kouchner had yet to visit Drenica, Dukkagjin or Malisheva, the areas most ravaged by the war.[10] Another indicator of neglect is the fact that UNMIK and the OSCE still persists in only having permanently staffed offices in Mitrovica, Prizren and Peja. For long periods of time, key areas would be utterly ignored by UNMIK's bureaucracy. In a well publicized case, it took a full five months after UNMIK assumed power for the appointed representative to the key region of Podujeva, David Violet, to go and meet with local civic leaders.[11] Such negligence is reflective of an administrative practice that has persisted until today for those communities far from the major towns.

REVISITING STATE POWER THROUGH THE EYES OF UNMIK

This process of neglect forces us to explore the relationship between state power and its constituents more closely. I see UNMIK as but a copy of institutional agents and their practices that have found ascendancy in the post-Enlightenment world. UNMIK's operational relationship with Kosova's population shares the intrinsic tensions of power over agency that have hampered social and political growth throughout the world. From the Soviet Union to a variety of operational models found in the West, the dominance of organizational and conceptual mediums situated in the modern state have transformed the world since the nineteenth century.[12] Categories, framed in pseudoscientific terms have found important operational niches in the reconfiguring of first Europe and later the Third World. Such categories – ethnicity, race, creed, class – while dependent on the coercive capacity of those who use them, have had enormous explanatory value in dealing with difference, a process which defined physical, cultural and ultimately moral boundaries for those who evoke them. Such boundaries have a way of solidifying distinctions, leading ultimately to tensions of interests as articulated exclusively in these terms. Such constructions are deemed essential to self-constitutive efforts, but as William Connolly has so brilliantly noted, they have important moralizing elements which close possibilities as opposed to expanding interaction.[13] Such inherent 'border-drawing' tendencies, I argue, build registers of power; those who can impose notions of right and wrong, terrorism and justice, shape the contours of human life in a given social space and determine the nature of 'self' for all.

This perspective has a distinctive bias to it. As Michael Shapiro observed, academic and political discourses fixated on the state have approached these limits only by way of legitimating the authority of nation-states, the dominant political order of our time.[14] According to policy makers and 'specialists' on the Balkans, it is the ethnic tensions between distinctive and spatially conceived actors – Albanians and Serbs – that shape the operational limits of intervention in Kosova's history.

In this context, as is often the case that when issues of sovereignty are involved (a cause célèbre for similarly orientated Western democracies), the use of a framework of analysis based on ethnicity inherently reinforces the state's ideological thrust. In the case of the Balkans, it is Yugoslavia (Serbia) which has set the terms of engagement with Bosnians, Croats and Kosovars on account of its sovereign membership as a recognized state. It justified mass murder by evoking sociological and political categories 'originating' from European traditions, lending further legitimacy to its voice in face of the cluttered, at times inept representations uttered by Serbia's victims. In other words, Kosova as seen in the media and the diplomatic corps is an 'ethnic' quagmire that pitted 'Albanian rebels' (sometimes called guerrillas, sometimes terrorists) against the 'security forces' of Serbia. The world, finding little sympathy for constructs that complicate their geostrategic fixation on the firmly defined nation-state, refused to engage 'Albanians from Kosova' on any other terms than as 'separatists', 'rebels', and/or 'victims'.[15] The language of exclusive, sovereign rights, the privilege of state over subject silenced 'Albanians' in their attempt to frame a historical narrative to assert 'rights' beyond the dictates of diplomatic protocol. The same holds true today, where it is UNMIK's state that holds the keys to expression, it is UNMIK that determines the validity and tenor of information that circulates to the outside world and the representative dynamics of the recently elected legislative body.

By way of recasting Kosova in the 1990s in terms readily used by the practitioners of genocide (whose actions served as the context for international intervention), the internal dynamics of Kosova's many communities were never considered. In a process Derrida would call 'coup du force', the internal dynamic of racist domination, articulated by a sovereign state, forced outside observers to articulate the crisis in terms privileging that perspective: a clash between ethnic groups within a sovereign state.[16] Not only was there no other way of identifying the principals but, as we shall see, the international community, trapped in these discursive conventions, has subsequently perpetuated Belgrade's racialist ethnography as it assumed authority over Kosova in June 1999.

To summarize this theoretical intervention, what has changed in Kosova since June 1999 is the nature of rule, not the discursive relationship between power and subject. 'Ethnic Albanians' are still the issue, a construct with distinguishable boundaries from others – a 'minority Serb population' and the international community – who ultimately must be reformed, guided and punished when applicable.[17] This persistent 're-sourcing' of essentialist categories, by way of mobilizing ethnicity as a explanatory tool to distinguish ruler from ruled, will ultimately create failures far more spectacular than the latest outbreak in Mitrovica.[18]

OPERATIONAL ASSUMPTIONS: NEW PERSPECTIVES IN ORDER

On the ground in Kosova, there are ways of monitoring the process of reducing Kosova's problems to an ethnic one which should prove important if we were to make comparisons elsewhere. First and foremost, the perpetrators of this post-war manifestation of the process are the foreign staff of the groups who have virtual control over Kosova's daily life. There is something of a pernicious NGO culture that permeates operations such as UNMIK's. Opportunism, privilege, corruption, and incumbent power comes with the territory; careers are enhanced and resurrected in situations which render indigenous structures as 'archaic and traditional', in need of reform and an infusion of Western democratic values. It is this same operational assumption of legitimate authority that is incongruent with the very human issues at play and has led to human disasters all over the world.[19]

Part of the tension is reflected in the vast discrepancy between official narratives, largely adopted uncritically by the outside world, and realities on the ground. There were local mechanisms in Kosova that historically maintained autonomous communities largely separated from both each other and the various states that attempted to annihilate them. These same patterns of communal agency were in operation in Kosova until June 1999 and had been important sources of power that UNMIK sought to eliminate. These communities, however, were not 'Albanian' social units. Rather, they were distinctive communities that operated beyond such boundaries of distinction.

As a historian, I have had a difficult time diverting my colleagues' attention from the assumed ethnic nature of events in Kosova's past. Contemporary historians, for instance, often appropriate the frequently noted uprisings in Kosova during the last 50 years of Ottoman rule for border-drawing ploys. These uprisings, however, were not nationalistic in nature, but distinctively local, emerging from communities that resisted state conscription and tax collection.[20] This same observation can be made throughout the twentieth century and proves particularly helpful in the 1990s. While the nature of the resistance to the state has changed, it would be a mistake to suggest rural Kosovars' resistance to Serbia's colonial state was driven by 'ethnic hatred'. Certainly the various efforts by Belgrade to demographically change the region have been framed in these terms, but closer inspection reveals important nuances to assumed sectarian and ethnic cleavages and the nature of resistance to Belgrade's colonialism. Rural populations traded with their 'ontological others' (Serbs, Bosniaks, Gorans and Roma); they often lived in the same village and even prayed at the same holy site.[21] Why this is pertinent to post-war Kosova is clear when we observe how the international community has framed the nature of the conflict as well as its ultimate resolution.

Informatively, for the Serbian state, it has been the same 'ethnic' separation recognized by UNMIK today that has driven policy in Kosova. Since the 1920s, Belgrade mobilized support for territorial expansion into Kosova by soliciting racial difference. This method of expanding state domination, often noted in other colonial settings, did not operate cleanly, however, largely because locals did not accept the discursive principles on which they sat. One could look at Belgrade's last ten years of policy in Kosova as a final attempt to reverse such realities.

Recognizing the contested terms of state attempts to consolidate control over a population exposes just how provocative and self-fulfilling the use of ethnic markers is in post-war Kosova.[22] This is all the more reason why the world should be appalled at UN administrators' adoption of ethnic categories to parcel out a number of operational domains for Kosova's population. Unless immediately reversed, any future interaction between Kosovars will be permanently based on criteria beyond their control; giving self-asserted nationalists veto over any policy inside Kosova.[23]

SOCIAL CODES THAT MAKE INDIGENOUS ORDER

We should take the refined understanding of how Kosova is an amalgamation of autonomous communities in analysing the political dynamics of the last ten years. It is in the last ten years that Milošević has almost completely monopolized political power among 'Serbs' in Kosova. Through strategies of mass migration, intimidating local opponents and enforcing an ethnic criteria for employment and education, Kosova's colonialization had reached its current, hyper-ethnicized phase by 1999. This had clear implications for Kosova's political order. In the Milošević era, the Democratic League of Kosova (LDK) represented itself to an outside audience as the administrative party for Kosova's Albanians.[24] Western European powers and the United States, seeking conventional means to put a lid on Kosova's conflict, supported the notion of a single representative party for 'all' Kosovars in the person of the 'pacifist' Ibrahim Rugova.[25] However, these often inflated self-representations did not resonate locally.

It is the popularity of the LDK among Western leaders that speaks of the political subjectivity of modern state systems which are incapable of dealing with multiple sources of power. As the logic goes, all communities must have leaders, and since Kosova was identified in terms of two dominant 'ethnic' communities, first by Milošević and then Rugova, the inherent dispersal of power among local communities never registered in diplomatic and academic circles. Again, while the LDK played a role for the international community impatient with local nuances, it could not penetrate dispersed organizational patterns using its big party strategies.

This is an important point to stress as similar strategies have been used to resurrect Ibrahim Rugova in order to assure his domination of the Kosova legislature set up by UNMIK. Much as has been done in 2001, the international community attempted to manage Kosova's political quagmire through patronage of one man. The local elections that first brought Rugova to power in 1991 were continuously represented as a reflection of a unified Kosovar polity.[26] Throughout the 1990s, Ibrahim Rugova's political strategy was to use this claim. These claims rang hollow, however, in the hundreds of villages and small towns of Kosova. The symbols of a 'shadow' state and claims of universal support were meant for an outside audience, while local Kosovars continued to contest Serb-state oppression by local means, within their own communities, often with little or no direction from the LDK. This fact could not be monitored by outside observers, however. The models of ethnicity in many ways imposed the structural requisite of Rugova in face of Milošević's totalizing strategies, making events in Kosova manageable only if actions remained fixed on these ethnic polarities. Unfortunately for the outside world, ethnicity in Kosova was filled with contradictions, leading ultimately to a dangerous misreading of factors on the ground.

The Kosova Liberation Army (KLA) is a perfect example of such contradictions within the models of ethnicity used to represent the region's history. The 'movement' was a by-product of earlier attempts at armed resistance in the 1980s. The principle actors of the KLA came from small communities in Drenica, Malisheva and other rural areas, largely marginalized by the political structures dominated by a Pristina-based elite. The early members of the KLA were socialized in an era which grew progressively more violent as Belgrade actively sought to racialize the state's traditional policies of repression. It is important to note that the KLA could only really develop among exiles living in Europe, reflective of a largely fragmented social order within Kosova itself. While outsiders often assumed the KLA maintained a political centre, insisted on naming a leader and asserting a founding ideology as it had been done with the LDK, in reality, the war in Kosova was fought with little central command for most of the time in question. Resistance to Serbian military and paramilitary units developed out of local militias which, in one shape or another, had been responsible for defending local communities for at least a century. Most of these small, largely untrained units never took part in any integrated defensive and offensive manoeuvres with other units elsewhere in Kosova; rather, they sought to defend local communities while framing, when appropriate, the struggle as one that enclosed the rest of Kosova.

During the 1998 and 1999 Serb-state offensives, such lightly armed, often ragtag units with their own code names and locally-elected commanders developed important autonomous pockets of resistance that relied on hit-and-run tactics to which Serbia's mechanized forces were vulnerable. These early KLA units operated under no centralized command, something that only emerged during the course of 1998 and 1999.[27] This is important to post-war Kosova for the international community has aggressively ignored these factors and adopted Belgrade's terminology to characterize the KLA and those who partook in the struggle against 40,000 heavily armed soldiers.

The categorical niceties of internationalism and the bureaucratization of the Kosova conflict by both Belgrade and the international community, represent failed attempts to rationalize Kosovar society and its resistance. This has ultimately led to failures in dealing with the realities on the ground. Much as in Bosnia, diplomacy and academic analysis drifted into the fantastical as policies and diplomatic measures were drawn along 'ethnic' lines, lending a cold state-centred rationale to mass rape and deportations as territorial and irreconcilable historical differences were cited.

UNMIK'S STRATEGIES

I suggest the international community has used its monopoly of administrative, and thus coercive, power to specifically attack autonomous sources of legitimacy embedded in local communities. It has done this, in large part, because there remains a discursive hierarchy in the practice of a 'state's' sovereignty that sets restrictive conceptual boundaries around its constituents for reasons of control. Specifically, the UN and to a lesser extent the OSCE articulate Kosovar ethnicity and use it for a variety of administrative strategies. I suggest this has introduced a new element into the daily lives of Kosova's population that has strategically modified local interactive patterns, ultimately hindering democratic development. A direct consequence of the uncritical application of the ethnic category by the international community is the detrimental effect it has on individuals and their perceptions of place. I call this internalized ethnicity a process that results in self-marginalization within Kosova's political, social and economic polity.

226

Again, through the crude stereotyping of Kosovar society in the context of a universalized Balkans, bounded in the rhetoric of ethnicity and all its inherent dangers, the international community has developed important justifications for its blatant attack on local networks of organization. The requirements today are such that references to archaic social structures, which have little analytical value to social scientists and even less so for bureaucrats, serve as the rhetorical justification for what I have observed as Pristina simply ignoring Kosovars' local concerns. In order to 'bring peace to Kosovo' [sic] everything that existed in Kosova structurally, culturally and spiritually had to be either eliminated or put under firm surveillance.[28] It is the added imposition of administrative structures that adopt criteria based on a collective identity, here ethnicity, that further simplified a far more fluid and hybrid population in the post-war period.[29] In the course of applying these simplifications, individuals and communities that did not adapt to these alien criterion emerged as a threat and were identified as such in highly charged messages relayed to the international media corps.

ADMINISTRATION CONVERGENCE: POWER DEMANDING UNIFORMITY

The bureaucratic necessities of a strong administrative state seeking to 'bring peace to Kosovo' [sic], demanded all external sources of legitimacy and economic and social production to be eliminated or channelled through Pristina. Through this imposition, only UNMIK had legitimate claim to authority in Kosova.[30] Upon entering Kosova, all administrative bodies, the 'self-declared' Provisional Government and the Republic of Kosova, run by the LDK, had to stop operations.[31] The KLA had to be disarmed and break ranks in three controlled stages as the new authority in Kosova assumed a monopoly of military force.[32] All 'Albanian' political parties, economic and social organizations had to be registered with Pristina or face persecution. All matters concerning education, legal complaints, water supply, road repair or mine clearance were no longer to be addressed by local means. Since Pristina did not recognize the authority of the local communities, it refused to allocate funding or material assistance to the many organizations ready to begin rebuilding Kosova from day one.

It is here that I suggest Kosovars themselves, while instinctively resistant to such efforts, set in the current situation, have had to abandon their inherited and largely intact principles of communal cooperation in order to survive in post-war Kosova. In the conditions set by Pristina, to survive UNMIK's brave new world means Kosovars have to abandon tried and true social practices. Because of the manner in which Pristina has coordinated the distribution of foreign assistance, these people, numbering in the hundreds of thousands, are existentially externalized from their familiar world and are forced to act within boundaries of behaviour set by the discourse of ethnicity. As individuals and members of now highly dependent communities seek assistance from all places, Pristina, they must do so in a discursive context that has largely marginalized them and empowered Pristina-based bureaucrats.

It must be remembered that one of the first measures taken by Pristina upon replacing Belgrade's forces was to formalize the disbanding of the KLA. It is important to note that local communities resisted in subtle ways the enforcement of disarming the KLA on the premise that KLA was a term too broadly applied. Since the KLA, as suggested above, was barely a formal military organization at the time of NATO intervention, the best way to have handled the question of post-war law and order was not to focus so much repressive attention on a largely non-existent organization. Since the KLA, as seen by the international community, was ethnically Albanian and its forces widely spread in Kosovar society and Pristina, and its military arm was enforcing the imposed disarmament, KFOR could not differentiate between KLA and someone who had no association with the structures of that organization. The end result was *all* 'Albanians' were suspected of being members of the KLA and were treated accordingly. This led to months of particularly questionable harassment on the part of Russian and French troops in such operations, spoiling an opportunity to empower locals in the need to help rebuild a social order in Kosova. Basically, UNMIK and KFOR, a military force that was not answerable to any legal checks, had conducted a process of 'bringing peace to Kosovo' [*sic*] that had an embedded bias towards 90 per cent of the population.

Any number of agencies located in Pristina throughout the post-war period have repeated this theme. A look at the problem with the post-war flight of the region's Serb-speaking population is particularly helpful in this sense. While a uniform condemnation of ethnic cleansing in reverse seemed, on the surface, just and appropriate, I argue there were strategic reasons for the launching of what was ultimately a smear campaign directed against 90 per cent of the population. The tone was set in Pristina by the legitimate and authorized administration of Bernard Kouchner. His various agencies had, for the first three months of UNMIK's administration, made it a policy to publicly condemn acts of violence against Serbs as 'revenge' attacks, acts of a 'barbaric and inhuman' nature perpetrated by Albanians.

There are two important points to make here. First, it is simply not true that Albanians undertook a 'systematic campaign to ethnically cleanse Serbs' from Kosova.[33] After numerous challenges at daily news conferences held in Pristina, however, it became clear that attempts to modify the implicit, and at times explicit, associational ploy operated by the various agencies that issued statements to the press were futile.[34] The campaign directed by UNMIK fed into the generalizations that ran rampant in the mass media and reinforced all assumptions about Kosova, its inhabitants and the legitimacy of UNMIK in its thankless task. At the time, the results were deemed largely positive by the spindoctors who manned Kouchner's press team: the Kosovar Albanians were on the defensive; everyone from Hashim Thaçi, to the farmer trying to pick up the shambles of his life had some explaining to do. Little did the press team at UNMIK headquarters know, the consequences for such slash-and-burn tactics would have dire consequences for the region's long-term stability.

This policy of applying pressure on all of Kosova's Albanians through a media campaign of guilt by association was done for one principal reason: there was a crisis of legitimacy that plagued the international community. While NATO forces were seen as saviours, the premise of UNMIK's introduction into Kosova was inherently contradictory to what the population sought – independence.[35] UNMIK's mandate, however, was not to develop an independent Kosova but one which would remain formally inside the 'recognized' borders of Serbia.[36] Kosova, as far as UNMIK was concerned, was a space that remained part of a hierarchy of order that produced 'angles of vision' requiring that it assumed goals that could produce a potential clash with a 'population' which had different aspirations.[37] This hierarchy was based on an assumption that Sovereign States were the principal forces that sustained order in the world; a hierarchy that directly excluded the inhabitants of Kosova from having a say in the day-to-day administration of the country. The subsequent angles of vision were predicated on goals adopted by the international community which believed it had the right to impose a level of administrative distance from what had just happened in Kosova in order to 'rebuild' Kosova as a 'multiethnic' province within Serbia's boundaries. This is a daunting task and probably an impossible sell if made directly to Kosovars.

The question of legitimacy, therefore, was key for Pristina if it hoped to produce results. Phrases such as 'security vacuum' and 'nonexistent social order' that lent immediate value to KFOR and UNMIK's role in Kosova, tie in the fact that many in the international community feared the KLA (read Albanians) would fill in those gaps. The result of this paranoia meant no 'Albanian' community could be allowed to rebuild on its own terms. According to self-assured statements, KFOR and UNMIK were to 'return' Kosova to a state of 'normalcy'. Such terms had an insulting disregard for Kosova's recent history built into them. Returning Kosova to a state of 'normalcy' or filling a 'security vacuum' were seen as queer concepts by 90 per cent of the population, who never in their lives thought there was any 'security' in Kosova or that there was anything desirable about what was 'normal' before the war. It became abundantly clear that the practitioners of this 'rebuilding' had little or no knowledge of what Kosovars had gone through, and the rhetoric of legitimacy, essential to establishing amicable relations with the media and security council members such as China and Russia, literally meant silencing Kosova's population. Hence a media campaign blaming 'Albanians' for the flight of a 'Serb' population that, by the admission of the UNHCR left 'before KFOR troops or "Albanians" could enter into Kosovo'.[38]

Despite the public statements, it was hard not to see that there was in fact a possibility of locally produced order, and even a mechanism to maintain security, in Kosova as the international community began to rumble in. KFOR troops, assuming their role as sole military force with great confusion, from day one met Kosovars who were 'coming down from the mountains' with a sense of trepidation. The anxiety was completely misguided and counterproductive. If one witnessed the first days of 'liberation' one saw countless examples of an orderly process taking place. NATO troops were guided by members of the KLA to pockets of paramilitaries who tried to melt into the Serb civilian population. KLA soldiers pinpointed mine fields and mass graves and helped keep crowds under control as tens of thousands of deportees moved frantically back from camps in neighbouring countries. A systematic effort to document crimes had produced thousands of names of those who were murdered, trucked away by Serb forces for destruction inside Serbia or left missing. Field hospitals and kitchens, which fed and cared for hundreds of thousands of 'internally' displaced people throughout the war were waiting to be re-established in the burnt out villages and cities. Finally, although without many of their former leaders (who were either murdered or spirited away to Serbian jails),[39] local communities began to re-establish local community boards addressing issues like water and electricity supplies, schools and a plan of action demonstrating a spirit of a population 'eager to rebuild before winter'.[40]

These manifestations of a resilient population were widely attacked by the international community in ways that are best understood by the discursive tactics of marginalization noted above. As members of an ethnic group, 'Albanians'' association with the war, regardless of whether they had been the targets of genocide, gave a strong rhetorical weapon to agencies seeking unchallenged control of the country. Again, the use of press conferences and the manipulation of events, using ethnicity as an explanatory tool, took place in order to destroy any possible opposition to a scheme that went inherently against the hopes and desires of 90 per cent of the population. The KLA, which if incorporated into a security system could have stopped the looting of homes perpetrated by criminals coming from Albania, were confined to barracks and disarmed. Local communities that had the manpower and the will to rebuild and provide safety for all under its jurisdiction, were denied building materials and money because no UNMIK agency was prepared to acknowledge anyone that represented a community in Pristina as 'democratically elected'.[41]

It is important to stress here that my critique of the operational tactics of UNMIK in no way attempts to defend or condone the murders that have taken place in Kosova since June 1999. The point I am making deliberately delegitimizes such attacks as I assert they do not represent Kosovars as a whole. I am pointing out a serious issue of how the international community has attempted to assert mastery over Kosova's population. It has adopted essentialist media policies, often racist in nature, which have effectively marginalized Kosova's population from effective self-responsibility while, at the same time, asserting collective guilt for criminal acts conducted by individuals.

Pristina, through mechanisms of selective reasoning and public pressure, has created a population under direct state rule by imposing a sense of 'dependent uncertainty' in their daily lives. There are no longer communities that can react as they have historically, to real, immediate problems of housing, mine clearance, health care, etc. with any sense of control. As of June 1999, 'Albanian' organizations were deemed to be part and parcel of a systematic policy of 'revenge' and a threat to altruistic, democratic efforts implemented by the modern, free world. Individual acts of revenge were lifted from their context and generalized. The murdered 'Serb', regardless of whether he was directly responsible for ethnic cleansing and murder, was a victim of 'reverse' ethnic hatred that needed to be eradicated. The perpetrator, often never found, was always the generic 'Albanian'.

The ethnic categorization of criminal behaviour is of particular interest here for it has led to a retention of real choices for individual communities. By implicating all 'Albanians', Pristina created a social ontology that forced its adopted 'communal' leaders, Rugova, Thaçi and others, to perform a definitional shift. By creating first the IAC and then the legislative body in this context, UNMIK established firm ground for engagement, ground for which the terms state that if you want to participate you must publicly distance yourself from these acts and accept institutional guidelines as set forth by Pristina. This has led to the effective silencing of real dissent. In particular, Hashim Thaçi, in June and July 1999 probably favourite in any election, is now diminished to a sorry addition to a council of puppets.

The process of 'dependent uncertainty' has also permeated to the 'simple' farmer who has lost everything. Any deviation beyond the permissible institutional and rhetorical space provided for the simple civilian is considered 'anti-democratic' and a threat. Being an 'Albanian' at once limits where one can go to voice one's complaints and how expressions of anger can be articulated before the international community. The problem is that that same administrative agency has not established institutions to address the very concerns expressed by Kosova's population.

There are direct relations between missing institutional systems and the operational husbanding of such duties by local communities. Justice is just one domain – schooling, water and electricity services, security and political administration have been others – in which UNMIK state aspirations clashed with realities on the ground. For nearly three years now, there has been a systemic marginalization of individuals which intensifies the sense of political powerlessness. The growing tenor of new bodies of political advocacy speak to these frustrations and fears, ultimately fulfilling the negative stereotypes imposed from the outside world as only radical voices gain attention. The 'ethnic' criteria has been used in post-war Kosova to strengthen distinctions between not only 'Serb' and 'Albanian', but those whose rhetoric has followed the guidelines set by the international community and those who resist. The more virulently 'nationalist' one is in northern Mitrovica, the greater one's attractiveness to small pockets of supporters have become, to the extent that individuals can now basically veto any directive initiated within the recently elected legislative body. One's anti-Serb or anti-Albanian credentials have become of great political value in the context of a Kosova divided discursively along ethnic lines.[42]

CONCLUSION

The underlying conclusion to the internationalization of Kosova is that it is a failure. I approached the issue from the perspective of its discursive place in the global vernacular of diplomacy and great power politics. There are of course significant issues of regional powers seeking greater influence, and the economic prizes are always appreciable in such international projects. The persecution of the air war, to halt mass murder, demonstrated the complexities involved in diplomacy and the widely divergent interests NATO members have in the Balkans. That in itself is deserving of an extensive study. Kosova since June 1999 cannot be reduced to one solely reflective of operational rigidities but I believe how it has been administered since June 1999 is in large part responsive to such methodologies of power.

What can be learned ultimately from Kosova is that its discursive place in a larger narrative framework has greatly determined the fate of the population's relationship with their patrons. Often, the interaction is shaded by extreme displays of *naïveté* on both sides and often, an uncomfortable level of trust has been granted to administrative bodies that do not have the best interests of local Kosovars at heart. The troubling conclusion here comes with a prediction that Kosova has not seen the last of the politics of murder. As violence percolates with the whims of well-protected 'activists' it is not clear how far the international community will be able to go in face of a new dynamic, one which has been largely shaped by Kosova's intimate exposure to Western norms of governance since June 1999.

NOTES

I wish to dedicate this chapter to all those who gave their lives for freedom and those who have felt pain because of someone else's hate.

1. See Isa Blumi, 'The Commodification of Otherness and the Ethnic Unit in the Balkans: How to Think About Albanians', *East European Politics and Societies* XII (1998), pp. 527–69.
2. By international community, I do not wish to suggest it is a monolith. There is enormous diversity within this rubric that, in the case of Kosova, has often quite opposite views as to what should be done, including the final 'legal' status of Kosova.
3. On the basis of UNSCR 1244 the UN has set up an administrative mechanism, United Nations Mission in Kosovo [*sic*] (UNMIK), to develop institutions that would retain Serbia's sovereignty but give Kosovars a 'high degree' of autonomy. For a full text of all relevant mandates see www.un.org/peace/kosovo/pages/kosovo12.htm.
4. For a history of this debate among anthropologists, see Marcus Banks, *Ethnicity: Anthropological Constructions* (London: Routledge, 1996).
5. For a strong critique of how ethnicity is ethnographically fixed in political and social structures, see Jack D. Eller and Reed M. Coughlan, 'The Poverty of Primordialism: the Demystification of Ethnic Attachments', *Ethnic and Racial Studies*, vol. 16, no. 2 (April 1993), pp. 183–202.
6. Judith Butler, *Bodies That Matter: On the Discursive Limits of 'Sex'* (New York: Routledge, 1993), p. 2. For understanding of the performative constitution of identity in terms of foreign policy see David Campbell, *Writing Security* (Minneapolis: University of Minnesota Press, 1998).
7. The hate speech decree (Reg. 2000/4), while only implemented in February 2000 has been in operation 'off the books' since August 1999. The criminalization of speech has the dangerous potential for silencing real opposition to provocation. See OSCE Press Release, 'Regulation against incitement of hatred is key for a democratic Kosovo' (9 February 2000).
8. See 'Main Tasks' at www.un.org/peace/kosovo/pages/kosovo12.htm.
9. IAC divisions were distributed to 'the political parties' of Kosova, most of which were (and still are) only focused on securing favour in Pristina. See www.un.org/peace/kosovo/pages/regulations/regs.html.
10. The fact that his advisors escorted Kouchner that very day for photo opportunities in Prakaz (only 'Albanian' reporters were notified) indicated the power of imagery they wanted to maintain and avoid a major embarrassment with locals. Photo opportunities aside, these same three districts remain the most neglected parts of the region.
11. Hasan Përvetica, 'Takim i përbashkët i partive politike të Podujevës me UNMIK-un', *Koha Ditore*, 13 October 1999.
12. See, for instance, Stephen A. Marglin, *Dominating Knowledge: Development, Culture and Resistance* (London: Clarendon, 1990).
13. See William E. Connolly, *Identity/Difference: Democratic Negotiations of Political Paradox* (Ithaca: Cornell University Press, 1991).
14. Michael J. Shapiro, *Violent Cartographies: Mapping Cultures of War* (St Paul: University of Minnesota Press, 1997), pp. 15–20.
15. Such operations of argumentation had been articulated by Michael Walzer as the 'legalist paradigm' which has enjoyed legitimacy in international relations. Mihael Walzer, *Just and Unjust Wars: A Moral Argument with Historical*

Illustration (New York: Basic Books, 1977).

16. Jacques Derrida, 'Force of Law: The "Mystical Foundation of Authority"', in Drucilla Cornell, Michael Rosenfeld and David Gray Carlson (eds), *Deconstruction and the Possibility of Justice* (New York: Routledge, 1992), pp. 14–19.

17. The checklist of councils and advisory centres set up by the OSCE, the 'lead organization for the institution-building tasks of UNMIK', are impressive. The underlying thrust of their mission is 'to promote the development of a mature, democratic society'. See the OSCE's Mission in Kosova website: www.osce. org/kosovo.

18. See 'Ethnic Rioting Eases in Flashpoint Kosovo City', *Reuters*, 23 February 2000.

19. See the excellent study of the 'aid culture' in James Ferguson, *The Anti-Politics Machine: 'Development', Depoliticization, and Bureaucratic Power in Lesotho* (St Paul: University of Minnesota Press, 1997).

20. Most Kosovar historians desperately seek to situate the late Ottoman period as one of uniform, nationalist revolt. Such imagery, duplicated by all post-war historians of the Balkans, fails to meet realities on the ground. See my 'The Dynamics of Identity: The Albanian in the Ottoman Empire', in Gisela Prochazka-Eisl (ed.), *ACTA Viennensia Ottomanica Akten der 13 CIEPO-Symposiums* (Wien: Vienna University, 1999), pp. 21–34.

21. The monastery in Deçan is a perfect example of how both 'Albanian' and 'Serb' locals developed locally informed myths about such permanent structures. For another example, see the ethnography of Ger Duijzings, 'Kosovo: The End of a "Mixed" Pilgrimage', *ISIM* no. 3 (July 1999), p. 9.

22. The number of variants to Kosova's Ottoman period is revealing in that none of the assumed ethnic markers, which today determine policy, fit realities on the ground. For instance, there are numerous occasions when 'Serbs' fought with the Ottoman army against rebellious locals, among whom were Albanian and Serb speakers. The same holds true in reverse. See Ottoman Archives located in Istanbul, Prime Minister's Archives, BBA, *Meclis-i Vükela Mazbatalari* 1086, 1317.N.26.

23. This is evidenced by the use of the 22 seats held by the 'Serb' community in the legislature in order to put pressure on UNMIK policies to realize, among other things, the return of the Serb military to Kosova.

24. See the party's website: www.kosova.com and its daily newspapers *Bota Sot* and *Rilindja*.

25. For Rugova's perspective see Ibrahim Rugova, *La question du Kosovo* (Paris: Fayard, 1994).

26. The overwhelming unity exhibited was behind a vote for independence (of the 87% of Kosovar residents who voted, 99.3% voted for independence) and not Rugova per se. Rugova, whose organization of the referendum strategically put him, as a political figure, in the spot light, probably was read from the outside as an indication of his popularity among Kosovars.

27. See interview with Rexhep Selimi in *Zëri*, 9 August 1999, pp. 12–17.

28. The OSCE only opened a NGO Council of local NGOs and established guidelines for NGO registration in late January 2000, a good seven months after the international community had taken over distribution of goods and services in the country. In the interim period, local NGOs were largely shut out of operations. See *OSCE Mission in Kosovo Update*, no. 1 (January 2000).

29. For a good summary of the first six months of international administration and how it has implemented some of these standardizations, see Shkelzen Maliqi, 'Special Report: Chaos and Complications in Kouchner's Kosovo', *Balkan Crisis Report* no. 107 (14 January 2000).

30. The International Crisis Group, in a report dated 31 August 1999, came to the same conclusion. See www.crisisweb.org/projects/sbalkans/reports/Kos27rep.htm#3.
31. See analysis of this process in Gjergi Dedaj, 'Dy qeveritë-thembra e Akilit për Kosovën', *Pasqyra* no. 13 (1–7 October 1999), pp. 9–10.
32. The process formally ended in September 1999. An entirely civilian structure has been created, subsequently, to provide positions for some 3,000 former members, the Kosova Defense Force (TMK in Albanian). See how the transition was articulated by the KLA in *Pasqyra* no. 12 (23–30 September 1999), pp. 22–5.
33. It is telling that as the failures of UNMIK's policies have mounted and Belgrade continued to exert influence on the 'Serb' minority, UNMIK shifted its policy. See www.kforonline.com.
34. For the period between July and September 1999, I conducted numerous interviews among UNMIK officials and attended the daily press briefings held at KFOR HQ in Pristina. See respectively the archives of www.kosovapress.com and www.nato/kosovo/press/1999 for sporadic, poor transcriptions of the question and answer periods.
35. Eloquently articulated in Shemsi Reçica, 'Pritja e madhe gjithëshqiptare', *Pasqyra* no. 12 (23–30 September 1999), p. 3.
36. This was reiterated during a visit by Kofi Annan to Pristina, whose insensitive, almost arrogant refusal to discuss anything beyond Kosova's continued attachment to Serbia, had incited weeks of angry editorials in local media. See Blerim Shala, 'Ngadhënjim apo dështim i përbashkët', in *Zëri*, 16 September 1999, pp. 3, 50.
37. Michel Foucault, 'Governmentality', in Graham Burchell, Colin Gordon and Peter Miller (eds), *The Foucault Effect* (Chicago: Chicago University Press, 1991), pp. 87–104.
38. UNHCR spokesman, Ron Redmond, KFOR press conference, Pristina, 12 August 1999.
39. A number which had been acknowledged by Kouchner himself to be much higher than previously admitted by his same office, 'Les extrémistes et les irresponsable ne l'emporteront pas', *Le Monde*, 15 February 2000. See also 'Kosovo Albanians in Serbian Prisons', International Crisis Group (26 January 2000) at www.crisis web.org/projects/sbalkans/reports.
40. Rory O'Sullivan, chief inspector in Kosova for the World Bank press conference, Brussels, 26 July 1999. One can resource the transcript of the press conference at www.worldbank.org/html/exdr/kosovo/kosovots072699.htm.
41. Often the fact that one or more of the members of these boards fought in the defence of his/her village, suggested to the world that this 'Albanian' was a member of the KLA and automatically disqualified them as 'legitimate' leaders in civilian life.
42. The growing number of war diaries among the politically wishful have led to a sharp rise in marking loyalty on the basis of participation in the war for liberation. See, for instance, Bardh Hamzaj's, *Rrëfimi për Luftën dhe Lirinë* (*Dialog me komandantin Ramush Haradinaj*) (Pristina: Zeri, 1999).

REFERENCES

Banks, M., *Ethnicity: Anthropological Constructions* (London, Routledge, 1996).
Blumi, I., 'The Dynamics of Identity: The Albanian in the Ottoman Empire', in G. Prochazka-Eisl (ed.), *ACTA Viennensia Ottomanica Akten der 13 CIEPO-Symposiums* (Wien: Vienna University, 1999), pp. 21–34.

Blumi, I., 'The Commodification of Otherness and the Ethnic Unit in the Balkans: How to Think About Albanians', *East European Politics and Societies* XII (Autumn 1998), pp. 527–69.

Burchell, G., Gordon, C. and Miller, P. (eds), *The Foucault Effect: Studies in Governmentality* (London: Harvester Wheatsheaf, 1991).

Butler, J., *Bodies That Matter: On the Discursive Limits of 'Sex'* (New York: Routledge, 1993).

Campbell, D., *Writing Security* (Minneapolis, University of Minnesota Press, 1998).

Connolly, W. E., *Identity/Difference: Democratic Negotiations of Political Paradox* (Ithaca: Cornell University Press, 1991).

Derrida, J., 'Force of Law: The "Mystical Foundation of Authority"', in D. Cornell, M. Rosenfeld and D. G. Carlson (eds), *Deconstruction and the Possibility of Justice* (New York: Routledge, 1992), pp. 14–19.

Duijzings, G., 'Kosovo: The End of a "Mixed" Pilgrimage', *ISIM* 3 (1999), p. 9.

Eller, J. D. and Coughlan, R. M., 'The Poverty of Primordialism: the Demystification of Ethnic Attachments', *Ethnic and Racial Studies*, vol. 16, no. 2 (1993), pp. 183–202.

Ferguson, J., *The Anti-Politics Machine: 'Development', Depoliticization, and Bureaucratic Power in Lesotho* (St Paul: University of Minnesota Press, 1997).

Foucault, M., 'Governmentality', in Graham Burchell, C. Gordon and P. Miller (eds), *The Foucault Effect* (Chicago: Chicago University Press, 1991), pp. 87–104.

Hamzaj, B., *Rrëfimi për Luftën dhe Lirinë (Dialog me komandantin Ramush Haradinaj)* (Pristine: Zeri, 1999).

Kaufmann, C., 'Possible and Impossible Solutions to Ethnic Civil Wars', *International Security* 20 (1996).

Maliqi, S., 'Special Report: Chaos and Complications in Kouchner's Kosovo', *Balkan Crisis Report* 107 (14 January 2000).

Marglin, S. A., *Dominating Knowledge: Development, Culture and Resistance* (London: Clarendon, 1990).

Mertus, J. and Mihelić, A., *Open Wounds: Human Rights Abuses in Kosovo* (Paris: Helsinki Watch, 1994).

Rugova, I., *La question du Kosovo* (Paris: Fayard, 1994).

Scott, J. C., *Seeing Like a State: How Certain Schemes to Improve the Human Condition Have Failed* (New Haven: Yale University Press, 1998).

Shapiro, M. J., *Violent Cartographies: Mapping Cultures of War* (St Paul: University of Minnesota Press, 1997).

Walzer, M., *Just and Unjust Wars: A Moral Argument with Historical Illustration* (New York: Basic Books, 1977).

12

The European Union and Humanitarian Intervention in Kosovo: A Test for the Common Foreign Policy

Cristina Churruca Muguruza

The sense of shame over past inaction in the first four years of atrocious wars in the former Yugoslavia (1991–1995) remains the main explanation for the European Union and its member states' engagement in the humanitarian intervention in Kosovo.[1] The EU gave its full support to the NATO air campaign to persuade the Federal Republic of Yugoslavia to accept a ceasefire in Kosovo and a political solution to the conflict in order to put an end to the humanitarian catastrophe in Kosovo.[2] They decided to intervene in order to stop the humanitarian catastrophe and they provoked a complex emergency. After the armed stage of the conflict the region was faced with the consequences of the military operation: the humanitarian, the political and the economic ones, with the necessary reconstruction of infrastructure. A new phase of the intervention was opened.[3] Kosovo came under UN Administration (UNMIK) and the European Union was in charge of the economic reconstruction involved with implementing the civilian aspects of rehabilitating and reforming.

One year later, although the international mission has made progress, the situation in Kosovo is still chaotic. There are serious challenges which can lead the intervention to failure. The ongoing violence is making the goal of a multi-ethnic Kosovo appear to be less and less achievable, the macro-economic problems remain unresolved and there is a lack of direction in the UN administration.[4] Underlying the continued tensions within Kosovo – as well as many of the practical problems experienced by UNMIK – is the failure of the international community to address the political solution to the conflict.

The aim of this chapter is to analyse whether the EU policy in the Balkans is able to address a complex political emergency such as Kosovo. In order to do so, the chapter first examines the new context of humanitarian intervention and what kind of challenge a conflict like the Balkans poses to the international community. It then shows how, in theory, the EU now has all the elements to formulate a common foreign policy towards the Balkans: the capability and the willingness to act. In this context the political and economic dimensions of the post-war European Union's policy in the Balkans is considered.

The main argument is that intervention requires a comprehensive strategy that addresses the underlying causes of conflict. This also includes the responsibility for the harm that invariably accompanies the good the intervention does. South-eastern Europe is the EU's crisis-driven back yard. The Balkans, as the centre of conflict, poses a challenge to the EU's crisis management capabilities. Thus, how the EU approaches its relations with this region is regarded as a test of the existence and effectiveness of a common foreign policy. In the face of Kosovo's 'humanitarian' intervention, the need for the European Union to develop a coherent and effective common foreign policy in the region has become a duty.

THE NEW CONTEXT OF HUMANITARIAN INTERVENTION: THE NEED FOR A POLITICAL APPROACH

The end of the Cold War has seen the introduction of a new dimension to the responsibility of the international community to intervene in internal conflicts involving gross violations of human rights which threaten to generate wider instability or unacceptable human suffering. In a series of resolutions adopted since 1991, the Security Council, bearing in mind its primary responsibility for the maintenance of international peace and security as set out in Article 24 of the UN Charter, has clearly recognized that massive and systematic breaches of human rights law and international humanitarian law constitute threats to international peace and security and therefore demand its attention and action.[5] The new humanitarian concern of the Security Council needs to be viewed in the light of the culmination of a complex process in the UN General Assembly which set up the new context for humanitarian action.[6]

As a consequence of this development, humanitarian intervention, instead of being a matter of self-help by states as during the Cold War, is now mainly a collective response with the purpose of implementing UN Security Council resolutions. Intervention is no longer understood as referring only to the use of force but it is now more about considering what kind of intervention, from humanitarian assistance to military intervention, including rehabilitation and reconstruction, should be brought into play in response to humanitarian crises.[7]

The closer connection between humanitarian crises and threats to international peace and security should be seen in general as a positive development. Static non-intervention norms seem to be giving way before a new international consensus whereby minimum humanitarian standards within states would be enforced by the international community. This development opens the way to see state sovereignty as a matter of responsibility, not just power.[8] However the balance sheet of intervention with a basically humanitarian purpose, sanctioned by the Security Council in the 1990s, reveals an inconsistent pattern of involvement. It shows selectivity and a reluctance to accept the risk of casualties and to make long commitments.[9] Moreover, while the UN has been incapable of responding effectively to several humanitarian crises, notably in Somalia, Rwanda and Bosnia, the impetus for peacemaking and peacekeeping, including military intervention, has passed from the Security Council into the hands of regional and subregional organizations, ad-hoc coalitions of UN member states and even individual states.[10]

Why were these and other crises not better managed? Part of the answer lies in a scarcity of information, but on most occasions the relevant information was available. In many cases where it was clear what was needed, governments lacked the necessary political will.[11] In others, part of the problem was attributable to confusion as to how best to respond; policymakers lacked a clear view of the options open to them.[12] Situations involving armed conflict and humanitarian crises challenge the capacity of response of the international community. In these conflicts the use of violence is not irrational, but is used as a medium to reap benefits at the expense of collective misery.[13] In Kosovo the brutal Serb military repression against the ethnic Albanian population during 1998 killed hundreds and displaced upwards of 300,000 people from their homes. The NATO air strikes that began on 24 March 1999 intending to end Serb violence in Kosovo were instead accompanied by escalating violence on the ground and a large refugee outflow that included organized expulsions. Within nine weeks of the beginning of the air strikes, nearly 860,000 Kosovo Albanians fled or were expelled (Albania (444,600), Macedonia (344,500) and Montenegro (69,900)) by the Serb forces.[14]

Complex political emergencies such as Kosovo pose a twofold challenge for the international community.[15] Firstly, there is a need to intervene to save lives and relieve the suffering. Secondly, these emergencies need to be addressed in a coherent manner with an appropriate mix of all available policy instruments (among others political, economic, social, legal, environmental and development measures). The provision of emergency aid must be combined with measures to protect human rights and rehabilitation measures with long-term strategies that address the underlying causes of the emergency. As complex political emergencies are the result of social vulnerabilities produced by deliberate economic, political and military strategies, if conflict is to be avoided or stopped the conditions leading to a predisposition to conflict should be reduced or eliminated.

Humanitarian interventions in complex emergencies pose a political dilemma. There is the question of when to intervene, which involves a difficult weighing up of the relationship between the scale and nature of the humanitarian need and other, international dimensions of the crisis. There is also the so-far unanswered question of whether intervention should take place, raising the contentious issue of criteria for selection and when and why the international community would be right to refuse to intervene. Also, the decision makers need to be clear about what they want to accomplish with the intervention, not only in the short term but also in the long term.[16]

Finally, the new context of humanitarian intervention demands a new political attitude to humanitarianism which recognizes that 'responsibility demands incalculability and unpredictability, while freedom requires that we be responsive to the harms that invariably accompany the good we should do. In short to live ethically, we must think and act politically.'[17]

THE EUROPEAN UNION'S CAPABILITY AND WILLINGNESS TO ACT IN THE BALKANS

When the Maastricht Treaty was agreed in December 1991, it committed the European Union (EU) 'to assert its identity in the international scene, in particular through the implementation of a common foreign and security policy including the eventual framing of a common defence policy, which might in time lead to a common defence' (Article B). To achieve this 'the Union will avail itself of the WEU to elaborate and implement decisions and actions which have defence implications' (Article J.4). Part of Article J.1 of the aim of the Common Foreign and Security Policy (CFSP) was to:

> preserve peace and strengthen international security, in accordance with the principles of the Charter of the United Nations as well as the principles of the Helsinki Act and the objectives of the Paris Charter; to promote international co-operation, and to develop and consolidate democracy and the rule of law, and respect for human rights and fundamental freedoms.

The Maastricht Treaty gave the EU the instruments to develop, for the first time, global foreign policy strategies, combining Community and CFSP measures, towards central and eastern Europe and Mediterranean neighbours. These strategies showed the EU's capability to develop a common foreign policy, namely to formulate policy objectives and the instruments to implement them. However, the EU failed to reach common decisions about reacting quickly to crisis situations. The record of the last years has shown that the EU has not been able to develop a coherent and effective foreign policy to help prevent or resolve conflict. The experience of the EU's policy towards Yugoslavia made it amply clear that it is the dose of political will, and not so much the perfection of instruments and procedures, that determines success in foreign policy.[18]

The willingness to act depends of the existence of a 'common interest'.[19] The common interest doesn't emerge automatically. It is the result of a process of overcoming narrow national interests for the sake of a shared common interest. Appropriate decision-making processes and appropriate structures help to create a common interest but they cannot supplement it.[20] Common interest begins by identifying which objectives and areas are important for the EU and why. The Council 'Report to the European Council in Lisbon on the Likely Development of the Common Foreign and Security Policy (CFSP) with a View to Identifying Areas Open to Joint Action vis-à-vis Particular Countries or Groups of Countries', adopted by the European Council in Lisbon in June 1992, confirmed the existence of important interests in common as the basic criterion for developing a CFSP.[21] The report points out certain factors to help determine important common interests:

1. the geographical proximity of a given region or country;
2. an important interest in the political and economic stability of a region or country;
3. the existence of threats to the security interests of the Union.

According to these factors the Council identified a limited number of geographical areas and, for each area, a number of horizontal issues in respect of which joint action would appear to be 'particularly beneficial for the attainment of the objectives of the Union'. These areas were: central and eastern Europe, in particular the Commonwealth of Independent States and the Balkans; the Mediterranean, in particular the Maghreb, and the Middle East. Regarding former Yugoslavia the essential aim of the EU at that time was 'to promote peace among the peoples and countries of the area and to contribute to safeguarding European security'.[22]

The common interest also arises from the existence of common values, which the EU wants to promote and defended in the international scene. The EU's foreign policy has, as its first objective, to safeguard the common values, fundamental interests and independence of the Union. The common values shared by the member states are laid down in Article F.1 (new Article 6.1) of the common provisions, which confirms their attachment to the principles of liberty, democracy, respect for human rights and fundamental freedoms and the rule of law. Furthermore, respect for human rights is one of the main prerequisites for membership of the European Union and a basic principle informing all its activities. This general objective is specifically stressed in the development cooperation policy, which should contribute to it (Article 177.2, former Article 130 U.2). On these bases, the protection and promotion of human rights has become the mainstay of the EU common foreign policy.[23] With regard to emergency situations, particularly in cases of violence against innocent civilians and refugees, the Union states that to the victims' need for assistance 'corresponds a duty of solidarity of the States concerned and of the international community'.[24]

Although former Yugoslavia was identified as a possible area of common interest and the Union's common values were at stake, the EU didn't take the resolute action that was needed. Early diplomatic and mediation efforts by the EU to stem conflict failed, largely because there was no political will. It could be argued that there was no 'Union' at the time. Neither was there any underlying policy, nor a structure of appropriate mechanisms that might have enabled the Union to contribute to effective international crisis management.[25] When the EU is able to develop a common strategy and despite the fact that Yugoslavia becomes the top priority of the CFSP, it is already too late.[26] Although it worked actively to search for a peaceful solution to the conflict, it failed again to provide protection to the civilian population.

In this context the Kosovo situation was to be forgotten. The need to restore the province's autonomy within Serbia was mentioned only once during the four years of open conflict.[27] Kosovo was not mentioned in EC or EU documents until the 'Declaration on recognition by the EU Member States of the Federal Republic of Yugoslavia', on 6 April 1996. The declaration states that the Union considers the development of good relations with the Federal Republic of Yugoslavia, and of its position within the international community, dependent on a constructive approach by the FRY to its international commitments including 'full respect for human rights, minority rights and the right to return of all refugees and displaced persons and the granting of a large degree of autonomy for Kosovo within the FRY'.[28]

It was not until the Kosovo crisis exploded that the EU finally manifested a willingness to act. The detonator of the international community's intervention in Kosovo was the massacres of Kosovo Albanians in February–March 1998. The brutal repression against the civilian population reminded the Union of the experience of its former inaction in Bosnia.[29] The Kosovo crisis served both as a catalyst and as a wake-up call for the European Union to accept finally its international responsibilities. The debate on the need to develop a European autonomous defence capacity for crisis management opened in October 1998 at the Pörtschach European Council symbolized the new attitude of the Union.[30]

Early in 1999, the EU threw its weight behind the search for a peaceful solution to the Kosovo conflict via the Rambouillet (February) and Paris (March) negotiations, supported by several parliament resolutions and council conclusions. After the failure of the last mediation effort the European

Council meeting in Berlin on 24–25 March issued a statement concerning Kosovo where it clearly stated its willingness to intervene:

> The international community has done its utmost to find a peaceful solution to the Kosovo conflict ... On the threshold of the twenty-first century, Europe cannot tolerate a humanitarian catastrophe in its midst. It cannot be permitted that, in the middle of Europe, the predominant population of Kosovo is collectively deprived of its rights and subjected to grave human rights abuses. We, the countries of the European Union, are under a moral obligation to ensure that indiscriminate behaviour and violence, which became tangible in the massacre at Racak in January 1999, are not repeated. We have a duty to ensure the return to their homes of the hundreds of thousands of refugees and displaced persons. Aggression must not be rewarded. ...[31]

THE EUROPEAN UNION'S STRATEGY IN SOUTH-EASTERN EUROPE

The Kosovo intervention obliged the Union to realize that the region's problems could not be addressed in isolation to each other. Faced with the emergency, the Union foresaw that, 'A political solution to the Kosovo crisis must be embedded in a determined effort geared towards stabilizing the region as a whole.'[32] With this aim the European Union defined its overall objective in the western Balkans as being 'the fullest possible integration of the countries of the region into the political and economic mainstream of Europe'.[33] Practical implementation of this new insight came with the Cologne European Council decisions of 10 June 1999 on developing a comprehensive approach to include all the countries in the region, and to devise a common strategy and a stability pact.

The Vienna European Council announced the adoption of 'EU Common Strategy towards the Western Balkans' in December 1998. The common strategies of the Union, the new CFSP instrument provided in the Amsterdam Treaty (Article 11) were to be implemented by the Union in areas where the Member States had important interests in common. The adoption of such a strategy would clarify the objectives, the duration and the means to be made available for the Union in the western Balkans. However, the announced strategy was not adopted. In the absence of a common strategy, the stabilization and association process for the countries of south-eastern Europe, an initiative launched by the commission in May 1999 with the aim of changing the nature of the contractual relations offered to these countries in the former Regional Approach, has become the centrepiece of the Union's policy in the Balkans.[34]

The process entails the development of a stabilization and association process of Bosnia and Herzegovina, Croatia, the Federal Republic of Yugoslavia (FRY), Macedonia and Albania. The objective is to give the countries of the region the prospect of increasing rapprochement with the EU, with the perspective of full integration into European structures. For that purpose the Union offers to these countries a new kind of contractual relations: Stabilization and Association Agreements (SAAs).

The agreements are being tailor-made, depending on the individual situation of each country. In general they will include formal political dialogue including that at regional level; further development of existing economic and trade relations to and within the area, with the prospect of setting up a free-trade area; further development and partial restructuring of existing economic and financial assistance; strengthened support for democratization and civil society; provisions on justice and home affairs and a commitment to approximate their legislation to that of the EU in various fields. The start of negotiations on such agreements is based on political and economic conditions to be fulfilled by these countries. They will have to gear their political, economic and institutional development to the values and models underpinning the Union: democracy, respect of human rights, and market economy. Regional cooperation is stressed particularly strongly, not as an alternative or precondition of European integration, but as a way to bring it about.[35]

The offer of a new contractual relationship with the prospect of future integration in the European Union is an important political sign to the countries of this region. However the possibility that all five countries fulfil the political and economic conditions in the near future is very unlikely. And even if they do, they will not come into force until the year 2004. It has proved feasible hitherto in Spring 2001 to conclude negotiations with Macedonia. Croatian democratization efforts after the change of government have qualified that country for an SAA, which was concluded in October 2001. Bosnia and Herzegovina continues to be extensively supported and jointly administered by the international community. Albania has still a very long way to go before any thought can be given to issuing a negotiating mandate. With the FRY such an agreement has been delayed by the rule of Milošević until October 2000 and the uncertainty over the status of Montenegro.[36]

The stabilization and association process is considered by the European Union to be an important contribution to the Stability Pact adopted on 10 June 1999. The Stability Pact to 'bring peace, stability and economic development to the region', led by the EU, lays down a framework for cooperation involving not only the Member States and the Commission for the EU as initiator, but also the United States, Russia and the countries of the region (Albania, Macedonia, Bosnia and Herzegovina, Bulgaria, Croatia and FRY, if it fulfils the conditions for its attendance, including neighbouring Hungary, Romania, Bulgaria, Slovenia and Turkey) plus regional and international organizations (UN, UNHCR, the Council of Europe and NATO) and international financial institutions (IMF, World Bank, EIB and EBRD).[37] The attempt is being made not to react country by country but to provide a wider mechanism for taking forward regional solutions and creating a regional dynamic which can ensure long-term and sustainable development. The special feature of this pact is that all participants sit together at the same table. The Stability Pact sets out principles and areas of action with the view to a common approach and specifies the role played by each party, that of the EU being to focus on the development of programmes to underpin democracy, stimulate the economy and foster contractual relations within the region. It is organized around three 'working round tables' on democracy and human rights, economic reconstruction, development and cooperation and on security issues.[38] A special representative of the European Union has been appointed to act as special coordinator of the Stability Pact to ensure achievement of the pact's objectives.[39]

As a consequence of its role within the Stability Pact and within the UNMIK, where it is in charge of the economic sector, the European Union has a central responsibility in the reconstruction and development of the region.[40] The Union is the single biggest donor of assistance. In 1999, the EU, not counting bilateral contributions by its member states, provided a total of €505 million for people throughout the region affected by the Kosovo intervention.[41] The financial allocation for the period 2000–2006 is envisaged to be €5.5 billion for the five countries. Including the €6 billion in pre-accession assistance for Romania and Bulgaria the assistance to south-eastern Europe amounts in total to €11.5 billion. To launch comprehensive assistance to the region and to consolidate the stabilization and association process it will be adopted in a new, single, legal framework. The main objective of the assistance is to help the countries to redirect their political, economic and institutional development in the short-to-medium term. This means concentrating the assistance on building-up and modernizing institutions and administrations so as to strengthen democracy, the rule of law, respect of human rights and minority rights and to provide the institutions and administrations concerned with the skills they need to embark on, and develop, economic and social policies based on market-economy oriented reforms.[42]

With regard to Kosovo, the Union has taken the lead in funding and coordinating its reconstruction. The Union provides about 70 per cent of all reconstruction assistance. Learning from the lessons of Bosnia, the EU has set up a European Agency for Reconstruction to respond to the urgent need for special measures to tackle the post-war reconstruction. The agency should enhance the effectiveness, speed and visibility of European operations, allowing them to be both decentralized and closely coordinated with the United Nations interim administration.[43] In addition to a comprehensive public reconstruction programme, so as to better target donor resources in support of the mission's priorities for reconstruction, the Union has presented an ambitious plan for privatizing Kosovo's medium and large-scale enterprises and for introducing the legal underpinning needed to establish a market economy.

BRIDGING THE GAP BETWEEN RHETORIC AND REALITY

The Lisbon European Council in March 2000 stated the Union's determination to ensure the success of the international effort in Kosovo. To this end it has recognized the need 'to provide support in a much more co-ordinated, coherent fashion, and to ensure that the efforts of the Union and its Member States receive appropriate recognition'.[44] In other words, the Union has lacked the ability to project its capacity in order to implement its foreign policy objectives.

On one side the complex and lengthy procedures of foreign policy formulation and decision making have impeded the Union from reacting rapidly and effectively to developments in the Balkans. The combination of the unanimity requirements constrain policymakers to the search of the lowest common denominator. Decision making is further complicated by inter-pillar frictions. On the other side, there has been inadequate coordination between EU and member state programmes. Additionally, the EU's assistance has not had the expected impact and has suffered from a lack of effectiveness and visibility.[45]

The degree of time lag and variation in development of the five potential SAA countries make it clear that these agreements do not contribute in the short term to the stabilization and development in the region. At its meeting in Lisbon on 23–24 March 2000, the European Council recognized that the Union had not clarified sufficiently what it means by offering 'the perspective of integration' to the countries of the region. The political significance of this process has not been well understood and some have seen it as a bureaucratic exercise instead of the political framework that it represents. The Union had to set out clearly the conditions to be met for each step of the stabilization and association process and more needs to be done to define the objective conditions which should be met at each stage.[46]

The success of the Stability Pact depends on linking political commitment to reform, and regional cooperation to practical and financial support from the international community. Yet the effectiveness of the Stability Pact and of European policy suffers from the multiplicity of institutions and frameworks involved in the region. There is a superposition of international initiatives some centred on the political aspects (the Royaumont process), others on the economic aspects like the SECI (South-East Cooperative Initiative) and the CEI (Central European Initiative).[47] There are also many actors involved in crisis management: special envoys, the High Level Steering Group, individual member states, etc. Consequently there is a high degree of duplication of work.

As regards the EU's assistance to the region, it has been extensive – €4.5 billion since 1991 not counting the contributions of member states. Unfortunately the aid has often been delivered very slowly and has been criticized for being bureaucratic and insufficiently targeted. The existence of two separate legal bases for support to the region, Phare and Obnova, each with their own different administrative and management procedures, has caused endless operational problems. Also the Phare programme has been redirected to serve the new priorities of enlargement and is therefore no longer suited to providing assistance for these countries. The European Union's expected contribution for 2000–2006 represents over half the World Bank assessment of what is needed. Still, this is only the Union's contribution. It does not include the member states. There are other independent evaluations which calculate that some €26 billion will be needed over a period of four years. In the long term more than €79 billion should be envisaged for a period of 12 years.[48] If the European Union wants to bridge the gap between rhetoric and reality, the member states should contribute at least the same amount.

In addition to its regional strategy, the EU supports the reconstruction of Kosovo, participating in KFOR and the UN Mission in Kosovo. In the summer of 1999 the EU countries were able to send 30,000 soldiers to Kosovo at a couple of months' notice, but at May 2000 they had not mustered more than 800 civilian police. One year after the end of the armed intervention, a climate of lawlessness and disrespect for the institutions of public order is perceived as the greatest failure of the international mission. The EU has not yet been able to meet the requests for legal experts and expertise-training to ensure the function of the judicial system and to support basic administrative structures. Also the EU-led Pillar Four of UNMIK, the economic reconstruction pillar, has suffered shortfalls in staff. Because of the EU's inability to recruit qualified staff on time, during the first year of the Kosovo mission, USAID (United States Agency for International Development) stepped in to partially fill the gaps by recruiting contract personnel. The problem has continued during the second year of UNMIK operation.[49]

The main task of Pillar Four is to transform the Kosovo economy into a modern market system. However implementation of EU's privatization plan and market reform has been held up by concerns among the UN staff and some Security Council members that it would prejudice the issue of Kosovo's final status. On the other hand it seems to be no alternative. The Kosovo budget cannot afford to subsidize loss-making public enterprises. Slowness in privatization is blocking the foreign investment needed to restart Kosovo's economy and causing a decline in foreign economic assistance.

Most important, Kosovo Albanians are becoming increasingly impatient with what they see as an international dilatoriness.[50]

In this context, it is necessary that the Union shows the same political and economic commitment to making peace work as it put into the armed intervention. Current EU instruments have to be reviewed and improved if the EU policy is to achieve the desired results. Yet, underlying many of the problems experienced by the European Union is its failure to address the political solution to the conflict. Neither the stabilization and association process nor the Stability Pact confront the issue. Both emphasize regional cooperation as a core element in a lasting solution to the problems of the region. Their failure is to ignore that a premise to regional cooperation is the political solution to the question of Kosovo and a democratic and cooperative change in Serbia. When the armed intervention began the EU clearly stated that:

> the international community's only objective is to find a political future for the Kosovo, on the basis of the sovereignty and territorial integrity of the Federal Republic of Yugoslavia, which does justice to the concerns and aspirations of all people in the Kosovo.[51]

UN resolution 1244 providing an interim international civilian administration for the people of Kosovo reaffirms this statement as the framework for the international community's efforts in the area. The problem is that this is no solution to the conflict. The UNSCR 1244 does not clarify the future status of Kosovo, neither did the Rambouillet Accords before. This makes the task of the UNMIK more difficult, further confuses both Serbs and Albanians and leaves space for self-serving misinterpretations and propaganda. Due to the high level of animosity between the ethnic Albanian and Serb communities, the idea of an autonomy within the FRY seems to be unrealistic at this point. Yet the only lasting peace and stability to the region will come from a political settlement that reconciles legitimate ethnic Albanian interests about the future of the province and long-term peace with Serbia.

Delaying facing reality is only aggravating the problem. If the European Union wants to bridge the gap between rhetoric and reality it should begin thinking about how a final settlement in Kosovo can be integrated into a broader package of regional security and economic and political measures. A stable, permanent settlement for Kosovo cannot be achieved in Kosovo alone. When the issue of Kosovo's final status is decided, the resulting structure will need to be embedded in a series of political, economic and security ties among the nations in the region. The EU could support growing cooperation between Macedonia, Albania and Montenegro. Sub-regional cooperation may turn out to be more efficient economically and politically than the broader, regional cooperation on which past international efforts have focused. The Union could also consider allowing Kosovo and Montenegro to participate, without prejudice to their final status in the stabilization and association process and include them in the Stability Pact. This would open real prospects for regional and European integration.

CONCLUSIONS

Situations involving armed conflict and humanitarian crises like Kosovo pose a twofold challenge for the international community. First of all there is a growing duty to intervene to save lives and relieve the suffering. Second, there is a responsibility to assume the consequences of the intervention. When the EU was finally clear that it wanted 'to do something' in Kosovo it should have had a clear strategy to back it. The intervention in Kosovo required a comprehensive strategy which addressed the underlying causes of conflict and which combined all available policy instruments.

Theoretically the Union should have a comprehensive approach towards the Balkans. It possesses now the capability to develop a common foreign policy and, what is even more important, it has got the willingness to act. The experience of the failure in Yugoslavia has helped to create a common interest in the need for the European Union to accept its international responsibilities and to act in future crises. Besides, learning from its former failures the Union has developed an elaborate approach to conflict prevention and resolution. Further, in Kosovo, the common interest coincided with its proclaimed common values.

Yet the capability and the willingness to act needs to be matched with adequate instruments. In the absence of a common EU strategy towards the western Balkans, the stabilization and association process for the countries of south-eastern Europe and the Stability Pact lack coordination. The stabilization process is unable to contribute to improve the current situation in the western Balkans. The political and economic conditions to be fulfilled make the prospect of concluding agreements with these countries very unlikely in the near future. As a consequence they don't benefit from the additional economic and financial assistance offered by the Union. The Stability Pact, led by the EU, is affected by the excess of actors and the duplication of work. Moreover, both the stabilization process and the Stability Pact avoid addressing the main cause of the current situation: the political solution of the question of Kosovo.

Facing its inability to encourage reform in these countries and to make a substantial contribution to the reconstruction of Kosovo, the EU has decided to reform its policy in the Balkans. To reform its policy won't be enough if the Union does not define a comprehensive strategy towards the western Balkans. If the Union felt that there was a moral obligation to intervene, now it has the duty to help resolve the conflict.

Finally, the Kosovo crisis has been both a catalyst and a wake-up call for the European Union to accept finally its international responsibilities.[52] The EU's decision to develop the necessary means and capabilities for crisis management shows a political will which was lacking before. An autonomous crisis management capability will enable the EU to develop an effective foreign policy. In the future the Union could employ the whole range of instruments from diplomatic activity, humanitarian assistance and economic measures, to civilian policing and military crisis management operations in support of international peace and security. Although it is the dose of political will, and not so much the perfection of instruments and procedures that determines a foreign policy, its success very much depends on the ability to project capabilities in order to implement foreign policy objectives. Without renewed commitment on the part of the member states, more consistency and coordination and increased financial support, the European Union won't be able to meet the challenge of 'humanitarian' intervention.

NOTES

This chapter was first submitted in September 2000. It is part of a research project 'Humanitarian Crisis: Theory and Practice. The Role of the European Union and Western European Union after the Amsterdam Treaty' carried out at the IFHV with support of a Marie Curie Grant of the TMR (Training and Mobility of Researchers) Programme of the EU.

1. There are increasingly critical voices questioning NATO reasons, mainly of the United States, for going to war. See, among others, the special report on Kosovo, 'Kosovo, histoire d'une crise' of *Le Monde Diplomatique* at http://www.monde-diplomatique.fr/cahier/kosovo/.
2. 'Statement by the European Council on Kosovo', *Conclusions of the Presidency*, Special European Council (Berlin, 24–25 March 1999), *Bull.* UE 3-1999, point I. 41.
3. On 10 June 1999, Kosovo came under UN Administration and the UN Mission on Kosovo (UNMIK) was set up under UN Security Council resolution 1244 in order to provide interim international civilian administration for the people of Kosovo. The Special Representative of the Secretary-General presides over the four sectors involved with implementing the civilian aspects of rehabilitating and reforming: civil administration, under the United Nations itself; humanitarian assistance, led by the Office of the UN High Commissioner for Refugees; democratization and institution-building, led by the OSCE and economic reconstruction, managed by the EU. See S/RES/1244 (1999).
4. See International Crisis Group, *Kosovo Report Card*, IGC Balkans Report no. 100, Pristina/Brussels, 28 August 2000 and Security Council, 'Report of the Secretary-General on the United Nations Interim Administration Mission in Kosovo' (S/2000/538).
5. See Security Council, 'Report of the Secretary-General on the Protection of Civilians in Armed Conflict' (S/1999/1257); also General Assembly and Security Council, Report of the Secretary-General pursuant to the statement adopted by the Summit Meeting of the Security Council on 31 January 1992, 'An Agenda

for Peace: Preventive Diplomacy, Peacemaking and Peacekeeping' (A/47/277-S/24111).

6. See O. Rambsbotham and T. Woodhouse, *Humanitarian Intervention in Contemporary Conflict* (Cambridge: Polity Press, 1996), pp. 70–85.

7. For this broader use of the term see, among others, O. Rambsbotham and T. Woodhouse, *Humanitarian Intervention*, and J. Harriss, *The Politics of Humanitarian Intervention* (London: Pinter for the Save the Children Fund, 1995).

8. See K. A. Annan, 'Peacekeeping, Military Intervention, and National Sovereignty in Internal Armed Conflict', in J. Moore (ed.), *Hard Choices* (Lanham, MD: Rowman and Littlefield, 1998), p. 57 and K. A. Annan, 'Two Concepts of Sovereignty', *Economist*, 18 September 1999.

9. See, for example, L. Minear, 'Humanitarian Action and Peacekeeping Operations', *International Peacekeeping*, January 1997–December 1997, pp. 7–18 and *Journal of Humanitarian Assistance*, at www.jha.sps.cam.uk/a/a024.htm (posted on 4 July 1997) and the reports and descriptions available at the web site of the International Crisis Group, www.intl-crisis-group.org/.

10. See M. Griffin, 'Blue Helmet Blues. Assessing the Trend Towards "Subcontracting" UN Peace Operations', *Security Dialogue* 30, 1 (1999), pp. 43–60.

11. See H. Dylan, 'Humanitarian Action in Protracted Crisis: An Overview of the Debates and Dilemmas', *Disasters* 22, 4 (1998), p. 283.

12. While the international community is continuously called upon to handle intrastate wars the usual ad hoc employment of its traditional instruments, in particular peacekeeping and humanitarian aid, has proved costly, sometimes ineffective or even counterproductive. See M. Plugh, 'Peacekeeping and Humanitarian Intervention', in B. White, R. Little and M. Smith (eds), *Issues in World Politics* (London: Macmillan, 1997), pp. 148–9.

13. See Security Council, 'Report on the Protection of Civilians in Armed Conflict'.

14. See UN High Commissioner for Refugees (UNHCR), *The Kosovo Refugee Crisis: An Independent Evaluation of UNHCR's Emergency Preparedness and Response* (10 February 2000), at www.unhcr.ch/evalute/kosovo/toc.htm.

15. A complex emergency is a 'profound social crisis in which a large number of people die and suffer from war, disease, hunger, and displacement owing to manmade and natural disasters, while some others may benefit from it'. The complexity of the emergency arises from the multi-dimensionality of the concepts as well as 'the politicized nature and persistence of the crisis'. R. Väyrynen, *The Age of Humanitarian Emergencies*, UNU/WIDER Research for Action paper no. 25 (Helsinki: 1996), p. 19. See also in this regard the reports and descriptions available at the web site of the Relief Web: Complex Emergencies, at www.reliefweb.int/w/rwb.nsf/WCE?OpenForm.

16. O. Rambsbotham and T. Woodhouse, *Humanitarian Intervention*, pp. 137–8.

17. M. Orlie, *Living Ethically. Acting Politically* (Ithaca, NY: Cornell University Press, 1997), p. 169, quoted in D. Campbell, 'Why Fight: Humanitarism, Principles and Post-structuralism', *Millennium* 27, 3 (1998), p. 519.

18. For an extensive record of the EU response to the Yugoslav crisis, see G. Edwards, 'The Potential and Limits of the CFSP: the Yugoslav Example', in R. E. Regelsberger, P. Schoutheete and W. Wessels, *Foreign Policy of the European Union*, pp. 173–95; S. Lucarelli, 'Europe's Response to the Yugoslav Imbroglio', in K. E. Jorgensen (ed.), *European Approaches to Crisis Management* (The Hague: Kluwer Law, 1997), pp. 35–63.

19. The concept of common foreign policy invokes the existence of interests in common. The Treaty on European Union makes a clear differentiation between

areas of common interest and matters of general interest on which the member states will inform and consult one another within the Council (Article 16, former Article J.2). The Treaty of Amsterdam has included the definition of CFSP 'common strategies to be implemented by the Union in areas where the Member States have important interests in common' (Article 13.2).

20. The almost non-existent preparatory phase of decision making in CFSP has hindered the search for a common interest. The reforms provided in the Amsterdam Treaty are designed to improve the ability of the EU to defend its common interests on the international scene and to strengthen its conflict management capacity.

21. European Council, Presidency Conclusions, European Council in Lisbon (26/27 June 1992), *Bull.* CE 6-1992, point I., Annex I.

22. Ibid.

23. See European Commission, *The European Union and the External Dimension of Human Rights Policy: From Rome to Maastricht and Beyond*, COM (95) 0567, OJ C 320, 28.10.96.

24. 'Declaration on Human Rights', appended to the 'Conclusions of the Luxembourg European Council of 28–29 June 1991', *Bull.* CE 6-1991, point I.45.

25. After the adoption of the Amsterdam Treaty, faced with its inability to respond to conflicts, the EU has elaborated an approach to crisis management. This policy is to take into account the 'human rights' component of conflict prevention and reacting to crises. See C. Churruca, 'The Development of Political/Humanitarian Strategies in Europe. The EU's Political and Humanitarian Objectives: A Contradiction in or a Logical Interdependence?', in H. Fischer (ed.), *Europa und die Zukunft der Humanitären Hilfe – Aus Krisen Lernen* (Bochum: IFHV, 2001).

26. To enlighten this statement it is enough to stress that of the 48 decisions (joint actions and common positions) adopted within the framework of the CFSP from November 1993 to December 1995, 21 (12 joint actions and 9 common positions) concerned Yugoslavia. Yugoslavia also became the major priority of humanitarian action.

27. European Council, 'Presidency Conclusions' (European Council Edinburgh 11/12 December 1992), *Bull.* CE 12-1992, I.

28. PESC/96/30, 1996-04-09.

29. The EU issued more than 20 declarations strongly condemning the brutal repression against the civilian population and demanding the respect of human rights and the political and peaceful solution of the conflict. During NATO's armed intervention against the FRY, from 23 March to 10 June, the European Council, the Parliament and the NATO Council, repeatedly condemned 'ethnic cleansing' and the atrocities in Kosovo, and called on the FRY authorities to meet the demands made by the international community. See the 'General Report on the European Union' (Luxembourg: OPOCE, 2000), no.751.

30. C. Churruca, 'Von Maastricht nach Köln: die Gestaltung der Westeuropäischen Union als ein integraler Bestandteil der Europäischen Union', *Sicherheit und Frieden* 2 (2000), pp. 176–86.

31. Presidency Conclusions, 'II. Statement on Kosovo', Berlin European Council (23 March 1999).

32. 'Declaration on Kosovo', Special Council Meeting – General Affairs – Luxembourg (8 April 1999), *PRESS/94/99*.

33. Presidency Conclusions, 'III. Western Balkans', Lisbon European Council, 23–24 March 2000, *Bull.* UE 3-2000, I.

34. Developing the regional approach set out by the EU in 1996–97 the Commission published a communication on 26 May proposing a new stabilization and association process, which was approved by the Council and adopted and confirmed by the Cologne European Council. See *COM (99) 235* 26 May 1999.

35. The conditions were established by the General Affairs Council on 29 April 1997, *COM (1999) 599*; *Bull.* 11-1999, point 1.5.54.

36. Communication from the Commission to the Council on Operational Conclusions, 'EU Stabilization and Association Process for Countries of South-Eastern Europe', COM *(2000) 49 final/2*, Brussels 2.3.2000.

37. See, Council of the European Union General Secretariat, 'Report on the Western Balkans presented to the Lisbon European Council by the Secretary General/High Representative Together with the Commission', *SN 2032/2/00 REV 2*, Brussels, 21 March 2000, p. 5.

38. In its structure and mechanisms the Stability Pact resembles the process of Helsinki being based on the insight that security, democracy and the rule of law on the one side, and economic development on the other, are two sides of the same coin neither of which can exist without the other.

39. Council Joint Action (1999/434/CFSP of 2 July 1999), *OJ* L 168, 3.7.1999. It was amended and prorogated by Council Joint Action 1999/523/CFSP and Council Joint Action 1999/822/CFS, 29 July 1999, *OJ* L 201, 31.7.1999.

40. See, Council Joint Action (1999/522/CFSP) of 29 July 1999 concerning the installation of the structures of UNMIK, *OJ* L 201, 31.7.1999 and Council Joint Action (1999/864/CFSP) extending Council Joint Action 1999/522/CFSP concerning the installation of the structures of UNMIK, *OJ* L 328, 22.12.1999.

41. €127 million of this total was specifically for reconstruction assistance within Kosovo, plus €7.7 million from 1998. €378 million was in humanitarian aid to the region as a whole, €101.7 million of which was for Kosovo itself. Of this €65.7 million had been contracted and €34.1 million paid as at 6 March 2000. See '1991–1999 EU assistance to South-Eastern Europe & Western Balkans Figures', at europe.eu.int/comm/external_relations/see_balkans_support_91_99. htm.

42. Commission of the European Communities, 'Proposal for a Council Regulation on assistance for Albania, Bosnia and Herzegovina, Croatia, the Federal Republic of Yugoslavia and the former Yugoslav Republic of Macedonia and amending Regulation (EEC) No 3906/89, Proposal for a Council Regulation concerning the European Agency for Reconstruction', *COM(2000) 281 final*, Brussels, 10.5.2000, p. 3.

43. This Agency was established by Council Regulation (EC) No 2454/1999 of 15 November 1999, *OJ* L 299, 20.11.1999.

44. Lisbon European Council, 'III. Western Balkans', 23–24 March 2000.

45. See, 'Report on the Western Balkans', pp. 5–7.

46. Ibid.

47. See, in this regard, N. Vukadinovic, 'Les enjeux de la stabilisation et de la reconstruction des Balkans', *Politique Étrangére* 1 (2000), pp. 151–61.

48. Ibid., p.157.

49. As at 24 May, 3,626 civilian police out of an authorized strength of 4,718 were deployed in Kosovo. This is well below the 6,000 that the advance party estimated would be necessary to police Kosovo effectively. There are also problems with the quality of police from some countries. In response to the shortfall in strength, UNMIK has, since its inception, been conducting joint operations with KFOR. See, 'Security Council, Report of the Secretary-General on the United Nations Interim Administration Mission in Kosovo', paras 31–8 and International Crisis

Group, *Kosovo Report Card*, pp. 42–5.
50. See International Crisis Group, *Kosovo Report Card*, 28 August 2000, pp. 35–41.
51. Presidency Conclusions, 'II. Statement on Kosovo', Berlin European Council (23 March 1999).
52. After the Amsterdam Treaty came into force on 1 May 2000, the Cologne European Council of 4–5 June 1999 marked a decisive step forward in enabling the EU to play its full role in the international scene. The heads of state and government resolved to strengthen the Common Foreign and Security Policy through the development of a military crisis management capability. See, in this regard, C. Churruca, 'Strengthening the European Union's Common Foreign Policy: the European Council's Decision to Develop an Autonomous Military Crisis Management Capability in the Context of Petersberg tasks', *Humanitäres Völkerrecht* 4 (2000), pp. 206–20.

REFERENCES

Annan, K. A., 'Peacekeeping, Military Intervention, and National Sovereignty in Internal Armed Conflict', in J. Moore (ed.), *Hard Choices* (Lanham, MD: Rowman and Littlefield, 1998).

Annan, K. A., 'Two Concepts of Sovereignty', *Economist*, 18 September 1999.

Campbell, D., 'Why Fight: Humanitarianism, Principles and Post-structuralism', *Millennium* 27, 3 (1998), pp. 497–521.

Cassese, A., '*Ex iniuria ius oritur*: Are we Moving towards International Legitimization of Forcible Humanitarian Countermeasures in the World Community?' Comment on: Bruno Simma, 'NATO, the UN and the Use of Force: Legal Aspects', *EJIL* 10, 1 (1999), pp. 24–31.

Churruca, C., 'Von Maastricht nach Köln: die Gestaltung der Westeuropäischen Union als ein integraler Bestandteil der Europäischen Union', *Sicherheit und Frieden* 2 (2000), pp. 176–86.

Churruca, C., 'Strengthening the European Union's Common Foreign Policy: the European Council's Decision to Develop an Autonomous Military Crisis Management Capability in the Context of Petersberg Tasks', *Humanitäres Völkerrecht* 4 (2000).

Churruca, C., 'The Development of Political/Humanitarian Strategies in Europe. The EU's Political and Humanitarian Objectives: A Contradiction in or a Logical Interdependence?' in H. Fischer (ed.), *Europa und die Zukunft der Humanitären Hilfe – Aus Krisen Lernen* (Bochum: IFHV, 2001).

Council of the European Union General Secretariat, 'Report on the Western Balkans presented to the Lisbon European Council by the Secretary General/High Representative together with the Commission', *SN 2032/2/00 REV 2*, Brussels, 21 March 2000.

Dylan, H., 'Humanitarian Action in Protracted Crisis: An Overview of the Debates and Dilemmas', *Disasters* 22, 4 (1998), pp. 283–7.

Edwards, G., 'The Potential and Limits of the CFSP: the Yugoslav Example', in R. E. Regelsberger, Ph. Schoutheete and W. Wessels, *Foreign Policy of the European Union* (Boulder, CO: Lynne Rienner Publishers, 1997), pp. 173–95.

European Commission, *The European Union and the External Dimension of Human Rights Policy: From Rome to Maastricht and Beyond*, COM(95)0567, OJ C 320, 28.10.96.

General Assembly and Security Council, position paper of the Secretary-General on the occasion of the 50th anniversary of the United Nations, Supplement to an

Agenda for Peace' (A/50/60-S/1995/1).

General Assembly and Security Council, 'Report of the Panel on United Nations Peace Operations' (A/55/305-S/2000/809).

General Assembly and Security Council, Report of the Secretary-General pursuant to the statement adopted by the Summit Meeting of the Security Council 31 January 1992, 'An Agenda for Peace: Preventive Diplomacy, Peacemaking and Peace-keeping' (A/47/277-S/24111).

Gnsotto, N., *Lessons from Yougoslavie*, Institute for Security Studies Western European Union, Chaillot Papers 14 (Paris, 1994).

Grasci, S., 'L'introduzione delle operazioni di peace-keeping nel Trattato di Amsterdam: profili giuridici ed implicazioni politische', *La Comunità Internazionale* vol. III (1998), pp. 295–326.

Grenaway, S., *Post-Modern Conflict and Humanitarian Action: Questioning the Paradigm* (posted 1999), at www.reliefweb.int/library/documents/paradigm.htm.

Griffin, M., 'Blue Helmet Blues: Assessing the Trend Towards "Subcontracting" UN Peace Operations', *Security Dialogue* 30, 1 (1999), pp. 43–60.

Harriss, J., *The Politics of Humanitarian Intervention* (London: Pinter for the Save the Children Fund, 1995).

Holme, T. T. and Eide, E. B. (eds), 'Peacebuilding and Police Reform', *International Peacekeeping* 6, 4 (special issue, Winter 1999).

International Crisis Group, *Kosovo Report Card*, IGC Balkans Report no. 100 (Pristina, Brussels: 28 August 2000).

International Monetary Fund, *The Economic Consequences of the Kosovo Crisis: An Updated Assessment Prepared by staff of the International Monetary Fund in consultation with the World Bank staff*, approved by Michael C. Deppler and G. Russell Kincaid (25 May 1999).

Jorgensen, K. E. (ed.), *European Approaches to Crisis Management* (The Hague: Kluwer Law, 1997).

Minear, L., 'Humanitarian Action and Peacekeeping Operations', *International Peacekeeping*, January 1997–December 1997, pp. 7–18 and *Journal of Humanitarian Assistance*, at www-jha.sps.cam.uk/a/a024.htm (posted 4 July 1997).

Le Monde Diplomatique, 'Kosovo, histoire d'une crise', at www.monde-diplomatique.fr/cahier/kosovo/.

Lewis, F., 'The Kosovo Mission of the United Nations is Being Left to Fail', *International Herald Tribune*, 10 March 2000.

Lucarelli, S., 'Europe's Response to the Yugoslav Imbroglio', in K. E. Jorgensen (ed.), *European Approaches to Crisis Management* (The Hague: Kluwer Law, 1997), pp. 35–63.

Orlie, M., *Living Ethically. Acting Politically* (Ithaca, NY: Cornell University Press, 1997).

Pagani, F., 'A new Gear in the CFSP Machinery: Integration of the Petersberg Tasks in the Treaty on European Union', *European Journal of International Law*, vol. 9, no. 4 (1998), pp. 737–49.

Plugh, M., 'Peacekeeping and Humanitarian Intervention', in B. White, R. Little and M. Smith (eds), *Issues in World Politics* (London: Macmillan, 1997), pp. 134–56.

Rambsbotham, O. and Woodhouse, T., *Humanitarian Intervention in Contemporary Conflict* (Cambridge: Polity Press, 1996), pp. 70–85.

Salmon, T., 'Testing Times for European Political Co-operation: The Gulf War and the Yugoslavia, 1990–1992', *International Affairs*, vol. 68, no. 2 (April 1992), pp. 233–53.

Security Council, 'Report of the Secretary-General on the Protection of Civilians in Armed Conflict' (S/1999/1257).

Security Council, 'Report of the Secretary-General on the United Nations Interim Administration Mission in Kosovo' (S/2000/538).

Simma, A., 'NATO, the UN and the Use of Force: Legal Aspects', *EJIL*, vol. 10, no. 1, pp. 1–23.

UN High Commissioner for Refugees, *The Kosovo Refugee Crisis: An Independent Evaluation of UNHCR's Emergency Preparedness and Response* (10 February 2000), at www.unhcr.ch/evaluate/kosovo/toc.htm.

Väyrynen, R., *The Age of Humanitarian Emergencies*, UNU/WIDER Research for Action paper no. 25 (Helsinki: 1996).

Vukadinovic, N., 'Les enjeux de la stabilisation et de la reconstruction des Balkans', *Politique Étrangére* 1 (2000), pp. 151–61.

Eberwein, W. D. and Chojnacki, S., 'Capacity and Willingness to Act: Two Constitutive Elements of Strategy Design', in H. Fischer (ed.), *Europa und die Zukunft der Humanitären Hilfe – Aus Krisen Lernen* (Bochum: IFHV, 2001).

Wallensteen, P. and Sollenberg, M. 'Armed Conflict and Regional Conflict Complexes', *Journal of Peace Research* 35, 5 (1998), pp. 621–34.

13

Questioning Reconstruction:
Reflections on Theoretical Foundations for
Conceptualizing Reconstruction in Kosovo

Jens Stilhoff Sörensen

FROM DEVELOPMENTALISM TO RECONSTRUCTION:
SHIFT IN AID POLICY

Parallel to the protracted Yugoslav crisis an important shift in the structure of international aid, or aid policy as an instrument, has taken place. This shift, which had already taken off in Africa in the 1980s and the features of which have become increasingly clear and general during the last decade, has been analysed as a logical response to the emergence of a number of regions marked by protracted political crises and institutional collapse coupled with internal wars and complex humanitarian emergencies.[1] One aspect of this shift was the idea of linking relief to development combined with the reprioritization of aid budgets, leaving larger budgets for humanitarian assistance at the expense of various forms of development aid. In the process an established set of ideas concerning development has become discursively replaced by a concept of so-called reconstruction.[2] The whole discourse of 'development' and 'development aid' was, as it were, embedded in the ideology and logic of bipolarism. In the same instance as the bipolar (Cold War) global power system has, at least for the time being, tended to be replaced by a unipolar (US), or in some aspects multi-polar, system a new basis for dealing with the so called 'periphery' in the global power system has emerged. But ideas of development are deeply rooted in social imagery.[3] Just as elements of the more specific political development theory, following its decline in the 1960s, started to reoccur in the 'liberal' or 'non-marxist' attempts to develop a new political economy of development,[4] it would be fair to say that develop-mentalism as a project has re-invented itself in relation to conflict and 'post-war reconstruction'. In a similar manner aspects of political development theory have found new ground in relation to the 'transition' view on post-communist societies.

Social reconstruction as discourse and practice implicates radical elements of a policy shift as well as new strategies and forms of policy implementation. In terms of policy 'reconstruction' brings forward the idea that whole societies can be transformed and reconstructed according to a certain liberal, democratic scheme. This includes the transformation to a liberal (market) economy as well as a transformation to democratic practices, rituals and institutions, including programmes for reconciliation, civil society building and multiculturalism as a political vision for conflict resolution and the social integration of multi-ethnic/polynational societies. In terms of implementation it involves a network of organizations with partly over-lapping and partly complementary functions. The result has been an increase in the subcontracting of non-governmental organizations (NGOs), which are financed to work directly, or via local partners, in the crisis area. In this manner NGOs have been increasingly financed to work in the field of social reconstruction or with democracy assistance, reconciliation, etc., with the perspective that they are reconstructing (or constructing) a civil society, supposed to function as an important agent in a *transition* to democracy.[5] The subcontracting of NGOs has been incorporated in the networks of institutions that are implementing this new practice.

In Bosnia-Herzegovina this model has been in place since the war. In addition to all traditional international actors (including various UN agencies, ICRC, IFRC etc.) a number of new institutions and organizations have developed. Virtually all traditional, as well as a range of new, methods are being tested in Bosnia-Herzegovina. All organizations there, including NATO, OSCE, OHR, UN, etc., are faced with open-ended mandates. Yet the result, four years after the war, is very little progress in terms of reconciliation, democratization, repatriation and social reconstruction.[6] What remains is a ceasefire and a limbo, on a territory where three centripetal ethnic 'forces' are institutionalizing themselves. The prospects for Kosovo, should this be reproduced, seem no brighter.

The concept of regional cooperation cum reconstruction, such as the intentions outlined in, for example, the 'Stability Pact for South Eastern Europe' (launched by the EU in summer 1999) and 'Toward Stability and prosperity: A Programme for Reconstruction and Recovery in Kosovo',[7] is perceived to be the main instrument or method to create political and social stability (and thereby also avoiding refugee flows). To this latter problem is connected the problem of how to conceptualize the situation in Kosovo. That is, how one is to understand and conceptualize the social, economic and structural processes and changes that Kosovo and the entire post-Yugoslav social and political space are experiencing. This chapter is concerned with the problem of conceptualization in relation to post-war reconstruction. Particularly I want to question the underlying assumptions for reconstruction and contrast them with an alternative systemic perspective, which suggests that in the Balkans in general, including Kosovo, we are witnessing a new form of political project and political economy rather than mere social and institutional breakdown. This perspective draws on a number of authors with whom we can see the contours of a new theoretical framework of political instability and internal war, which poses fundamental challenges to aid policy and reconstruction. In a rough division three competing perspectives seem available: various forms of transition (to liberal democracy); war as social transformation and war as social breakdown. This chapter is a searchlight and the conclusions are tentative, but it attempts to point in a direction of where the questions on reconstruction should be posed.

THE TRANSITIONAL PERSPECTIVE AND RECONSTRUCTION IN KOSOVO

The Stability Pact for south-eastern Europe (and also the Dayton Agreement) indicates three measures for support: reconciliation, regional cooperation and social reconstruction.

Regional Cooperation cum Reconstruction

Regional cooperation includes aid policy and the ideas of a so-called reconstruction plan for the Balkans (sometimes labelled 'a Marshall Plan for the Balkans'). The document on the Stability Pact outlines a series of intentions and competences for various actors. There are, however, no concrete ideas about viable solutions for the region, or how underlying problems should be tackled. The idea of a Balkan reconstruction plan is indeed the necessary departure for any future economic development or stability in the region. The problem is how to realize it. An analogy with the Marshall Plan is weak though. First the Marshall Plan was launched in the wake of a complete restructuring of the global economy and international system. There was a new basis for international trade as the gold standard had finally collapsed in the period before the Second World War. New institutions were constructed for regulating trade and the international economy as such. Secondly, the Marshall Plan was implemented largely in industrial societies that had chiefly cooperative governments, or as in the case of Germany, were occupied after an unconditional surrender. Third, the Marshall Plan was launched towards a Keynesian background with the State as an important agent in development. Moreover, the Marshall Plan was a real transfer of resources to which current aid has no parallel.[8]

Social Reconstruction includes democratization, institutional reconstruction, the development of 'civil society', political liberalization, institutional capacity building, good governance and the like, aiming also at creating an idea or a concept of multicultural coexistence and co-operation. Social reconstruction is naturally incorporated in the idea of regional cooperation–integration, just as a dimension in reconciliation (alternatively it could be labelled an umbrella for the above). We can analytically separate it however, since regional cooperation is not equivalent to social reconstruction. Social reconstruction could, at least in theory, be undertaken without regional cooperation. It seems, however, unrealistic to expect any development of a formal market economy without regional integration, just as it seems impossible to have social reconstruction without a functioning formal economy. However, regional cooperation could be understood minimally merely as certain governmental performances, bilateral agreements and fulfilment of international obligations (especially in relation to political liberalization, minority protection and refugee repatriation policy) being conditional in order to receive credits, physical reconstruction assistance and integration into Euro–Atlantic institutions. This also sets a limit for the involvement of bilateral assistance. Social reconstruction goes further as it contains the reconstruction of a whole institutional framework (including such as international support to restructure the banking sector, pension systems, etc.). These instruments can be divided into institutional cooperation, multilateral or bilateral assistance to governmental bodies, and non-institutional cooperation i.e., support for civil society, media and NGOs, etc.

These practices have been a main idea in post-Dayton reconstruction thinking for Bosnia-Herzegovina.[9] The institutional work has, however, largely become directly controlled by the international bodies in Bosnia-Herzegovina, which has evolved into a protectorate. We may essentially treat these various organizations as a network of an emerging system of global governance.

Although the NGO-subcontracting seen as civil society safeguarding democracy is an assumption highly problematic in itself,[10] it has fitted well with the change in the aid-policy approach.[11]

A Programme for Reconstruction

The 'Programme for Reconstruction and Recovery in Kosovo'[12] outlines a kind of 'damage and deficiency' assessment (my label) of Kosovo, and suggests concrete measures for rebuilding institutions, infrastructure and revitalizing the local economy. It is fairly clear that the assumptions in the document are that Kosovo has an 'illness' which can be diagnosed as 'war damages' combined with 'transition and development problems'.[13] This is also stated explicitly in the European Commission and World Bank information document called the 'Regional Reconstruction and Development Programme'. This diagnosis can be questioned though. Post-communist transition in eastern Europe has been interpreted in the framework of democratization and liberalization, i.e., as if the main trend is a struggle for *transition* to democracy and market economy. The discourse on transition has been widely criticized for ignoring specific national and regional characteristics, idealizing Western institutions and for presupposing a linear process of change.[14]

Although the transition approach itself has undergone changes and had varying conceptions in the 1990s, such as for example the 'shock-therapy' versus the 'gradualist' approach as well as variations in the importance acknowledged to institutions,[15] the fundamental principles have remained much the same, and although the implicit evolutionism in the transition approach has been questioned it nevertheless remains the dominant way of conceptualizing post-communist change.[16]

A fundamental assumption is that the societies and states in question have suffered a structural and institutional breakdown inducing, as well as being increased by, violent conflict. This is interpreted as an abnormal situation in contrast to a more harmonious development, which is the norm. It is also understood that reconstruction (rather than development in the discourse of the late 1990s) of the societies through effective and accountable institutions with the introduction of a market economy through privatization as well as promoting the rule of law, securing property rights, etc., as a corner stone for a functioning market economy, will promote a more stable environment and promote development. This is symptomatic of how development discourse has reinvented itself through conflict, and the idea that it is conflict as such that is the abnormal evil that has destroyed the socio-cultural environment and increased poverty.

While the Stability Pact so far has had little to say in concrete terms, the 'Programme for Reconstruction and Recovery'[17] seems to see no political problem at all. Here all the issues are technical. The problem of Kosovo is firstly located firmly in the concept of 'post-war trauma' and of 'transition'.[18] Then, while it is stated that the future of Kosovo lies in a 'full reintegration within the region',[19] the priorities for support are a strengthening and reforming of existing institutions,[20] rebuilding infrastructure, small scale agriculture, small enterprise and supporting transition to a market economy.[21] The strengthening of existing institutions is not treated as a political problem with regard to inter-ethnic relations but appears merely technical. The institutional dimension is, however, central to the problem of inter-ethnic relations; consequently, also central to future security and stability of the region, as well as for any future reintegration or regional cooperation, and should therefore need a detailed analysis. Moreover, the political formula and status for Kosovo will have implications on people's loyalties and influence both institutional aspects and political behaviour.[22] Similarly, the recommendation of encouraging a private sector is located within a transitional conceptual framework. Although the

Programme for Reconstruction and Recovery acknowledges that there are 'worrying reports about the development of organized illegal groups, possibly linked to criminal networks in neighbouring countries or in the diaspora'[23] and although there are no functioning institutions and no existing *state*, the Programme for Reconstruction and Recovery indicates that the social agent for development is one of private enterprises and entrepreneurs relying on a free market. While it is noted that 'markets have been lost',[24] the task seems to be merely the creation of a judicial climate and legal framework, so that a market can be reconstructed, and to provide incentives so that the grey economy can join the formal sector.[25]

Although the Stability Pact acknowledges the need for regional reintegration and cooperation, that is, a larger market, for the formal economy to develop and grow, as well as a necessity for regional security and stability, it has no means or instruments to support this. The Programme for Reconstruction and Recovery by contrast, does not enter into these political problems (which are implicitly suggested in the Stability Pact).

In effect the programme sketches out a reconstruction, or rather construction, of an economy and political management which has not existed in the area before, and which is based on a theoretical model derived from a liberal, democratic, Western perspective. Moreover, within the various models of capitalist development, that is, with a simple distinction between the social-market model (as in the German case), the state mercantilism model (as in the Japanese case) and the Anglo-American, laissez-faire neo-liberalist model,[26] it appears from the reconstruction plan that the social agent for development is neither the state, nor any corporatist model, but the rules of the free market, where the institutional-political framework and the state, are merely to guarantee certain institutions and regimes, such as property rights, contracts, etc. The international protectorate will ensure a 'fixing of the space for capitalism'.[27] This laissez-faire neo-liberalist approach has gained strength relative to other models of development internationally. In the reconstruction plan the issues of agency for development or of the structural conditions, let alone the systemic, are absent. The analysis has had to give way for a technicalized inventory list which functions more like a manual for reconstruction and transition, much in the same way as you can have manuals for technical devices. With some of the details amended, this might have been produced for any other developing or 'post-conflict' country on the globe.

Such assumptions do, however, avoid systemic connections. An alternative way of conceptualizing post-communist change is the one I will call 'adaptation to marginalization'. Here we can draw on a number of authors using metaphors such as: marginalization,[28] new medievalism,[29] re-peripheralization, re-traditionalization,[30] polarization, bifurcation[31] and transition to feudalism.[32] The basic framework is an integrated macrostructural perspective for the understanding of local processes.

GLOBALIZATION AND MARGINALIZATION ADAPTATION: THE SYSTEMIC VIEW

Although the Yugoslav experience has its own particular dynamics due to its social and ethnic structure, its power relations, and its own efforts and strategies to develop and integrate into the global economy, the macro-structural context enriches the analysis on local ethnic mobilization, internal war and consequences for international conflict management, aid policy and international security. The neo-liberal ideology which gained strength in the 1980s and entered the 1990s as the sole alternative after the end of bipolarism and the reshaping of capitalism during the post-Cold War period seem to have wiped out any competing political projects (at least as far as political agendas in the West are concerned). However, as the character of the international economy or of global capitalism, since the 1970s, has been the formation of and increasing integration in three economic blocks (west Europe, North America and south-east Asia) the areas outside these blocks have been excluded and increasingly marginalized.[33] While the dynamic factors of world economy and international trade, increasingly have taken place within and between these blocks, the effect in other areas has been increasing marginalization or peripheralization as systemic economic crises, in areas like eastern Europe has rolled back earlier achieved development gains. The development gap has grown wider, as have income disparities, and in this new periphery we have also witnessed political instability, increased migration and a steady rise in internal wars.[34]

As Kaldor notes, these 'new wars' share many things in common, whether in Africa or in the Balkans, and they involve a blurring of the distinctions between war, organized crime and large-scale violations of human rights and, although they are localized, they involve a myriad of transnational connections.[35] Kaldor also suggests that they are a part of a process, which is more or less a reversal of the process through which modern states evolved.[36] Duffield views conflict from a perspective of social transformation and notes that there has been a strong trend of redefining political authority within those unstable areas.[37] Political separatism and regional fragmentation has accelerated in the periphery. While some states have been redefined as ethno-nationalist projects there have, in other areas, been warlord structures emerging, which have fashioned so called weak or failed states, where the resource base has been insufficient for a formal state monopoly.[38] In the former Yugoslavia and in Bosnia a similar trend has been noted, where an 'ethno-nationalist elite' has expanded illegal economic activities including drug trafficking, trade in stolen goods and pure robbery and looting of the indigenous population.[39] This, is a complement to achieving control over factories and the industrial infrastructure in a highly dubious privatization process.[40] So, while 'transitional thinking' – for example by economists advocating 'shock therapy' in the early 1990s, as

263

well as by the more gradualist oriented – regards state disintegration, socio-economic exclusivism, and ethno-nationalism in the Balkans and the successor states in the former Soviet Union area as a temporary normative breakdown due to abnormal occurrences and the trauma of communism, we may instead regard these developments as the emergence of new forms of political projects connected to a particular kind of political economy. Rather than mere social breakdown they represent social change and transformation. This transformation is, however, largely based on exclusion of large groups of people. In Serbia, for example, this social change has continued forcefully throughout the 1990s with a consolidation of the new elites parallel to an economic redistribution, 'primitive accumulation' of resources, expansion of criminal forms of economy and a change in social stratification.[41] These new forms of political economy in the marginalized areas may, for example, through the informal trade networks, be just as 'internationalized' as liberal economies in the core areas. While the formal economy of these marginalized areas has broken down and shows meagre performance, the informal economy can be linked up with broader trans-national networks. Such processes have been noted in Africa as well as in Bosnia. Similarly, the financing of the KLA in Kosovo has drawn on international networks and trans-border trade, including remittances by the diaspora,[42] as well as trade in illegal goods, such as narcotics, and been linked up with wider international networks of illegal trade and money laundering.[43] This does not mean that all economic activities are of this kind, rather it is to say that there is a development of alternative forms of integrating in international trade networks and in the global economy as means of provision.

Also, in the struggle for resources, the development of a parallel economy, and indeed war itself, is a rational activity. As William Reno notes it can be seen with reference to economic motivations that are specifically related to the intensification of transnational commerce in recent decades, and to the political economy of violence inside a particular category of states.[44] Reno calls this category of states 'Shadow States' in which political instability is manipulated to become the norm:

> Another key element of the Shadow State is the ruler's effort to prevent individuals from gaining unregulated access to markets, unless they demonstrate to the ruler that they can contribute to his personal power. A Shadow State ruler may then logically seek to make life *less secure* and *more materially impoverished* for subjects.[45]

The individuals who can demonstrate to the ruler that they can contribute to his power are 'clients' in a patron–client relationship with the ruler or indeed with a client of the ruler in a clientelist network developing through the society. Such networks, which are found in Africa,[46] were also strengthened throughout Yugoslav society during the 1970s and 1980s where informal ties became increasingly important as the economic crisis deepened and Yugoslavia became increasingly marginalized in the international division of labour,[47] and have consolidated throughout the war in, for example, Bosnia,[48] just as in other parts of eastern Europe.[49]

The processes of integration and disintegration are closely connected parts of what we may call globalization. Duffield describes this as the bifurcation of the world system, and claims that

> as conventional forms of economy are disappearing in the periphery one can no longer assume that a process of modernization will eventually raise life-chances here, or that an exploitative relation necessarily links the centre and the periphery.[50] Reflecting such changes, earlier modernization and dependency theories have fallen from fashion.[51]

Similarly, Hoogvelt concludes that the periphery is no longer needed for the global capitalist system, and that developmentalism has given way to exclusion and containment.[52]

Robert Cox has noted that 'Neoliberalism is transforming states from being buffers between external economic forces and the domestic economy into agencies for adapting domestic economies to the exigencies of the global economy'.[53] Inspired by Karl Polanyian,[54] Cox is expecting some counter-movement to the restructuring of the global economy.[55] Also Hettne and Gill take their departure in a Polanyian framework in understanding systemic changes that have been in process since at least the 1980s.[56] The collapse of the Soviet Union and planning economies in eastern Europe are a symptom of those changes as much as they reinforce them.[57] One dimension of such a counter-movement from a global point of view may be the development of parallel economies clustered around clientelist structures in marginalized areas.[58] Although connected to formal economic decline and social exclusion they represent new forms of political projects, with new forms of legitimacy, rather than mere social breakdown. Induced by empirical evidence[59] this perspective is in stark contrast to transitional logic for eastern Europe or much of the development theory for Africa.[60]

Peripheralized Balkans

This perspective is highly relevant for Kosovo as well as most of the post-Yugoslav space. Ethnicity achieves its meaning in social and economic contexts. The mobilization of nationalist sentiments and instrumentalization of inter-ethnic conflicts in Yugoslavia is intimately connected to a wider social, economic, structural and institutional breakdown and transformation. This had strong effects on the legitimacy of the political system and the existing social contract, which evolved into an identity crisis.[61] One of the important root causes behind the crisis was the structural problems built into the system, which in connection with the changes in the international economy, and the strategies of foreign creditors and finance institutions, would pose paramount problems to the modernization project.

As discussed in detail by Schierup, the social contract, formed at the local level between the local and regional political–bureaucratic elites and manual workers throughout Yugoslav society took the form of patron–client relationships where the elite (the patrons) guaranteed work and a minimal income for the new manual workers (the clients) in return for loyalty, thus providing legitimacy for the elite.[62] These networks were revitalized and strengthened through the 1970s and 1980s where the local and republican political–bureaucratic elites came to defend protectionist economic interests through political means. These networks came to take features of an increasingly traditionalistic character.[63]

This process was even further strengthened and fuelled by the disintegration of the 'real socialist' structure and the deterioration of the self-management system. As there was no other structure replacing it, this left a vacuum in which masses of the working population inevitably looked for any type of protection.[64] As Yugoslavia faced a failure in its modernization project[65] and became increasingly marginalized in the international economy there was a kind of 'retraditionalization' of the local community.[66] The crisis also had particularly problematic consequences in Kosovo, which was the most underdeveloped province in Yugoslavia. The Albanian community in Kosovo, which was still characterized largely by the *fises* (clans, tribes) and village communities, also had to rely on traditional links in the development of an Albanian parallel system, divided from the Serbian state through the 1990s, as a response to the withdrawal of autonomy.[67] Just as Yugoslavia was peripheralized in the international economy, Kosovo was a periphery within Yugoslavia. The parallel system of the 1990s was ethnically closed, since it was a response to the discriminatory practices of the Serbian regime (although there were elements of economic cooperation with the Serbian, and other, minorities). In terms of the economy though it was not isolated since it was financed partly by tax collections (3 per cent of income) in the diaspora and voluntary contributions, as well as through aid money coming in from foreign donors and aid agencies.[68] Indeed several institutions in the parallel society, particularly the media, depended on the latter. At the same time the institutional framework in Serbia deteriorated and also Serbs living in Serbia were suffering under an increasing dissolution of the social contract.[69] A process of state breakdown and attempts of statebuilding went hand in hand and a destruction of pluralism, and of alternatives to the authoritarian regime, has continued effectively within different spheres of society since the so-called anti-bureaucratic revolution of the late 1980s.[70] This 'atomization' of society has also prevented alternative political alliances.

Ethnicity and the State

Commenting on the European pattern of state-making Charles Tilly prefers the analogy of organized crime to that of the development of a social contract.[71] Rulers of medieval Europe not only relied on indirect rule via local magnates, they also commissioned bandits and outlaws in times of war. Although the king relied on the forces of the feudal lords in order to fight a war, between themselves feudal lords and local magnates were rivals, and sometimes rivals to the king. For this reason they reliably produced civil wars. The development of a police force was a method of maintaining internal control, while at the same time reducing the threat the military would pose. This separation and creation of a division of armed men, one for internal, the other for external purposes, was an important aspect in state-making.

Tilly's analysis seem to have parallels with, for example, the regional war in central Africa or the situation in the Balkans. In some areas, like the former Yugoslavia, where it is not even clear how many states will emerge, we seem to have a new process of state building, as state making also follows the logic of the ethno-nationalist rhetoric and the recognition of new territories for self-determination.[72] Terms like 'neo-medievalism' and 'new feudalism' have also been suggested as metaphors for post-socialist developments.[73]

Although local elites like, for example, the ethno-nationalist elite[74] in the Yugoslav successor states, were struggling for power in and creation of political constituencies, it is not certain that internal wars represent an initiation of state building that parallels the early European pattern. Instead, local rulers and strongmen may have economic motivations to maintain a certain level of instability. By manipulating political violence, speeding it up or slowing it down, economic gains can be made and keep business going. This may be an actual alternative to building expensive state institutions. Through non-territorial elements, such as the global networks that are drawn upon, there may be a new type of geography emerging where one can see a distinction between classical bureaucratic states and states without effective bureaucratic institutions, but which are states in formal terms. As Reno has noted, for example, many rulers in Africa have preferred to conserve resources and instead devoted them to payouts among key strong-men in return for obedience.[75] Reno also noted that they create rival mini-shadow states based on direct, personal accumulation, rather than on control of bureaucratic institutions.[76] This is also what Griffiths observed in Bosnia, where the ethno-nationalist elite not only exploited and robbed the local population in their own area of control, but in addition used displaced persons and refugees as an instrument for maintaining the instability necessary for preserving and recreating patron–client relationships.[77] Ordinary corruption, robbery and trade in legal and illegal goods form the economic base as well as asset transfer from ethnic cleansing.[78] A lack of rule of law is necessary in order to preserve the use of patronage. Similar observations have been made in Croatia, where property rights are uncertain and disputed,[79] laws are discriminatory and implemented in a discriminative way, court decisions are arbitrarily enforced and members of the military, particularly, violate laws and court decisions.[80] A certain level of insecurity is necessary to maintain clientelism.

This view suggests that 'war' and 'peace' are relative concepts rather than separate states.[81] Consequently that political and social instability is durable and must be seen as a long-term response, rather than a temporary normative breakdown. Or, indeed as an alternative way of integrating into the international economy drawing upon international networks in addition to local resources.

CRIMINALIZING THE PERIPHERY: WAR AS SOCIAL BREAKDOWN

A view which is in contrast to the transition perspective, and seems to be related to 'marginalization adaptation' is the perspective of social breakdown in the periphery induced by globalization. Representative of this is Mary Kaldor's perspective of the 'new wars' being a symptom of social change and social breakdown, where the political economy of the new wars is transnational and where the distinction between war and crime is blurred and would better be described as a slowing down or speeding up of political violence.[82] Globalization is understood as a process of inclusion and exclusion and Kaldor notes a cleavage between those who take part in global processes and those who are excluded. This enables her to make a distinction of a bipolar relationship between 'cosmopolitans' versus 'particularists/ nationalists' where the cosmopolitan view explicitly is the more 'modern', 'democratic' and 'civic', with assets and resources available that the locals do not have.[83] The problem with this perspective is that it mutates. After having analysed the transnational links and connections to the local 'war economy', and the economic and social exclusions at a systemic and structural level, the analysis slides towards an actor-oriented perspective in order to 'criminalize' those actors together with the entire political economy and political systems, which they are assumed to propagate. This 'slide' to a focus on actors and subjects is unfortunate since it disconnects the political actors from the structural environment in the last instance and thereby reduces the political project that is being created to a matter of individual behaviour and greed. While this perspective starts off by analysing how the macro-structures and systems produce exclusion and a particular economy of the 'new wars', it suddenly seems to be due to entrepreneurship among local agents. The first half carries features of dependency theory, while the latter half suddenly hosts elements from modernization theory and has evolved into a covert, liberal, 'universal values' yardstick. This tendency is also a risk with a careless application of Castells' view.[84]

Instead the analysis must emphasize on the one hand the connection and structural features between the two, e.g., how local entrepreneurship is reflecting a much wider systemic crisis while, on the other hand, also seek to understand the social structures in the local society, the nature of transformation and the new forms of political legitimacy within them. Namely, it is not the system as such which induces changes in the local societies, but the way in which pre-existing social conditions interact with the system. This is where we find room for agency. With a sole emphasis on the system there would be no room for agency and we would end up with macro-determinism in which it would be equally meaningless to criminalize the periphery.

Criminalizing the periphery has become a political tool for legitimizing international intervention by, for example, NATO (the war-fighting machine of the 'cosmopolitans'), in the societies and territories of the locals/nationals, albeit under a terminology of 'policing' or 'cosmopolitan law-enforcement' (while the idea of policekeeping may seem moral it would be naive to think of NATO as a pursuer of humanitarian values).[85] However, here only one side of the 'systemic coin' comes into focus and therefore the roots of the problem are never addressed, while the symptoms are 'criminalized'. If internal war is viewed 'only' as crime and social breakdown, rather than as also containing new forms of political projects and social transformation, and therefore as long-term adaptations to marginalization, the 'cosmopolitan policing' would develop into a long-term global governance project by the 'core' into the 'periphery' reminiscent to colonialism. In effect it can, therefore, serve only to legitimize the new forms of global governance that we have seen in action in post-Dayton Bosnia and in Kosovo, as well as serving as a justifying and legitimizing of theoretical assumptions for various forms of intervention and protectorates. This type of policekeeping will, however, never come to terms with the structural exclusion and marginalization of the areas concerned, just as it will not be able to transform the social, economic and political structure of the society. Attempts to eliminate the symptoms in this manner would require that the whole area be ruled by colonial means. In practice, however, governance includes partnership with local actors which are formed on pragmatic and strategic, rather than on moral and legal, grounds. Moreover, just as, for example, Kosovo contained a parallel system to the Serbian one between 1990 and 1999, similar forms of resistance might be expected should such ambitions be renewed.

Local rulers may be criminal, and the political projects may be more or less repulsive, but the point is that the political economy of the new periphery *has adapted* to marginalization, and also partly integrated into the global economy albeit in economically non-conventional ways. While the formal economies reveal disastrous or meagre performance, the informal systems may serve as a providing line, sometimes the only one, for a large number of people, just as there are new forms of legitimacy as well as order for *some* people (while excluding others). Criminalizing the actors obviously does not change anything at the systemic level. Agents act within the limits of the possible[86] and although alternative political alliances are possible there are structural and systemic restraints to its potential performance in terms of economic integration and development. For example, a country at the periphery of the world economy, which has been isolated through sanctions (e.g., Serbia including Kosovo) may also have to provide its supply by non-liberal means. In terms of agency the struggle is then between reviving a formal economy that can be integrated in the global economy – the same problems Yugoslavia was struggling with in the 1970s and 1980s – and the structure and organization of new forms of political economy and political project, already in place. In a way similar to the struggle between the reformists of Ante Markovic and the local political–bureaucratic elites in Yugoslavia in 1990.

A parallel can be made with Polanyi's counter-movement of fascism.[87] This political project could be eliminated only after a complete reorganization of the international system and the international economy. Only in connection to a complete reintegration into a new international economy (of course after a disastrous Second World War) did the political project that replaced fascism and nazism in Europe develop. With this perspective reconstruction is not technical. It is essentially a political problem, which needs a different set of questions than those posed by transitional thinking or conventional neo-liberal economics as in the Reconstruction Programme for Kosovo. These questions need to address systemic connections to economic marginalization; which type of social agent can promote modernization in the new international economy. Questions about the geography of global capitalism are relevant, such as whether it is possible to reconstruct an economy in a particular territorial space without also addressing the systemic logic of capitalism. Which political alliances and constructions are necessary for the social stability required in order to obtain regional cooperation and integration on its own terms, and so on.

POWER STRUCTURES AND DEVELOPMENT:
REVISITING BRENNER

As important as the macrostructural perspective is, it is not global trade patterns, technological transfers, financial aid and international capitalist development as such that can explain the particular development within a region. Rather, it is in which ways these interact and coincide with internal conditions, and among internal conditions; what is especially important is the character of social relations and power-structure. Here I am inspired by Robert Brenner and his contribution to understanding transition from feudalism to capitalism in pre-industrial Europe.[88] Brenner argued that it was the local class-relations (i.e., social relations and power structure) which conditioned the transition and the direction social change and economic development would take. This focus was in contrast to other perspectives, which emphasized either trade and financial factors or demographic aspects.[89] Perspectives on pre-industrial transition have also influenced transitional thinking and the aid policy debate. While one should not exaggerate this parallel, the theoretical aspects may still be useful. (Pre-industrial western Europe and the contemporary periphery, obviously have far greater differences than parallels.)

The forms of clientelism that strengthened and developed around, or sometimes parallel with, local bureaucracy as Yugoslav society decentralized were determining structures in the economic development of Yugoslavia. Hereby they also conditioned strategies for development and integration into the world economy. Namely, it was the power-structure in Yugoslavia, both the formal which had been decentralized since the constitution of 1974, and the informal local ties[90] that determined the outcome of the struggle for economic reforms between the attempts of Ante Markovic, who strove to pursue a macro-economic policy, and the local and regional, more protectionist, elites in their struggle for political constituencies in the immediate years before Yugoslavia's breakup. Regional and local political and bureaucratic elites defended local economic interests through political means. This would come to sustain economic fragmentation and make macro-economic strategies impossible, particularly since there were no other integrating factors in the society, such as free business or labour associations.[91] The power struggle and internal cleavages of the elites in Yugoslavia (including the one in Kosovo) were also an important prerequisite for the consequent ethno-nationalist mobilization and preparation for war. The cleavages that developed within the elites, which eventually also transformed into personal conflicts, increased in the second half of the 1980s. The elites could, through the control of institutions, also provide an organizational framework for conflicts within the society by mobilizing their respective layers among the population.[92] Just as Brenner criticized the fact that 'class-relations' were 'abstracted out' from economic models in the study of transition from feudalism to capitalism, so the local power relations and the nature of the political economy, are often neglected in current transitional thinking and market-economy prescriptions for eastern Europe. In the Reconstruction Programme these are ignored rather than problematized. These local structures are likely to be more important than aid flow and external trade relations.

Local political-bureaucratic elites have shaped developments in all the Yugoslav successor states during and after the wars, as they were legitimized by the international community. Local warlords in Bosnia-Herzegovina adapted to and used humanitarian assistance, and became legitimized in the process of negotiated access by external agents, as external agents had to negotiate access and make transports secure.[93] The legitimization of these actors by the international community partly reflects the realism with which agents are confronted. The development of the KLA and of Hashim Thaçi as a power-factor in Kosovo was strongly influenced by international factors, such as the effects in Kosovo of the Dayton Agreement, and how it was perceived among Albanians, as well as the direct legitimization of the KLA and Hasim Thaqi as a leader, by the US Government.[94]

It is my hypothesis that it is this interaction (within the structural limits) with the local power structure, that determines development and how the region will adapt to, or find a place in, the global, or macro-regional, economy. While it is tempting to emphasize the institutions of capitalist states as central to its development,[95] it is not, as Reno has noted, the property holders who insist on state protections of their rights to property and *from* the predations of the state itself,[96] as has been suggested by Douglass North.[97] According to Reno the melding of rule, profit and war cut out the interests of local property holders.[98] For example in the former Soviet Union and other post-communist states, the collapse of central control did not transfer property rights to a new class of autonomous owners who could assert these rights against the states.[99] The privatization process in some of the Yugoslav successor states (for example Croatia) resulted in the concentration of the banks, factories, industries, etc. in the hands of the ruling political elite. A process which included bribery and coercion. So it is also not the institutions that are determining the development of a formal (capitalist) economy, since – while these probably are fundamental to such developments – they are a reflection of power relations (or 'class power'), and shaped by them. In former Yugoslavia, for example, such institutions as the self-management system, as well as the whole constitutional structure, were determined by outcomes of struggles among the elites.

With this hypothesis the new power structures will be a determining factor in future aid and reconstruction attempts, just as local power structure and social ties provided hindrance for Yugoslavia's internal economic development, as it was exposed to an increasingly interdependent, asymmetric, global economy in the 1960s and 1970s as well as the disastrous effects of the export-led development strategy imposed by the international credit institutions in the 1980s.[100]

The fragmentation of the formal economy of the region and the political antagonism are fundamental problems. Any formal economic development would have to be based on a regional economy. This is, however, where the problems originated in the first place. To base a Balkan reconstruction plan on regional economic cooperation and integration will in this instance be extremely difficult, since the social structures and local power structure have been formulated around an economic base which is in direct contrast and opposition to this, and since the international institutional set-up has to form partnerships with some of these actors.

In Kosovo this problem has been particularly accentuated. The international community is faced with the problem of rebuilding an institutional framework and state institutions. These will have to be based either on pre-existing Yugoslav–Serbian structures, which the Albanian population has adapted to living completely outside of for almost a decade, or the only existing foundations which are the parallel structures formed during the 1990s. The latter are ethnically homogeneous Albanian structures which developed in response to the withdrawal of autonomy in 1989–90, and which throughout the 1990s developed into a complete parallel system to the official FRY state institutions.[101] The society has also been radicalized as the leadership of Ibrahim Rugova, with his passive resistance method, was marginalized in favour of more violent and radical elements, as those under the leadership of Hashim Thaçi (although this may be changing rapidly in the fluid political environment). The above mentioned approach would therefore provide paramount challenges to ethno-pluralism and most probably exclude non-ethnic Albanians. The other, equally problematic, alternative would be to build new structures from scratch, from *nihil*, in parallel to an already existing political economy and political project.

A GOVERNANCE SYSTEM CLOSED?

The international set-up in Kosovo resembles a protectorate in much the same way as in Bosnia. This institutional network is what we may call 'global governance' in action. In order for this type of governance, an authoritative foundation upon which the reconstruction is based, to function, and in order to implement policies, there has to be a building of strategic alliances and partnership forms with local actors. This includes certain forms of inclusion and exclusion, and legitimizes certain actors (such as the partnership with Hashim Thaçi), while ignoring or excluding others. Inclusion or exclusion is based partly on pragmatic reasons, partly on strategic interests and partly on political criteria. The reconstruction programme does not, however, enter into any analysis of the problems related to this process, just as it does not deal with any structural or political problems related to the political economy. Its purpose is to function as a document that can mobilize donors and governments, rather than being a blueprint for Kosovo as such. The donors and aid agencies need this type of depoliticized technical agenda in order to respond. Within the donor community or aid industry, this logic functions in an optimal way regardless of its effects on society in Kosovo. It cannot deal with macro-structures to which itself is a part. This is not to

273

say that the governance system is autistic or forms a closed system. However, it is not particularly open either: rather it is a porous system through which information has to be carefully filtered and adjusted in order to become incorporated into the system. The systemic perspective does not seem to fit any pore.

NOTES

1. M. Duffield, 'Evaluating Conflict Resolution: Context, Models and Methodology', Discussion Paper (Bergen: Christian Michelsen Institute, 1997); J. S. Sörensen, 'Pluralism or Fragmentation', in *WarReport: Reconstruction in Bosnia* (London: Institute for War and Peace Reporting, 1997).
2. M. Duffield, 'Lunching with Killers', in C.-U. Schierup (ed.), *Scramble for the Balkans: Nationalism, Globalism and the Political Economy of Reconstruction* (London: Macmillan, 1999).
3. A. Escobar, *Encountering Development: The Making and the Unmaking of the Third World* (Princeton, NJ: Princeton University Press, 1995).
4. V. Randall and R. Theobald, *Political Change and Underdevelopment* (London: Macmillan, 1985).
5. See Sorensen, 'Pluralism or Fragmentation'.
6. D. Chandler, *Bosnia – Faking Democracy After Dayton* (London: Pluto Press, 1999); H. Griffiths, 'A Political Economy of Ethnic Conflict, Ethno-Nationalism and Organized Crime', in *Civil Wars*, vol. 2, no. 2 (Summer 1999), pp. 56–73.
7. 'Towards Stability and Prosperity: A Programme for Reconstruction in Kosovo', EU Commission and World Bank in support of the UN Mission in Kosovo, November 1999.
8. During its first year the US transferred 13% of its total budget to just 16 European states (more if Japan is included). In 1997, it transferred just 0.5% in aid to the underdeveloped world generally.
9. Compare Chandler, *Bosnia*.
10. Ibid.
11. Compare Duffield, 'Lunching With Killers'.
12. Ibid. This programme was prepared by the EU Commission and the World Bank, with support from UNMIK, November 1999.
13. Also mentioned at, for example, p. 1 and p. 2.
14. M. Duffield, 'Post-Modern Conflict: War Lords, Post-Adjustment States and Private Protection', in *Civil Wars*, vol. 1, no. 1 (Spring 1998), pp. 65–102; compare B. Likić-Brborić, 'Globalization, Governance and the Political Economy of Transition', in Schierup, *Scramble for the Balkans*.
15. Compare Likić-Brborić, 'Globalization'.
16. R. Craig Nation, unpublished synopsis presented at a conference of the International Network 'Europe and the Balkans' (Bologna: February 2000).
17. 'Towards Stability and Prosperity: A Programme for Reconstruction in Kosovo'.
18. Ibid., for example, p. 1 and p. 2.
19. Ibid., p. 2.
20. Ibid., p. 3.
21. Ibid., *in passim*.
22. Susan Woodward, *Kosovo and the Region: Consequences of the Waiting Game* (London: Centre for Defence Studies, Kings College, 1999).

23. 'Towards Stability and Prosperity: A Programme for Reconstruction in Kosovo', p. 17.
24. Ibid., p. 12.
25. Ibid., p. 11.
26. S. Gill, 'Theorizing the Interregnum: The Double Movement and Global Politics in the 1990s', in B. Hettne (ed.), *International Political Economy: Understanding Global Disorder* (London: Zed Books, 1995).
27. The expression is borrowed from the title of a presentation by Neil Smith, held at the Institute of Geography in Lund (May 2000).
28. For example R. Cox, 'Critical Political Economy', in Hettne, *International Political Economy*; S. Gill, 'Theorizing the Interregnum'.
29. P. Cerny, 'Neomedievalism, Civil War and the New Security Dilemma: Globalization as Durable Disorder', in *Civil Wars*, vol. 1, no. 1 (Spring 1998), pp. 36–64.
30. C.-U. Schierup, *Migration, Socialism and the International Division of Labour: the Yugoslavian Experience* (Aldershot: Ashgate, 1990); C.-U. Schierup, 'Memorandum for Modernity', in Schierup, *Scramble for the Balkans*.
31. Duffield, 'Evaluating Conflict Resolution' and 'Lunching With Killers'.
32. K. Verdery, *What Was Socialism and What Comes Next?* (Princeton, NJ: Princeton University Press, 1996).
33. A. Hoogvelt, *Globalization and the Post-Colonial World: the New Political Economy of Development* (London: Macmillan, 1997); Duffield, 'Evaluating Conflict Resolution'; Cox, 'Critical Political Economy'; Gill, 'Theorizing the Interregnum'; compare M. Castells, 'The Information Economy and the New International Division of Labour', in M. Carnoy et al. (eds), *The New Global Economy in the Information Age* (University Park, PA: Pennsylvania State University Press, 1993); P. Hirst and Thompson, *Globalization in Question* (Cambridge: Polity Press, 1996). While Hirst and Thompson question the discourse on globalization as such, their study also provides material for the point that the dynamic factors of international economy increasingly is taking place within and between the three economic blocs, with the rest of the world being marginalized in the international economic system (which is one of the main points for this purpose).
34. Although subject to definition the number of wars have increased radically since around 1960. See J. K. Gantzel, 'War in the Post World War II World: Empirical Trends, Theoretical Approaches and Problems on the Concept of Ethnic War', paper presented at Symposium on Ethnicity and War (San Marino: Centre for Inter-disciplinary Research on Social Stress, 1994).
35. Mary Kaldor, *New and Old Wars: Organized Violence in a Global Era* (Cambridge: Polity Press, 1999), p. 2.
36. Ibid., p. 5.
37. Duffield, 'Evaluating Conflict Resolution' and 'Lunching With Killers'.
38. Duffield, 'Evaluating Conflict Resolution'; compare W. Reno, 'Commercial Agendas in Civil Wars', in M. Berdahl and D. Malone (eds), *Greed and Grievance: Economic Agendas in Civil Wars* (Boulder, CO and London: Lynne Rienner Publishers, 2000), pp. 43–68.
39. Compare: Griffiths, 'A Political Economy of Ethnic Conflict'.
40. Ibid.
41. See M. Lazić, 'Stratification under Conditions of the Socialist Society and the Civil War', in D. Janjić and S. Maliqi (eds), *Conflict or Dialogue* (Subotica: Open University, 1994), p. 65; and M. Lazić, 'Old and New Elites in Serbia', in D. Janjić (ed.), *Serbia Between the Past and the Future* (Belgrade: Institute for

Social Sciences and Forum for Ethnic Relations, 1997), p. 92.

42. C. Hedges, 'Kosovo's Next Masters', *Foreign Affairs*, vol. 78, no. 3 (May/June 1999), pp. 24–42.

43. M. Chossudovsky, 'Kosovo "Freedom Fighters" Financed by Organized Crime', Transnational Foundation for Peace and Future Research (1999), at www.transnational.org/features/crimefinansed.html.

44. See Reno, 'Commercial Agendas', p. 2.

45. Ibid., p. 5 (my abbreviations).

46. Ibid.

47. See Schierup, 'Memorandum for Modernity' and *Migration, Socialism*.

48. See Griffiths, 'A Political Economy of Ethnic Conflict'.

49. Compare Verdery, *What Was Socialism?* for Romania.

50. See Duffield, 'Evaluating Conflict Resolution'.

51. Ibid., p. 1; compare F. H. Cordoso, 'North–South Relations in the Present Context: A New Dependency?' in M. Carnoy et al. (eds), *The New Global Economy*, pp. 155–7.

52. See Hoogvelt, *Globalization*, part 2.

53. See Cox, 'Critical Political Economy', p. 39.

54. K. Polanyi's *The Great Transformation – the Political and Economic Origins of Our Time* (Boston: Beacon Press, 1944–1957).

55. See Cox, 'Critical Political Economy'.

56. B. Hettne, 'Introduction: The Political Economy of Transformation', in Hettne, *International Political Economy*; and B. Hettne, 'Globalization and the New Regionalism: The Second Great Transformation', in B. Hettne et al. (eds), *Globalism and the New Regionalism* (London: Macmillan, 1999); Gill 'Theorizing the Interregnum'.

57. See also M. Castells, *End of Millennium – The Information Age: Economy, Society and Culture*, vol. III (New York: Blackwell, 1998).

58. The comparison with the Polanyian 'double-movement' has also been suggested by I. Iveković in his 'Modern Authoritarian Ethnocracy: Balkanization and the Political Economy of International Relations' in Schierup, *Scramble for the Balkans* with the view that the first phase of this would be the 'utopian vision of capitalism' in the European east, the privatization, dismantling of the state etc., and the second phase 'bringing the state back in' reshaping state control over the productive forces, with this second phase including a protectionist reaction by nationalist elites. Also the second phase being a fragmentation of the periphery (to the first movement of an integrating core) in order to be better digested by the global economy (Iveković, p. 79).

59. Ibid.; Duffield; Reno; Griffiths; Verdery; compare also Schierup 'Memorandum for Modernity'.

60. While the term 'development' is normally used for Africa, the term 'transition' seems to be preferred for eastern Europe.

61. See D. Janjić, 'National Identity Building Process in Post-Communist Society: Serbian Case 1989–96', in S. Bianchini and P. Shoup (eds), *State Building in the Balkans – Dilemmas on the Eve of the 21st Century* (Ravenna: Longo editore, 1997).

62. See Schierup, *Migration, Socialism* and 'Memorandum for Modernity'.

63. See Schierup, 'Memorandum for Modernity', p. 40.

64. M. Stanojević, 'Industrial Regulations in Post-Self-Management Society', in T. Kuzmanic and A. Truger (eds), *Yugoslavia War* (Ljubljana and Schlaining: Peace Institute and Austrian Study Centre for Peace and Conflict Resolution, 1992).

65. See Schierup, 'Memorandum for Modernity'; Likić-Brborić.

66. See Schierup, 'Memorandum for Modernity'.

67. Compare: S. Maliqi, *Kosova – Separate Worlds* (Pristina: MM Society and Dukagjini Publishing House, 1998); D. Kostovičevá, *Parallel Worlds: Response of Kosovo Albanians to Loss of Autonomy in Serbia 1989–96* (Keele: Keele European Research Centre, 1997).

68. See Kostovičevá, *Parallel Worlds*; J. S. Sörensen, *The Threatening Precedent – Kosovo and the Remaking of Crisis* (Umea: Merge, 1999).

69. See D. Janjić, 'National Identity Building Processes'.

70. See E. Gordy, *The Culture of Power in Serbia* (University Park, PA: Pennsylvania State University Press, 1999).

71. C. Tilly, 'War Making and State Making as Organized Crime', in P. Evans et al. (eds), *Bringing the State Back In* (Cambridge: Cambridge University Press, 1985), p. 172.

72. When EC countries like Germany recognized the new states in the Balkans they applied a territorial principle (the administrative borders of the republics within the Yugoslav Federation) and did not pay much attention to nationalities or minorities within those borders, thus producing a new minority problem in diminishing circles, and by this also maintaining a fundamental problem in the conflict. This fact has actually been argued (quite forcefully and convincingly) to escalate the war, which at least is true for the war in Bosnia-Herzegovina. For example: M. Glenny, *The Fall of Yugoslavia* (London: Penguin, 1992); H. Wiberg, *Jugoslaviens sondersprangning* (Lund: TFF, 1992), H. Wiberg, 'The Dissolution of Yugoslavia: A Study of Interaction', in F. D. Pfetsch (ed.), *International Relations and Pan-Europe* (Münster: Lit Verlag, 1993), pp. 361–87; J. S. Sörensen, 'Bosnien-Hercegovina: Mellan Demokrati och Etnokrati', in N. Milivojevic et al. (eds), *Bortom kriget* (Stockholm: Carlssons, 1996).

73. For example Cerny, 'Neomedievalism'; Verdery, *What Was Socialism?* The analogy was used by Hedley Bull (reference in Cox, 'Critical Political Economy'), but perhaps referring to something slightly less sinister.

74. I would refer to the political, bureaucratic and military elite who formed nationalist oriented parties (or actually they reflect political movements) in the various republics within the former Yugoslavia and still maintain power within their respective republics or entities (most of them of course former communist party members). This would include local patrons and warlords who have benefited from war and political conflict.

75. See Reno, 'Commercial Agendas in Civil Wars', p. 4.

76. Ibid., p. 7.

77. See Griffiths, 'A Political Economy of Ethnic Conflict', pp. 67–70.

78. Ibid.

79. I. E. Koch, *Protection of Property Rights in the Republic of Croatia – The Law on Temporary Taking Over and Administration of Specified Property* (OSCE Mission to the Republic of Croatia, May 1997).

80. Several Human Rights reports, for example by the Helsinki Committee, describe this. Also observations by local NGOs such as Otvoreni Oci in Split which is regularly monitoring enforcement of court decisions regarding disputed tenancy rights. These are also my personal observations after having lived and worked for two years in Croatia. For example, in 1997 I attended several attempts to enforce court decisions. These attempts were always 'staged' where the military or military police local patrons were involved. It remains to be seen if the new government installed in 2000 can bring changes to this.

81. See Kaldor, *New and Old Wars*.

82. Ibid.
83. Ibid.
84. See Castells, *End of Millennium*.
85. The targeting of civilians in the NATO attack on Yugoslavia would be enough to question this (Sörensen, *The Threatening Precedent*). If the 'police', by contrast, should be the UN, one might assume that, from the above criticized perspective, there is too much 'non-cosmopolitan periphery' in the UN for this purpose!
86. F. Braudel, *The Structure of Everyday Life: The Limits of the Possible* (New York: Harper & Row, 1981).
87. See Polanyi, *The Great Transformation*.
88. R. Brenner, 'Agrarian Class Structure and Economic Development in Pre-Industrial Europe', *Past and Present*, no. 70 (February 1976), pp. 30–75.
89. Brenner argued against two other perspectives which we may call the 'commercialization model', and the 'cyclic Malthusian model'. According to the commerce model it was the development of a market and increase in trade, which was a key factor in the transition to capitalism and it's later development, since they broke up the feudal ties and paved the way for capitalist development. The cyclic Malthusian model (developed by Postan, in 1966, in polemic to the commercial perspective to deal with the fifteenth and sixteenth centuries) instead emphasized that demographic aspects, such as increasing population will lead to increasing land rent and lower wages on the one side, and population diffusion resulting in trade on the other, and that here we would find the causal links to the demise of feudalism and the development of capitalism. In contrast to these models, Brenner placed class relations in the centre. He argued that those in medieval Europe led to strong exploitation, which in turn led to an increasing erosion of cultivated land and the cultivation of more, increasingly lower quality, land. This resulted in a productivity crisis which in turn led to a demographic crisis. This then resulted in increasing pressures at feudal estates and so on. So, here the demographic aspect comes in later in the explanation. These discussions also have impact on the perceptions of the current transition problems in developing countries and particularly in the European east and the Balkans.
90. See Schierup, 'Memorandum for Modernity' and *Migration, Socialism*.
91. Ibid. (both works).
92. V. Goati, 'The Impact of Parliamentary Democracy on Ethnic Relations in Yugoslavia 1989–96', in D. Janjić (ed.), *Ethnic Conflict Management – the Case of Yugoslavia* (Ravenna: Longo editore, 1997).
93. Compare Duffield, 1994; Griffiths, 'A Political Economy of Ethnic Conflict'.
94. See Sörensen, *The Threatening Precedent*.
95. N. Rosenberg and L. E. Birdzell Jr., *How the West Grew Rich: The Economic Transformation of the Industrial World* (New York: Basic Books, 1986); D. C. North and R. P. Thomas, *The Rise of the Western World* (Cambridge: Cambridge University Press, 1973).
96. Ibid. (both works).
97. See North and Thomas, *The Rise of the Western World*.
98. See Reno, 'Commercial Agendas in Civil Wars', p. 21.
99. Ibid.
100. See R. Chepulis, 'The Economic Crisis and Export-Led Development Strategy of SFR Yugoslavia', Paper for Mediterranian Studies Seminar (Dubrovnik: IUC, April 1984); B. Young, 'Nothing From Nothing is Nothing', in Schierup, *Scramble for the Balkans*.

101. See for example, Maliqi, *Kosova – Separate Worlds*; Kostovičevá, *Parallel Worlds*; Sörensen, *The Threatening Precedent*.

REFERENCES

Braudel, F., *The Structure of Everyday Life: The Limits of the Possible* (New York: Harper & Row, 1981).

Brenner, R., 'Agrarian Class Structure and Economic Development in Pre-Industrial Europe', *Past and Present*, no. 70 (February 1976), pp. 30–75.

Carnoy, M. et al. (eds), *The New Global Economy in the Information Age* (University Park, PA: Pennsylvania State University Press, 1993).

Castells, M., *End of Millennium – The Information Age: Economy, Society and Culture*, vol. III (New York: Blackwell, 1998).

Cerny, P., 'Neomedievalism, Civil War and the New Security Dilemma: Globalization as Durable Disorder', in *Civil Wars*, vol. 1, no. 1 (Spring 1998), pp. 36–64.

Chandler, D., *Bosnia – Faking Democracy after Dayton* (London: Pluto Press, 1999).

Chossudovsky, M., 'Kosovo "Freedom Fighters" Financed by Organized Crime', Transnational Foundation for Peace and Future Reseach (1999) at www.transnational.org/features/crimefinansed.html.

Chepulis, R., 'The Economic Crisis and Export-Led Development Strategy of SFR Yugoslavia', Paper for the Mediterranean Studies Seminar (Dubrovnik: IUC, April 1984).

Duffield, M., 'Evaluating Conflict Resolution: Context, Models and Methodology', Discussion Paper (Bergen: Chrsitian Michelsen Institute, 1997).

Duffield, M., 'Post-Modern Conflict: War Lords, Post-Adjustment States and Private Protection', in *Civil Wars*, vol. 1, no. 1 (Spring 1998), pp. 65–102.

Escobar, A., *Encountering Development: The Making and the Unmaking of the Third World* (Princeton, NJ: Princeton University Press, 1995).

Gantzel, J. K., 'War in the Post World War II World: Empirical Trends, Theoretical Approaches and Problems on the Concept of Ethnic War', paper presented at Symposium on Ethnicity and War (San Marino Centre for Inter-Disciplinary Research on Social Stress, 1994).

Glenny, M., *The Fall of Yugoslavia* (London: Penguin, 1992).

Goati, V., 'The Impact of Parliamentary Democracy on Ethnic Relations in Yugoslavia 1989–96', in D. Janjić (ed.), *Ethnic Conflict Management – The Case of Yugoslavia* (Ravenna: Longo editore, 1997), pp. 53–94.

Gordy, E., *The Culture of Power in Serbia* (University Park, PA: Pennsylvania State University Press, 1999).

Griffiths, H., 'A Political Economy of Ethnic Conflict, Ethno-Nationalism and Organized Crime', in *Civil Wars*, vol. 2, no. 2 (Summer 1999), pp. 56–73.

Hedges, C., 'Kosovo's Next Masters', *Foreign Affairs*, vol. 78, no. 3 (May/June 1999), pp. 24–42.

Hettne, B. (ed.), *International Political Economy: Understanding Global Disorder* (London: Zed Books, 1995).

Hettne, B., 'Globalization and the New Regionalism: The Second Great Transformation', in B. Hettne et al. (eds), *Globalism and the New Regionalism* (London: Macmillan, 1999).

Hoogvelt, A., *Globalization and the Post-Colonial World: the New Political Economy of Development* (London: Macmillan, 1997).

Janjić, D., 'National Identity Building Processes in Post-Communist Society: Serbian Case 1989–96', in S. Bianchini and P. Shoup (eds), *State Building in the Balkans –*

Dilemmas on the Eve of the 21st Century (Ravenna: Longo editore, 1997), pp. 339–62.

Kaldor, M., *New and Old Wars: Organized Violence in a Global Era* (Cambridge: Polity Press, 1999).

Koch, I. E., *Protection of Property Rights in the Republic of Croatia – The Law on Temporary Taking Over and Administration of Specified Property* (OSCE Mission to the Republic of Croatia, May 1997).

Kostovičevá, D., *Parallel Worlds: Response of Kosovo Albanians to Loss of Autonomy in Serbia 1989–96* (Keele: Keele European Research Centre, 1997).

Lazić, M., 'Stratification under Conditions of the Socialist Society and the Civil War', in D. Janjić and S. Maliqi (eds), *Conflict or Dialogue* (Subotica: Open University, 1994), pp. 54–68.

Lazić, M., 'Old and New Elites in Serbia', in D. Janjić (ed.), *Serbia Between the Past and the Future* (Belgrade: Institute for Social Sciences and Forum for Ethnic Relations, 1997), pp. 86–101.

Maliqi, S., *Kosova – Separate Worlds* (Pristina: MM Society and Dukagjini Publishing House, 1998).

North, D. C. and Thomas, R. P., *The Rise of the Western World* (Cambridge: Cambridge University Press, 1973).

Polanyi, K., *The Great Transformation – the Political and Economic Origins of Our Time* (Boston: Beacon Press, 1944–1957).

Randall, V. and Theobald, R., *Political Change and Underdevelopment* (London: Macmillan, 1985).

Reno, W., 'Commercial Agendas in Civil Wars', in M. Berdahl and D. Malone (eds), *Greed and Grievance* (Boulder, CO and London: Lynne Rienner Publishers, 2000), pp. 43–68.

Rosenberg, N. and Birdzell, L. E. Jr., *How the West Grew Rich: The Economic Transformation of the Industrial World* (New York: Basic Books, 1986).

Schierup, C.-U., *Migration, Socialism and the International Division of Labour – The Yugoslavian Experience* (Ashgate: Aldershot, 1990).

Schierup, C.-U. (ed.), *Scramble for the Balkans: Nationalism, Globalism and the Political Economy of Reconstruction* (London: Macmillan, 1999).

Sörensen, J. S., 'Pluralism or Fragmentation', in *WarReport: Reconstruction in Bosnia* (London: Institute for War and Peace Reporting, 1997).

Sörensen, J. S., *The Threatening Precedent – Kosovo and the Remaking of Crisis* (Umea: Merge, 1999).

Stability Pact for South Eastern Europe, Cologne, 10 June 1999.

Stanojević, M., 'Industrial Relations in Post-Self-Management Society', in T. Kuzmanic and A. Truger (eds), *Yugoslavia War* (Ljubljana and Schaining: Peace Institute and Austrian Study Centre for Peace and Conflict Resolution, 1992).

Tilly, C., 'War Making and State Making as Organized Crime', in P. Evans et al. (eds), *Bringing the State Back In* (Cambridge: Cambridge University Press, 1985).

'Towards Stability and Prosperity: A Programme for Reconstruction in Kosovo' (World Bank, November 1999).

Verdery, K., *What Was Socialism and What Comes Next?* (Princeton, NJ: Princeton University Press, 1996).

Wiberg, H., *Jugoslaviens sondersprangning* (Lund: TFF, 1992).

Wiberg, H., 'The Dissolution of Yugoslavia: A Study of Interaction', in F. D. Pfetsch (ed.), *International Relations and Pan-Europe* (Münster: Lit Verlag, 1993), pp. 361–87.

Woodward, S., *Kosovo and the Region: Consequences of the Waiting Game* (London: Centre for Defence Studies, Kings College, 1999).

PART V
REGIONAL IMPLICATIONS OF
THE KOSOVO CONFLICT

14

Regional Perspectives for an Independent Kosovo – Albania and Macedonia

Aldo Bumci

The Albanian question as such has existed since 1912. Although the Serbs were able to incorporate large ethnic Albanian territories, as the course of history showed, they could not do away with the Albanian question. The large and growing number of Albanians, with a well-developed national consciousness, combined with their regional compactness and homogeneity made sure that the Albanian question would continue to exist.[1] Yet it existed only as a domestic question without posing a danger to regional stability. It was only after the dissolution of Yugoslavia that the Albanian question became salient at the regional level. The main factor that contributed to the internationalization of the Kosova issue was the weakness on the Serbian side. In terms of the elements of national power Serbia is much weaker than former Yugoslavia. Serbia was also suffering from international isolation, economic sanctions and the side effects of the wars in Bosnia and Croatia. Thus, the collapse of communism, disintegration of Yugoslavia and Serbia's pariah status provided greater opportunities for the Albanians to challenge Belgrade. In addition, the demographic trends in Kosova further strengthened Albanians' position. The population ratio of Albanians to Serbs was roughly nine-to-one, while the gap in the growth rate was even larger.[2] This discrepancy between the ability of the Serbs to control Kosova in the short run, and Albanian calculations that time works for them, made the tackling of the Kosova issue extremely difficult, as both sides had adopted diametrically opposed goals.

Two interrelated questions arise when we examine the question of the Kosova's future status. What status for Kosova – independence or autonomy – would bring a sustainable solution, and which one would contribute to regional stability? The prevailing attitude prior to the NATO bombardment was that any solution to the Kosova question had to be found within the border of Yugoslavia. The objections to Kosova statehood were grounded in the fear that this would cause region-wide instability by undermining Macedonia and unravelling the Dayton agreement for Bosnia. The spillover of the conflict from Kosova to Macedonia in particular occupied the thinking of Western policy makers. The war in Kosova was seen as jeopardizing Macedonian security under different scenarios.[3]

However, both the international community and Serbian politicians squandered the opportunity offered to them by the peaceful resistance of Albanians in order to reach an accommodation. Until the escalation of the conflict in March 1998, the mediation efforts of the international community were incoherent and primarily declaratory.[4] Though until 1998 the international community and Kosovar Albanians had exercised no real pressure on Serbia, this does not mean that the Serb authorities had no reason to start a dialogue with the Albanians in order to find an accommodation. In retrospect, we could say that Serbia lost a golden opportunity by not restoring autonomy to Albanians. Despite Albanian demands for independent statehood, Serbia might have been able, through constitutional arrangements similar to those of 1974, to shift the political dynamics to its advantage. The political atmosphere in Serbia, however, was not conducive to reaching a settlement. There was no significant difference between the opposition and Milošević who had built his political career on Kosova and the abolition of its autonomy and had ruled out any possibility that autonomy could be restored. This intransigent attitude of the political class perfectly reflected Serb public opinion on the issue: 41.8 per cent of Serbs believed that the solution was to be seen in the forcible expulsion of Albanians while only some 27.2 per cent manifested some democratic tolerance and would be willing, at best, to grant cultural autonomy.[5]

The disillusion with the pacifist way and the international community combined with Serb repression and intransigence, led to an increase of KLA activity and the outbreak of conflict in early 1998. Despite the fact that the conflict continued, no military action was taken to stop it. The West was reluctant to intervene fearing that this would help the Albanians win independence and destabilize the region. This indicated that the West was more interested in preventing statehood for Kosova than solving the conflict. At this point the political aims of both the international community and Milošević converged.[6] The renewed Serb offensive that was tolerated by the West created hundreds of thousands of refugees. Thousands crossed into Montenegro, Albania and Macedonia, but the majority remained displaced within Kosova. The vivid memories of the Bosnian war made it very difficult for the Western policy makers to justify their policy in front of their public. In order to prevent the humanitarian catastrophe NATO threatened air strikes.

The course of 1998 illustrated very well the vicious circle of Serb–Albanian conflict. While the Serbs were unable to put down the guerrilla movement, the Albanians could not win independence by themselves, which would have resulted in a war of attrition spilling into Albania and Macedonia. Many analysts criticized the West's policy, on the grounds that by ruling out independence to Kosova as an acceptable solution, it was legitimizing Milošević's goals, thus leading to a protracted war. They argued that dangers to regional stability do not come from the independence of Kosova but from a policy that prolongs the life of Milošević's doomed federation. As Janusz Bugajski argued, as long as Kosova remained part of Serbia–Yugoslavia, Milošević, by manipulating the Albanian question, could spread the conflict to Macedonia and Montenegro to detract attention from the Kosovar crisis, and present the Albanians as a destabilizing factor. Additionally, with the Kosova question unresolved, the chance for democratization in Serbia was blocked, which meant the continuation of the authoritarian regime of Milošević. During the Yugoslav wars of secession the West failed to identify Serbia as the main source of instability in the region, however, as Mort Abramowitz maintained, the time had come to face the Serbian problem as ëthe only real exit strategy' from a decade of conflicts. The independence of Kosova would narrow Milošević's room to manoeuvre, so that any crises that he could generate would not be any longer a threat to the region. Zbigniew Brzezinski rightly pointed to the fact that the conflict in Kosova is not confined to Albanians and Serbs alone, but involves a wider picture. It is insightful to look at those who support the use of force to stop the ethnic killing and cleansing in Kosova (Western democracies) and those who oppose it (Belarus and the regime in Russia). 'Two visions of European future are thus colliding.' The real question that policy makers should confront 'is not whether Kosova should become independent, but in what context self-determination can be reasonably exercised'.[7]

During the 78-day NATO campaign two things became clear. The longer the conflict lasted the greater were the dangers that it would spill over to neighbouring countries. It also became clear that Milošević and his clique, not the Albanians whether in Kosova, Macedonia or Albania, as it was feared, were behind such a scenario. Mainly through the refugees crisis but also by using other means Milošević hoped that he could destabilize Albania, Macedonia and Montenegro. Milošević used the conflict with NATO to step up pressure on Montenegro's leadership. The danger of the new development was indicated by the fact that the army was now being used to exercise pressure, as Djukanovic declared that Montenegro would remain neutral and did not recognize the state of war. Many observers thought that the aim of the army was to stage a military coup, which was prevented from materializing by a force of 15,000 well-armed police, controlled by Djukanovic.[8] Macedonia, in particular, was targeted as being the most vulnerable. As stated by the Macedonian Deputy Prime Minister and Interior Minister at a press conference: 'Macedonia is under pressure from powerful subversive activities instigated from abroad with the aim of involving the country in the so-called Kosovo scenario.'[9] The leaders of the Democratic Party of Albanians Arben Xhaferi and Menduh Thaci, also pointed to the same pressure that has been brought to bear on Macedonia. Xhaferi said that through the refugee crisis Milošević expected to radicalize the two communities and bring them to the situation where they would have adopted diametrically opposite views on NATO air strikes and the issue of refugees in Macedonia, thus precipitating a governmental crisis and even inter-ethnic conflict.[10] However, Milošević could not succeed in destabilizing the country, as the Deputy Prime Minister noted: 'All the institutions of the system are working perfectly which is also due to the high level of the inter-ethnic relations in Macedonia.'[11] At this point it is worth looking briefly at the relationship between Kosova Albanians and Macedonia.

THE RELATIONSHIP BETWEEN THE KOSOVA ALBANIANS AND MACEDONIA

Here we will not be looking at the ties that exist between Albanians in Kosova and Macedonia, whether family ties or those developed as result of Pristina's status as the centre of Albanians in former Yugoslavia. What matters is the political behaviour and agendas of these two communities.

The generally held belief among many regional analysts is that the two communities are locked in a quasi-automatic relationship: '... the situation in Kosova is always closely watched by all Albanians in Macedonia and often an important pointer to future action in the republic ...'[12] or 'an explosion in one area will instantly radicalize the other'.[13] However, this way of reasoning is deeply flawed because it removes the action of Albanians in Macedonia from its historical context; it overlooks the differences between the two communities and it is not supported by historical facts.[14]

In November 1968 massive demonstrations broke out in Pristina, followed almost a month later by similar ones in Tetova, demanding that Albanian inhabited areas of Macedonia join Kosova in a seventh republic. It is important to note that Albanians throughout Yugoslavia had gone through the same repressive policies of the Rankovic era. As a consequence their protest should not be seen as simply 'inspired' by events in Kosova, but primarily as a reaction to their conditions in Macedonia, as part of Yugoslavia at large, that existed at the time. In stark contrast to the magnitude of the demonstrations held in Kosova, in March–April 1981, which had necessitated the intervention of the army, no serious political disturbance occurred in Macedonia. The situation had remained calm during the demonstration in Kosova, 'and only later in June were there reports that insurrectionary literature was being distributed and Albanians were involved in activities like sloganeering.'[15] Nevertheless, the Macedonian authorities seized the opportunity provided by the campaign against Albanian nationalism to roll back the educational and cultural rights of

Albanians in Macedonia, and to further marginalize them. Actually, the policies of the Serbophile Macedonian leadership were even more repressive than those implemented in Kosova.[16] The Macedonian authorities could not take such drastic measures without the support of Belgrade, and the two closely coordinated their anti-Albanian campaign. At this point Macedonian authorities were aligned with Milošević. In 1989 while Serbia adopted amendments that abolished Kosova's autonomy, Macedonia, too, changed its constitution redefining the state as 'a national state of the Macedonian people' in contrast to the 1974 constitution which defined the republic as 'a state of the Macedonian people and Albanian and Turkish minorities'.[17] Following the abolition of autonomy in 1989, massive demonstrations were staged in Kosova, however, the situation in Macedonia had remained relatively calm.[18] Surprisingly enough, there was a strong cooperation between Belgrade and Skopje but not between Pristina and Tetova. What is more indicative is the different methods that Albanians of Kosova and Macedonia chose to pursue after the collapse of Yugoslavia. The Albanians of Kosova boycotted Serbia's political system, started to build their own parallel system and declared the independence of Kosova as the only legitimate goal. In contrast, the Albanians of Macedonia, even though they were facing a weaker state lacking repressive capabilities, chose to participate in political life showing that they were following their own local agenda. This last development clearly indicated the differences between Albanians in Kosova and Albanians in Macedonia, and the political realities they face.

The conflict in Kosova provided further evidence against those advocating the 'domino theory'. During the euphoric spring of 1998 when it was said that the KLA controlled 30–40 per cent of Kosova's territory no tension was recorded in Macedonia. That was also the case during the refugee crisis, despite the frequently not very decent behaviour of Macedonian authorities towards the Albanian refugees.[19]

The Macedonian crisis, which started in early 2001, further shows that the political agendas of Albanians in Kosova and in Macedonia are different. First, the political wing of the National Liberation Army declared that they respected the territorial integrity of Macedonia and were fighting for equal rights of Albanians vis-à-vis Macedonians, and their demands were similar to those of Albanian political parties in Macedonia that participated in the state structures.[20] The fact that even those who have taken up arms and are labelled as extremists recognize the territorial integrity of Macedonia, shows that Macedonia is a Balkan reality accepted by all and that ethnic politics/conflict is confined to this republic's borders. In addition, as the crisis unfolded Albanian political parties joined the national unity government, thus preventing further radicalization between the two communities. Second, the guerrillas continued their armed struggle in Macedonia despite the fact that Albanian leaders in Albania, Kosova and Macedonia had unequivocally condemned violence declaring that they were for the stability of Macedonia and the use of force was not in the interest of Albanians.[21] The Albanians in Kosova were especially concerned that violence in Macedonia would harm their quest for independence as many were pointing to Kosova as the source of instability in the region. However, this did not serve as a reason for Albanian guerrillas in Macedonia to stop their fight. This happened only after the Ohrid political agreement was reached on 13 August 2001.

AN INDEPENDENT KOSOVA DOES NOT POSE A THREAT TO REGIONAL STABILITY

The international community is in general reluctant when it comes to the question of recognizing new states. The principle of self-determination is usually seen as subordinate to that of territorial integrity. In this context the independence of Kosova is perceived as constituting a dangerous precedent. However, even from a legal perspective the case could be made in favour of Kosova's independence. As an international legal analyst argues: 'Kosova has been an extraordinary episode in the modern history, but not because some new destabilizing principle was established. Rather, Kosova is the rare case where the strict conditions set by international law of secession were met.'[22] This does not mean that there is general agreement about the legal arguments, however, it is significant because it shows the qualitative difference that exists between the Serb and Croat territories in Bosnia and Kosova, with the latter resembling more former Yugoslav republics that have won their independence. As Anthony Borden rightly argues, Kosova existed as a separate entity during Yugoslavia with its administrative borders and, if not *de jure* a de facto republican status, whereas Serb and Croatian territories in Bosnia were formed in the 1992–95 war through genocide.[23] The arguments against Kosova's independence do not seem to be legal, but rather political, as Montenegro's independence is also opposed despite the fact that its status is similar to the other former Yugoslav republics that have won their independence. As a journalist from Podgorica noted: 'In its drive for independence Montenegro is in the straitjacket of Kosova. In dealing with Kosova the international community is determined to keep alive a third Yugoslavia that is unviable and effectively, already dead.'[24]

At the regional level, the independence of Kosova does not pose a threat to Macedonian security. The fact that none of the scenarios involving Macedonia turned out to be true, despite the favourable conditions that existed in the early 1990s such as lack of diplomatic recognition, military weakness and a general turbulent situation that existed in the Balkans, indicates two things. That an independent Macedonia has had a sobering effect in the region, and/or the cost of military involvement far exceeds the benefits.

To evaluate the impact of the independence of Kosova on Macedonia and the region we need to look at the regional policies and interests of the Albanian state, since its support is vital for achieving any pan-Albanian goal.

Although the disintegration of Yugoslavia further fragmented the Albanians in the Balkans, the establishment of an independent Macedonian state was in the interest of Albania and the Albanians in general. The decision of Macedonia not to remain in Yugoslavia weakened Serb regional standing and separated Greece and Serbia, while showing that the threat from the Albanians was not considered serious enough to force Macedonians to remain in Yugoslavia. In addition, both countries shared similar interests. They were being squeezed by the Greco–Serb axis[25] and could offset some of the pressure by developing close economic and political ties.[26] Due to these considerations Tirana strongly supported Macedonia's stability and independence, and urged the Albanians of Macedonia to work toward this end.

During Gligorov's visits to Albania in June 1992 Berisha supported the Albanians' demand for constituent nation status in Macedonia, and linked the recognition of Macedonia with the latter's respect for Albanians rights there. However, Albania recognized *de jure* Macedonia immediately after the UN recognition of Macedonia in April 1993, notwithstanding the Macedonian authorities' failure to address any of the Albanian grievances. Albania's position was reversed because Tirana considered that *de jure* recognition of Macedonia would improve the atmosphere between the two countries thus creating the conditions for solving the status of Albanians in Macedonia.[27]

A similar change occurred on the issue of Macedonia's membership in OSCE that had been vetoed by Albania (and Greece). In the end Albania had lost the leverages that could have been used against Macedonia without extracting any concessions regarding the rights of Albanians in Macedonia. Albanian leaders, whether in Tirana, Pristina or Skopje, have converged on the importance of Macedonia's independence. While Albania showed interest in the welfare of the ethnic Albanians the issue was not the main factor shaping bilateral relations. As we trace the development of Albanian–Macedonian relations we notice that the overriding security concern – stability of Macedonia – prevailed over other interests.[28] During the Greek-imposed embargo on Macedonia, Albania and Bulgaria provided Macedonia with alternative trade routes, without trying to capitalize on Macedonia's weakness. Although the relations between Macedonian authorities and the Albanians in Macedonia provided considerable room for intervention Tirana did not exploit it.[29] The policy of the socialist-led government toward Macedonia, similar to the Democratic Party's policy, continued to subordinate ethnic ties to security concerns and maintenance of good relations. Following the outbreak of war in Kosova in March 1998, the two countries increased their cooperation in the security area as well, to prevent arms, drug trafficking and illegal border crossings.[30] The cooperation between Albania, Macedonia and Montenegro increased during the Kosova crisis, as these countries were trying to avoid the destabilizing effects of Milošević's policies, and cope with the refugee crisis. As we noted earlier, Tirana strongly condemned the use of violence in Macedonia, while calling on the Macedonian government to open immediately a dialogue with the legitimate Albanian representatives to address their grievances. Against Skopje's accusations that arms were being smuggled on the Albanian–Macedonian border, Tirana demanded that international observers and NATO monitor the border.

Apart from geo-strategic considerations the attitude of Tirana toward Skopje has also been influenced by the way Tirana perceives the problem of Albanians in Macedonia. For the Albanian political class it is Kosova that constitutes what we know as the Albanian national question, whereas the case of Albanians in Macedonia is seen as 'one of equal rights within the existing state'.[31]

No matter how quick and solid the economic recovery of Kosova and Albania is, both of them, but Kosova more so, will depend, for the foreseeable future, on international guarantees for their security. It is difficult to see, then, how they could become a threat to another country. There exists a strong security link between Kosova and Macedonia. During the Kosova crisis Macedonia was under the continuous threat that the conflict could spill over. While the preferable solution for both the international community and Macedonians would have been an autonomous status of Kosova within FRY, it became clear that this would have only prolonged the conflict. Partition of Kosova, too, could not have provided peace and security because it would have set a very dangerous precedent for Macedonia. This link was clearly shown on the firm stance of the international community against any federal arrangements in Macedonia as basis for the political solution of the 2001 crises. Opposing Serb proposals were made by Nebojsa Covic to create Serb and Albanian entities in Kosova. At the same time, Albanians are well aware that if a war breaks out in Macedonia not only the borders of Macedonia but also those of Kosova, at least, would be subject to change. The independence of Kosova, thus, would turn Albanians into a status quo force. As Janusz Bugajski argues, 'the independence of Kosova rather than provoking calls for a greater Albania would actually resolve the Albanian question and pacify their demands.'[32]

ALBANIA AND KOSOVA

On 28 November 1912 the Albanians declared their independence. The newly established Albanian state did not correspond to the vision of the Albanian national movement, which struggled for a state that would incorporate all Albanian-inhabited territories. However, it was not merely a question of injustice done to the Albanians, the very existence and viability of the new state was in question. Albanian leaders had always advanced economic and geopolitical arguments in addition to the ethnic factor to support their goal. Cut off from its territories with a strong Albanian population allocated to Serbia, Montenegro and Greece, the prospect of Albania to achieve economic development, with all the implications of this on the social and political dimensions, were bleak.[33]

After the First World War prominent Albanian figures from Kosova participated in the political life of Albania and even held positions as cabinet members. They advocated the continuation of the armed struggle for the recovery of the lost territory. The weak Albanian state, however, was unable to provide assistance.[34] Although recognized as an independent state in 1912, Albania's existence after the First World War was once again questioned. As the Albanians were struggling to maintain their truncated state, the focus of attention shifted away from the national question. The majority of Albanian politicians believed that Albania could not afford to wage a war against Yugoslavia. Rather, the energies and resources should be channelled toward the strengthening of the state. Thus no irredentist vision was implanted into the state 'ideology'.[35] Against such a background the Albanian politicians that advocated the continuation of the armed resistance appeared as the 'odd men out'. They were seen as a source of instability, a factor obstructing the strengthening of the state.

A weak and vulnerable state, Albania has always been preoccupied with its own survival. The best way to achieve this was by not focusing on the national question. This was a clear dimension of Albanian foreign policy during the inter-war period as well as during the communist era. However, the two periods differ significantly in their domestic policies toward the national question. During the inter-war years the policies pursued by the Albanian state in education and cultural fields placed Kosova in the national memory.[36] It is at this level, the domestic one, that communist rule caused the greatest harm to the national question. The process of political socialization in the Albanian education system 'narrowed' the concept of Albanian nation. Thus, even though the title of books such as *History of Albania* and *History of Albanian Literature*, or phrases such as 'the struggle for national liberation' sounded all-encompassing in their scope, they covered only the Albanians living in the Albanian state. The struggle of the Albanians for national liberation against Serb rule, or their literary achievements was not presented in these books.[37] Moreover, there was a dearth of media coverage and publications on Kosova.

In the 1970s, reflecting the rapprochement between Albania and Yugoslavia as a result of the Soviet invasion of Czechoslovakia and Yugoslavia's interest in strengthening relations with Albania, Kosova was assigned the bridge-building role between the two countries. The contacts between Tirana and Pristina in educational and cultural fields assisted Albanians in

Kosova in building their own institutions in these areas. The fact that Albanians of Kosova adopted the standard literary language that was in use in Albania greatly facilitated the cultural exchanges and prevented the development of cultural differentiation. However, the contacts between Albania and Yugoslavia and Kosova as a result could have been even more intense, but the Albanian leadership was unwilling to establish close links fearing ideological 'contamination' from the Yugoslav branch of socialism. Even during this period the contacts between Tirana and Pristina were limited to a small group of Albanian intellectuals.

Apart from the 'shrinking' of the concept of nation, communist rule also weakened the nationalist and patriotic feelings among the population, though not intentionally. Albanian nationalism was no longer based on the culture, traditions and historically accumulated experience of the nation, but on the socialist ideology. As an Albanian analyst put it, 'nationalist sentiments were cultivated more like a vague ideological and romantic feeling toward the glorious and the only communist country in the world, rather than toward the nation and people itself.'[38] The authorities extensively employed nationalistic and patriotic slogans to justify their isolationist and repressive policies and the economic hardships that the country was going through. In the end, the result of such policies and practices alienated the population from anything that involved nationalist and patriotic rhetoric. This was the general mood that characterized Albanians as they entered the post-Cold War era.

The collapse of communism and disintegration of Yugoslavia marked a new era in the relations of Albania and Kosova. Prominent figures in Kosova criticized the slow pace of reforms in Albania, arguing that democratization of Albania would be of great assistance to Kosova, and openly supported the Democratic Party. Against this the Albanian Labour (Communist) Party and later on its successor Socialist Party started a 'well co-ordinated campaign to discredit visiting ethnic Albanians and drive a wedge between them and local Albanians.'[39]

In post-communist Albania, the national question became a foreign policy priority. In the past, as shown, Albania had tried to enhance its security by not focusing on the national question; however, under the new circumstances this foreign policy line could no longer provide security. The outbreak of Yugoslav wars presented an ominous threat from Serbia. If the war spread to Kosova, then Albania would have, ultimately, been dragged into it as well. Such a development would have been catastrophic for Albania. The avoidance of war became the overriding foreign policy security. The new national security strategy adopted by Albania stated that while Albania recognized the inviolability of borders, thus rejecting the idea of national unification and supporting a peaceful resolution of the problem, it also declared that if Serbia started its ethnic cleansing campaign in Kosova, Albanians would react as one nation, which could lead to a larger Balkan war.[40] This foreign policy stand was meant to serve as a deterrent against the Serbian threat and to urge the USA and other Western countries to become more involved in the region.

In all its endeavours, the Albanian state closely coordinated its activities with the Kosova shadow government. Albania was the only country that had recognized the Republic of Kosova. This close cooperation at the institutional level strengthened the firmness of Albanians in Kosova to carry on their resistance in a peaceful way.[41] Despite the great progress that was made in inter-Albanian cooperation, problems did exist. The relationship between Albania and Kosova, though conducted through institutional channels, had remained confined to two political forces, the Democratic Party (DP) and the Democratic League of Kosova (LDK), or even, some would say in between two individuals: Berisha and Rugova.[42] The DP and LDK did not try to reach out to other political forces in Albania and Kosova in order to establish a wider and open dialogue on the national question.[43] This lack of consensus on the national question proved to be very costly for the Albanians when the crisis broke out. Moreover, Rugova publicly supported Berisha and DP policies during national elections and the referendum on the constitution. This attitude undoubtedly increased the already existing gap between Rugova and the Socialist Party. Whereas Berisha, by strongly supporting Rugova and his peaceful policies, and by maintaining contacts only with him, contributed to the marginalization of the other political figures in Kosova.

Until late 1996, Albanian foreign policy remained unchanged. It continued to support Rugova's peaceful policies and urge the US and Western countries to exercise pressure on Belgrade to initiate negotiations with Pristina. By late 1996 the relations between Berisha and Rugova deteriorated as Berisha called on the Albanians of Kosova to stage peaceful protests in support of the Serbian opposition arguing that the democratization of Serbia was important for the resolution of the Kosova question.[44] For the first time Berisha was openly challenging Rugova's position, who maintained that the protests were an internal Serbian affair, and that there was no difference between Milošević and the opposition. The rift between Berisha and Rugova became clear as the press in Kosova started attacking Berisha.[45] Whether the move of Berisha marked the beginning of a more assertive policy by Albania is difficult to say due to the outbreak of the crisis in Albania.

After the 1997 crisis Albania not only ceased to be a factor in Balkan politics but also presented to the world the image of a country that was unable to govern itself, which in turn badly damaged the quest of the Albanians in Kosova for statehood. However, the collapse of the Albanian state did not force the Albanians in Kosova and Macedonia to reconsider their objectives. The political agendas of the Albanians in Kosova and Macedonia reflected these communities' historical experiences and the dynamics of power in their particular and immediate environments.[46] These political movements have developed independently from Tirana and do not rely on its support for their survival.

Albanian foreign policy toward Kosova during the Socialist-led government changed dramatically. In order to win the West's support Nano presented himself as a moderate force charting a new course that was in contrast to the nationalistic policies of Berisha.[47]

The meeting between Nano and Milošević during the Crete summit of the Balkan countries in November 1997 was the embodiment of the new Albanian foreign policy. In a total policy reversal, Tirana had carried out talks with Belgrade on Kosova, when only the legitimate leaders of the Kosovar Albanians were entitled to carry out those talks. Similar to the meeting between Albanian and Yugoslav foreign ministers at the UN a month earlier, this meeting had taken place without consultations with the Kosovar Albanian leadership. For Nano the full observation of human rights and democracy in Kosova would be considered as sufficient conditions to initiate a dialogue with Belgrade.[48] Unlike traditional cases when the mother country determines the political behaviour and acts as a legitimate representative of its minorities in the neighbouring states – Turkey toward its minorities in Bulgaria and Greece, or the latter toward its minority in Albania – Albania simply has never been able to play the role of the mother state. Consequently, Tirana cannot represent Kosovar Albanians and decide about their fate. The new foreign policy adopted by Nano had obviously changed from being a factor of support for Kosovar Albanians to one of pressure. In line with this policy Nano criticized Kosovar parallel institutions saying that they were not a solution but, on the contrary, they radicalized the societies that had created them.[49]

The new policy line of Tirana was strongly criticized by the Kosovar Albanians, which asked the 'government in Tirana to give the same support as its predecessor' and reminded it that the 'relations between Albania and Kosova are not ones of a mother–daughter country'.[50] The contacts between Tirana and Pristina had almost broken down and Rugova refused to visit Tirana. As events unfolded it became clear that a kind of 'alliance' had developed between Nano and those opposing Rugova in Pristina. Even after the outbreak of war in Kosova, in March 1998, the government's attitude remained restrained and ambivalent.[51] The need to win the West's support in order to shore up his position at home, was the main driving force behind Nano's foreign policy. Despite widespread corruption and marginalization of the opposition the West continued to support the socialist-led government.[52] Following the violence that was sparked as a result of the assassination of Azem Hajdari, a leading Democratic Party figure, Nano was forced to resign and was succeeded by Pandeli Majko. The foreign policy pursued by Majko changed substantially from his predecessor's. It became more assertive, and increased considerably his support for the Albanians in

Kosova.[53] The current policy of the Socialist government is that Tirana respects the will of Albanians in Kosova.

As noted earlier, the policies of the communist regime in Albania combined with daunting economic problems had weakened the nationalistic feelings among the population. Prominent Albanian writer Ismail Kadare described the situation prevailing in Albania as follows: 'In Albania there is no national hysteria. On the contrary the Albanians have gone to the other extreme that of too great indifference.'[54] The attitude of political parties in Albania toward Kosova was not a factor that influenced the election results.[55] The plight of Albanians in Kosova did not work as a cohesive factor for the political forces in Albania. It was only with the refugee crisis that Albanians started to become more aware of the fact that their future was linked to that of Kosova as well.

The refugee crisis 'galvanized Albanians in a new sense of national purpose'.[56] The government and the opposition called a truce, while the people at large revealed an unprecedented sense of solidarity by providing food, clothing and even by sheltering more than half of the 480,000 refugees that had fled to Albania in their homes, despite the difficult economic conditions. While through the refugee crisis Milošević hoped to destabilize Albania (and other neighbouring countries), the crisis accelerated the process of national integration. After several decades of being kept apart the two parts of the Albanian nation 'met' each other. Finally the 'Berlin Wall' dividing the Albanians had fallen.

Despite the greater opportunities that new Balkan realities have offered to the Albanians, since the conflict the influence of Albania in Kosova, and the level of cooperation between the two, is rather symbolic. A number of factors ranging from economic and political conditions in Albania and Kosova, to the attitude of the West accounts for this.

The lack of willingness of the political forces to reach a consensus and normalize political life has hampered the process of Albania's recovery from the 1997 crisis. Albania is suffering from weak state institutions, rampant corruption, serious problems with law and order, despite recent improvements, and high unemployment. These huge internal problems that the country faces provide no room for Albania to divert its attention to Kosova. In addition, political cooperation between political forces in Albania and Kosova has been plagued by lack of consensus, and has been conducted largely on an ideological basis: the Socialist Party maintaining close contacts with Hashim Thaci and other left-wing forces, and the Democratic Party with the Democratic League of Kosova. The visit of the Albanian President, Rexhep Mejdani, to Kosova on 24 May 2000, clearly illustrates this. Despite the historical significance of this visit, as the first visit of an Albanian President to Kosova, the Democratic League of Kosova, chaired by Ibrahim Rugova, boycotted it. As shown earlier, the relations between Rugova and the Socialist-led government had deteriorated due to the foreign policy pursued by the Socialists but also by the latter's support of Hashim Thaci, former political leader of KLA and now chairman of the Democratic Party of Kosova. Unless and until political consensus is achieved between Albanian political forces on the basic rules of the game, any initiative to establish political forums at the pan-Albanian level is likely to fail. Another important principle that should be respected in the political cooperation between Tirana and Pristina is that of equality. Albania has not been able to, and cannot, play the role of a mother country, consequently the political class of Albanians in Kosova cannot accept a paternalizing attitude from Tirana.

Economic cooperation, too, is far from realizing its full potential. Albania's poor infrastructure and the security situation in the northeast of the country, combined with double taxation of the goods that go through Albania to Kosova, have created an unfavourable environment that hinders economic relations. The development of economic relations with Kosova is especially crucial for the economic well-being of northern Albania.

The 1999 refugee crisis has provided a sound basis for integration at the social level by creating direct contacts between Albanians on both sides of the border. The free movement of people, for the first time in several decades, is one of the main driving forces behind this process of national integration. The increased interest of Albanians on both sides of the border for each other is reflected in the greater coverage by Albanian media of the events in Kosova and vice-versa. Plans to unify the education systems will further strengthen the ties between the two communities. Unlike the generations of Albanians who grew up during the communist period, in total isolation from each other, for Albanians today, Kosova is no longer abstract and distant, but concrete and real.

The processes that are outlined above – in political, economic and social levels – will proceed rather slowly due to the preoccupation of both Albania and Kosova with their internal problems, but also as a result of the Western attitude that has a great leverage on both of them. The Western attitude is reflected in the lack of high-level visits from Albania to Kosova following the end of NATO bombardment, and the fact that Tirana opened an office in Pristina only after many other countries had done so. As an analyst from Albania notes:

> Every initiative coming from Albania is seen with suspicion from the international community, which fears the idea of Greater Albania. Paradoxically, the Albanians in Albania are stimulated to integrate with the Macedonians, Bulgarians, Montenegrins within the Stability Pact, but they are hindered in integration with the Albanians on the other side of the border.[57]

Yet the question is not integration per se, but the pace and the context within which it will take place. The process of integration between Albanians in Albania and Kosova might be retarded, but cannot be opposed because it is compatible with the values and objectives of the main trend in the continent – European integration.

Enhanced cooperation at all levels between Albania and Kosova and the strengthening of the Albanian factor in the Balkans might appear threatening to neighbouring countries. In order to dissipate such fears Kosova and Albania could enter into treaties with their neighbours.[58] Moreover, what could provide greater guarantees and assurances is the fact that Albania and Kosova will be part of a larger process of regional cooperation and integration aiming at EU and NATO membership.

A NEW REGIONAL ORDER FOR THE BALKANS

The inability to establish regional cooperation is a salient characteristic of the Balkans. As an analyst from the region notes: 'Balkan countries find it difficult to build their co-operation arrangements on the basis of their own interests and needs.'[59] The war in Yugoslavia reinforced this legacy by slowing down regional cooperation, and amplifying countries' suspicions of each other. The Balkans could be characterized as a region with a high interdependence on the security affairs, yet having little meaningful interaction in other areas.

The end of the conflict in Kosova has ushered in a new era for the Balkans. The presence of NATO provides the indispensable foundation for the construction of an inter-state order and genuine future cooperation. As the analyst Josef Joffe argues in a very insightful article 'Europe's American Pacifier' security is the cause and not the consequence of western European cooperation.[60] The same message is conveyed by the Macedonian Foreign Minister when he stresses that Macedonia sees the US role in Albania as a reassuring factor.[61] In a self-help system states tend to assume the worst. Had NATO not intervened in the Balkans, each state would have been left to its own devices to face the southward spread of the Yugoslav conflict, with dire consequences for regional security. NATO presence addresses the question of security interdependence. The launching of the Stability Pact, despite its shortcomings, and the project of creating a free trade zone in south-east Europe is the best proof of the changed regional environment. For the first time in the history of the Balkans the West has an institutional approach for the whole region.

NOTES

1. I. Banac, *The National Question in Yugoslavia* (Ithaca, NY: Cornell University Press, 1993), p. 306.
2. International Crisis Group, 'Kosovo: Spring Report' (20 March 1998).
3. J. Shea, *Macedonia and Greece* (Jefferson, NC: McFarland, 1997), pp. 320–1. S.

Troebst, 'Macedonia: Powder Keg Defused?', *RFE/RL Research Reports* 3, no. 4 (28 January 1994), pp. 35–6.

4. S. Troebst, *Conflict in Kosovo: Failure of Prevention? An Analytical Documentation 1992–1998*. ECMI Working Paper 1 (Flensburg: ECMI, 1998).

5. Quoted in Troebst, *Conflict in Kosova*.

6. A. Borden, 'Rambouillet and Aftermath: Kosovo Fudge', *Balkan Crisis Report* 4, 26 February 1999.

7. M. MacDonagh, 'Why is a Free Kosovo ruled out?' *New Statesman*, 7 August 1998; J. Bugajski, 'Independent Kosova', *Christian Science Monitor*, 19 August 1998; Z. Brezinski, 'Get Serious', *National Review*, 3 May 1999; R. Gutman, 'Tragedy of Errors', *New Republic*, 26 October 1998; M. Abramovic, 'Again a Deal with Milosevic?' *Washington Post*, 11 April 1999.

8. M. Doobs, 'Montenegro Easing Away From Serb Ally', *Washington Post*, 25 June 1999, Z. Ivanovic, 'The Last War Begins', *Balkan Crisis Report* no. 37 (25 May 1999).

9. *Skopje Radio Macedonia Network*, 28 March 1999, in FBIS-EEU-1999-0328, 28 March 1999.

10. *ALBPRESS*, 21 April 1999; *Demokratsiya*, 5 April 1999, in FBIS-EEU-1999-0445, 5 April 1999.

11. *Skopje Radio Macedonia Network*, 1700 GMT, 28 March 1999, in FBIS-EEU-1999-0328, 28 March 1999.

12. H. Poulton, *Who are the Macedonians?* (London: Hurst & Company, 1995), p. 133.

13. V. Capelli, 'The Macedonian Question Again ...', *Washington Quarterly* 21, no. 3 (Summer 1998).

14. I. Blumi, 'The Question of Identity, Diplomacy, and Albanians in Macedonia', *International Journal of Albanian Studies*, at www.albanian.com/IJAS/vol1/is1/art4.html.

15. S. Ramet, *Nationalism and Federalism in Yugoslavia, 1962–1992* (Bloomington, IN: Indiana University Press, 1992), pp. 196–7; Blumi, 'The Question of Identity'.

16. M. Glenny, 'The Macedonian Question: Still No Answer', *Social Research* 62, no. 1 (Spring 1995), p. 147.

17. E. Biberaj, *Albania in Transition* (Boulder CO: Westview Press 1998), p. 256; Ramet, *Nationalism and Federalism*, p. 233.

18. See Poulton, *Who are the Macedonians*, p. 133.

19. *Reuters*, 7 April 1999; *ENTER*, 8 April 1999; *ALBPRESS Bulletin*, 3 April 1999.

20. 'An Optimist In Panic: An Interview with Arben Xhaferi', *Balkan Crisis Report*, 236, 6 April 2001

21. 'Albania calls for Macedonian Stability', *RFE/RL Newsline*, 12 March 2001; 'Macedonian Albanian Parties Call for Peace', *RFE/RL Newsline*, 21 March, 2001; 'Kosovar Leaders Appeal for Peace', *RFE/RL Newsline*, 26 March, 2001.

22. J. Tepperman, 'Freedom for Kosovo is Not a Dangerous Precedent', *International Herald Tribune*, 23 June 1999.

23. See Borden, 'Rambouillet and Aftermath: Kosovo Fudge'.

24. See *AFP*, 25 June 1999; Ljubinka Cagarovic, 'Belgrade v. Podgorica: the New Cold War', *Balkan Crisis Report* 1, 4 February 1999.

25. Quoted in J. Shea, *Macedonia and Greece*, pp. 281–2, 338.

26. V. Turpovski, 'The Balkan Crisis and the Republic of Macedonia', in C. Danopolous and K. Messas (eds), *Crises in the Balkans* (Boulder CO: Westview Press, 1997), pp. 141–3.

27. R. Austin, 'Albanian–Macedonian Relations, Confrontation or Co-operation?',

RFE/RL Research Reports 2, no. 42 (22 October 1993), p. 4.

28. See Biberaj, *Albania in Transition*, pp. 239–40.

29. K. Blazevska and K. Mehmeti, 'Steering Through the Regional Troubles', in Institute for War and Peace Reporting & Search for Common Ground (eds), *The New Accommodation* (London & Skopje: 1998).

30. See *ATA*, 17 March 1998.

31. R. Barnett (ed.), *Toward Comprehensive Peace in South East Europe* (New York: The Twentieth Century Fund, 1996), pp. 76–9.

32. See Bugajski, 'Independent Kosovo'.

33. H. Ferraj, *Skice e Mendimit Politik Shqiptar* (Tirane: Koha, 1998), pp. 151–2; J. Swire, *Albania: The Rise of a Kingdom* (New York: ARNO Press & The New York Times, 1971), pp. 150–3.

34. I. Banac, *The National Question*, pp. 150–3.

35. M. Baze, *Shqiperia dhe Lufta ne Kosova* (Tirane: Koha, 1998), p. 40.

36. Ibid., p. 29, Ferraj, *Skice e Mendimit Politik Shqiptar*, pp. 196–70.

37. See Ferraj, *Skice e Mendimit Politik Shqiptar*, pp. 327–31.

38. A. Isaku, 'Opening the Albanian Dossier', *War Report* 41 (May 1996), p. 27.

39. See Biberaj, 'The Albanian National Question', p. 245.

40. See Biberaj, *Albania in Transition*, p. 251.

41. See Baze, *Shqiperia dhe Lufta ne Kosova*, p. 28.

42. F. Schmidt, 'Balancing the Power Triangle', *Transition*, 1, no. 8, 26 May 1995, p. 39; L. Zanga, 'The Question of Kosovar Sovereignty', *RFE/RL Research Reports* 1, no. 43 (30 October 1992).

43. *Koha Jone*, 8 June 1994, in BBC Monitoring Service, 21 June 1994.

44. *ATA* news agency, 28 December 1996.

45. See Baze, *Shqiperia dhe Lufta ne Kosova*, p. 51.

46. I. Blumi, 'The Question of Identity ...'

47. See Baze, *Shqiperia dhe Lufta ne Kosova*, pp. 55–6.

48. *Reuters*, 4 November 1997.

49. *ENTER*, 7 February 1998.

50. *Kosova Daily Report*, Pristina, 3 November 1997, in BBC Monitoring Service, 5 November 1997.

51. International Crisis Group, 'The View From Tirana: The Albanian dimension of the Kosova crisis', 10 July 1998.

52. D. McAdams, 'Don't Look Now: Another Albanian Nightmare', *Human Events* 54, issue 39 (16 October 1998), p. 6.

53. *Reuters*, 22 January 1999.

54. I. Kadare, 'Dealing a Blow to the Dictatorship,' Interview with Ismail Kadare, *Transition* 1, no. 20 (3 November 1995), p. 64.

55. *The Economist*, 21 May 1994.

56. International Crisis Group, 'Albania: State of a Nation' (1 March 2000).

57. R. Lani, 'Another "Unfinished Peace"', *AIM Tirana*, 4 May 2000.

58. See Bugajski, 'Independent Kosovo'.

59. R. Vukadinovic, 'Balkan Co-operation Realities and Prospects', in S. Larrabee (ed.), *The Volatile Powder Keg*, A RAND Study (The American University Press, 1994), p. 189.

60. J. Joffe, 'Europe's American Pacifier', *Survival* (July/August 1984), pp. 174–80.

61. L. Tindemans et al. (eds), *Unfinished Peace* (Washington: Carnegie Endowment for International Peace, 1996), p. 11.

REFERENCES

Abramovic, M., 'Again a Deal with Milosevic?' *Washington Post*, 11 April 1999.

AFP, 25 June 1999.

ALBPRESS, 21 April 1999.

ATA, 17 March 1998.

ATA, 28 December 1996.

Austin, R., 'Albanian–Macedonian Relations, Confrontation or Co-operation?' *RFE/RL Research Reports* 2, no. 42 (22 October 1993), p. 4.

Banac, I., *The National Question in Yugoslavia* (Ithaca, NY: Cornell University Press, 1993).

Barnett, R. (ed.), *Toward Comprehensive Peace in South East Europe* (New York: The Twentieth Century Fund, 1996).

Baze, M., *Shqiperia dhe Lufta ne Kosove* (Tirane: Koha, 1998).

Biberaj, E., *Albania in Transition* (Boulder CO: Westview Press, 1998).

Biberaj, E., 'The Albanian National Question: The Challenges of Autonomy, Independence, and Separatism', in M. Mandelbaun (ed.), *The New European Diasporas* (New York: Council of European Relations Press, 2000), pp. 214–88.

Blazevska, K., and Mehmeti, K., 'Steering Through the Regional Troubles', in Institute for War and Peace Reporting & Search for Common Ground (eds), *The New Accommodation* (London & Skopje: 1998).

Blumi, I., 'The Question of Identity, Diplomacy and Albanians in Macedonia', *International Journal of Albanian Studies*, at www.albanian.com/IJAS/vol1/is1/art4.html.

Borden, A., 'Rambouillet and Aftermath: Kosovo Fudge', *Balkan Crisis Report* 4, 26 February 1999.

Brezinski, Z., 'Get Serious', *National Review*, 3 May 1999.

Bugajski, J., 'Independent Kosova', *Christian Science Monitor*, 19 August 1998.

Cagarovic, L., 'Belgrade v. Podgorica: the New Cold War', *Balkan Crisis Report* 1, 4 February 1999.

Capelli, V., 'The Macedonian Question … Again', *Washington Quarterly* 21, no. 3 (Summer 1998), pp. 129–35.

Daalder, I., 'What Holbrooke Wrought', *Weekly Standard*, 28 June 1999.

Demokratsiya, 5 April 1999, in FBIS-EEU-1999-0445, 5 April 1999.

Doobs, M., 'Montenegro Easing Away From Serb Ally', *Washington Post*, 25 June 1995.

ENTER, 7 February 1998.

Ferraj, H., *Skice e Mendimit Politik Shqiptar* (Tirane: Koha, 1998).

Glenny, M., 'The Macedonian Question: Still No Answer', *Social Research* 62, no. 1 (Spring 1995), pp. 143–60.

Gutman, R., 'Tragedy of Errors', *New Republic*, 26 October 1998.

International Crisis Group, 'Kosovo: Spring Report', 20 March 1998.

International Crisis Group, 'The View From Tirana: The Albanian dimension of the Kosova Crisis', 10 July 1998.

International Crisis Group, 'Albania: State of a Nation', 1 March 2000.

Isaku, A., 'Opening the Albanian Dossier', *War Report* 41 (May 1996).

Ivanovic, Z., 'The Last War Begins', *Balkan Crisis Report* 37, 25 May 1999.

Joffe, J., 'Europe's American Pacifier', *Survival* (July/August 1984), pp. 174–80.

Kadare, I., 'Dealing a Blow to the Dictatorship,' Interview with Ismael Kadare, *Transition* 1, no. 20 (3 November 1995).

Koha Jone, 8 June 1994, in BBC Monitoring Service, 21 June 1994.

Kosova Daily Report, 3 November 1997, in BBC Monitoring Service, 5 November 1997.

Lani, R., 'Another "Unfinished Peace"', *AIM Tirana* (4 May 2000).

MacDonagh, M., 'Why is a Free Kosovo Ruled Out?' *New Statesman*, 7 August 1998.

McAdams, D., 'Don't Look Now: Another Albanian Nightmare', *Human Events 54*, issue 39, 16 October 1998.

Poulton, H., *Who Are the Macedonians?* (London: Hurst & Company, 1995).

Ramet, S. P., *Nationalism and Federalism in Yugoslavia, 1962–1992* (Bloomington, IN: Indiana University Press, 1992).

Reuters, 22 January 1999.

Rizopoulos, N., 'An Independent Kosovo', *World Policy Journal 15*, no. 3 (Autumn 1998).

Schmidt, F., 'Balancing the Power Triangle', *Transition 1*, no. 8, 26 May 1995, pp. 34–9.

Shea, J., *Macedonia and Greece* (Jefferson, NC: McFarland, 1997).

Skopje Radio Macedonia Network, 28 March 1999, in FBIS-EEU-1999-0328, 28 March 1999.

Swire, J., *Albania: The Rise of a Kingdom* (New York: ARNO Press & New York Times, 1971).

Tepperman, J., 'Freedom for Kosovo is not a Dangerous Precedent', *International Herald Tribune*, 23 June 1999.

The Economist, 21 May 1994.

Tindemans, L. et al. (eds), *Unfinished Peace* (Washington: Carnegie Endowment for International Peace, 1996).

Troebst, S., 'Macedonia: Powder Keg Defused?', *RFL/RL Research Reports 3*, no. 4 (28 January 1994), pp. 33–41.

Troebst, S., *Conflict in Kosovo: Failure of Prevention? An Analytical Documentation, 1992–1998*. ECMI Working Paper 1 (Flensburg: ECMI, 1998).

Turpovski, V., 'The Balkan Crisis and the Republic of Macedonia', in C. Danopolous and K. Mestas (eds), *Crises in the Balkans: Views from the Participants* (Boulder, CO: Westview Press, 1997), pp. 135–52.

Vukadinovic, R., 'Balkan Co-operation Realities and Prospects', in S. Larrabee (ed.), *The Volatile Powder Keg, A RAND Study* (Washington: The American University Press, 1994).

Zanga, L., 'The Question of Kosovar Sovereignty', *RFE/RL Research Reports 1*, no. 43, 30 October 1992.

15

Kosovo Independence and Macedonian Stability: Is There Any Alternative to the Nationalistic Discourse?

Goran Janev

In a ten-year agony what was the largest state in the Balkans, the Socialist Federative Republic of Yugoslavia, is falling apart. Most of the republics of former Yugoslavia decided to change their statehood status from the one of federal units into full-scale independent states. Under Milošević's leadership Serbia participated in all violent conflicts aimed at preventing this from happening and lost all of the wars, including the war over Kosovo. Once an autonomous province, this subunit of Serbia decided to secede too. Without the intervention of NATO, the greatest military conglomerate in the world, the outcome of the fight of Kosovo Albanians against the Serbian forces would be rather different from the one we can observe now. Today, the prospects for independent Kosovo are greater than ever and this carries along a number of concerns for the balance of power and regional security in the Balkans. South of Kosovo, Macedonia, with a numerous Albanian population, may be dramatically affected, its stability and even its existence are at stake.

Nationalistic discourse makes us believe that current Kosovo territory is not where the border of the liberated Albanian state will be. Whether Kosovo will be annexed to the already existing Albania or not is a source of a lesser anxiety. Another, closely related issue, raises greater unease in the region, especially in the country where the imagined entity would stretch over, Macedonia. Following this reasoning, recognition of Kosovo independence is unlikely to come from Macedonia. Nevertheless, with the progress of democratization in Kosovo, which is well behind at the moment, especially with the taming and suppressing of nationalistic forces in Kosovo, its recognition, even by Macedonia, should be a lesser difficulty. Unfortunately, two years from NATO intervention Albanian extremists did open other fronts, one in Serbia proper, in the Presevo valley, and another in

north-western Macedonia. On both fronts NATO mediated peace agreements after fierce fighting.

Regardless of the reasons why, whether it is because of fear, compassion
or perverted pleasure, violence in the Balkans attracted great attention.
Mass media was there to take its piece and academia, although slowly, is
taking its share too. It is hard to be sufficiently critical of the sensationalism
that is created around the Balkans' troubles.[1] The Balkans' troubles are
troubles of inept dealing with nationalism as a social movement, and
nationalism in academia as well. In this chapter I will explore this situation,
on both levels, in greater length especially in regard to the situation in
Macedonia as influenced by the latest events in Kosovo.

DISINTEGRATIVE TREND

Although dramatic, processes of disintegration in the Balkans are not that
special or unique. It is, rather, a global trend that rages all around the planet.
Very illustrative are the latest developments in the political sphere in eastern,
as well as western, Europe that are characterized by an ongoing process
which might best be described as a disintegrative trend. Orthodoxy holds
that the current process of disintegration is the product of the pursuit of
self-determination, the natural right of every people. It is claimed that
nationalism – the ideological fuel of the principle of self-determination – is
merely harvesting its fruits. As I will argue, this conclusion results from a
cursory analysis of the phenomenon and leads only to a descriptive level of
understanding. Nationalism possesses great mobilization power, however,
either nationalism as phenomenon is not understood yet in its full richness,
or there are some other mechanisms behind or below nationalistic appear-
ances, because the power that makes people ready to die or kill for it,
remains unexplained.[2]

Exercising nationalistic rhetoric, we can say that the disintegration of
Yugoslavia, what was left of it, and of Macedonia, is a precondition for an
eventual integration of the Albanian community across the borders. At the
cost of two nation-states, a third, ethnically tidier, will be created. Clearly,
a nationalistic world-view offers no comfort for all the participants in
nation-state politics. Accepting this perspective we are forced to manipulate
concepts like segregation, self-determination, national liberation and so
forth. Commentators and observers of the social world, by adopting this
conceptual framework, even involuntarily, enforce and validate nationalistic reasoning. Arguably, there is another aspect in the inter-ethnic
dynamics that is by and large overlooked and left out of the analyses of
ethnic phenomena. Analysis of the politics of ethnic dynamics is commonly
packed into the framework of nationalistic reasoning. Studies conducted
within this framework operate with sharp, clear-cut, distinct units.[3] Ethnic

groups, rather than nations, are seen as a solid blocks that aim at political consolidation. Discussing them on that level does no good for decreasing dangerous confrontation between 'imagined communities'.

Arguably, an anthropological perspective to these phenomena might help us to unearth the mechanisms underlying the processes of ethnic politics. I am taking the case of the inter-ethnic dynamics in the Republic of Macedonia in regard to the latest developments in Kosovo. Macedonia and Kosovo are connected through the most direct medium, that of the people. The Albanians living in Macedonia are closely related to the Albanians in Kosovo and this establishes a strong and important link between Macedonia's and Kosovo's political development through this group of people.[4]

The Balkans Map Changed After All: Kosovo No Longer Part of Yugoslavia

Slightly over decade ago in Yugoslavia a multi-party system was introduced but instead of improved democratization we witnessed the growth of radical nationalism in every corner of the now dissolved country.[5] At that time, in wider Serbia and in Kosovo, Milošević had already established his authoritarian regime, and expression of political beliefs on the part of Albanians was suppressed and pushed underground. Consequently this led to the creation of a parallel system, an underground society, that was organized and run by the 'government' of the self-proclaimed Republic of Kosovo. Antagonism between oppressed Kosovo Albanians and the Milošević's regime was growing day by day, until it resulted in extremist actions by the KLA. The failure to reach agreement between warring sides resulted in controversial military action undertaken by NATO forces.

The military intervention of NATO forces in Kosovo in the spring of 1999 ended with the withdrawal of the Serbian military forces from the province. As the Yugoslav Army and Yugoslav police forces retreated from Kosovo, NATO troops under the name Kosovo Protection Forces (KFOR) took their positions. Additionally, Serbian administrative rule was substituted with the UNMIK administration. Hence, Kosovo existence is already outside the Federal Republic of Yugoslavia. Under the UN Security Council Resolution 1244, FRY's territorial integrity is guaranteed and Kosovo is not to secede from the federation, but in reality any Yugoslav control over Kosovo in future is ended for good. The will of Kosovo Albanians to remain forever beyond the reach of Belgrade is undeniable. Searching for reasons that led to this outcome of the long fight for autonomous government in Kosovo by its dominant Albanian population needs no exhaustive inquiry here and is well argued in other chapters of this book. In this chapter I explore the consequences of the status of Kosovo as an independent political entity, especially in regard to the inter-ethnic balance in the neighbouring Republic of Macedonia.

Albanian Extremism and its Threats to Macedonia

Reading the Macedonian newspapers and following broadcasts in the Macedonian language, from independence until today, it is not hard to realize that Macedonians, although the majority, feel threatened by the ethnic Albanian minority living in the country.[6] The possibility of the creation of Greater Albania is perceived as threatening to the Republic of Macedonia's territorial integrity. Therefore, Macedonians will be reluctant for any form of Kosovo independence, which is understood as a serious step towards the creation of a national state that will embrace all Albanians and the territories they populate. Popular belief holds that the realization of such a project will lead to the separation of the north-western part of Macedonia which would become part of the Greater Albanian national state. It should not be a great surprise that this idea raises heavy opposition among the Macedonians. In order to back up this statement that implies the existence of tight connections between Kosovo's and Macedonia's Albanians and of their mutual nationalistic goal, more attention will be given to this particular aspect.

When it became obvious to the Kosovo Albanians that Rugova's 'Gandhism' was not bearing the fruits they hoped for, they readily invested their support with the emerging armed movement that promised liberation from Belgrade's regime. With NATO's persuasive intervention this promise became reality. After Serbian occupation was ended and before UNMIK became more organized, KLA fighters filled the power-control void that emerged in Kosovo. The expulsion of Serbian military, police and para-military units brought about indisputable change in the lives of Kosovo Albanians.

Besides being relieved of the occupier they rejoiced in a rather peculiar way. The international community became largely disappointed when the policy of an ethnically cleansed Kosovo took hold again and victims turned into victimizers. This time Kosovo was not cleansed of Albanians, but of Serbs, Roma, Bosniaks and Croats.[7] Although not wanted, this reversal is not unexpected. By the force of arms KLA imposed itself as the main political factor in the province during and after the military campaign against Yugoslavia. Their bitterness can be partially understood, but their actions of retaliations cannot be accepted or justified. Armed extremists are more powerful than the rest of the political actors in Kosovo would like. Their power comes from the ability to take whatever action they want, whenever they want.[8] It goes without saying that this kind of power is very dangerous.

In principle this kind of power is dangerous because the polity has no control over it in any way. The use of arms as an argument is not a political instrument and is against democratic principles. Furthermore, in the naive belief that they are the ones who won the war, KLA structures want control over Kosovo territory for themselves and they are reluctant just to drop their weapons and leave the stage quietly. Using illegitimate power means nothing else but the rule of brutal force and qualifies as extremism in achieving political goals. Therefore it can be concluded that extremism is clearly present in Kosovo. Moreover, this extremism expresses itself not only in the use of means for 'political action', but also in its final goal: 'liberation' of all Albanians. Since there is a large number of Albanians living in Macedonia it is natural that non-Albanians in this country feel threatened by the liberation actions on its territory. The KLA was never fully disarmed. It was transformed into the Kosovo Protection Corpus. It is an army with a most powerful air force and, using pseudonyms, goes ravaging around Kosovo unpunished. Since the beginning of spring 2001 Macedonian state territory has been attacked a number of times by National Liberation Army (KLA) forces from Kosovo territory.[9]

INTER-ETHNIC RELATIONS IN MACEDONIA BEFORE THE START OF THE NATIONAL LIBERATION ARMY'S ACTIVITIES

Inter-ethnic relations in Macedonia were never as tense and openly hostile as in Kosovo. Nevertheless, the latest developments in this province bear heavy consequences for Albanian–Macedonian relations in this country too. The level of politicization of ethnicity and its polarization in Macedonia was never the same as in Kosovo, although in Macedonia, since the independence from the Yugoslav federation, the major characteristic of the political life has been the ethnicization of the politics.

In Macedonia, ethnic Albanians' political parties, organized on an ethnic basis, started exploiting the unfavourable social position of the ethnic Albanians in Macedonia in order to present themselves as defenders of their people. The more radical they became, the more popular they were. The situation is the same in the Macedonian camp. Following their overwhelming victory in the last parliamentary elections, the radical Albanian, Democratic Party of Albanians, and the hard-core Macedonian nationalist party, Internal Macedonian Revolutionary Organization Democratic Party for Macedonian National Unity, although unlikely bedfellows, almost overnight jumped into a marriage of interest.[10] The slogan of their government coalition was 'relaxation of inter-ethnic relations'. The situation in Macedonia, besides the exposure to influences from Kosovo, also has its own peculiarities and what follows is a further elaboration of Macedonia's ethnic politics.

Contemporary Macedonian society is undergoing a painful transition towards a fuller democracy and market economy. It is widely accepted in contemporary literature that the Macedonian struggle for independence and stability is constantly under threat from outside forces.[11] This is true as long as the perspective taken is macro-sociological. Giving more credit for political actions to the individual actors on the lower level – if it is not just political parties jabbering – the real threat to the stability of Macedonian society comes from within. The key to this danger is best described with one value-laden phrase: inter-ethnic relations.

Clearly, inter-ethnic relations is a problematic category. However, it is taken as adequate for the purposes of this investigation. It is commonly used to describe the tensions between Macedonia's two major ethnic, linguistic and religious communities: Christian Macedonians and Muslim Albanians. In a country of barely two million people, ethnic Macedonians are the largest group numerically (1.32 million). Ethnic Albanians in Macedonia total some 440,000. They are concentrated in the north-western part of the country and because of this spatial concentration they can be seen as occupying homogeneous territory, a part of the country that belongs to them. This perspective is created by the growing confrontation between these two most politically active and viable groups. Before turning to Macedonian–Albanian ethnic tensions in greater detail, it is worth remembering that there are around thirty other ethnic groups in the country, including Vlachs, Turks, Roma and Serbs. However, their political demands and actions are unlikely to escalate into violent conflict and, after all, their numerical strength if poor. In this chapter I intend to explore why exactly Macedonians and Albanians became so sharply divided on an ethnic basis. I suggest that the answer lies in the politicization of ethnicity, a product of both the reinvigorated nationalism in the region, Kosovo in particular, and of Macedonian internal dynamics that offers fertile soil for this harmful ideology.

Statistical Figures and Ethnicity Issues in Macedonia

Since statistical categories are very questionable analytical tools, I wrote this section only because of their strong impact on reality. In other words, borrowed from Perry, in Macedonia there is a special feature of politics, or of numbers: the politics of numbers.[12] Nevertheless, some information, as expressed in numbers, is very revealing. The main source for these figures is the 1994 census and the literature and analysis based on it.[13] The total population of the Republic of Macedonia is 1,945,932 inhabitants. By declared ethnic affiliation there are 1,295,964 (66.6 per cent) Macedonians; 441,104 (22.7 per cent) Albanians; 78,019 (4.0 per cent) Turks; 43,707 (2.2 per cent) Roma; 40,228 (2.1 per cent) Serbs; 8,601 (0.4 per cent) Vlachs; 36,427 (1.9 per cent) others and 1,882 (0.1 per cent) not stated.

According to the type of settlements the Macedonian population is 59.80 per cent urban and 40.20 per cent other.[14] The Albanian population is mostly rural (296,894 live in the rural category and only 145,093 live in urban settlements).[15]

The Albanian population, around one-quarter of the total population, is the largest group besides Macedonians, and naturally in certain regions it can be found as a majority population. This is the case in the north-western part of Macedonia, bordering with Albania in the west and in the north with Kosovo. In Tetovo municipality, not the town itself, there are 128,050 Albanians (74 per cent of the population), in Gostivar 68,926 (63 per cent), in Kichevo 26,073 (49.2 per cent), in Struga 28,351 (45.2 per cent), and in Debar 11,311 (44.4 per cent). Albanians are also significant in Kumanovo 47,178 (36.9 per cent), and in the capital, Skopje, 113,426 or (20.8 per cent) are spread around all of its five municipalities, in numbers from 15,019 to 31,784, in proportions from 10.2 per cent to 26.9 per cent.

Education is counted as a very important channel for upward social mobility and, in the case of the Albanian population, it is a black hole rather than a channel. In 1992/93 there were 27.3 per cent ethnic Albanian pupils in primary schools and only 7.2 per cent in secondary schools. Clearly, Albanian children are failing to make the transition to secondary school. Only 2.8 per cent of enrolled students at the universities in 1993/94 were Albanians. The special provisions for the enrolment of the students belonging to the ethnic minorities in Macedonian universities are having some effects. Under the minorities quota, proportional to the ethnic distribution, a certain percentage of the intake is reserved for members of minority groups, so the percentage of the Albanians in university grew to 9.57 per cent in the academic year 1998/99.[16] On the other hand, Macedonians have completely different educational 'behaviour'. In primary schools in 1992/93 the ratio of Macedonians was 63.6 per cent, in secondary schools 88.0 per cent and at the universities 91.4 per cent.[17]

The Albanian population demands the creation of an Albanian-language university. The Albanian political elite mobilized the whole ethnic group to support these demands. Although denied government support or recognition, a university was set up in Tetovo, financed by the Albanian community. Once more the two biggest ethnic groups are put in an antagonistic position.[18] The Macedonian constitution provides for minority language education at both the primary and secondary levels, but not at university level. However, this 'linguistic' problem spreads into areas of social life too.

According to local government law, in municipalities where significant minority populations live, that minority's language is to be used alongside Macedonian in official documents. But this law fails to satisfy the demands of Albanian politicians in Macedonia. They maintain that Albanian should be recognized alongside Macedonian as an official language at the national level too.

Religion constitutes a further dimension to the 'big divide' between Albanians and Macedonians in the Republic of Macedonia. Robert W. Mickey argues that:

> Although the Albanian are a minority, the focal point of ethnic conflict in Macedonia, is predominantly Muslim, and although other Islamic communities with significant grievances are present in Macedonia as well, this stand-off concerns the group status of Albanians as a large minority, i.e. the question about who 'owns' Macedonia.[19]

Macedonian Albanians are mostly, if not absolutely, Muslims 425,376 (98.2 per cent) (Catholics 877 (0.2 per cent) and Orthodox (942) (0.2 per cent)). On the other hand, Macedonians are mainly Orthodox, 1,229,147 (94.8 per cent), (Christians 27,104 (2.1 per cent), Catholics 4,144, Protestants 1,081 and Muslims 15,139 (1.2 per cent)). This leads to another gap between these two groups. Commenting on the data from the 1993 research project 'The National and the Confessional Distance in the Republic of Macedonia', the authors argue that: 'the most significant results are those which illustrate the "closing in" of the confessional groups on themselves, which has increased in the last few years. Indeed, even the increase in the single year since 1992 was striking'. Their analysis stresses the worsening inter-faith relations.[20]

Another big difference between these two groups is their demographic characteristics. The 'reproductive behaviour' of Albanians in Macedonia is characterized by a higher birth rate. Macedonians usually have one or two children, whereas Albanians have four or more.[21] Related to this is the fact that 43.1 per cent of the Albanian population is in the 0–19 years age group, and in the same age group there are 33.2 per cent out of the Macedonian population.[22] The Albanian population's reproductive rate is decreasing, but the myth that 'they will multiply faster and will outnumber us' is not losing ground.

The factors listed above combined contribute to the image of Macedonia as a society divided along ethnic lines. We are left without choice when it comes to accepting this reality if we follow the line of the arguments presented above, especially if we take into account what ethnic political parties are making out of it. But I argue that there is one level of social life largely unexplored in existing literature. The informal organization of these two groups is usually left unaccounted and I will turn attention to this issue before turning back to the 'existing' division of Macedonian society and the potential of this division to be turned into the destructor of the country.

INFORMAL ORGANIZATION OF ALBANIANS AND MACEDONIANS IN MACEDONIA

The 'conflict' between Macedonians and Albanians cannot be attributed solely to the nationalistic ideologies of the ethnically based political parties. It would be naive to believe that these political programmes were simply imposed upon the people. Even then, such an explanation would not suffice to explain their mass appeal among the members of different ethnic groups. I argue that the informal political organization of the ethnic groups, after the abuse by the political parties, is at the root of the ethnic divide in Macedonia. In other words, informal political organization of the ethnic groups is the precondition for the ethnic divide, but it is not the reason why there is any ethnic division in the society. The processes of industrialization and urbanization, followed by the increased bureaucratization, of Macedonian society in the last half of the twentieth century, should imply greater rationality in its management. However, the informality of the mobilization of ethnic groups is still at the core of society's organizational principles. Only by locating and analysing the hidden, invisible, informal mechanisms that lie behind political actions we can create a more realistic picture than the one that 'paints over' everything with the colour of nationalism.

The weak or alienated state, a historical constant in Macedonia, invites the formation of alternative social organizations.[23] Despite the formation of the Macedonian state some 50 years ago, when the local population started to fully participate in the work of state institutions for the first time, family-based ties remained more important than the principles of institutional organization, that is, administrative procedures are mediated by personal relationships. If one does not have a direct link to the provider of a service then a broker is introduced into the relationship. This principle generates a self-perpetuating system, which takes various forms. The lines of contact might take unexpected directions, since there are no rules regulating who can help whom and, consequently, who owes a favour, apart from the obligation to kin. Kinship ideology is still very strong and pervasive in all aspects of Macedonian social life. Because of normative constraints it is very hard to turn away kin in need. These practices helped the ethnic Macedonians, when seen as an ethnic group, to achieve a dominant position. As a result, ethnic Albanians in Macedonia were forced to maintain and strengthen their own historical kinship structure. I am taking the kinship idiom as a basic organizational principle of these two groups. I am not doing so in disregard of other factors of overt political action, but I argue that improving our knowledge of the more personal level can reveal new aspects of the political life of Macedonian society.

Additionally, Macedonia cannot be analysed as an isolated unit.[24] The recent tragedy in Kosovo brought to light the close connections between that region and Macedonia, and, in particular, the strong influence that the former exerts on the latter. It showed that inter-Albanian informal organization transcends international boundaries. The popular view holds that this solidarity results from a shared ideal to create a Greater Albania. I argue that the reason for this solidarity is non-ideological. In the relativist and manipulative quality, and especially the flexibility of kinship and other informal social institutions, we can seek for a more profound understanding of the principles of social organization. This understanding, when set in the realm of ethno-politics, should reveal the basic mechanisms of the ongoing negotiation, or struggle, over resources in society.

At this point, we can briefly look at inter-ethnic relations in Macedonia in these terms. The historical understanding of the ever-present fixed boundary between Albanians and Macedonians contributes greatly to the vision of two separate and divided ethnic groups, or nations, as each of them perceives themselves. I will argue that, modifying this view, we can say that we are dealing with two separate kin groups. Each of them pursues the improvement of the hold over resources. The distribution of wealth will be, we can assume, even unconsciously reserved for the next of kin, not given over to the 'others'. Unfortunately, this view is too naive compared to the widely accepted nationalistic ideology. The dominance of the nationalism in the Republic of Macedonia, results from ethnicization of politics, that is in Macedonia, politics is *ethnic* politics.

Recent events in neighbouring countries have made the ethnic situation in Macedonia even more uneasy. The Kosovo problem can be traced back to the treatment of the Albanian population as a national minority in SFR Yugoslavia. Although as a group they outnumbered Montenegrins, Macedonians and Slovenians, unlike those groups the Albanians did not enjoy the right to organize their own republic within the federal state. Back in 1968 Albanians from Kosovo and Macedonia pronounced their will to have the status of a constituent nation with its own federal unit in Yugoslavia.[25] This demand was silenced in a rather harsh way and pushed that part of Albanian political movement underground. It erupted once more in 1981 with the student demonstrations in Pristina and once more the measures taken against it were brutal. Kosovo remained under Serbian rule and Serbia later fell into the hands of Milošević – who came to power by exploiting the Kosovo situation – and it was obvious to everyone that it was only a question of time before it will erupt again. Macedonia and Macedonian Albanians came into focus only after Kosovo exploded and the flood of refugees poured into the tiny country with a fragile ethnic balance, especially after the KLA/NLA continued with liberation of the Albanians from the Slavic occupiers.

To understand better the Macedonian inter-ethnic relations dynamic, a very rough and general historical picture is required before turning in greater detail to recent events.

Historical Sketch

Only after the Second World War was the Macedonian state finally organized. It should be noted that Macedonia had been occupied and its people kept away from the direct governing of the state for centuries. That led to a culture of distrust of state officials and, consequently, a focus on the people who could be trusted. It should not be surprising that well into the 'socialist revolution' people were creating networks of relatives and friends.[26] Almost five decades of propagated, nominal near-equality, opened the channels of social mobility to almost everyone in Macedonia. The system was supposedly built on meritocracy, but nepotism was never fully eliminated.

The last decade of independent rule in Macedonia is known as a transition period, like elsewhere in the post-communist world.[27] With social habits that were developed throughout history, imposing new standards of behaviour is, once more, perceived as alien to the local population, and reaction to it is turning to traditional forms of organization once more. Today, again, the state is seen as an alien entity. It is perceived as a barrier to personal advancement. Only people with special connections benefit from it.

If this can be said for the general population, it is not surprising that Albanians feel even more estranged from the Macedonian state. After the liberation war, during the socialist revolution, the Macedonian nation was rapidly catching its neighbouring countries in establishing nation-building institutions. This process of nation-building obviated the needs of Albanians in Macedonia. The forces of nationalism, in combination with the network system organized by Macedonians who became dominant in the life of the republic, made Albanians a discriminated against, but not a persecuted population. Albanians responded the way they knew best, by organizing their own network system of alliances and coalitions based on kinship. I argue that this natural adaptation to the social environment, when seen through nationalistic glasses, creates the vision of a society divided along ethnic lines. But nationalism was not created in the Balkans and its artificiality and incompatibility with the traditions of this region brought the notorious troubles to it.

EMERGENCE OF THE BALKAN NATION-STATES AND THE BEGINNING OF THE BALKANIZATION PROCESS

The politics of the Balkans must be perceived as a regional whole when analysed. Besides the numerous particularities and differentiated developments of specific countries, all of it might be seen as a part of a bigger analytical unit. Especially if we accept that the Balkans became divided into smaller political units only after the entrance of the nationalistic ideology. Since nationalism was imported to the Balkans we can say that it became

312

Balkanized only after it became Europeanized.[28] Ever since the Balkan peninsula was 'Europeanized' it became one big battlefield. Nationalists from the region organized countless 'liberation' wars. Not without success, local nationalist leaders regularly promoted – and still do – chauvinism, xenophobia, racism, intolerance, distrust and hatred. Often this state of affairs is dubbed 'Balkanization'. It is taken to mean, among many other things, the primitive, uncivilized, raw, wild, violent and merciless promotion of national causes.

There are two perspectives on Balkanization, one from outside the region and the other from within. The former can be nicely summed up and presented in its full misunderstanding as 'the prospect of further fragmentation'.[29] Political turmoil in the Balkans at the beginning of the twentieth century resulted in the collapse of two great empires. The disintegration of these empires, and the consequent wars, promoted this territory as eternally fragmenting. Moreover, the break up of Yugoslavia in the last decade only enforced this perspective. The internal perspective, on the other hand, offers an explanation for the troubles of the Balkan people as a repercussion of the forced 'Westernization' of the region. The process of Westernization of the Balkans began in the age of nationalism and being coterminous with it, unfortunately still lasts today.

Some Balkan nations were better organized than others in conducting their nationalist projects and were more capable of gaining state territory. Others were less successful. This is the main generator of the never-ending stability crisis in this troubled region. Almost no single Balkan nationalist territorial ideal was fulfilled. To make this happen the territory of the Balkan peninsula would have to stretch over half of the European continent. Every Balkan ethnic group has embraced nationalism and made claims on territory. In regard to Albanians, in the speech of nationalism, their national body was butchered in three parts, and uniting it is the only natural thing every Albanian should strive for. To a certain extent the same goes for Macedonians. The great difference between these two 'projects' is to be found in the ways of political fighting they adopted. While Albanians in Kosovo and in Macedonia, as of late and to the present, resorted to arms, Macedonians in Greece, Bulgaria and Albania did not do so. The positive outcome of the Kosovo conflict, that is, fulfilled liberation from the Serbian regime, only fuels the hopes of the extremists that the violent principle did bear fruit. Nevertheless, we can see how, in Macedonia, two 'unresolved' national questions are brought into conflict through their frustrations from previous losses.

Balkanization (Fragmentation) of Macedonia?

After the outbreak of violence in spring 2001 it became obvious that, contrary to the widely accepted view that Macedonia's stability is threatened from outside, the real danger comes from nationalistic forces within the country. The external threat is recognized by a number of authors writing about the Macedonian situation.[30] All of its neighbours act unfavourably, in a number of ways, with respect to the future of Macedonia. This reasoning about neighbouring countries threatening Macedonian territory is highly speculative. However, it cannot be ruled out, on precondition that internal actors are turned into agents of the national cause of some of the neighbouring countries. Nevertheless, what seems most threatening is a possibility of a civil war, that is, ethnic war between ethnic Albanians and ethnic Macedonians in Macedonia. Certainly, for such an unhappy development both sides should be blamed. For their part in the relationship of distrust, the behaviour of Macedonians towards Albanians does not help much to prevent the further division of Macedonian society along ethnic lines. However, Macedonians have no interest in challenging the territorial integrity of the country. In the current situation, which is a result of a longer process, the provocation comes from the ethnic Albanian camp, and one must admit that the provocation was not just a small and innocent nationalistically romantic action, like distributing flyers or painting graffiti. The concentration of ethnic Albanians in the western part of Macedonia makes conflicting territorial claims an additional source of armed conflict, if other preconditions are met.

There are a number of reasons to locate the radical Albanians in Macedonia as the only existing force that can lead to the country's disintegration. The radical elements might take advantage of the ethnic Albanians' cohesiveness. It would be unreasonable to blame the Macedonian Albanians en masse, but when the situation deteriorated the common Albanian, as a member of his group, was left without choice. Not helping the National Liberation Army's soldiers is national treachery. If the observation of the strong kin obligation among Albanians is correct, we can note that helping kin takes priority over the state. Furthermore, ethnic minority Albanian politicians in Macedonia have presented the state as foreign and illegitimate. Adding to this, all Macedonian governments since independence only contributed to this alienation felt by ethnic Albanians in Macedonia.

Coming from training camps in Kosovo and from the ranks of the never-disbanded Kosovo Liberation Army, fighters of the National Liberation Army started shooting and killing Macedonian armed forces in March 2001.[31] They never stopped to talk about their fight as fight for the human rights of Macedonian Albanians, but indeed, they are fighting for the liberation of their nation from the Macedonian occupiers.[32] Hundreds were killed and injured, and thousands of refugees were created as a consequence of innumerable, merciless, terrorist attacks and the response of the security forces. With the involvement of the Western international community and NATO structures, who felt obliged to intervene in this mess, political leaders of the four biggest political parties, two Macedonian and two Albanian, signed the Framework Agreement for constitutional changes on 13 August 2000. The fighting did not stop immediately. Over 60,000 Macedonians are registered as internally displaced, and probably the same number of ethnic Albanians went to Kosovo to avoid the explosions and bullets.

Six months of armed conflict and fierce nationalistic rhetoric gravely harmed normal inter-ethnic communication. Both Macedonians and Albanians became more nationalistic, out of fear, anger and hate for the 'others' and loyalty, pride and love for the own group. All of this mix, fostered by irresponsible actors from the Macedonian political scene, finally contributed to the successful ethnic division of Macedonian society. Fear of territorially dividing the country is also the main reason why Macedonians see radical Albanians as the greatest enemies of the state and why recognition of Kosovo independence now seems most unlikely. Most importantly, the NLA succeeded in severely breaking inter-ethnic bridges and makes redundant most of the argumentation in this chapter that speaks against the power of nationalism.

CONCLUSION

All of these factors, put together, demonstrate how the widely accepted picture of Macedonia as a society with deep ethnic division has been created. From a perspective of popular belief, political speeches, journalists' reports and macro-sociological studies this picture is correct. Nevertheless, I do not agree with the accuracy of the above presentation. Distanced from nationalistic reasoning, a serious and all-encompassing study should strive to bring to light the unaccounted aspects of informal organizing. This should reveal non-politicized kin-networks that instrumentalize the collaboration between its members. Closely related people tend to help each other under unfavourable social conditions. In Macedonia, the existing informal organization before the introduction of the multi-party system was a natural repository heavily exploited by ethnic political parties. Furthermore, politicization on an ethnic basis may harden group distinctiveness and bring animosity towards the 'others', the 'enemies'. But 'others' turn out to be enemies only when they are a threat to 'us' and that is possible only within nationalistic reasoning.

The way out of this dangerous and unfortunate situation in Macedonia, as painted above, in the wider Balkan region and elsewhere, is not that hard to find. The abandonment of nationalism as an ideology that distracts the perception of reality is not an easy task, but that task must be undertaken for the sake of ending the suffering that nationalism has caused since its emergence. That the disease of nationalism is spread efficiently all over the globe is acknowledged fact. I would only like to challenge the assumption that its students are immune to it. While striving to understand its

315

mechanisms, principles and appeal, we forget to distance ourselves from it. The picture of nationalism as created by the scholar, on an abstract theoretical level or while dealing with a particular situation, contains the nationalism malady in itself. As in modern marketing, the important notice is given only in small print. The Macedonia–Kosovo case, and especially the relations between Macedonians and Albanians in Macedonia should help show clearly that nationalism is an ideology that is fed by scholars too. Adopting the language of nationalism and treating humans as group phenomena, that is, nations, serves only the descriptive level of under-standing, which is of the lowest heuristic quality and helps only to strengthen the nationalistic worldview. All the noise about the potentiality of the ethnic clash in Macedonia comes from the overemphasized importance of nationalistic leaders and their recruited followers. We can say that Macedonian citizens are cleverer then the observers and the politicians since, even after months of fighting between Albanian extremist groups and Macedonian security forces, common people did not get involved. This is not supposed to suggest that the actions of nationalists that threaten basic security norms should be neglected or ignored, but more attention must be paid to the more specific, harder to find, evidence on the micro level, since generalization only helps advancing nationalism's curse.

NOTES

1. M. Todorova, *Imagining the Balkans* (Oxford: Oxford University Press, 1998), and V. Goldsworthy, *Inventing Ruritania: The Imperialism of the Imagination* (New Haven: Yale University Press, 1999). These two recent works give us a precious insight into Western perceptions of the Balkans. With a pedantic precision Todorova analyses the historical and political writings on the peninsula and its people, while Goldsworthy focuses on the literary and entertainment industry developed around the exploitation of Balkan exoticism.
2. B. Anderson, *Imagined Communities* (London: Verso, 1991).
3. Eric Wolf, 'Race, Culture, Ethnicity: Perilous Ideas', *Current Anthropology*, vol. 35, no. 1 (1994). Eric Wolf points out that social scientists' need for distancing from these concepts as their uncritical use inflicts damage to the social reality.
4. See 'The Albanian question in Macedonia: Implications of the Kosovo Conflict for Inter-Ethnic Relations in Macedonia', International Crisis Web, at www.risisweb.org/projects/macedonia/reports.mac03main.htm; and S. Clement, 'Macedonian Albanians and Kosovo Albanians: Towards the Bosnian Model', in T. Veremis and E. Kofos (eds), *Kosovo: Avoiding Another Balkan War* (Athens: University of Athens, 1998).
5. Ethnicity as a major impediment to the emerging democracies was pointed out rightly in D. Horowitz, 'Democracy in Divided Societies', *Global Issues in Transition*, no. 6 (January 1994).
6. Albanian political leaders refuse to be treated as minority in the Republic of Macedonia and insist on equal status with majority Macedonians.
7. J. Briza, *Minority Rights in Yugoslavia* (London: Minority Rights Group, 2000), pp. 12–14.

8. On the political violence in the province see V. Surroi, *Kosovo Tributes*, at www.iwpr.net/index.pl5?archive/bcr/bcr_20000915_1_eng.txt; also L. Semini, *Kosovo Election Campaign Violence*, at www.iwpr.net/index.pl5?archive/bcr/bcr_20000915_2_eng.txt.

9. The acronym KLA and NLA reads UÇK in Albanian in both cases.

10. Actually, this party was never registered officially due to the programme of the party that aims at constitutional changes

11. S. R. Bollerup and C. D. Christiansen (eds), *Nationalism in East Europe: Causes and Consequences of the National Revivals and Conflicts in Late-Twentieth-Century East Europe* (London: Macmillan, 1997), p. 210; also R. Miller and M. Ivanović, 'Macedonia: the Creation of a Nation and the State out of Ethnic Conflict', in T. D. Sfikas and C. Williams (eds), *Ethnicity and Nationalism in the East-Central Europe and in the Balkans* (Aldershot: Ashgate, 1994), p. 312.

12. D. M. Perry, 'The Republic of Macedonia: Finding its Way', in K. Dawisha and B. Parrott (eds), *Politics, Power, and the Struggle for Democracy in South-East Europe* (Cambridge: Cambridge University Press, 1997).

13. The 1994 Census of the Population, Households, Dwellings and Agricultural Holdings was organized with the technical and financial assistance of the Council of Europe and the European Commission, working in cooperation with the International Conference on the Former Yugoslavia and the Economic Commission for Europe of the United Nations (Statistical Office of the RM 1996). Such a complex body was involved because the Albanian population boycotted the 1991 Yugoslav Census, claiming that they would be deliberately undercounted (and in the Republic of Macedonia – at that time the Socialist Republic of Macedonia and still part of the Yugoslav Federation – for not providing them with census forms in their language).

14. *The 1994 Census of Population, Households, Dwellings and Agricultural Holdings in the Republic of Macedonia, Population According to Declared Ethnic Affiliation, Religious Affiliation, Mother Tongue and Citizenship* (Skopje: Statistical Office of Macedonia, 1996).

15. See M. Najcevska and N. Gaber, *Survey Results and Legal Background Regarding Ethnic Issues in the Republic of Macedonia* (Skopje: Institute for Sociological, Political and Juridical Research, 1995).

16. Albanians in Macedonia, 'Minorities at Risk Project', at www.bsos.umd.edu/cidcm/mar/macalban.htm.

17. See Najcevska and Gaber, *Survey Results*.

18. Around the Tetovo University issue we can clearly see how the 'radicalization' shifts from one to the other ethnic Albanian party. When Tetovo University was set up PDP was a part of governing coalition and DPA was marking the traitors of the Albanian cause. Now in power DPA is content with the OSCE High Commissioner's proposition for the formation of a teachers' college, and PDP is talking of betrayal of Albanian ideals.

19. R. Mickey, 'Citizenship, Status, and Minority Political Participation: The Evidence from the Republic of Macedonia', in Nonneman, Niblock and Szajkowski, *Muslim Communities in the New Europe* (Berkshire: Ithaca Press, 1996).

20. M. Najcevska, E. Simoska and N. Gaber, 'Muslims, State and Society in the Republic of Macedonia: The View from Within', in Nonneman, Niblock and Szajkowski (eds), *Muslim Communities in the New Europe* (Berkshire: Ithaca Press, 1996).

21. A. Jovanović, *Planirawe na semejstvoto vo Republika Makedonija – Demografski i socioloski aspekti* (Ph.D. dissertation, Skopje: University of Sts Cyril and

Methodius, 1994); and J. Trifunoski, *Albansko stanovnistvo u Makedoniji: antropogeografska i etnografska istrazzivanja* (Belgrade: Knjizevne Novine, 1988)

22. *1994 Census.*

23. E. Gellner and J. Waterbury (eds), *Patrons and Clients In Mediterranean Societies* (London: Duckworth, 1977), p. 4. Gellner points out that an incomplete centralization of the state will 'lead to the emergence of informal brokers-patrons'. In this view, effective centralized bureaucracies or market economies prevent the emergence of alternative power structures. What we have had in Macedonia for centuries is weak, and consequently deviant, functioning of state mechanisms.

24. Within the social sciences it is widely agreed to treat states and societies as fixed differentiated units. This positivistic domination culminated in the functionalist or structural–functionalist phase, which coincides with the establishment of nationalistic ideology. The atomization of the social world that emerged from this perspective was most warmly embraced by nationalist ideologues and that makes it relevant for us. That this discourse of atomization is illogical was noticed by a number of authorities in social sciences. See L. Drummond, 'The Cultural Continuum: A Theory of Intersystems', *Man*, vol. 15, no. 2 (1980); E. Wolf, *Europe and the Peoples Without History* (Berkeley: University of California Press, 1997); U. Hannerz, *Cultural Complexity* (New York: Columbia University Press, 1992); and M. Castells, *The Information Age: Economy, Society and Culture*, Vols I, II, III (Oxford: Blackwell, 1998), who contributed greatly to overcoming the mosaic representation of the world.

25. See Clement, 'Macedonian Albanians and Kosovo Albanians'. Also in 'Albanians in Macedonia', *Minorities at Risk Project*, at www.bsos.umd.edu/cidcm/mar/macalban.htm. Arben Xhaferi, the leader of the main Albanian political party in Macedonia today, was imprisoned at the age of 20 for his participation in this demonstration.

26. See E. A. Hammel and C. Yarbrough, 'Social Mobility and the Durability of Family Ties', *Journal of Anthropological Research*, vol. 29, no. 3 (1973), and E. A. Hammel and D. Soc, 'Lineage Cycle in Yugoslavia', *American Anthropologist*, vol. 75 (1973). The importance of the specific forms of social and economic organization, which are clearly based on kinship ties, are undeniable for the development of normative aspects of Balkan people's culture. Hammel and Soc and Hammel and Yarbrough record the continuation of kin ties in new urbanized and industrialized setting since the Second World War in Yugoslavia. Also A. Simić, 'Ageing in the US and Yugoslavia: Contrasting Models of Integrational Relationships', *Anthropological Quarterly*, vol. 50, no. 2 (1977), p. 58. In his comparative analysis of integrational relationships in the US and Yugoslavia, for the family prototype of the latter, Simic claims 'not only have archaic forms of household organization persisted in many rural areas, but more generally, even in urban centres, the ideology of kinship solidarity has survived almost intact'. Although these studies were concerned with Yugoslavia in general, Albanian and Macedonian populations were taken under consideration too.

27. This term is hardly applicable to the Macedonian situation. Transition implies transformation of one social system into something else. Economic life in Macedonia was destroyed which makes transition a term distant from reality. The Macedonian institutional system was ruined and now it is about to be rebuilt, under the omnipresent gaze of the International Monetary Fund and World Bank, which forces out the welfare state and pushes towards maximized rationalization.

28. See M. Todorova, *Imagining the Balkans*. Todorova's analysis of the development of the Balkanism discourse as product of Western academia's ethnocentrism is

very successful, yet fails to admit a certain distinctiveness from the political culture of Western Europeans. Also see M. Hertzfeld, *Anthropology Through the Looking-Glass* (Cambridge: Cambridge University Press, 1987). Hertzfeld provides us with a careful analysis of Eurocentric hegemonic discourse that packs south-eastern Europeans into the category of exotic 'Other'. However, regardless of the just opposition to the exotic view of the Balkans, we must recognize that the Balkan region and western Europe had different historical developments and the outcome simply cannot be the same.

29. See C. Cviic, *Remaking the Balkans* (London: RIIA, Pinter, 1991), p. 2

30. See S. R. Bollerup and C. D. Christiansen, *Nationalism in East Europe*, p. 210; R. East and J. Pontin (eds), *Revolution and Change in Central and East Europe* (London: Pinter Publishers, 1997); Miller and Ivanović, 'Macedonia', p. 312; and B. Szajkowski, 'Macedonia: An Unlikely Road to Democracy', in G. Pridham and T. Gallagher (eds), *Experimenting with Democracy: Regime Changes in the Balkans* (London: Routledge, 2000), p. 249.

31. See Kosovci, Kriminalci i Platenici, *Aktuel*, 24.08.2001, on the origins of NLA.

32. NLA communiqué no.4, cited in ICG April 2001 report *Macedonian Question: Reform or Rebellion.*

REFERENCES

Academy of Sciences of the Republic of Albania – Institute of History, *The Truth on Kosova* (Tirana: Encyclopaedia Publishing House, 1993).

'Albanians in Macedonia', *Minorities at Risk Project*, at www.bsos.umd.edu/cidcm/mar/macalban.htm.

Anderson, B., *Imagined Communities* (London: Verso, 1991).

Banks, M., *Ethnicity, Anthropological Constructions* (London: Routledge, 1996).

Barth, F. (ed.), *Ethnic Groups and Boundaries* (Oslo: Universitetsforlaget, 1969).

Bollerup, S. R. and Christiansen, C. D. (eds), *Nationalism in East Europe: Causes and Consequences of the National Revivals and Conflicts in Late-Twentieth-Century East Europe* (London: Macmillan, 1997).

Briza, J., *Minority Rights in Yugoslavia* (London: Minority Rights Group, 2000), pp. 12–14.

Campbell, J. K., *Honour, Family and Patronage: A Study of Institutions and Moral Values in a Greek Mountain Community* (Oxford: Clarendon Press, 1964).

Castells, M., *The Information Age: Economy, Society and Culture*, Vols I, II, III (Oxford: Blackwell, 1998).

Clement, S., 'Macedonian Albanians and Kosovo Albanians: Towards the Bosnian Model', in T. Veremis and E. Kofos (eds), *Kosovo: Avoiding Another Balkan War* (Athens: University of Athens, 1998).

Cviic, C., *Remaking the Balkans* (London: RIIA, Pinter, 1991), p. 2.

Drummond, L., 'The Cultural Continuum: A Theory of Intersystems', *Man*, vol. 15, no. 2 (1980).

East, R. and Pontin, J. (eds), *Revolution and Change in Central and East Europe* (London: Pinter Publishers, 1997).

Gellner, E. and Waterbury, J. (eds), *Patrons and Clients In Mediterranean Societies* (London: Duckworth, 1977), p. 4.

Goldsworthy, V., *Inventing Ruritania: The Imperialism of the Imagination* (New Haven: Yale University Press, 1999).

Grillo, R., *Pluralism and the Politics of Difference: State, Culture and Ethnicity in Comparative Perspective* (Oxford: Clarendon Press, 1998), p. 12.

Hammel, E. A. and Soc, D., 'Lineage Cycle in Yugoslavia', *American Anthropologist*, vol. 75 (1973).

Hammel, E. A. and Yarbrough, C., 'Social Mobility and the Durability of Family Ties', *Journal of Anthropological Research* vol. 29, no. 3 (1973).

Hannerz, U., *Cultural Complexity* (New York: Columbia University Press, 1992).

Hertzfeld, M., *Anthropology Through the Looking-Glass* (Cambridge: Cambridge University Press, 1987).

Horowitz, D., 'Democracy in Divided Societies', *Global Issues in Transition*, no. 6 (January 1994).

International Crisis Group, 'The Albanian question in Macedonia: Implications of the Kosovo Conflict for Inter-Ethnic Relations in Macedonia', 11 August 1998.

Jovanović, A., *Planirawe na semejstvoto vo Republika Makedonija – Demografski i socioloski aspekti* (Ph.D. dissertation, Skopje: University of Sts Cyril and Methodius, 1994).

Mickey, R., 'Citizenship, Status, and Minority Political Participation: The Evidence from the Republic of Macedonia', in Nonneman, Niblock and Szajkowski, *Muslim Communities in the New Europe* (Berkshire: Ithaca Press, 1996).

Miller, R. and Ivanović, M., 'Macedonia: the Creation of a Nation and the State out of Ethnic Conflict', in T. D. Sfikas and C. Williams (eds), *Ethnicity and Nationalism in the East-Central Europe and in the Balkans* (Aldershot: Ashgate, 1994), p. 312.

Najcevska, M. and Gaber, N., *Survey Results and Legal Background Regarding Ethnic Issues in the Republic of Macedonia* (Skopje: Institute for Sociological, Political and Juridical Research, 1995).

Najcevska, M., Simoska, E. and Gaber, N., 'Muslims, State and Society in the Republic of Macedonia: The View from Within', in Nonneman, Niblock and Szajkowski (eds), *Muslim Communities in the New Europe* (Berkshire: Ithaca Press, 1996).

Perry, D. M., 'The Republic of Macedonia: Finding its Way', in K. Dawisha and B. Parrott (eds), *Politics, Power and the Struggle for Democracy in South-East Europe* (Cambridge: Cambridge University Press, 1997).

Semini, L., *Kosovo Election Campaign Violence*, at www.iwpr.net/index.pl5?archive/bcr/bcr_20000915_2_eng.txt.

Simić, A., 'Ageing in the US and Yugoslavia: Contrasting Models of Integrational Relationships', *Anthropological Quarterly*, vol. 50, no. 2 (1977), p. 58.

Surroi, V., 'Kosovo Tributes', *Balkan Crisis Report*, no. 172 (2000).

Szajkowski, B., 'Macedonia: An Unlikely Road to Democracy', in G. Pridham and T. Gallagher (eds), *Experimenting with Democracy: Regime Changes in the Balkans* (London: Routledge, 2000), p. 249.

The 1994 Census of Population, Households, Dwellings and Agricultural Holdings in the Republic of Macedonia, Population According to Declared Ethnic Affiliation, Religious Affiliation, Mother Tongue and Citizenship (Skopje: Statistical Office of Macedonia, 1996).

Todorova, M., *Imagining the Balkans* (Oxford: Oxford University Press, 1998).

Trifunoski, J., *Albansko stanovnistvo u Makedoniji: antropogeografska i etnografska istrazzivanja* (Belgrade: Knjizevne Novine, 1988).

Wolf, E., *Europe and the Peoples Without History* (Berkeley: University of California Press, 1997).

Wolf, E., 'Race, Culture, Ethnicity: Perilous Ideas', *Current Anthropology*, vol. 35, no.1 (1994).

16

Serbia After the Kosovo War:
The Defeat of Nationalism and Change of Regime
Florian Bieber

The war in Kosovo has had different kinds of impact on the population of Yugoslavia and on most Serbs. Obviously the NATO bombing inflicted much suffering among the civilian population. In addition, it placed the Yugoslav regime for the first time in *visible* conflict with and opposition to the international community. Prior to the NATO bombing, the confrontation between the regime and Western countries had never before taken such direct and explicit form. The bombing of Serb positions in Bosnia in 1995 occurred at a moment when Milošević had already broken most links with the Serb leadership in the Republika Srpska. The sanctions between 1992 and 1995, and since 1999 – although having a detrimental effect on the population of Serbia – never positioned Western countries in the same confrontation as the war in early 1999. The war in Kosovo, or rather the wars, the bombing of Yugoslavia by NATO on one side and the campaign of mass expulsions and murder in Kosovo by the Yugoslav army and paramilitary groups on the other, had contradictory effects on Serbia itself and on nationalism, which has been a dominant phenomenon in Serbian politics of the past decade.

This chapter will seek to put forth some considerations on the role nationalism played prior to and during the Kosovo war in Serbia. It will also highlight some of the consequences of the loss of Kosovo in the Serbian political scene after June 1999. First, the chapter will explore the role of the government in mobilizing a 'patriotic' policy vis-à-vis Kosovo, and the public support (or the lack thereof) it managed to secure. It will then highlight the impact of the loss of Kosovo on the political opposition, and the impact of Kosovo on the regime change in September/October 2000. In its concluding parts, the chapter will discuss the role of conspiracy theories in relation to nationalism, as reinforced by the war in 1999, and discuss some of the post-war attempts to address the crimes committed in the name of the Serbian people.

THE 'PATRIOTIC POLICY' OF THE GOVERNMENT

There is little evidence that the government actually enjoyed widespread support for its policy of expelling as many Albanians as possible during the NATO bombardment of Yugoslavia. While support for Milošević and his Socialist Party continuously declined throughout the 1990s, the lack of criticism for the government's nationalist policies from large segments of the 'real' and 'false' opposition, have created the appearance of a broad consensus over the policies pursued in Kosovo.

The last elections in Serbia, which took place in 1996 and 1997 focused less on national issues than any previous election. Instead, they represented attempts by parts of the electorate to vote for a 'normalization' of Serbia, as indicated by the victory of the opposition alliance *Zajedno* in local elections in November 1996. The elections for the Serbian presidency in the following year reflected general dissatisfaction with the internal squabbling of the democratic opposition, as witnessed by the rise of Vojislav Šešelj as the alternative to the Socialist Party and its candidates Zoran Lilić and later Milan Milutinović. Despite the importance of other issues during the election, the question of Kosovo nevertheless featured prominently in the electoral campaign. The government continued to advance a position that proposed dialogue and 'compromise' with the Albanian population, but that rejected any significant degree of territorial autonomy, rendering the offer de facto worthless. The Yugoslav Left (JUL) generally, sought to portray the more 'conciliatory' wing of the government, as exemplified by the following statement by Ljubiša Ristić, its president:

> It was our duty and obligation to launch dialogue with our fellow-countrymen of Albanian ethnicity with a view to finding a solution to their status and their participation in the political life of the country. Obviously such a dialogue cannot be initiated with those who stubbornly insist upon separation of Kosovo, its independence and separatism ... Hence the left coalition will not talk about Kosovo as a state or Republic within the FRY.[1]

The dominant Socialist Party, on the other hand, supported a similar policy, while taking a stronger line against separatism, linking it with 'foreign enemies', as its first presidential candidate, Zoran Lilić explained:

> ... [we] will have to fend off the attacks of those who would like to spoil [what we achieved]. There are such people in Vojvodina, Kosovo and Metohija, in Raška and beyond our borders. If we cannot prevent

the intentions of our foreign enemies, we can neutralize the intents of those who live within our borders ... I am referring to those who are seeking territorial autonomy, a state within a state. That will not happen in Serbia.[2]

Only one attempt was made by the regime to garner legitimacy for its policy towards Kosovo after the elections of 1997 with the referendum held in April 1998. The referendum only addressed foreign mediation in the escalating conflict, however. A poster of the Yugoslav Left in English serves as a good (and amusing) example of the government position: 'Citizents [*sic*]! Do you agree that strangers should interfere with what you do in your country? No. We all think the same!'[3] Although the 75 per cent rejection was celebrated by the regime as a 'historical "No"' comparable to the 1941 coup against the German–Yugoslav alliance and the 1948 break with the Soviet Union, it rather demonstrated (illustrated) the regime's understanding of democracy by holding a referendum at very short notice, and posing a strongly biased question with little concrete meaning for the outcome.[4] A few months later the Holbrooke–Milošević agreement over the stationing of up to 2,000 unarmed OSCE observers in Kosovo (Kosovo Verification Mission, KVM) exposed the referendum as being nothing more than a bluff.

The intensification of the conflict in Kosovo, largely triggered by the brutal response to the growing Kosovo Liberation Army (KLA), prompted a shift in the policy of the Socialist Party of Serbia. In the early phase of Milošević's rule, while it still existed as the League of Communists of Serbia, the party combined the rhetoric of a centralized Yugoslavia with calls for a strong Serbia. Between 1991 and 1993, the new Socialist Party shifted toward a more outright nationalist position, justifying the wars in Croatia and Bosnia. Starting with the later phase of the Bosnia war until the beginning of the Kosovo conflict, the party adopted a 'pro-peace' line and presented itself domestically and internationally as a factor and guarantor of stability.[5] Since 1998, the Socialist Party has positioned itself as a 'patriotic' party and has engaged in more blatant acts of outright authoritarianism than in the previous eight years.

Between April and October 1998, the Yugoslav regime attacked the opposition on three fronts: on the question of Kosovo, the universities and the media, thereby dealing successive painful blows from which the opposition was unable to recover quickly, and which effectively weakened their resolve.[6] A new university law passed in May 1998 eliminated the autonomy of the universities and demanded a written declaration of loyalty to the regime. This law confirmed a political climate of

> authoritarian consolidation of the political regime in Serbia, which is manifested in increasingly overt regime's reliance on forms of direct and indirect repression and increasingly more open production of

uncertainty, insecurity and fear, destruction and suppression of the autonomous enclaves of civil society resisting the existing authoritarian rule.[7]

In the wake of the first threats by NATO to bomb Yugoslavia, the government imposed severe restrictions on the freedom of the media, leading to the progressive closure of most independent media outlets. The confiscation of the equipment of the important independent daily *Naša Borba* in October 1998 exemplifies the ways in which the regime used the crisis in Kosovo to eliminate opposition from all sides. The ban was justified because the newspaper had published reports from Kosovo critical of the government, including statements by Adem Demaçi, the KLA spokesman at the time:

> The publishing of invalid political assessments by representatives from terrorist organizations, including the supplement titled 'Demaqi's Preconditions', spreads fear, panic and defeatism and is contrary to the resolutions by the Federal Parliament and the People's Assembly of the Republic of Serbia, since non-existent and unrecognized organizations are thus given an opportunity to jeopardize the territorial integrity and sovereignty of Yugoslavia.[8]

Both the army and police campaign in Kosovo, and the suppression of the opposition within Serbia, need to be considered in the context of the strong opposition to the regime during the demonstrations in the winter of 1996/97. The 'normalization', which Serbia began to experience as it emerged from five years of participation in wars, sanctions and an overall breakdown of social order, proved to be more threatening to the regime than all the previous years of crisis. While the regime succeeded in dividing the opposition and narrowly winning the presidential elections in Serbia, the high level of dissatisfaction among large segments of the population remained. After 1995, the independent media succeeded in broadening their scope and reaching beyond their traditional audience in Belgrade, especially through the Association of Independent Media (ANEM). The military campaign in Kosovo not only justified calls for unity behind the political leadership, but also firmly placed on the political agenda the single issue – Kosovo – where political opposition presented few alternatives to the regime. Despite a variety of plans on a future status for Kosovo launched by various opposition parties and intellectuals – from the partition of Kosovo to regionalization of Serbia – few demonstrated the willingness to engage in a constructive dialogue with the Kosovo Albanian political elite.[9] As a result most opposition parties remained silent during the early phase of the Kosovo war, partly out of fear, partly out of lack of alternatives and partly because of the reduction of their political space resulting from the conflict between the countries symbolizing their political aims (West) and their home

324

country (Serbia).[10] The Serbian Renewal Movement of Vuk Drašković, formerly the biggest opposition party, entered the federal government shortly before the beginning of the war and leaving in April 1999, while most other opposition forces continued their resistance to any cooperation with the regime throughout the war.

THE LOSS OF KOSOVO

Although the regime sought to portray the war in Kosovo as having ended in a victory the facts that Kosovo left the control of the regime and of the exodus of Serbs from the province in the months following the war, meant that the defeat the regime suffered in the war could not be disguised. The loss of Kosovo has been the most significant defeat of Serbia in the past decade. Neither the expulsion and emigration of Serbs from Croatia, nor the failure to secure a stronger Serbian republic in Bosnia has had a similar impact as the end of Serbia's rule over Kosovo. Although Kosovo formally remains part of Yugoslavia, there is little doubt that it will not be administered by Belgrade authorities in the immediate future, if ever again.

The months following the war saw the emergence of widespread protest against the regime, especially in smaller towns throughout Serbia. These protests were mostly not nationalist in nature in the sense of accusing the regime for abandoning the province, but rather criticizing the regime for having engaged in a war which led to a result that could have been achieved peacefully in March 1999. Also, some towns, especially Čačak, governed by the popular opposition mayor Velimir Ilić, resisted the regime for placing weapons in civilian areas and not adequately protecting civilians during the conflicts. These protests, and citizen's parliaments, lost their energy and had dwindled in numbers by autumn 1999, mostly due to the inability of opposition parties to capitalize on the dissatisfaction.[11] However, they demonstrated a highly dissatisfied population throughout Serbia, including smaller towns and cities in southern Serbia, which were previously under tight control of the regime.[12]

Political competition between leading politicians of the opposition rendered the participatory path to a change of government unlikely, as it would be improbable that one opposition leader would entrust the other with taking a high office. Most of the opposition's energy in the winter 1999/2000 was devoted to garnering a degree of unity which would allow it to engage in a joint strategy against the regime and prevent the desertion of parts of the opposition to the government. The inability of the opposition to make a clear conceptual break with the nationalist rhetoric of the regime, the internal disunity and the lack of a clear alternative, has led some observers to identify the opposition as the fourth pillar of power of the regime.[13] During spring 2000, the opposition did slowly manage to establish some degree of unity, by establishing a joint opposition platform in January 2000 and with the calling of Yugoslav elections the adoption of a joint list of candidates and a political programme, which contained a relatively detailed plan for political, social and economic recovery.[14]

The election campaign in August and September 2000, which lead to the victory of the opposition, rested essentially on three pillars. Firstly, the movement 'Otpor', consisting mostly of students and pupils mobilized against Milošević, put unity of the opposition on the top of the political agenda. Secondly, the joint opposition campaign mostly sought to promote the programme of economic reform, paying only little attention. Thirdly, the presidential candidate Koštunica did pay great importance to Kosovo, travelling there during his campaign and criticizing the international administration for its failure in protecting Serbs.[15] These multi-level campaigns, although eventually successful, highlighted the lack of agreement within the opposition over the issue of Kosovo. There is no consensus today on whether the loss of Kosovo remains mainly on the surface of the political agenda, with no significant role in internal Serbian politics, or whether the stance of political parties on Kosovo does determine their success or failure. Vladan Batić, president of the Christian Democratic Party insisted, in an interview in November 1999, that the issue of Kosovo is very low on the list of priorities of the electorate, in sixth place after poverty and quality of life, crime and corruption, democracy and human rights, the participation in international organizations, and the return of the young generation in exile.[16] This trend seems to be confirmed by an opinion poll carried out in September 1999 when, among the four most important issues the population fears, a renewed war with NATO was in third place, after the fear of illness in the absence of proper health care and a civil war followed by the fear of hunger.[17] On the other hand, the former leader of the Civic Alliance in Serbia, Vesna Pešić has argued that nationalism is still an important force in Serbian politics, among the government as well as among the opposition.[18]

Along these lines the united Serbian opposition issued a statement in January 2000, asking the international community to act against 'all attempts by criminals to infiltrate the territory of Kosovo ... [and] against Albanian terrorists and thieves in Kosovo'.[19] Most pronounced on the issue of Kosovo, was Vojislav Koštunica throughout the war and in its aftermath. He and his Democratic Party of Serbia have strongly condemned the international administration and claimed that it acts in collusion with the Albanian leadership in establishing an independent Kosovo.[20] Koštunica emphasized the need to challenge Milošević on the national question:

> In Serbia the national question will have a significant impact [during elections] because of the situation in which Serbia is because of the bombing, because of the propaganda of Milošević. One cannot put it aside. We must have an answer to that. Large part of the Serbian

opposition is not aware of this fact. So it is underestimating the importance of the national issue. We have to try to find ... the possibility to compromise between the importance of the national issue and the importance of Serbia being a normal member of international organizations ... I think that part of the opposition underestimated this national issue of Kosovo.[21]

Despite the variation of importance attributed to Kosovo after the war by the former opposition, its programmatic visions of the province remain very much alike. The coalition which came to power in October 2000, as well as the now marginalized Serbian Renewal Movement, accept the international administration of the province for a long transition period, while emphasizing the need to keep the province as part of Serbia and/or Yugoslavia. As the minimum demands of the political representation of Serbs and Kosovo Albanians in regard to a final status of the province lack common ground, only little political discussion in Serbia has focused on proposals for a final settlement. Most attention concentrates on the return of Serbian refugees to Kosovo and the improvement of the security situation for Serbs. With the participation of most Kosovo Serb political leaders in the opposition, any discussion on the status of Kosovo after the change of regime is more likely to include the interests and position of Kosovo Serbs.[22]

THE KOSOVO WAR AS A CONSPIRACY

The seemingly united front of NATO countries determined to wage a (limited) war against Yugoslavia, and the limited criticism of this policy from Russia, China and non-European countries, all seemed to confirm the romantic notion of Serbia standing alone, the whole world thereby heightening the real and perceived isolation of Serbia.[23] The war also gave rise to a number of other conspiracy theories that point to more sinister reasons for NATO's waging the war: geopolitical domination, economic interest, and the desire to divide the Balkans into small, powerless states. As Marko Živković's work on Serbian nationalist narrative points out, the policy of the West, combined with the historical experience of great power interference, did little to discredit conspiracy theories and in fact helped undermine their critics.[24]

Since their beginning, the wars of Yugoslav succession have been accompanied by conspiracy theories from all sides. Even before the outbreak of the hostilities, the media in Serbia, as well as in the other republics, reported imaginary plans by the 'other side' or some outside powers to dominate or destroy Yugoslavia or at least the nation in question.[25] While the media war has been adequately documented elsewhere, conspiracy theories, as one of the main tools of the propaganda campaign in the media and through other channels of communication have not been adequately explored. First, let us consider these theories as a tool of nationalism.

A conspiracy theory is unconfirmed information which seeks to explain events as resulting from an elaborate plan, often a secret and clandestine project. The root of any conspiracy theory is the rumour, an unofficial piece of information spread by word of mouth. Sudhir Kakar has explained the role of the rumour in the example of riots between Hindus and Muslims in India:

> At the high point of a riot, the content of the rumours is at its most threatening and the speed at which they circulate are the highest. For it is at this particular time when three of the four conditions for the generation and transmission of rumours – personal anxiety, general uncertainty, and topical importance – are at their highest level. The ... condition [of] credulity [is] no longer in operation since, at high levels of anxiety, disbelief in rumour is suspended, that is, rumours will be believed regardless how farfetched.[26]

Conspiracy theories have functioned along the same lines during all phases of the war. The dissemination of such theories by newspapers further contributed to their widespread belief. Another reason for their acceptance is the sheer number of them. The proliferation of such theories has overwhelmed public opinion to the extent that a significant proportion of the theories are believed to be true, or at least that there 'has to be a kernel of truth' within the reports. There is, however, another level of relevance of the conspiracy theories. Beyond the element of misinformation and discrediting of information conspiracy has been defined as 'joining or acting together, as if by sinister design'.[27] The conspiracy is beyond the realm of those affected by it. Again, comparable to the rumour as Kakar described it, '[d]eriving from and reinforcing the paranoid potential which lies buried in all of us, they were the conversational food which helped the growth of a collective ... body'.[28] The conspiracy clearly delineates between two sides in a conflict – black and white – and allows the supposed victims to interpret even seemingly positive acts by the other side as a part of a larger, inevitably sinister plan.

Accordingly, under threat from a conspiracy, members of the 'own' nation not participating in the 'own' national project become 'traitors'.[29] The modern traitors were the members of the Serbian opposition and independent media who protested and criticized the war.[30] The government and its media organs defined treachery in Serbia. This task became easier with the media law passed in October 1998 that also institutionalized the dichotomy of 'patriotic' versus 'pro-Western media'.[31] As a result, most of the anti-regime media were not only branded as traitors but also banned, decimating one of the last niches of independence in Serbia. Once again, traitors were jeopardizing Serbian unity: 'By invoking an external conspiracy with its connections to internal traitors, the latent function of this theory is to assist the internal mobilization and unification of the population.'[32]

Beyond reaffirming the nation's collective identity and enforcing the perceived differences from the 'other' – the enemy – the conspiracy theory further emphasizes the helplessness and the victimhood of those affected by the conspiracy. As conspiracy assumes a group acting against the interest of the 'victim', it describes per definition the relationship between perpetrator and victim. The victim, however, is not only the weaker element in the relationship; the victim also inevitably belongs to the group that is 'just', regardless of the conspirators' claim, as their true intentions remain obscure and hidden, and therefore sinister and 'unjust'. Such an interpretation enables the self-perceived victims to deny reality to the point of justifying their own crimes. Consequently, the instigators of violence and ethnic hatred can redefine the balance of guilt through the claim of battling a conspiracy.

In the case of Kosovo, the crimes that have been committed by some Albanians against Serbs since the beginning of the international administration function within this structure to 'prove' the premeditated nature of war, and help not only to justify the Yugoslav resistance to Western intervention, but also the previous decade of repression. In the aftermath the regime attempted to retain the country in a state of emergency, which was being fed increasingly openly with conspiracies, plots and rumours. Especially the United Yugoslav Left (JUL) of Slobodan Milošević's wife Mira Marković engaged in 'uncovering' plots of domestic and international enemies seeking to destroy, kill or undermine the government. Goran Matić, member of JUL and federal minister of information, frequently went public in 1999 and 2000 with reports about various spy and assassination rings.[33] While primarily serving to legitimize suppression of the opposition and independent media, it also intended to extend the state of siege symbolized by the Kosovo war in 1999. However, public perception diverged from the increasingly obscure accusations of the regime.

Nevertheless, the international isolation of Serbia, the experience of recent years in conjunction with its instrumentalization of the regime has extended the power of conspiracy theories beyond the power of Milošević. He is frequently identified in Serbia as an American stooge, who helped in the destruction of Yugoslavia and the establishment of American control in the region.[34] Even after the end of the 'extended Kosovo War' with the change of regime on 5 October 2000, the conspiracy theory as an element of contemporary nationalism is alive without a broad and comprehensive discussion of the wars and crimes of the 1990s.

ADDRESSING THE PAST

While the war in Kosovo has contributed to and reinforced the isolation in which Serbia found itself in 1999/2000, intensifying the effectiveness of nationalism, it has also had some contrary effects. The direct involvement of the Yugoslav government in the expulsion of Albanians from Kosovo, and the crimes committed at that time, have established a clear line of responsibility that was not as visible in the case of the previous wars in Croatia and Bosnia.

The crimes committed by Yugoslav military and paramilitary forces were first addressed by the 'usual suspects' – NGO activists, members of human rights groups, and independent trade unions – in an open letter to their Albanian friends in April 1999:

> We are writing to you in these difficult moments of our shared suffering. Convoys of Albanians and other citizens of Kosovo, among whom many of you, were forced to leave their homes. The killings and expulsions, homes destroyed and burnt, bridges, roads and industrial buildings demolished – paint a sombre and painful picture of Kosovo, Serbia and Montenegro, as indicating that life together is no longer possible. We, however, believe that it is necessary and possible. The better future of citizens of Kosovo, Serbia and Montenegro, of Serbs and Albanians, as citizens of one state or closest neighbours, will not arrive by itself, or over night. But it is something we can and must work on together, as we have many times in the past, not so long ago.[35]

This clear opposition to the actions of the regime, however, came from many of the same groups and individuals that had protested against the regime during the previous wars. Their protests, thus, did not indicate a significant shift in public opinion, or among a different segment of the intellectual elite for that matter, toward a more differentiated evaluation of Serbian responsibility in the war.

Yet after the war, some members of the intellectual establishment began speaking out more openly against the crimes committed. In July 1999, a number of writers, including the member of the Serbian Academy of Sciences and Arts, Predrag Palavestra, demanded the punishment of those responsible for crimes against civilians, because otherwise 'guilt and shame for that crime would fall on the entire Serb people'.[36] Similarly a number of nationalist intellectuals, including Dobrica Ćosić and Matija Bećković, demanded Slobodan Milošević's resignation at the annual convention of the Serbian Academy in July 1999.[37] One must be cautious with an evaluation of such statements, however, as demands for resignation from nationalist intellectuals frequently reflect a dissatisfaction with the failure to win wars, rather than an outrage with the crimes committed in the process.

Segments of the Serbian Orthodox Church have been more outspoken than many intellectuals on the issue of responsibility. While the Church has been critical of the regime in the past, past criticism generally focused on the government's refusal to adopt the Church's demands. During the war in Bosnia, the Church had come into conflict with the regime for not siding with the more traditionalist and church-friendly Serb leadership in Bosnia. The war in Kosovo, however, led to a shift in the Church's position. On 15 June 1999, the Holy Synod of the Serbian Orthodox Church demanded the resignation of Milošević and the federal government, and their replacement with 'new persons, eligible [acceptable] to the home and foreign public'.[38] Bishop Artemije, at the Diocese of Raška and Prizren (including Kosovo), emerged as the most outspoken critic of the regime's policy in Kosovo and has since became a leading political representative of the Serbs remaining in Kosovo.

Nevertheless the confrontational line has been eroded with Patriarch Pavle's participation at the reception for the Day of the Republic on 29 November 1999 hosted by the Yugoslav president. Pavle's visit prompted an open letter by Bishop Artemije outlining the critical position towards the regime that he and other members of the Church had adopted:

> I beseech you in the name of the living God never to put us again in a situation in which we cannot face our flock and our people. After all that Mr. Milošević has done to the Serbian (and not only Serbian) people in the last ten years; after the tragedy he has brought in Kosovo and Metohija both on the Albanian and the Serbian people, and especially in the last two years; after the Serbian Orthodox Church has resolutely demanded Milošević's resignation and stepping down so as to save the people and the state ... your acceptance of Milošević's invitation and the fact that you personally congratulated him for the birthday of a state that died ten years ago, a birthday which this year has turned into 'the national celebration of the abolition of the monarchy' of the Serbian people, has shocked and puzzled many of our brethren archpriests, honourable clergy and monkery and the vast majority of orthodox Serbs ...[39]

Breaking with the nature of previous criticism of the regime, the bishop further criticized the Serbian Orthodox Church for having supported the regime and breaking with Milošević 'only when it became dissatisfied with his success in waging wars'.[40] The war in Kosovo has thus exposed a deep split within the leadership of the Serbian Orthodox Church, which in the past decade tried to walk the tightrope of calling for inter-confessional

331

dialogue and reconciliation on one hand, and supporting Serb nationalist policies on the other.

Bishop Artemije met with Hashim Thaçi and a delegation of Kosovo Albanians in early July 1999 to sign a joint statement calling for the return of refugees and the creation of a multi-ethnic Kosovo.[41] The discussion of the responsibility for the Kosovo war on the part of the Yugoslav government and Serbian nationalism, and a re-examination of Serbia's role in this and past wars, have been severely hampered by the continuing violence against Serbs in Kosovo, which has shifted the attention away from a critical evaluation of nationalism in Serbia.

In an extremely polarized political climate, these first steps are signs of courage, which express also the high degree of frustration of a significant, but nevertheless marginalized, group of public figures. But these steps reveal the limitations of such an attempted reconciliation. They are part of ongoing attempts between some Serbian intellectuals and counterparts from other parts of former Yugoslavia to engage in dialogue which not only address the issues of guilt, responsibility and reconciliation, but also more pragmatic issues, such as a political solution to the conflict.[42] This dialogue cannot yet be interpreted as pertaining to the reconciliation of the two nations. Especially as the Serbian representatives of this dialogue have remained disregarded by the public mainstream and were often branded as 'traitors'.[43]

Only the change of regime in Serbia opened the door to engaging in a more comprehensive process of dialogue and addressing past crimes.[44] The former opposition in Serbia is today divided on the issue of addressing responsibility, which is mostly a result of their role in the past. While some smaller parties (i.e., Civil Alliance of Serbia) have been vocal critics of the wars in the 1990s, others, including Yugoslav President Vojislav Koštunica[45] have in one way or another endorsed some of the crimes committed by the Serbian regime in Croatia, Bosnia and Kosovo. In the immediate aftermath of the change of power in Serbia, two events symbolized the change in regard to discussing responsibility. Only a few days after the change of regime the independent television station 'Studio B' showed a documentary describing the rise of Milošević and showing crimes committed by the Serbian armies during the wars of the past decade.[46] Less than a month after the change of power, Koštunica similarly stated that 'I am ready to accept the guilt for all those people who have been killed … For what Milošević had done, and as a Serb, I will take responsibility for many of these, these crimes.'[47] These two events signify the fact that only a change of regime enabled a broader process to address responsibility during the wars, as the human rights activist Nataša Kandić emphasized recently, 'We [Serbs] must come to terms with the crimes committed in our name. If Koštunica wants to fulfil his promise to make Serbia a "normal place", he must spearhead that process.'[48]

PROSPECTS

Only with the end of the rule of Milošević, nearly a decade after the collapse of the second Yugoslavia, has a dialogue on the territorial and political system of Serbia become possible. However, the issue of Kosovo remains unresolved, potentially even after a formal settlement of the final status of the province. Serbian social scientist Božidar Jakšić asserted before the beginning of the war that

> the anathema of highly set national goals would hurt Serbs, if Kosovo really remains 'an internal affair of Serbia'. The reason is simple: Serbia lacks the material, organizational and moral strength for solving this problem. Many years ago, Leon Trotsky, reporting from the Balkan front in the year 1912, insightfully remarked: 'With the annexation of Kosovo, Serbia got a millstone around the neck of its development'.[49]

In 1998, Dragan Štavljanin similarly wrote that '[b]earing in mind the complexity of the Kosovo situation, it seems impossible for Serbia to become a fully democratic society as long as Kosovo is part of it'.[50] Even with the de facto loss of Kosovo, the failure to put the issue to rest has the danger of continuing to bear a negative impact on democratization in Serbia. A conditional independence, as suggested by the Independent Commission for Kosovo,[51] seems to be the most probable long-term outcome for the province, if this is pursued too hastily and prematurely, however, it might run the risk of endangering the process of democratization and reform in Serbia.

NOTES

1. *Republika*, 1 September 1997, quoted from S. Biserko and S. Stanojlović (eds), *Radicalization of the Serbian Society: Collection of Documents* (Belgrade: Helsinki Committee for Human Rights in Serbia, 1997), pp. 60–1.
2. *Večernje Novosti*, 8 September 1997, quoted from Biserko and Stanojlović (eds), *Radicalization of the Serbian Society*, p. 67.
3. The fact that the posters were in English indicates that at least part of the intended message of the referendum was towards the outside.
4. D. Štavljanin, 'The Ethnification of Politics – A Case Study: Serbia', *Montenegro Journal of Foreign Policy* 3, no. 3/4 (1998), p. 52.
5. See the analysis of the political campaign in 1997 in S. Biserko and Stanojlović (eds), *Radicalization of the Serbian Society*, pp. 13–75.
6. I am grateful to Marina Blagojević for her ideas on this topic.
7. S. Vujović, 'The Society, State and University in Crisis', *Sociologija* 60, no. 4 (October–December 1998), p. 484.
8. Edict of the Ministry of Information of the Republic of Serbia, no. 651-03-292/98-01 (15 October 1998).

9. A. Kumer, M. Polzer-Srienz and M. F. Polzer, 'Politische Ordnungsvorstellungen der Regierungund Oppositionsparteien Serbiens sowie einiger ausgewählter serbischer und albanischer Gruppierungen', in J. Marko (ed.), *Gordischer Knoten Kosovo/a: Durchschlagen oder Entwirren?* (Baden-Baden: Nomos, 1999), pp. 35–44; S. Troebst, *Conflict in Kosovo: Failure of Prevention? An Analytical Documentation, 1992–1998.* ECMI Working Paper 1 (Flensburg: ECMI, 1998), pp. 12–16.

10. See V. Illić, *Srpska opozicija tokom i posle NATO bombardovanja*, Helsinške Sveske 2, *Potencijal za Promene* (Belgrade: Helsinški Odbor za Ljudska Prava u Srbiji, 2000), pp. 86–135.

11. The general distrust towards the regime and opposition in autumn 1999 is visible in an opinion poll published in *Vreme* from September 1999, asking for the figure most likely to lead the country out of the crisis, serves as a valuable indicator of public opinion in Serbia. The most trusted person in this respect remained Slobodan Milošević, although he could only obtain the confidence of a mere 9% of those surveyed. He was followed by Dragislav Avramović, the former head of the Yugoslav Central Bank who is widely credited with ending hyperinflation in 1994, who received 7% and Vuk Drašković with 4%. All other political figures, including Šešelj, Djindjić and Panić, each earned no more than 2%. The clear winner of the poll was 'nobody'. *Vreme*, 25 September 1999.

12. M. Milošević, *Politički vodič kroz Srbiju 2000* (Belgrade: Medija Centar, 2000), pp. 62–4; the change in attitudes is also visible in public opinion survey, see especially S. Mihailović (ed.), *Javno mnenje Srbije. Između razočarenja I nade* (Belgrade: Centar za proučavanje alternative, 2000).

13. The other pillars of the regime are the army, media and financial resources; D. Pavlović, 'Srpska opozicija pred lokalne izbore', *Reporter*, 1 March 2000. On this topic see also, M. Djurković, 'Nadziranje i podvođenje', *Republika*, 1 December 1999, pp. 19–24.

14. G17plus, *Program Demokratske Opozicije Srbije za Demokratsku Srbiju* (Belgrade, 2000).

15. *NIN*, 7 September 2000.

16. *Vreme*, 13 November 1999.

17. *Blic*, 25 October 1999.

18. *Reporter*, 2 February 2000.

19. *Betaweek*, 13 January 2000.

20. See, for example, the press statement 'Kouchner Amputates Kosovo', Information Service of the Democratic Party of Serbia, 7 April 2000.

21. V. Koštunica, interview with the author, 20 July 2000.

22. International Crisis Group, *Balkans Briefing: Reactions in Kosovo to Koštunica's Victory*, 10 October 2000.

23. See E. Gordy, 'Why Milošević Still?', *Current History* 99, no. 635 (March 2000), p. 101.

24. M. Živković, *Stories Serbs Tell Themselves*, unpublished Ph.D. dissertation (University of Chicago, 2000), ch. 6.

25. A number of interviews with leading intellectuals published in *Politika* in 1991 demonstrate the widespread usage of such theories. The interviews have been published as M. Vučelić (ed.), *Conversations with the Epoch* (Belgrade: Serbian Ministry of Information, 1991).

26. S. Kakar, *The Colors of Violence: Cultural Identities, Religion, and Conflict* (Chicago and London: University of Chicago Press, 1996), p. 35.

27. *American Heritage Dictionary of the English Language*, edn 3 (1996), electronic version.

28. See Kakar, *The Colors of Violence*, p. 35.
29. Betrayal became one of the main motives of the commemoration of the Kosovo battle in 1989. On 28 June 1989, the most important Serbian daily, *Politika*, ran the headline 'The Serbian people celebrated its heroes, but also recognized its traitors'. O. Zirojević, 'Das Amselfeld im kollektiven Gedächtnis', in T. Brenner, N. Popov and H.-G. Stobbe (eds), *Serbiens Weg in den Krieg* (Berlin: Arno Spitz Verlag, 1998), p. 60.
30. Unidentified men assassinated the publisher Slavko Čuruvija in Belgrade in April 1999, after he had been accused of treachery in government media. Zoran Djindjić was forced to seek refuge in Montenegro after his criticism of the war resulted in similar accusations.
31. See, for example, *IWPR Media Focus*, 11 January 1999.
32. J. Zupanov, D. Sekulic and Z. Sporer, 'A Breakdown of the Civil Order: The Balkan Bloodbath', *International Journal of Politics, Culture and Society* 9, no. 3 (1996), p. 404.
33. In October 1999, Matić claimed, for example, that the enemy attempted to smuggle Dinar notes into the country to undermine the currency (*Reuters*, 27 October 1999); in November Matić identified opinion polls as part of a propaganda campaign against the regime (*Politika Ekspress*, 4 November 1999); the same month Matić announced the arrest of a French spy-ring code-named 'Spider' which supposedly sought to assassinate Milošević, and later implicated Bernard Kouchner in the 'Spider' group (*Danas*, 10 December 1999); Matić later accused Drašković and other opposition politicians of being in contact with the French spies (*Danas*, 24 December 1999); Matić joined Šešelj in February 2000, in accusing the independent media in Serbia of pursuing terrorist aims (*Borba*, 14 February 2000); Otpor was later blamed by Matić as being responsible for the assassination of Boško Perošević (*Human Rights Watch*, 1 June 2000); in August the minister revealed the arrest of four Dutch would-be assassins of Milošević (*Borba*, 2 August 2000).
34. See the article by P. Maass, *New York Times*, 24 October 2000.
35. 'Letter to Albanian Friends from Non-Governmental Organizations', Belgrade, 30 April 1999, distributed electronically (on file with author).
36. S. Kostić, 'Awakening of Intellectuals. Who is Responsible for War Crimes?' *AIM Podgorica*, 4 July 1999.
37. Ibid.
38. The journalist reporting on the decision notes cynically that 'Milošević has officially become disagreeable even to God'. V. Vujić, 'Pre-Election Revival in Serbia', *AIM Podgorica*, 17 June 1999. The full text of the declaration is available at www.decani.yunet.com/resign.html.
39. B. Matić, 'Divisions in the Serbian Orthodox Church', *AIM Podgorica*, 21 December 1999.
40. Ibid.
41. *Betaweek*, 8 July 1999. The statement is available at www.decani.yunet.com/serbalb.html.
42. Troebst, *Conflict in Kosovo*, pp. 79–80, 91; Helsinški Odbor za Ljudska Prava u Srbiji, *Srpsko-Albanski Dijalog*, Ulcinj, 23–25 June 1997 (Belgrade: Prometej, 1997).
43. Albanian Intellectuals have run a similar risk. Veton Surroi described the crimes committed by Albanians against Serbs as bringing 'shame on all Kosovo Albanians, not just the perpetrators of violence. And it's a burden we will have to bear collectively.' Veton Surroi, 'Kosovo Fascism, Albanian's Shame', *IWPR Balkan Crisis Report*, 25 August 1999. His statements were followed by an accusation

that he was a spy for Serbia by the KLA Newsagency Kosovapress, see *RFE/RL Newsline*, 6 October 1999.

44. On the (past) hurdles to reconciliation see F. Bieber, 'Pomirenje u bivšoj Jugoslavji. Slučajevi Francuske i Nemačke kao modeli', in A. Fatić (ed.), *Problemi Srpske politike* (Belgrade: Centar za Menadžment, 2000), pp. 92–111.
45. Koštunica has been particularly criticized for posing with a Kalašnikov in Kosovo in the Summer of 1998. *NIN*, 19 October 2000.
46. *Guardian*, 10 October 2000.
47. *New York Times*, 25 October 2000. The interview for the US station CBS was also broadcast in Yugoslavia. Later some controversy emerged around the interview with claims by advisors to the president that the interview had been 'incorrectly' edited (*AFP*, 26 October 2000). Nevertheless, the interview marked an important step towards a discussion on the subject of responsibility.
48. N. Kandić, 'Our Unfinished Business in Serbia', *Washington Post*, 22 October 2000.
49. B. Jakšić, 'Kosovo – Prokletstvo Etnonacionalnih Ciljeva' in Božidar Jakšić, *Balkanski Paradoksi* (Belgrade: Beogradski Krug, 2000), p. 147.
50. See Štavljanin, 'The Ethnification of Politics', p. 61.
51. Independent International Commission on Kosovo, *The Kosovo Report: Conflict, International Response, Lessons Learnt* (Oxford: Oxford University Press, 2000), pp. 283–94.

REFERENCES

AFP, 26 October 2000.
American Heritage Dictionary of the English Language, edn 3 (1996), electronic version.
Betaweek, 8 July 1999.
Betaweek, 13 January 2000.
Bieber, F., 'Pomirenje u bivšoj Jugoslavji. Slučajevi Francuske i Nemačke kao modeli', in A. Fatić (ed.), *Problemi Srpske politike* (Belgrade: Centar za Menadžment, 2000), pp. 92–111.
Biserko, S. and Stanojlović, S. (eds), *Radicalization of the Serbian Society: Collection of Documents* (Belgrade: Helsinki Committee for Human Rights in Serbia, 1997).
Blic, 25 October 1999.
Borba, 14 February 2000.
Borba, 2 August 2000.
Danas, 10 December 1999.
Danas, 24 December 1999.
Djurković, M., 'Nadziranje i podvođenje', *Republika*, 1 December 1999, pp. 19–24.
Edict of the Ministry of Information of the Republic of Serbia, no. 651-03-292/98-01 (15 October 1998).
G17plus, *Program Demokratske Opozicije Srbije za Demokratsku Srbiju* (Belgrade, 2000).
Gordy, E. 'Why Milošević Still?', *Current History* 99, no. 635 (March 2000), pp. 99–103.
Guardian, 10 October 2000.
Helsinški Odbor za Ljudska Prava u Srbiji, *Srpsko-Albanski Dijalog*, Ulcinj, 23–25 June 1997 (Belgrade: Prometej, 1997).
Human Rights Watch, 1 June 2000.
Illić, V., *Srpska Opozicija tokom i posle NATO bombardovanja*, Helsinške Sveske 2,

Potencijal za Promene (Belgrade: Helsinški Odbor za Ljudska Prava u Srbiji, 2000), pp. 86–135.

Independent International Commission on Kosovo, *The Kosovo Report: Conflict, International Response, Lessons Learnt* (Oxford: Oxford University Press, 2000).

Information Service of the Democratic Party of Serbia, 'Kouchner Amputates Kosovo', 7 April 2000.

International Crisis Group, *Balkans Briefing: Reactions in Kosovo to Koštunica's Victory*, 10 October 2000.

IWPR Balkan Crisis Report, 25 August 1999.

IWPR Media Focus, 11 January 1999.

Jakšić, B., 'Kosovo – Prokletstvo Etnonacionalnih Ciljeva', in Božidar Jakšić, *Balkanski Paradoksi* (Belgrade: Beogradski Krug, 2000), pp. 145–50.

Kakar, S., *The Colors of Violence: Cultural Identities, Religion, and Conflict* (Chicago and London: University of Chicago Press, 1996).

Kandić, N., 'Our Unfinished Business in Serbia', *Washington Post*, 22 October 2000.

Kostić, S., 'Awakening of Intellectuals. Who is Responsible for War Crimes?' *AIM Podgorica*, 4 July 1999.

Koštunica, Vojislav, interview with the author, 20 July 2000.

Kumer, A., Polzer-Srienz, M. and Polzer, M. F., 'Politische Ordnungsvorstellungen der Regierungund Oppositionsparteien Serbiens sowie einiger ausgewählter serbischer und albanischer Gruppierungen', in J. Marko (ed.), *Gordischer Knoten Kosovo/a: Durchschlagen oder Entwirren?* (Baden-Baden: Nomos, 1999), pp. 35–44.

'Letter to Albanian Friends from Non-Governmental Organizations', Belgrade, 30 April 1999.

Matić, B., 'Divisions in the Serbian Orthodox Church', *AIM Podgorica*, 21 December 1999.

Mihailović, S. (ed.), *Javno Mnenje Srbije. Između razočarenja i nade* (Belgrade: Centar za proučavanje alternative, 2000).

Milošević, M., *Politički vodič kroz Srbiju 2000* (Belgrade: Medija Centar, 2000).

New York Times, 24 October 2000.

New York Times, 25 October 2000.

NIN, 7 September 2000.

NIN, 19 October 2000.

Pavlović, D., 'Srpska opozicija pred lokalne izbore', *Reporter*, 1 March 2000.

Politika Ekspress, 4 November 1999.

Reporter, 2 February 2000.

Reuters, 27 October 1999.

RFE/RL Newsline, 6 October 1999.

Štavljanin, D., 'The Ethnification of Politics – A Case Study: Serbia', *Montenegro Journal of Foreign Policy* 3, no. 3/4 (1998), pp. 41–65.

Troebst, S., *Conflict in Kosovo: Failure of Prevention? An Analytical Documentation, 1992–1998*, ECMI Working Paper 1 (Flensburg: ECMI, 1998).

Vreme, 25 September1999.

Vreme, 13 November 1999.

Vučelić, M. (ed.), *Conversations with the Epoch* (Belgrade: Serbian Ministry of Information, 1991).

Vujić, V., 'Pre-Election Revival in Serbia', *AIM Podgorica*, 17 June 1999.

Vujović, S., 'The Society, State and University in Crisis', *Sociologija* 60, no. 4 (October–December 1998), pp. 481–508.

Zirojević, O., 'Das Amselfeld im kollektiven Gedächtnis', in T. Brenner, N. Popov and

H.-G. Stobbe (eds), *Serbiens Weg in den Krieg* (Berlin: Arno Spitz Verlag, 1998), pp. 45–61.

Živković, M., *Stories Serbs Tell Themselves*, unpublished Ph.D. dissertation (Chicago: University of Chicago, 2000).

Zupanov, J., Sekulic, D. and Sporer, Z., 'A Breakdown of the Civil Order: The Balkan Bloodbath', *International Journal of Politics, Culture and Society* 9, no. 3 (1996), pp. 401–22.

Abbreviations

ANEM	Association of Independent Media
BPA	Banking and Payment Authority
BTF	Balkans Task Force
CEI	Central European Initiative
CEU	Central European University
CFSP	Common Foreign and Security Policy
CNN	Cable News Network
CSCE	Conference for Security and Cooperation in Europe
DPKO	Department of Peacekeeping Operations
EBRD	European Bank for Reconstruction and Development
ECMI	European Centre for Minority Issues
EIB	European Investment Bank
EU	European Union
FRY	Federal Republic of Yugoslavia
IAC	Interim Administration
ICJ	International Court of Justice
ICTY	International Criminal Tribunal for the Former Yugoslavia
IDP	Internally Displaced People
IMF	International Monetary Fund
JIAS	Joint Interim Administrative Structure
JUL	United Yugoslav Left (Jugoslovenska Levica)
KFOR	Kosovo Force (NATO Peacekeeping Force)
KLA	Kosovo Liberation Army
KVM	Kosovo Verification Mission
LBD	United Democratic Movement
LCY	League of Communists of Yugoslavia
LDK	Democratic League of Kosova (Lidhja Demokratike e Kosovës)
NATO	North Atlantic Treaty Organization
NGO	Non-Governmental Organization
NLM	National Liberation Movement
OSCE	Organization for Security and Cooperation in Europe
OTP	Office of the Prosecutor

PGK	Provisional Government of Kosovo
RTS	Radio and Television Serbia (Radio-Televizije Srbije)
SAA	Stabilization and Association Agreement
SCR	Security Council Resolution
SECI	South-East Cooperative Initiative
SFRY	Socialist Federal Republic of Yugoslavia
SPS	Socialist Party of Serbia (Socijalističa Partija Srbije)
TC	Transitional Council
UÇK	Kosovo Liberation Army (Ushtria Çlirimtare e Kosovës)
UN	United Nations
UNCHS	United Nations Centre for Human Settlements
UNEP	United Nations Environmental Programme
UNHCR	United Nations High Commission for Refugees
UNMIK	United Nations Interim Administration in Kosovo
UNPREDEP	United Nations Preventive Deployment Force
UNPROFOR	United Nations Protection Force
UNSC	United Nations Security Council
UNTAC	United Nations Transitional Authority in Cambodia
UNTAES	United Nations Transitional Administration of Eastern Slavonia
USAID	United States Agency for International Development
WCRP	World Conference on Religion and Peace
WEU	Western European Union

Index